Build with Claude Cod

From zero to deployed apps with AI-assisted development

Taeho Jo

<packt>

Build with Claude Code

Portfolio Director: Pavan Ramchandani
Portfolio Manager: Mohd Riyan Khan
Project Manager: Divij Kotian
Content Engineer: Rounak Kulkarni
Technical Editor: Vidhisha Patidar
Indexer: Pratik Shirodkar
Proofreader: Rounak Kulkarni
Production Designer: Vijay Kamble
Growth Lead: Prajwal S

First published: August 2026

Production reference: 1250826

Published by Packt Publishing Ltd.
Grosvenor House
11 St Paul's Square
Birmingham
B3 1RB, UK.

ISBN 978-1-80778-179-8
`www.packtpub.com`

This book is dedicated to my wife and two daughters. Without their love and encouragement, neither the Korean edition nor this English edition would have been possible.

– Taeho Jo

Foreword

I still remember the moment coding stopped feeling like typing. I had asked an AI agent to build something I would normally have scoped as two days of work: read the ticket, explore the codebase, write the fix, run the tests, explain the change. I watched it do all of that in the time it took me to finish a coffee. My first reaction was not excitement. It was the quiet, slightly uncomfortable recognition that my profession had just changed shape, and that everything I believed about how software gets built needed to be re-examined.

I have spent the years since living inside that change. At Avanai, the company I co-founded, we build and deploy AI agents for some of the largest enterprises in Europe and US; a large part of my work is standing in rooms full of experienced engineers, consultants, and domain experts, teaching them to work with these tools. I have given this training in corporate headquarters and at developer meetups, to teams of five and audiences of hundreds. And I can tell you what I see in every single room: the gap is no longer between people who can code and people who cannot. The gap is between people who know how to direct an AI coding agent and people who are still typing everything themselves.

Claude Code sits at the center of that shift. It is, to my mind, the clearest expression yet of what agentic coding means: not autocomplete, not a chat window that produces snippets for you to paste, but a genuine collaborator that reads your project, forms a plan, uses tools, checks its own work, and iterates. The first time you watch it navigate an unfamiliar repository and come back with a working change, you understand that the unit of software work is no longer the line of code. It is the intention, clearly expressed.

That is precisely why a book like this matters, and why Taeho Jo is the right person to write it. What impressed me about Taeho is the arc of his career: a senior software engineer at Macromedia Korea (now part of Adobe) who became a bioinformatics researcher and professor, someone who has used computation his whole life not as an end in itself but as an instrument for solving hard, real problems in medicine and science. He is also a proven teacher. His earlier book on deep learning became a standard textbook at dozens of universities because he has the rare ability to make a complex subject feel learnable without making it feel small. He brings both halves to this book: the engineer who respects the craft, and the scientist who cares about what the craft is for.

My advice for reading it is simple: do not read it. Work it. Keep Claude Code open in one window and this book in the other, and build something real as you go, however small. These tools reward practice over theory more than any technology I have ever taught, and the confidence you are looking for lives on the other side of your first twenty hands-on hours. This book is the most direct path I know to those hours being well spent. We are living through the greatest expansion of who gets to build software since the personal computer. It is a rare privilege to watch a door this large swing open. The book in your hands is an invitation to walk through it.

Aemal Sayer

AI Expert

Contributors

About the author

Taeho Jo is an Assistant Professor at the Indiana University School of Medicine, where he applies deep learning to Alzheimer's disease research, from discovering genetic variants to analyzing brain imaging and biomarkers. He created SWAT and a family of models including Deep-Block, TrUE-Net, and DuAL-Net. He holds a PhD in computational biology.

He is also the developer of AlphaGenome MCP, an open-source tool that connects the AlphaGenome genomics model with Claude Code and Claude Desktop, allowing scientists to run complex analyses using plain language.

Before entering academia, he worked as a software engineer at Macromedia Korea, now part of Adobe. His Deep Learning for Everyone has been a bestseller and university textbook in Korea for years, while his guide to Claude Code reached number one in the IT category at major bookstores across the country. *Build with Claude Code* is the English edition of that book.

I would like to thank my family for their patience and support during the long hours I spent on this book. I am also grateful to Dr. Andrew J. Saykin for suggesting a rare-variant study with AlphaGenome, which grew into the MCP and, ultimately, this book.

At Packt, I would like to thank Mohd Riyan Khan for setting the direction of the book for English-speaking readers and guiding it through every stage of publication; Divij Kotian for smoothly managing the project from start to finish; and Rounak Kulkarni for his careful reading and valuable feedback on the manuscript. My thanks also go to the entire Packt team for their support throughout the publication process.

This book began its journey in Korea, and I am also deeply grateful to the team at Hanbit Media who made it possible: Min-Ah Park, who led the editorial team and supported this book from the start; Jeongah Seok, whose careful and dedicated editing shaped the Korean edition, Hwa Jeong Seong, whose marketing helped this book reach its readers, and Yesol Hong, who supported the English edition throughout the process.

About the reviewer

Hari Prasad Renganathan is a Senior AI Engineer and 2x Founder specializing in Agentic AI, RAG systems, and AI platform architecture. A Columbia University graduate, he has built and deployed production AI systems across fintech, gaming, sales, and startups, including multi-agent systems used for complex financial and business workflows. He has also founded products used by thousands of users and mentors 900+ aspiring engineers. Beyond engineering, Hari is a TEDx speaker and creates practical AI content for a community of 70,000+ professionals.

Table of Contents

Chapter 7: Building a Development Team with Claude Code AI Agents 253

Chapter 9: Answers to Review Questions 361

Preface

Not long ago, building software meant one thing: learning to code first. You could have a clear picture of what you wanted to build and still be stopped at the door because you did not speak the language of programming. AI-assisted development has changed that. With Claude Code, the conversation itself becomes the interface, and describing what you want is the first real step toward building it.

This book is a hands-on guide to that way of working, often called vibe coding. You will not read about it in the abstract; you will build. A webpage in *Chapter 1*. A marketing portfolio in *Chapter 2*. A handwriting recognition program in *Chapter 3*, a to-do app in *Chapter 4*, and a quiz game in *Chapter 5*. By *Chapter 6*, you will be connecting AI models through APIs. In *Chapter 7*, you will be directing a team of AI agents, and in *Chapter 8*, you will deploy a database-backed service that anyone can open in a browser.

Along the way you will learn the things that separate a lucky result from a repeatable one: writing prompts that get what you actually want, keeping AI honest about the content it generates, managing projects with `CLAUDE.md` and custom commands, and extending Claude Code with MCP servers, skills, and plugins.

Along the way, you will learn what separates a lucky result from a repeatable one: writing prompts that get you what you actually want, verifying AI-generated content, managing projects with `CLAUDE.md` and custom commands, and extending Claude Code with MCP servers, skills, and plugins.

The goal is not to turn you into a traditional programmer. It is to make you someone who can turn an idea into working software, with AI as a genuine development partner rather than just an assistant.

Who this book is for

Whether you're a beginner or an experienced professional, this book equips you with the skills to turn ideas into real, working software. It is ideal for product managers, marketers, researchers, educators, entrepreneurs, and anyone interested in AI-assisted development. Early-career software engineers will also find it valuable. If you've ever wanted to build applications but felt limited by your coding skills, this book provides a practical and accessible path to get started.

What this book covers

Chapter 1, My First Vibe Coding, introduces vibe coding and compares the main types of AI coding tools, from web-based chatbots to model-selection tools and dedicated tools such as Claude Code. You will trace how AI evolved from neural networks to today's large language models and build your first webpage using Claude artifacts.

Chapter 2, Maximizing AI's Potential with Effective Prompts, teaches the principles behind prompts that get results, including the 5W1H framework and structured templates. You will draft a product proposal with AI, then apply a four-step strategy to build a complete marketing portfolio.

Chapter 3, Getting Started with Claude Code, walks you through installing Claude Code on Windows, macOS, or Linux and completing the initial setup. You will build a working handwriting recognition program using the MNIST dataset, then use CLAUDE.md and a hierarchical project structure to expand it into a web version.

Chapter 4, Practical Use of Claude Code, shows you how to combine Claude on the web with Claude Code in the terminal to build a to-do management app. Along the way, you will learn essential commands, work faster with Auto-Approve mode, manage your context window, improve a UI from a screenshot, and reference files directly in your prompts.

Chapter 5, Systematic Development and Management Through Game Creation, uses a quiz game to teach you how to verify AI-generated content and guard against hallucinations. You will then automate repetitive work with your own custom commands, chain them together into workflows, and add a data storage and ranking system.

Chapter 6, Giving Claude Code Wings with APIs, explains what APIs are and how to choose an AI model, whether through an integration platform such as OpenRouter or by connecting directly. You will learn to manage API keys safely and build FridgeChef, an application that combines image recognition and text generation to suggest recipes.

Chapter 7, Building a Development Team with Claude Code AI Agents, introduces sub-agents that take on roles such as code reviewer, optimizer, and UX designer, each with its own model and permissions. You will then assemble a full AI development team, including a product manager, backend and frontend developers, a QA engineer, and an AI integration specialist, and put it to work on two real applications.

Chapter 8, Extending Claude Code with MCP, Skills, and Plugins, shows you how to push Claude Code beyond its built-in capabilities. You will connect MCP servers, including Notion, Sequential Thinking, Playwright, and GitHub; work with skills and the plugin marketplace;

deploy your project with Vercel; and connect it to a Supabase database to create a service anyone in the world can use.

To get the most out of this book

To get the most out of this book, you do not need any prior programming experience. The book is written so that complete beginners can follow along, while readers with some coding background will simply move faster through the early chapters. Where a project calls for a specific language, such as the Python program you build in *Chapter 3*, Claude Code writes and runs the code for you, so there is nothing extra to learn upfront.

You will need a computer running Windows, macOS, or Linux, along with a stable internet connection. *Chapter 3* walks you through installing Git and Claude Code from scratch, and *Chapter 8* introduces Node.js when you start working with local MCP servers.

Starting from *Chapter 2*, you will need a paid Claude subscription of at least the Pro plan. The hands-on exercises from *Chapter 3* onward involve higher token usage, so the Max plan is worth considering for a smoother experience. Later chapters also use free accounts on OpenRouter, Notion, GitHub, Vercel, and Supabase; each one is set up step by step in the relevant chapter, and the free tiers are sufficient for everything in this book.

The best way to use this book is to build alongside it. Type the prompts, run the commands, and experiment. When your results differ from what you see on the page, that is not a mistake but part of working with AI. Most sections end with review questions, and the answers are provided at the back of the book.

The code bundle contains the complete projects you build throughout the book, from the first webpage and the handwriting recognition program to the to-do app, the quiz game, FridgeChef, the agent-built applications, and the deployed shopping list service. Use them to compare against your own results, to pick up from any chapter without starting over, or as a foundation for your own ideas.

Download the example code files

This book includes a complete downloadable code bundle containing all the example projects and files used throughout the chapters. We recommend downloading the bundle so you can follow along smoothly and experiment with the examples. These are also available in the book's GitHub repositor `https://github.com/PacktPublishing/Build-with-Claude-Code`.

Use the bundle as a practical starting point. Modify it, extend it, and apply what you learn by creating your own variations as you progress through the chapters.

Get the code bundle

If you bought the book directly from Packt:

1. Go to `packtpub.com`
2. Click your profile picture and select **Your Orders**
3. Find this book and click **Download Code**

If you bought this book from Amazon or any other channel partner:

1. Go to `packtpub.com/unlock` or scan the following QR code:
2. Search for this book
3. Sign up or log in to your free Packt account
4. Upload your proof of purchase and download the code bundle locally

Usage note: You're free to use and modify this code for personal learning and non-commercial projects.

> Note
>
> **AI usage disclaimer**
>
> This book was written by the author and originally published in Korean. AI-assisted tools, including Claude and DeepL, were used to support translation into English, vocabulary checks, proofreading, and image-quality enhancement. All translated and adapted content was reviewed by the author, technical reviewer, and Packt's editorial team to preserve the meaning and technical accuracy of the original work. AI tools were used only to assist the adaptation process and did not replace expert authorship or review.

Download the color images

Your purchase includes a color, DRM-free PDF copy of this book, ideal for viewing color images, screenshots, and diagrams. Refer to *Free benefits with your book section* at the end of the *Preface* to unlock your PDF copy.

Conventions used

There are a number of text conventions used throughout this book.

`CodeInText`: Indicates code words in text, database table names, folder names, filenames, file extensions, pathnames, dummy URLs, user input, and Twitter handles. For example: "To edit the `CLAUDE.md` file, enter the `/memory` command in Claude Code."

A block of code or Claude prompt is set as follows:

```
Convert this PRD into step-by-step prompts for use in Claude Code.
Summarize it into 5 key steps and create clear instructions for each step.
```

Any command-line input or output is written as follows:

```
claude mcp add supabase -s local -e SUPABASE_ACCESS_TOKEN=<Supabase API token>
-- cmd /c npx -y @supabase/mcp-server-supabase@latest
```

Bold: Indicates a new term, an important word, or words that you see on the screen. For instance, words in menus or dialog boxes appear in the text like this. For example: "In the **Generate New Token** window, enter `my_first_project` in the **Name** field and set **Expires** in (token validity period) to **30 days**. Then, click the **Generate token** button to complete the setup."

> **Note**
>
> Warnings or important notes appear like this.

> **Tip**
>
> Tips and tricks appear like this.

Get in touch

Feedback from our readers is always welcome.

General feedback: If you have questions about any aspect of this book or have any general feedback, please email us at `customercare@packt.com` and mention the book's title in the subject of your message.

Errata: Although we have taken every care to ensure the accuracy of our content, mistakes do happen. If you have found a mistake in this book, we would be grateful if you reported this to us. Please visit `http://www.packt.com/submit-errata`, click **Submit Errata**, and fill in the form.

Piracy: If you come across any illegal copies of our works in any form on the internet, we would be grateful if you would provide us with the location address or website name. Please contact us at `copyright@packt.com` with a link to the material.

If you are interested in becoming an author: If there is a topic that you have expertise in and you are interested in either writing or contributing to a book, please visit `http://authors.packt.com/`.

Free benefits with your book

This book includes free benefits designed to support your learning and help you apply what you learn effectively. Activate them now for instant access (see the *How to unlock* section for instructions).

Here's a quick overview of what you can instantly unlock with your purchase:

How to unlock

Scan the QR code (or go to `packtpub.com/unlock`). Search for this book by name, confirm the edition, and then follow the steps on the page.

UNLOCK NOW

Note: Have your invoice handy. Purchases made directly from the Packt website don't require an invoice.

Share your thoughts

Once you've read *Build with Claude Code*, we'd love to hear your thoughts! Scan the QR code below to go straight to the Amazon review page for this book and share your feedback.

`https://packt.link/r/1807781798`

Your review is important to us and the tech community and will help us make sure we're delivering excellent quality content.

Part 1

Foundations of Vibe Coding

This part covers the foundations of vibe coding: working with Claude on the web, writing prompts that get real results, and installing Claude Code to build your first programs. With detailed explanations and practical examples throughout, even absolute beginners can follow along without feeling overwhelmed.

This part of the book includes the following chapters:

- *Chapter 1, My First Vibe Coding*
- *Chapter 2, Maximizing AI's Potential with Effective Prompts*
- *Chapter 3, Getting Started with Claude Code*
- *Chapter 4, Practical Use of Claude Code*

1

My First Vibe Coding

A new era of coding has begun. The way we write software is changing with the rise of AI-assisted development and Vibe Coding. You no longer need to struggle with code on your own. That's because AI can act as your coding partner, guiding you through the entire process of turning your ideas into reality. In this chapter, we'll explore the basic concepts of Vibe Coding and the features of AI assistants, and we'll experience the new world of coding by actually trying Vibe Coding for ourselves.

Learning objectives:

- Understand the types and features of AI assistants
- Create your own webpage using AI models

> Note
>
> **Download the code bundle and the PDF version of this book**
>
> Your purchase includes a DRM-free PDF copy of this book, the code bundle, and a range of exclusive benefits. To unlock everything, follow the *Free benefits with your book* section in the *Preface*.

My coding partner, AI assistant

> Note
>
> **Key terms**: Vibe Coding | Model Selection Tool | Dedicated Model
>
> We explore and compare various Vibe Coding tools, from web-based chatbots to dedicated AI tools. We'll also examine how AI technology has evolved and how these tools fit into modern development workflows.

Before you begin

When you think of a programmer, you might picture someone staring intently at a screen and working through problems alone. This book will completely change that image. Coding today is not a solitary journey. That's because you have an AI partner who brainstorms ideas with you, answers your questions whenever you ask, and sits right beside you to write code together. This is the new way of programming presented by **Vibe Coding**.

Let's embark on a journey into Vibe Coding with your AI partner!

You've probably heard of large-scale AI models known as **Large Language Models (LLMs)**. The reason these models serve as powerful tools in coding is that they've been trained not only on natural language but also on vast amounts of programming code and technical documentation. As a result, LLMs can recognize the syntax and patterns of programming languages and generate code in response to natural-language instructions. Developers who recognized this potential gradually began applying LLMs to actual coding, and this marked the beginning of a new development paradigm known as "Vibe coding."

Vibe Coding

Vibe Coding refers to a new development approach that moves beyond the traditional programming method, where humans write code line by line, to a new paradigm where programs are implemented through dialogue with AI. Coined in February 2025 by OpenAI co-founder Andrej Karpathy, this term describes a process in which a person explains an idea to the AI in natural language; the AI interprets this and suggests code and execution methods, and the person reviews and modifies these suggestions to gradually improve the code's quality.

One of the key ideas behind Vibe Coding is that it lowers the barrier to software development. This is because LLMs have learned from vast amounts of text and source code, enabling them to understand human requests and generate context-appropriate code.

As a result, you no longer need to spend years learning development skills to an expert level; as long as you have an idea, you can easily complete a program through a conversation with AI. This has provided new opportunities for beginners who were previously frustrated by the act of writing code itself, while offering a way for experienced developers to dramatically increase their productivity.

The following figure shows the results of asking ChatGPT and Claude to create a calendar web app. After a brief moment of thought, the AI immediately generated the web app's script, and you can see the calendar webpage working in the preview window.

ChatGPT:

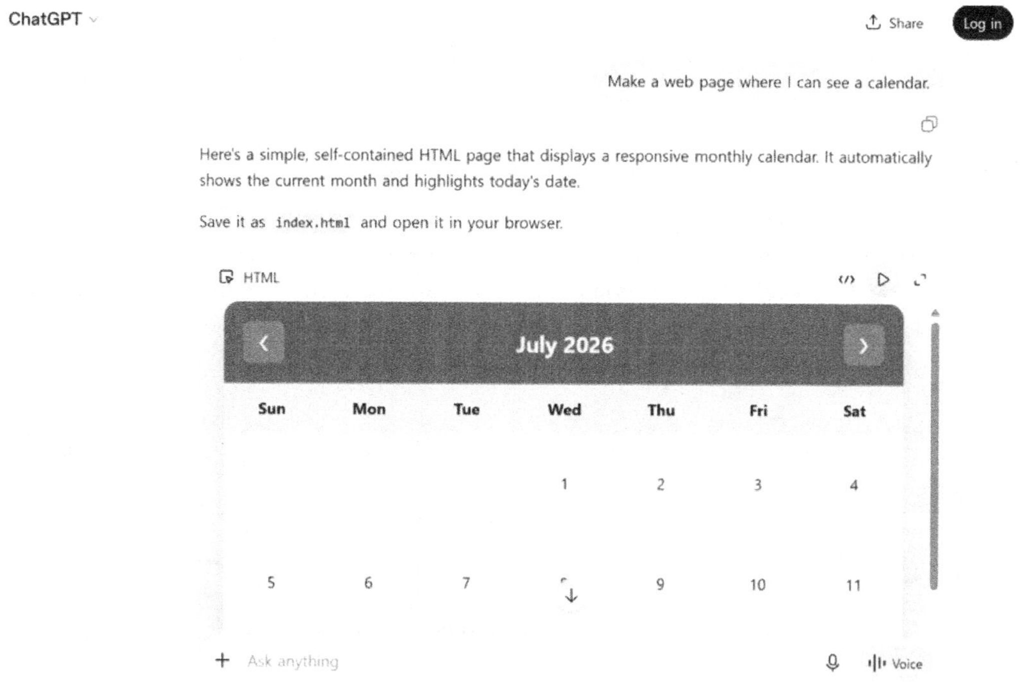

Figure 1.1: Asking ChatGPT to build a calendar app

Claude:

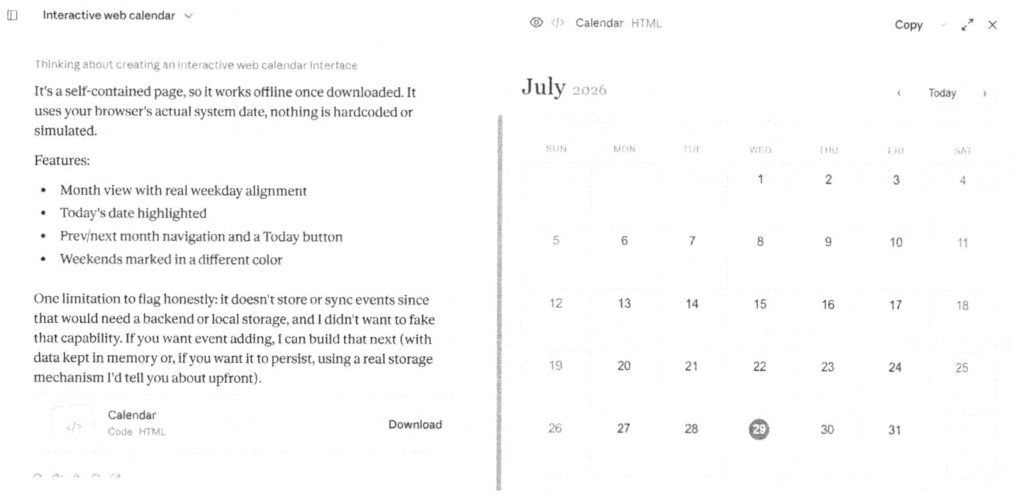

Figure 1.2: Claude generating the calendar app in an artifact

However, there were a few drawbacks to coding through a web chat interface. You had to manually copy the code generated in the chat window and paste it into your development environment, and due to the nature of web-based AI chat services, there were limitations when it came to accessing files on my computer or managing the entire project holistically.

The emergence of AI integration tools

To address these limitations, new tools have emerged that directly integrate AI into developers' actual work environments. These tools are designed not just to generate code, but to provide AI support throughout the entire development process. AI-integrated programming tools can be broadly classified into two types:

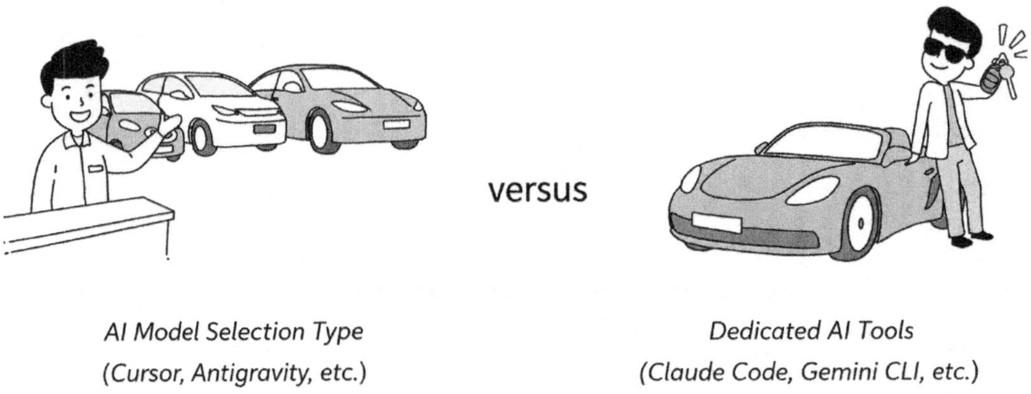

Figure 1.3: AI model selection type versus Dedicated AI tools

Model selection type

The first approach is the model-selection type. Much like renting a car, this approach allows users to choose from multiple LLMs within the same development tool. Since the code editor and AI are integrated, users can conveniently write and edit code within the user interface without having to copy and paste. Representative tools include Cursor and Antigravity.

The model selection approach offers the advantage of allowing users to conveniently choose the language model that best suits their needs from a variety of options. However, just as you pay for gas and rental fees when renting a car, you may have to pay a subscription fee for the tool itself in addition to the cost of using the model, as is the case with **Cursor**. On the other hand, there are tools like **Antigravity** that are offered for free, so it's important to check each tool's pricing policy in advance.

Dedicated model type

The second approach is the dedicated model approach. This involves installing a specific AI language model directly on your computer, which is similar to owning your own car. Representative examples include Claude Code, based on Claude, and Google's Gemini CLI.

Since you install the dedicated software provided by the AI model's developer, you only pay for the model itself without any additional costs. A key advantage is that you can directly access local files, allowing you to effectively manage your entire project.

These tools generally operate via a **Command Line Interface** (**CLI**), where you enter commands directly into the terminal. The terminal's text-based interface may seem unfamiliar to first-time users, but there's no need to worry. As you follow the instructions in this book and learn step by step, you'll find that it's not as difficult as you might think. In fact, you'll come to realize that you can work much faster and more accurately than by clicking with a mouse.

Note

GUIs and CLIs

There are two main ways for users to interact with computers. One is the **Graphical User Interface** (**GUI**), the common method where you use a mouse to click on graphical elements such as icons, buttons, and windows on the screen.

The other is the Command Line Interface (CLI), which involves directly entering text commands into a window called the command prompt (`cmd`) to control the computer. For example, `mkdir temp` is a command to create a new directory named `temp`. While the CLI may seem difficult at first glance, it is fast and lightweight, making it far more efficient than the GUI—especially for experts managing servers or automating repetitive tasks.

The tools used in Vibe coding are constantly evolving, but while their appearances may differ, their essence remains the same. They are simply different interfaces built on top of the powerful LLM engine. You just need to choose the tool that best suits your needs and situation.

The performance of LLMs is continuously improving, so you can expect similar results regardless of which model you use for basic coding. However, as the difficulty of the task increases, context understanding and system integration become more important.

This book primarily uses Claude and Claude Code. Claude provides the underlying AI capabilities, while Claude Code brings those capabilities into a command-line coding workflow.

> **Note**
>
> Claude's market share is more than double that of other tools (*Menlo Ventures, 2025 Mid-Year LLM Market Update: Claude holds 42 percent of AI code generation versus 21 percent for OpenAI*).

In this section, we've taken a look at the overall landscape of AI coding tools. In the next section, we'll run a project directly through the Claude web interface and get started with our first Vibe Coding session. Next, in *Chapter 2*, we'll learn how to write structured prompts, and starting in *Chapter 3*, we'll dive into the world of full-fledged Vibe Coding using the powerful tool known as Claude Code.

Deep dive: the birth and evolution of AI

Today's AI assistants, which are revolutionizing industries and astonishing people, are the result of long-standing efforts to create human-like AI. The history of **Artificial Intelligence (AI)** began in the 1940s with early work related to "neural networks." Attempts to have machines learn from given data, identify patterns within it, and make predictions have steadily evolved, and around 2010, this field became more widely known as "deep learning."

Early deep learning models used in image processing and generation, as well as sequential data processing, include **Convolutional Neural Networks (CNNs)**, **Generative Adversarial Networks (GANs)**, **Autoencoders (AEs)**, and **Recurrent Neural Networks (RNNs)**. A brief overview is as follows:

- **CNN**: A filter-based hierarchical structure that autonomously learns features within images; used in image classification and recognition
- **GAN**: A structure in which a generator and a discriminator compete to improve performance; specialized for generating new data
- **AE**: A self-supervised neural network with an encoder-decoder architecture; excels at extracting and reconstructing the core representation of data
- **RNN**: A neural network architecture designed to learn patterns in sequential data; commonly used for text and time-series data

Subsequently, transformers overcame the limitations of RNNs through the attention mechanism and have become the foundational technology for large language models such as ChatGPT and Claude.

The advancement of deep learning has been accompanied not only by image-based models but also by the development of **Large Language Models (LLMs)** capable of processing and generating natural language. In particular, the introduction of the "Transformer" model, announced by a Google research team in 2017, marked a turning point that led to a breakthrough in language models.

OpenAI recognized that large-scale investments in transformer-based infrastructure would lead to performance improvements, and released the Generative Pre-trained Transformer GPT series. By the time it reached version 3.5, it was successfully commercialized under the name ChatGPT.

Subsequently, Anthropic, founded in 2021 by former OpenAI researchers with a focus on AI safety, developed Claude, which has established itself as the most popular AI tool in the coding field today. After that, Google, a latecomer to the field, launched Gemini, while xAI is driving today's AI boom by successively unveiling large language models such as Grok.

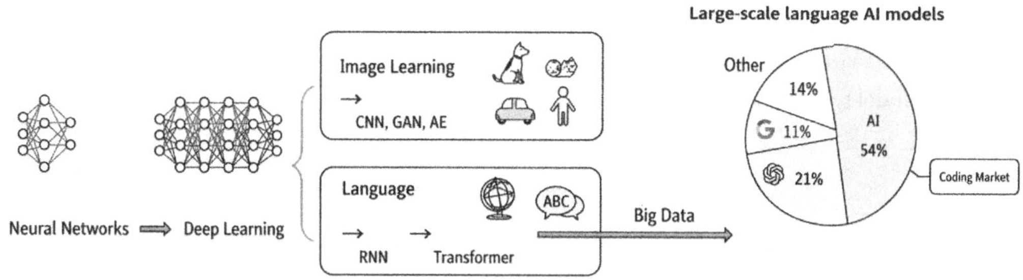

Figure 1.4: The evolution of AI from neural networks to LLMs

Wrapping up

Key takeaways summarized in 3 keywords:

- **Vibe coding** is a new development approach in which you create code by conversing naturally with AI.
- **Model-selection tools** offer the advantage of being able to choose from a variety of language models.
- **Dedicated model-based tools** are designed to provide deeper integration with a specific model or model family.

Review questions

1. The following are types of Vibe Coding tools. Complete the table by providing a representative tool for each category:

Category	Description	Representative Tools
Web-based chatbot	A method that can be used directly on the web without installation; copy-and-paste required	
Model selection type	A method where you can choose from multiple language models; may incur additional costs	
Dedicated model type	A method where you install and use a specific language model; allows direct access to local files	

Table 1.1: Fill in the appropriate tool names

2. Read the following descriptions and select the appropriate concept (term):
    1. A new development approach in which you explain an idea to AI as if in conversation, the AI proposes code, and you review and refine it to completion → (_)
    2. A virtual partner in the programming process that answers questions and writes code alongside you → (_)
    3. An AI coding tool, like a rental car, that lets you choose from multiple LLMs → (_)
    4. An AI coding tool, like a personal vehicle, that involves installing a specific model for in-depth use → (_)

Now that you've seen what Vibe Coding is and how AI coding tools have evolved, let's put it into practice by creating your first webpage with Claude.

Create my first webpage

> **Note**
>
> **Key terms:** Artifact | Prompt | Publish | Customize
>
> Claude offers an "Artifact" feature that allows you to create web pages and applications using only conversation.

> In this section, we'll create your own webpage through step-by-step exercises, covering everything from creating an account and opening Artifacts to building, publishing, and customizing a webpage. You'll understand the core workflow of web development and experience "Vibe Coding" without writing a single line of code.

Before you begin

A basic web page is created by combining three elements: HTML, CSS, and JavaScript. HTML creates the skeleton, CSS refines the colors and layout, and JavaScript adds functionality and interactivity. Traditionally, developers wrote all this code themselves, but Vibe Coding offers a different approach. If you explain the desired features and design to the AI in detail, it will automatically combine these three elements to create a fully functional webpage.

Figure 1.5: An AI partner writes the HTML, CSS, and JavaScript for you

How about having your own start page where you can see all the information you need at a glance every morning when you turn on your computer? Now, let's create a personalized start page that includes the weather, news, a clock, and a search function.

Getting started with Claude

First, open your web browser, go to the official Claude website (`https://claude.ai`), and log in. If this is your first time using Claude, follow the on-screen instructions to create an account.

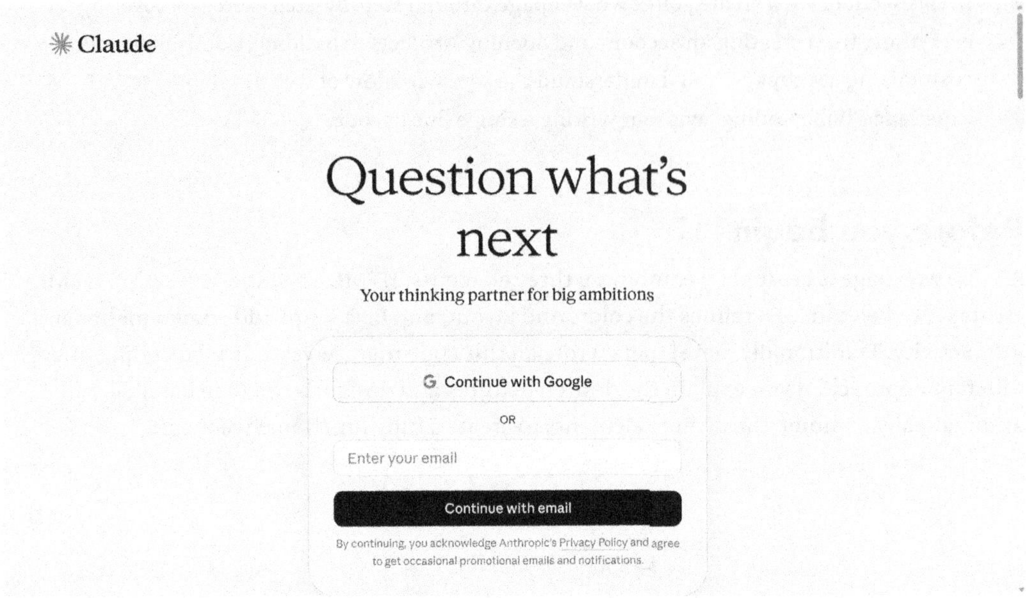

Figure 1.6: The Claude login page at claude.ai

Tip

For seamless account management, we recommend clicking **Continue with Google**. If you're asked whether to install the desktop version, click **Skip**. We'll be testing this on the web for now.

After successfully logging in, click the **New Chat (+)** icon on the left sidebar to proceed to the following screen.

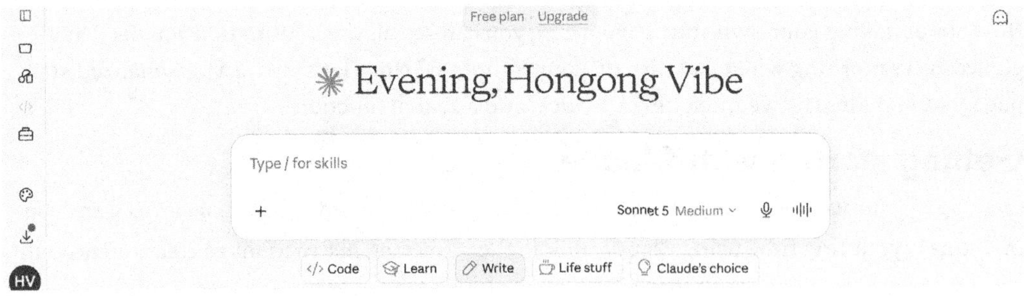

Figure 1.7: The Claude chat screen after logging in

Creating a webpage with Claude Artifacts

Claude offers a special feature called "*artifacts*." Artifacts are panels that are separate from the conversation window, allowing you to immediately see actual, functional results that go beyond simple text-based communication. They are particularly useful for creating reports, charts, and simple web pages, making them ideal for quickly validating ideas. Additionally, since previous versions are saved with every edit, you can experiment freely without hesitation, naturally learning how to refine your prompts step by step.

Opening a new artifact

Now, we'll use Artifacts—one of Claude's core features—to create a simple webpage. Before we begin, let's open a new Artifact and prepare to chat with the AI.

1. Click the *Artifacts* icon in the left sidebar of the Claude chat window.

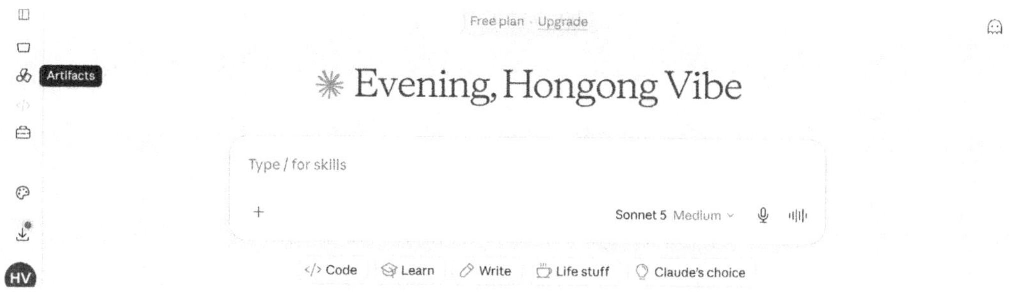

Figure 1.8: Clicking the Artifacts icon in the left sidebar

2. Click the **New artifact** button.

Figure 1.9: Clicking New artifact on the Artifacts page

3. Click **Start from Scratch** in the Artifact categories.

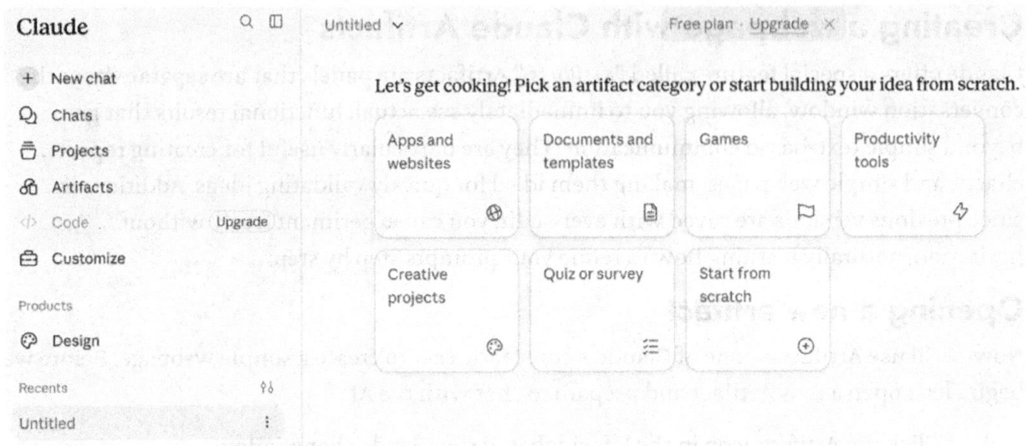

Figure 1.10: Choosing a category for the new artifact

4. Claude will ask what kind of app or website you want to create. Select **Start from scratch**.

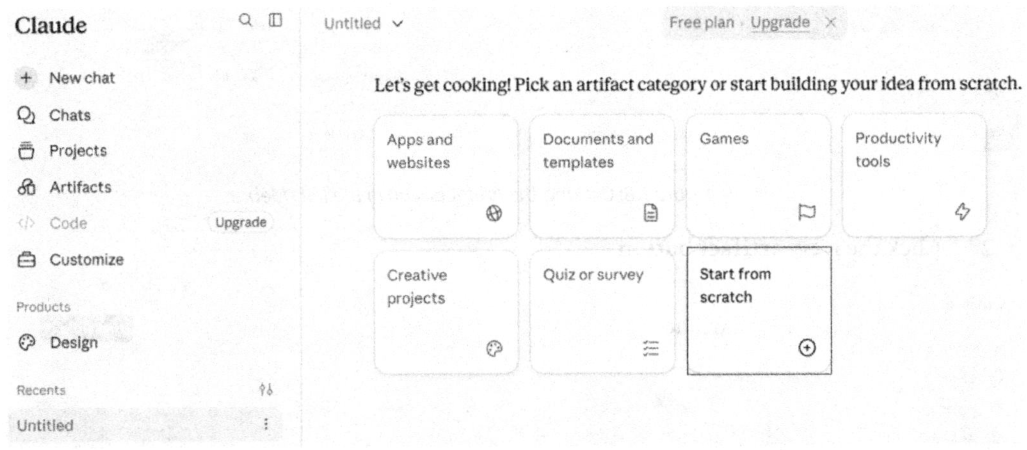

Figure 1.11: Selecting Start from scratch from the category list

Now you're ready to give Claude your first prompt.

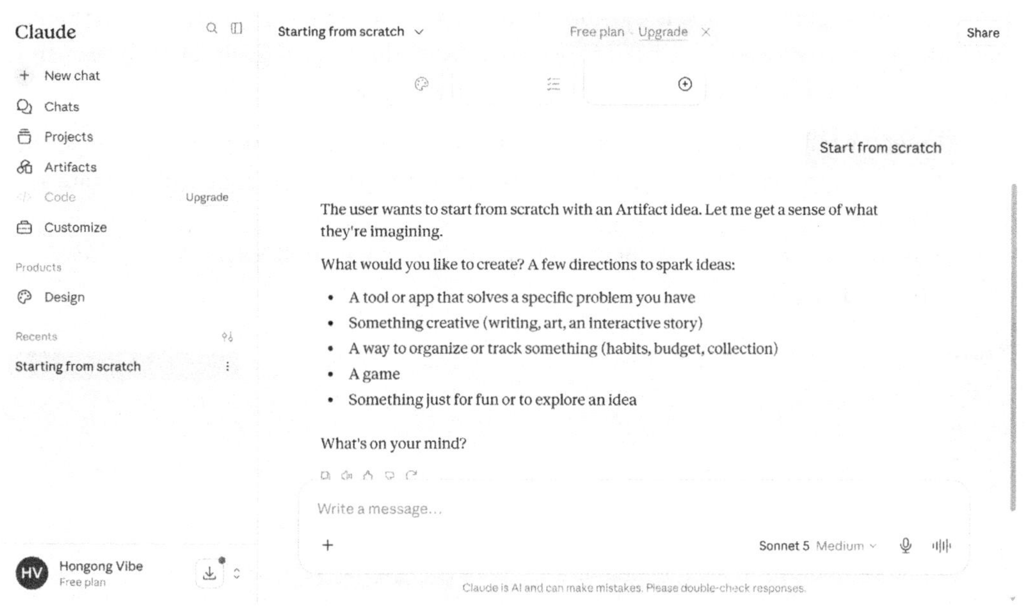

Figure 1.12: Claude ready to receive your prompt

Now that your artifact is ready, let's create the actual webpage and publish it to the web.

Creating and publishing a web page

A key aspect of Vibe Coding is that you can ask the AI to code using natural language, without any programming terminology. The requests or instructions you give the AI are called prompts.

In Vibe Coding, a prompt is not just a simple instruction; it is a key resource that determines the direction and quality of the desired output. The more specific and contextually relevant the prompt is, the more likely the AI is to generate code and ideas that match your intent. Conversely, vague or abstract prompts can lead to unnecessary revisions and rework, reducing efficiency.

The website we're going to build is the homepage of a web app that displays today's date and time with a search bar. There's no need to overcomplicate things. Let's make our request using comfortable, natural language—without any programming jargon.

1. Enter the following text into the prompt input field in the chat window, then press the *Enter* key to submit your request. Upon receiving the prompt, Claude will generate a response:

   ```
   I want to create my own personal start homepage with today's date and time and a search bar.
   ```

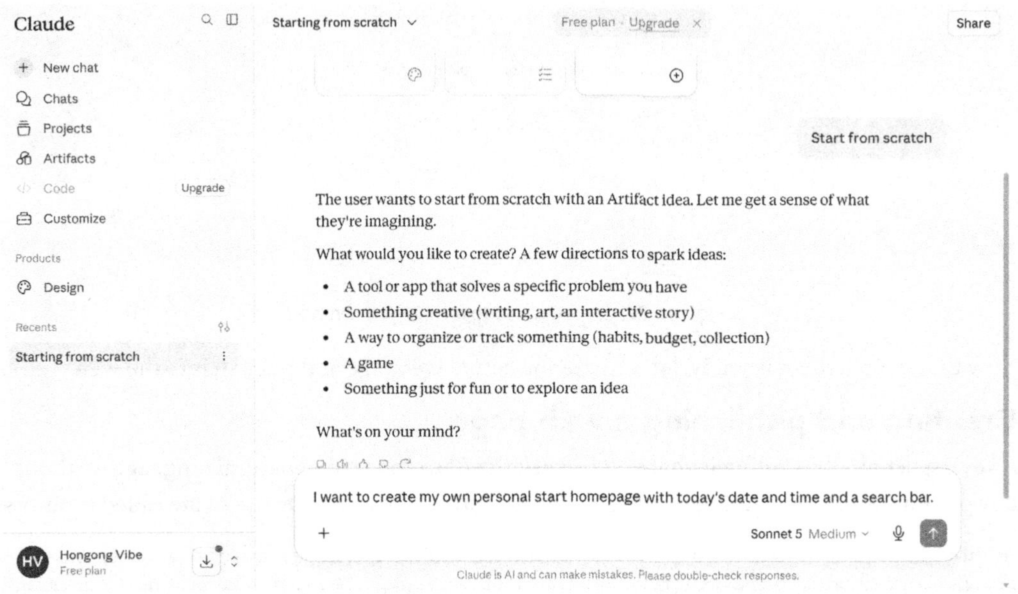

Figure 1.13: Entering the start page prompt

2. You'll be asked a few quick questions. The questions may vary depending on the prompt you entered, so choose the options that best match your preferences. Here, the first question asks for a clock format; let's select **24-hour**.

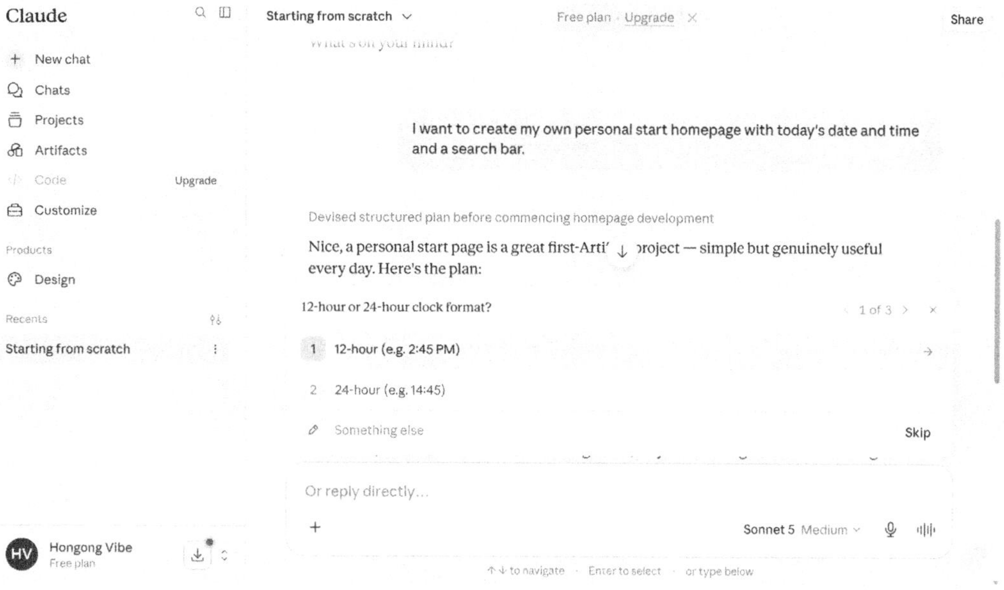

Figure 1.14: Answering Claude's first question

3. Next, a screen appears where you can choose a search engine. Here, let's select **Google**.

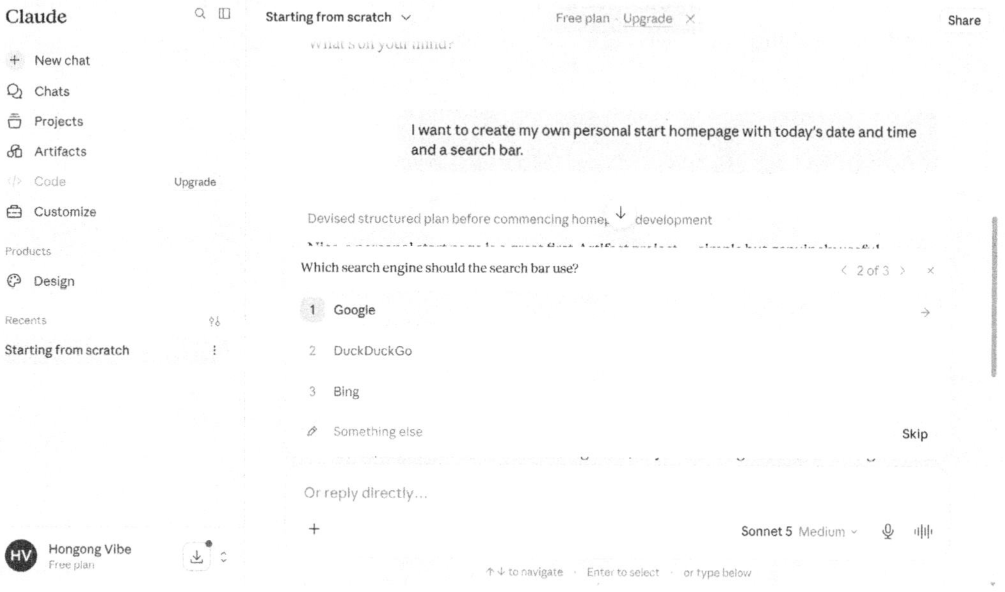

Figure 1.15: Selecting Google as the search engine

4. Finally, choose a design style. Here, let's select **Minimal & clean (light)**.

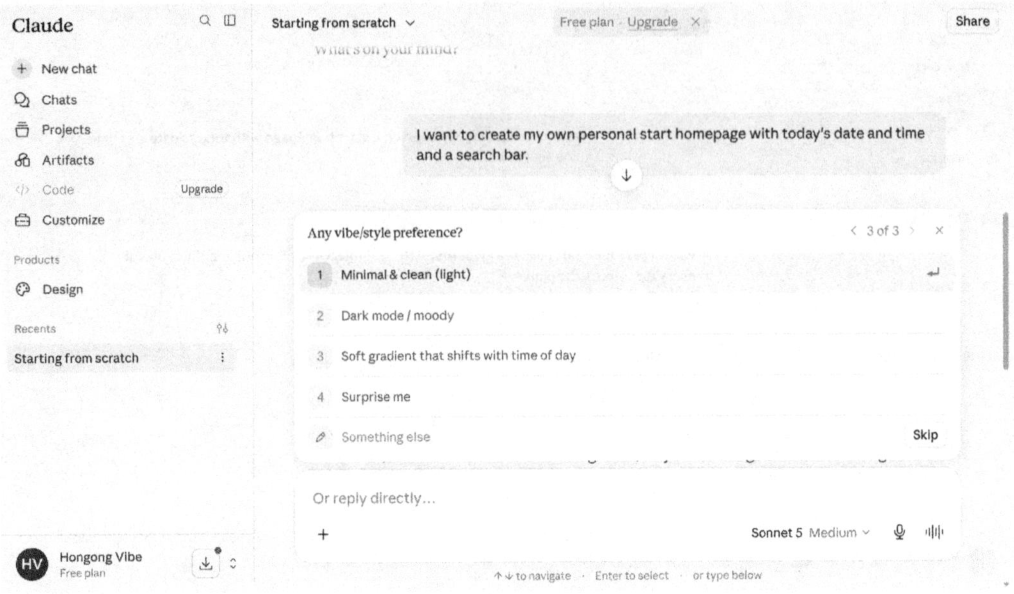

Figure 1.16: Choosing a design style

5. After a moment, a homepage incorporating all your requested features will be generated. On the left, you'll see a summary of the features Claude has implemented, and on the right, you'll see the screen in action.

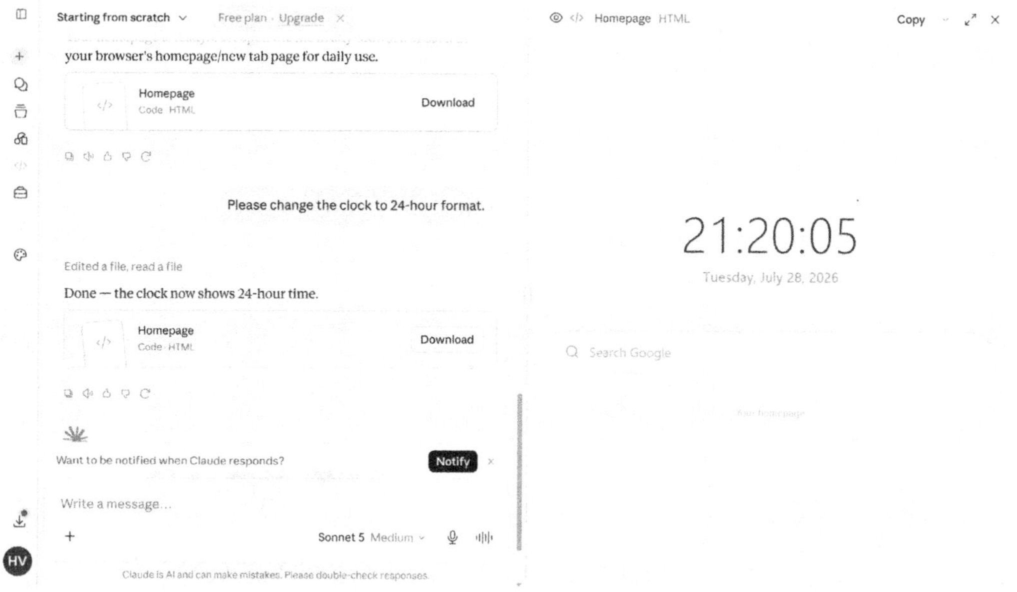

Figure 1.17: The generated start page with clock, date, and search

6. To share the completed website with others or access it through a public link, open the menu next to the *Copy* button in the upper right corner and select **Publish artifact**. When the **Publish artifact** window appears, click **Publish & copy link** to copy the shareable link.

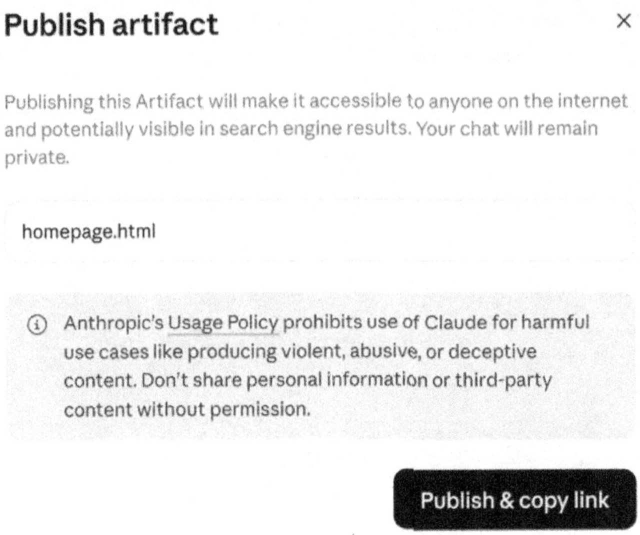

Figure 1.18: Publishing the artifact and copying the shareable link

7. Paste the copied link into a new browser tab to open the published website. Let's check if the search function actually works. Type `Today's Stock News` into the search bar and press the *Enter* key.

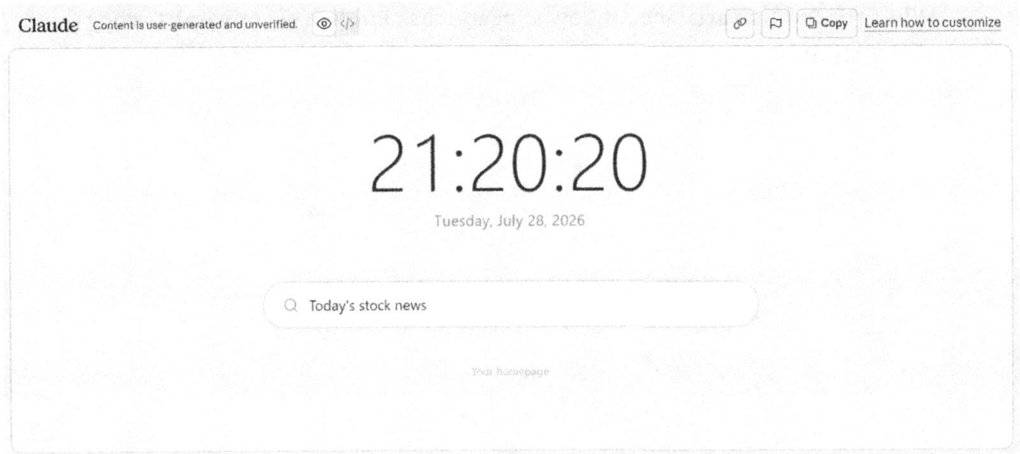

Figure 1.19: Testing the search bar on the published page

8. The results open in a new browser tab. If nothing happens on the published page (external links can be blocked there), click **Download in the chat** to save the HTML file, open it in your browser, and search there.

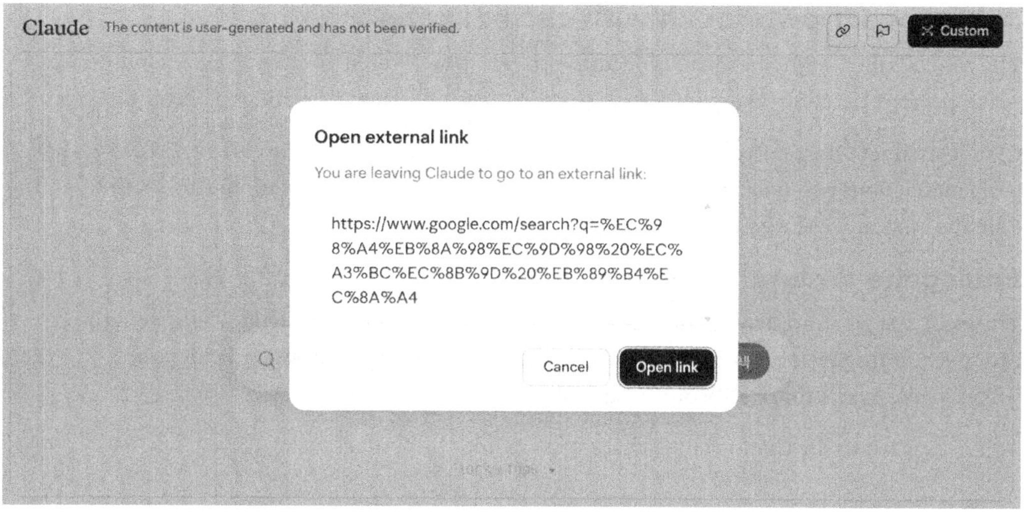

Figure 1.20: Confirming the external link to Google search

9. The Google search results page will open, displaying results related to **Today's Stock News**.

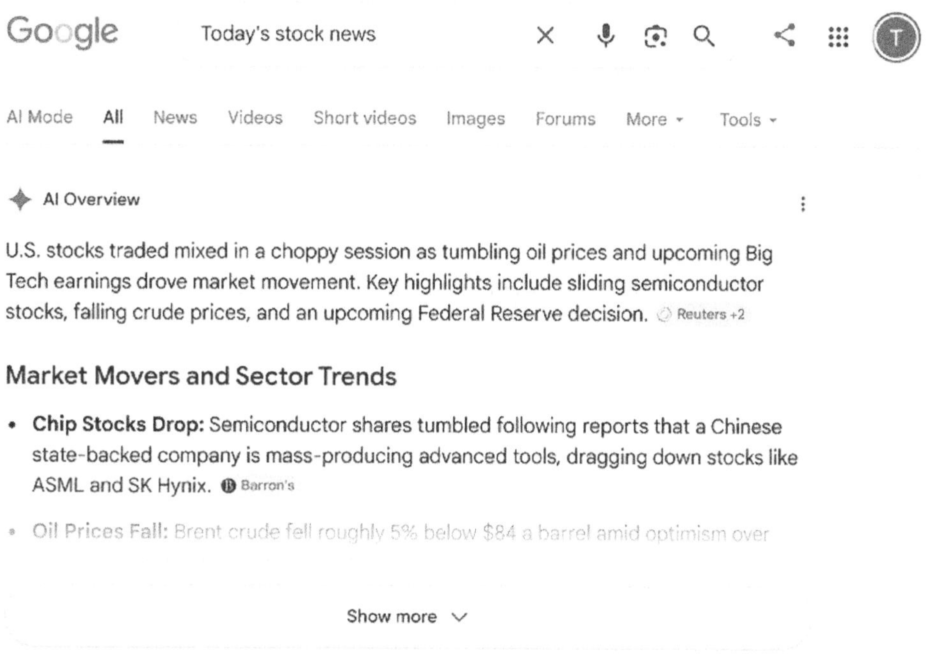

Figure 1.21: Google search results opened from the start page

Adding your own touch with customization

The core of Vibe Coding lies in *editing* and *customization*. Even if your first result isn't perfect, it's important to refine it step by step in the direction you want to achieve a better final result.

Claude Artifact offers customization features. These features allow you to create results that truly match your personality and needs without relying solely on the AI. In this section, we'll edit and customize the generated start page ourselves.

Editing the design

The webpage generated by Claude looks good enough, but since the design was generated randomly, it might not match your preferences. Let's modify the design to suit your preferences. Again, there's absolutely no need to edit the script yourself.

1. Return to the Claude chat where you created the artifact.

Figure 1.22: The published page seen by other visitors

2. Enter the following in the prompt field to request a design change:
   Prompt: `Please modify this design to match the Google style.`

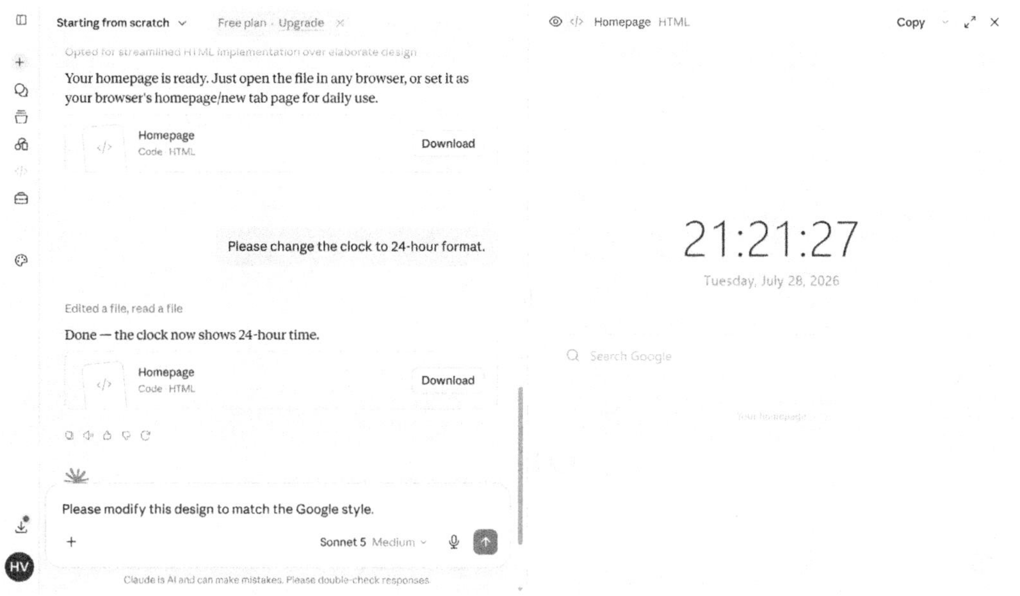

Figure 1.23: Requesting a Google-style design change

3. Claude understands the request and generates CSS and HTML code to modify the design.

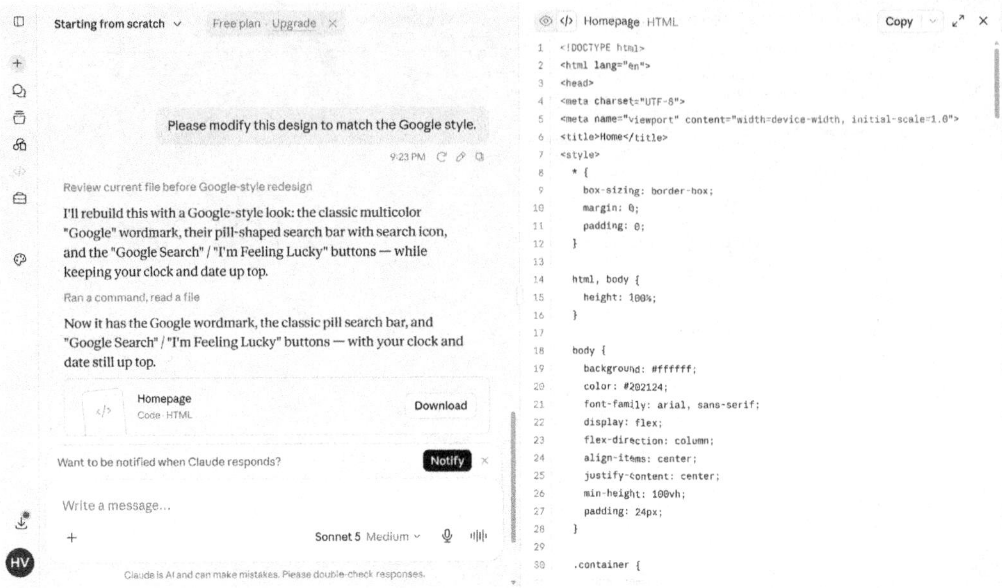

Figure 1.24: Claude rewriting the CSS and HTML for the new design

4. Wait a moment, and the webpage's design will be updated to resemble Google's homepage. By using this customization feature, you can modify the design of the artifact or add new features.

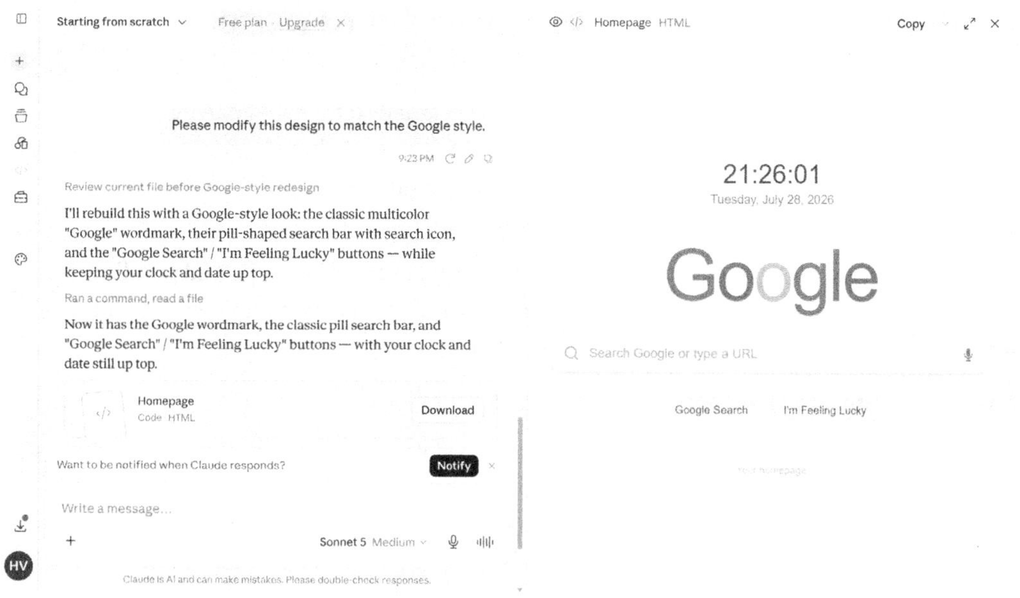

Figure 1.25: The start page restyled to look like Google

You've just experienced your first Vibe Coding session. In a short amount of time, without writing a single line of code, you've created a personal page featuring date, time, and search functions—all through a conversation with AI. What's more, it's a fully functional web page. This is the power of Vibe Coding.

Note

Importance of prompts

You've had the amazing experience of easily creating a webpage through conversation, even without any development knowledge. However, you likely discovered an important fact during this process: a specific request, such as "a home page with date and search functions," yields more satisfying results than a vague request like "make me a website."

AI needs specific instructions to accurately understand our intentions. In the next chapter, we'll delve into strategic communication methods—specifically, how to write effective prompts—to maximize AI's potential.

Deep dive: Unlocking a more powerful AI partner with a Claude subscription

The hands-on exercises up to this point have been designed so that they can be followed using Claude's free plan, but the free plan has limited usage—after exchanging dozens of messages, the conversation may be interrupted. In addition, during periods of heavy traffic, lower-priority access can result in slower speeds or restricted availability.

Starting from *Chapter 2*, a paid Claude subscription (Pro or higher) is required to follow the course material. Since the hands-on exercises in *Chapter 3* and beyond involve higher token usage, you may also want to consider the Max plan.

Subscribing to a Claude paid plan

Claude offers two paid plans: the Pro plan, which is relatively affordable and allows you to try out all features—including Claude Code—and the Max plan, which is designed for larger projects or longer conversations. Additionally, if you subscribe to the Max plan, you can upgrade to the Max (20x) option, which provides the highest usage limits of any plan.

Using Claude Code for Vibe Coding requires a lot of conversations, so it's essential to choose a plan that fits your usage patterns. You can upgrade or downgrade your selected plan at any time.

1. Click your profile at the bottom of the Claude chat window, then select the **Upgrade Plan** menu from the list that appears.

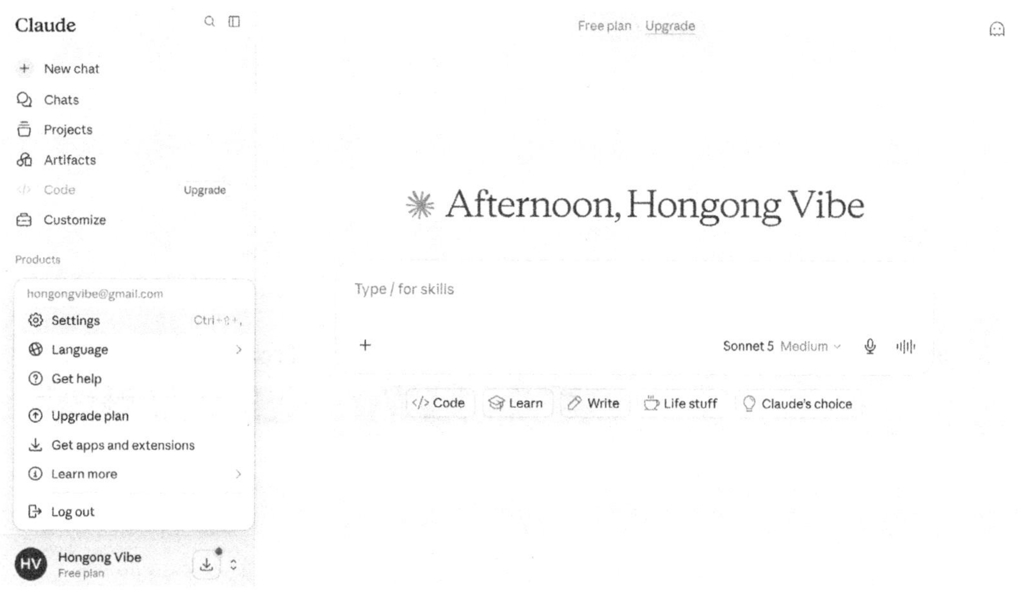

Figure 1.26: Opening the Upgrade plan menu from the profile

2. Select either the **Pro** or **Max** plan. Choose the plan that fits your budget. If you're starting with Pro, click the **Buy Pro Plan** button; if you're purchasing Max, click the **Subscribe to Max Plan** button.

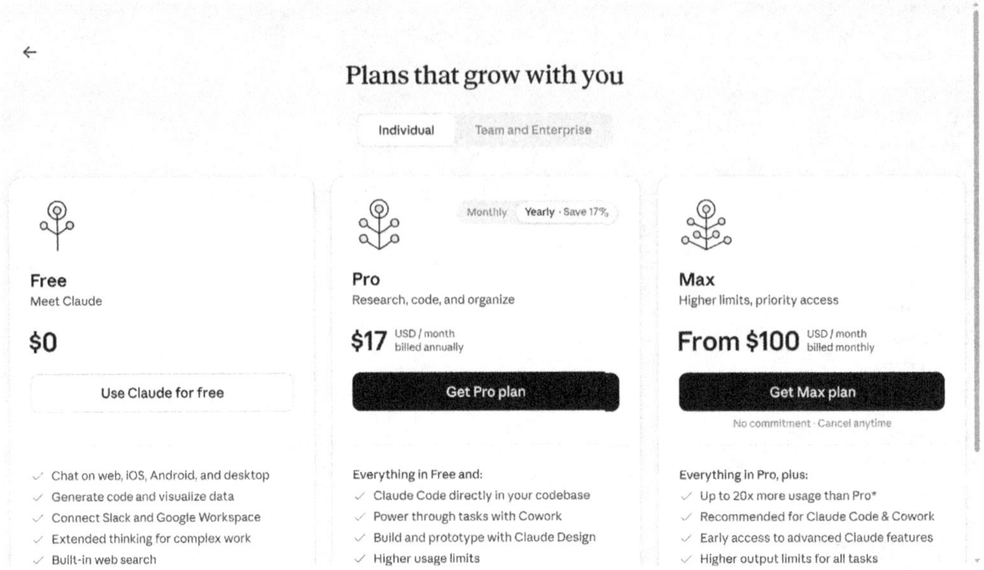

Figure 1.27: Comparing the Free, Pro, and Max plans

3. Enter your payment information to complete your subscription.

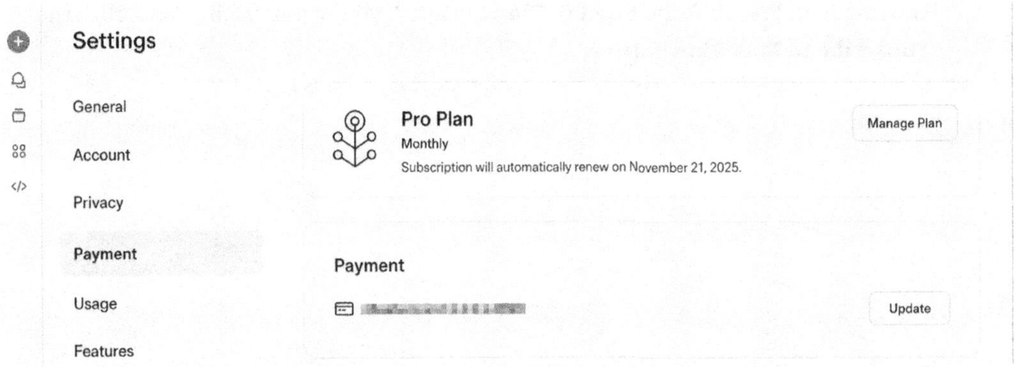

Figure 1.28: Billing settings confirming the active Pro subscription

Paid plan comparison

The following table compares the prices, usage limits, and features of the three plans offered by Claude. Review the table and choose the plan that best suits your needs:

	Free	Pro	Max (5x)	Max (20x)
Monthly fee	$0	$20	$100	$200

	Free	Pro	Max (5x)	Max (20x)
Usage	Limited usage	Approximately 5 times that of the Free plan	About 5 times that of the Pro plan	About 20 times that of the Pro plan
Features	Advanced models not available	Model selection available; Claude Code usage allowed	Pro features + priority access, web search available	Max features + maximum usage
Ideal user profile	Users who occasionally engage in light conversations	General users who regularly use Claude for work	Users who want to work on a variety of topics and long-term projects using Claude Code	Users who want to use Claude Code with the highest usage limits

Table 1.2: Comparison of the plans offered by Claude

Tip

The **Max (20x)** plan is available after selecting the Max plan and choosing the $200 option. For the hands-on exercises in *Chapter 3* and beyond, the Max plan or higher is recommended.

Wrapping up

Key takeaways summarized in 4 keywords:

- **An Artifact** is the workspace where Claude generates code and provides a live preview.
- **A prompt** is the request or instruction you deliver to AI.
- **The Publish** feature shares your creation online and generates a shareable link.
- **Customize** is the process of making further modifications on top of an existing design.

Review questions

1. Select the correct sequence that represents the development of AI assistants:
    - Deep learning → Neural networks → Transformer → LLM
    - Neural networks → Deep learning → Transformer → LLM
    - Transformer → Deep learning → Neural networks → LLM
    - LLM → Transformer → Deep learning → Neural networks
2. Select the statement that is *NOT* a feature of CLI-based models such as Claude Code.
    - Direct access to the local file system is possible.
    - The entire project can be managed in an integrated manner.
    - Tasks are performed using terminal commands.
    - Both the tool usage fee and the AI model cost must be paid.
3. Select the correct answer for the special workspace in Claude used when generating code or documents.
    - Prompt
    - Artifacts
    - Terminal
    - Command Line Interface (CLI)
4. To share a webpage you have built with others, you must click the (__) button.
5. To modify an already-published webpage, you must click the (__) button.

2

Maximizing AI's Potential with Effective Prompts

You have already taken your first steps into Vibe Coding by completing your own web page. However, we can't say we've fully experienced the true value of AI yet. This is because, when collaborating with AI, the results vary significantly depending on the commands you issue via prompts. A single well-written prompt can yield better results, shorten development time, and eliminate the need for dozens of revisions. In this chapter, we will learn prompt-writing techniques designed to unlock AI's full potential.

Learning objectives:

- Understand the components of effective prompts and create them
- Use AI to draft structured project proposals
- Break down complex projects into steps for efficient execution.
- Diagnose and resolve issues when AI responses do not meet expectations.

The secrets of prompts that awaken AI

> Note
>
> **Key terms**: Prompt | 5W1H | PRD | Template
>
> You'll learn the basic principles of prompt writing to unlock the full potential of AI. You'll understand the importance of specific and clear instructions and create a structured question template based on the 5W1H principle. Using this, you'll practice the process of writing a professional proposal for your portfolio.

Before you begin

AI is a vast repository of knowledge that has been trained on massive amounts of language data. However, the only way to communicate with this enormous storehouse of knowledge—accumulated by humanity over centuries—is through a single small prompt window. A prompt is similar to entering a destination into a navigation system. While you won't get precise directions from a command like "Take me somewhere nice," if you enter "the fastest route from Times Square to Central Park," you'll be able to reach your destination via the most efficient route.

Therefore, to maximize the potential of AI within the constraints of language, it is essential to write clear and specific prompts. The first spell to awaken the sleeping giant that is AI is a well-crafted prompt.

The importance of prompts

The most important starting point in any AI-driven task is the prompt. No matter how capable an AI may be, it's difficult for it to produce the expected results if it doesn't properly understand what we want. In other words, it's no exaggeration to say that the quality of the results depends on the quality of the prompt. So, what exactly makes a good prompt?

The characteristics of a good prompt:

A good prompt is not simply a long or elaborate description; it must meet three criteria: **clarity**, **specificity**, and **context**:

- **Clarity**: Avoid ambiguous language and clearly convey the desired outcome.
- **Specificity**: You must specify in detail the features or conditions required for the output.
- **Context**: Explain why it is needed and in what situations it will be used so that the AI can provide a more precise response.

When these three elements are met, the AI can produce much higher-quality results.

Limitations of ambiguous prompts:

Vague instructions can confuse the AI and lead to results that differ from what was expected. Let's look at the following example to see what limitations an unclear prompt can reveal.

Prompt: `Create a cool, personalized homepage for me.`

This prompt cannot be considered a good one. The term "cool" is far too vague. It's unclear whether the user wants a sleek design, powerful features, or both. Faced with such a vague request, the AI is at a loss as to which of the hundreds of possibilities to choose.

If specific requirements are missing, the AI will have no choice but to determine all elements arbitrarily, and there is a high likelihood that the output will differ from the user's expectations or preferences.

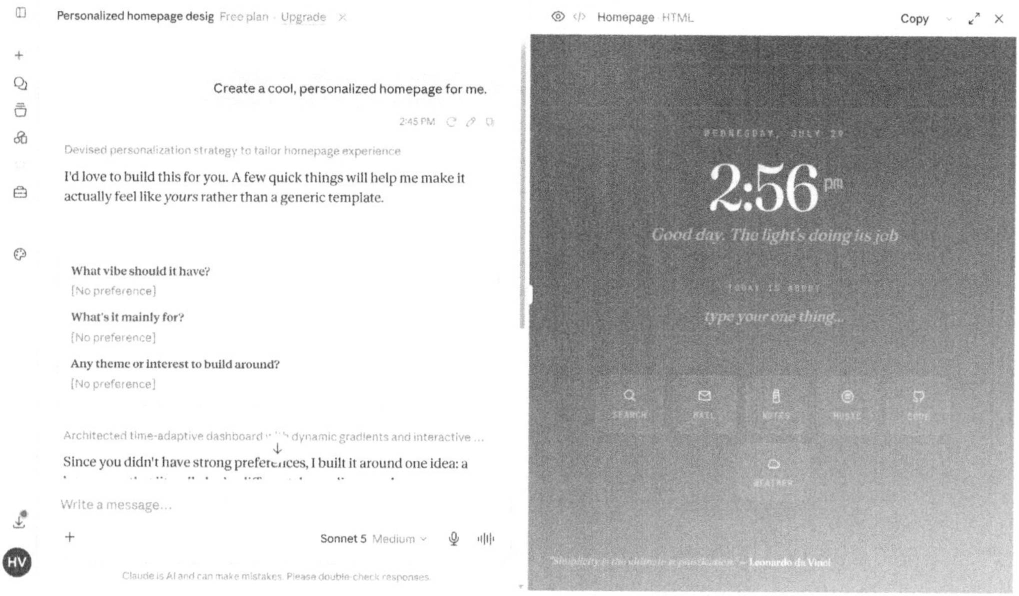

Figure 2.1: An arbitrary design generated from a vague prompt

The AI will arbitrarily set the style and features and generate results at random.

Improving AI and prompts

It's not easy to write a perfect prompt right from the start. How about the prompt we used in the previous exercise?

Prompt: `I want to create my own personal start homepage with today's date and time and a search bar.`

It's definitely better than the previous example. At least you specified which features are needed. However, it still lacks details such as the design, which search engine to use, and whether there are any other necessary features.

Many people struggle with this when writing prompts. They think, "I want to be more specific, but I'm at a loss as to what to ask for and how to phrase it." It feels even more difficult because there's no single "right" answer.

However, we've already solved this problem. Since the prompt lacks specific instructions, we designed it so that Claude can ask for the necessary information first and fill in the gaps

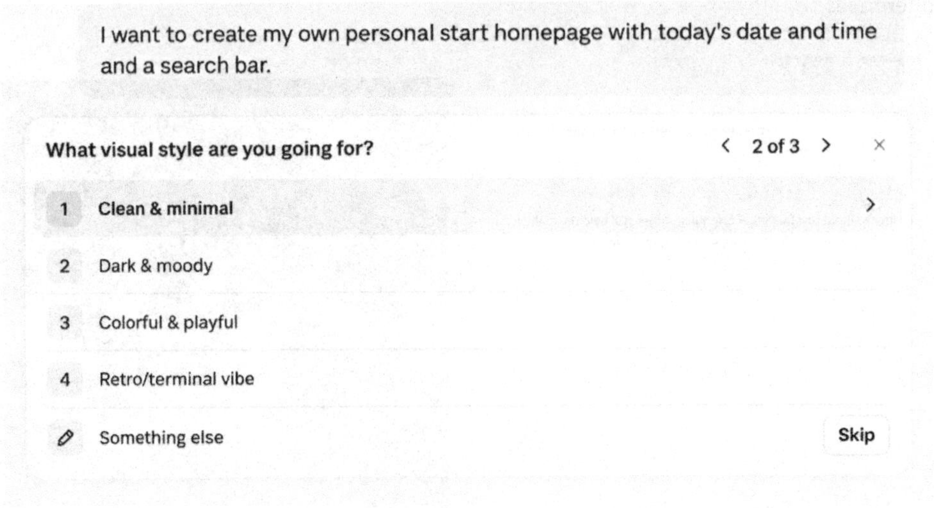

Figure 2.2: Claude asking clarifying questions about the design style

As I answered this question, I gradually set specific conditions one by one, such as "Light Mode" and "Google Search." At first, I only specified the date, time, and search bar, but as I answered Claude's follow-up questions, I naturally decided on the design style and search engine as well.

If you combine the options selected above into a single prompt, you can write it as follows.

Prompt: `I want to create my own homepage with a clean, light-mode design that includes today's date and time, and a Google search bar.`

Figure 2.3: A clean light-mode start page from the refined prompt

The apps we'll be building in the future will be far more complex and diverse than a "personal webpage." We can't expect Claude to kindly present us with options every time. Therefore, it's important to organize the necessary conditions in advance and communicate them clearly from the start.

The question has now shifted to, "How can we create better prompts with AI?" If you start a conversation without first meeting the criteria of clarity, specificity, and context, there's a high likelihood that the programming process will begin with a prompt that lacks polish. Outputs created this way also pose significant challenges during the revision process.

Writing good prompts that yield high-quality results requires a bit of practice. Let's learn this systematically through hands-on practice.

Drafting a product proposal

Researchers write research proposals before beginning their studies, architects draw up blueprints before breaking ground, and filmmakers prepare screenplays before shooting. Similarly, software teams write a **Product Requirements Document (PRD)** before they start coding.

> Note
>
> **PRD**: Clearly define what to build | Present the project's purpose and background | Specify requirements and implementation methods
>
> **A good prompt**: Specifically instructs on what needs to be done | Explains why it's needed and the context | Details the required features and conditions

It is worth noting that, in Vibe Coding, the product plan serves as a highly effective prompt. A good prompt clearly outlines the task at hand, provides context, and includes specific requirements. Similarly, since the product plan is a document that systematically organizes what to build, why it is needed, and how it should work, its fundamental purpose is the same.

Core elements of planning

So, how do you create a good planning document that serves as the foundation for a good prompt? While the content of a planning document will naturally vary depending on the field and purpose, there are common elements that apply to all of them. These are the core questions known as the **5W1H**:

- **Why**: Why are we creating this?
- **Who**: Who is this for?
- **What**: What are we going to create?
- **When**: When is it used?
- **Where**: Where is it used?
- **How**: How will it be created?

These six questions provide the most basic framework for defining a project. "Why" clarifies the purpose, "Who" defines the target audience, and "What" specifies the functionality. Then, "When" and "Where" help identify the context of use, and "How" determines the implementation method.

This kind of systematic thinking is essential for creating a good product proposal. The first step in crafting a prompt is to ask these six questions. As you fill in each element and engage in a dialogue with the AI, your vague ideas will evolve into a concrete proposal and, in turn, into a clear prompt. This is the starting point for effectively utilizing AI.

In particular, since we will be dealing with software—such as programs, web pages, and applications—it is most appropriate to follow the structure of a PRD, which specifies functions and requirements. Considering this, it becomes clear that among the *5W1H*, "What" and "How" should be emphasized even more.

A product planning document developed through dialogue

As we've already seen in the previous example, it's more effective to gradually refine a product plan through dialogue with AI rather than striving to write it perfectly from the start. This involves asking questions and responding to the AI's follow-up questions to develop the plan into an increasingly concrete and systematic form.

First, let's use the 5W1H framework to create a general-purpose basic question template that can be applied to any project. It should include the following elements:

- All elements of the 5W1H framework must be appropriately included
- The implementation approach must be specified in detail
- You must provide a technical description of specific features for the AI. Check to see if the following basic question template meets these conditions.

Basic question template for effective prompts

```
I'm trying to build [what]. The main feature is [specific feature description].
It's for [who], and it's needed to [why/solve a specific problem]. Please write
a detailed PRD with technical guidance on how to implement it.
```

Now let's try using this template in practice. For example, let's assume you're a freelance marketer preparing to enter the job market and need a portfolio webpage. Here's an example of a prompt based on the basic question template:

Basic Question Template: `I'm trying to build a portfolio webpage. The main feature is an impactful layout that allows recruiters to grasp my capabilities within 30 seconds. It is designed for a marketer preparing to transition into freelancing, and is essential for presenting myself as a competitive candidate. Please write a detailed PRD, including technical direction on how to implement it.`

Now, let's enter this into Claude.

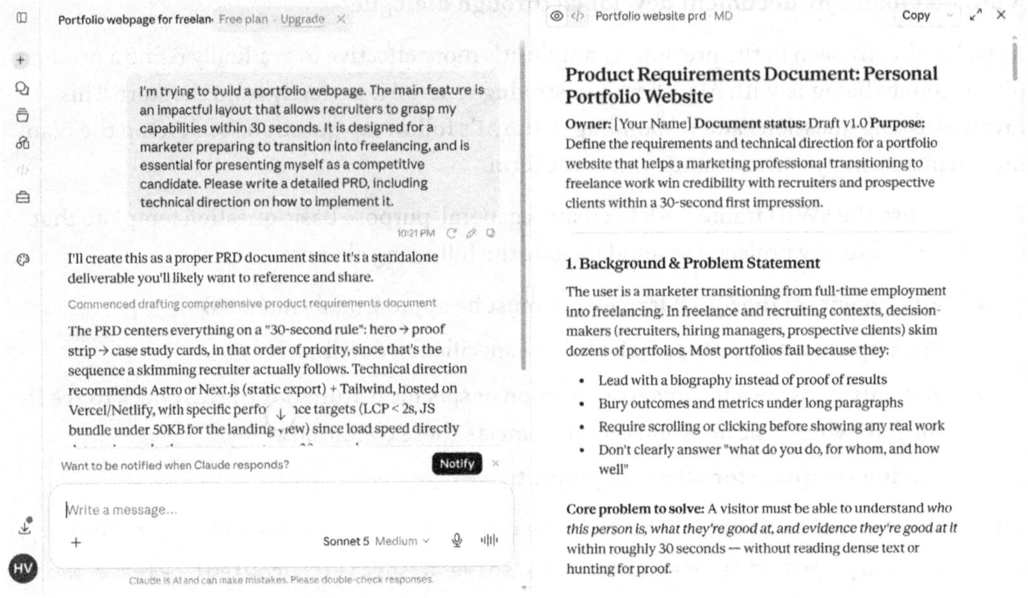

Figure 2.4: Drafting the portfolio PRD from the basic question template

The results may vary slightly depending on the user.

Take a look at what items are included in the "Portfolio Website PRD for Freelance Marketers" suggested by Claude. If the content is long, you can ask it to summarize it by section.

By using a template to write a prompt with accurate and specific instructions, as described above, you can successfully create a product proposal for your project. All you need to do is read the completed proposal and decide whether to use it as is or modify it as needed. This process itself is the key to preparing a high-quality prompt.

In this section, we've confirmed that prompts are the key to unlocking AI's potential. We were able to collaborate with AI throughout the process of creating a good prompt. By utilizing the 5W1H template, anyone can write a systematic proposal, which in turn serves as a powerful prompt.

In the next section, we'll apply this principle in practice by creating a job-hunting portfolio. We'll learn the process of turning an abstract idea into a fully functional web page.

Both prompts and PRDs are based on principles. These principles consist of six questions: Why, Who, What, When, Where, and How.

Wrapping up

Key takeaways summarized in 4 Keywords:

- **A prompt** is the primary way to communicate your intent to AI and is the key factor that determines its performance.
- The systematic thinking framework composed of Why, Who, What, When, Where, and How is abbreviated as **5W1H**.
- The product planning document used by developers is called a **PRD**.
- **A template** is a reusable question structure designed to help you write effective prompts.

Review questions

1. Select the option below that is *not* a characteristic of a good prompt.
    1. Clarity: It specifically conveys the desired result.
    2. Specificity: It provides detailed instructions on the required features or conditions.
    3. Creativity: Requires the output to be surprising.
    4. Providing context: Explains why it is needed and in what situations it will be used.
2. Fill in the blank: Both prompts and PRDs are based on the (__) principle, which consists of six questions: Why, Who, What, When, Where, and How.
3. What are the two questions that should be particularly emphasized in a PRD for software development?
    1. Why, Who
    2. What, How
    3. When, Where
    4. Who, Where
4. Which of the two prompts below is better? Why?
    1. "Create a cool, personalized homepage for me."
    2. "I want to create my own homepage that includes today's date and time, as well as a search bar."

Real-world application: completing your marketing portfolio

> Note
>
> **Key terms**: 4-Step portfolio strategy | Sections | Framework | Features | Design | Review
>
> So far, we've explored the principles for creating effective prompts and how to write a proposal document. In this section, we'll conduct a hands-on exercise to complete a marketing portfolio webpage with the help of AI. Based on the PRD, you'll apply the 4-step prompt strategy and experience the entire process of turning an idea into an actual webpage.

Before you begin

HTML can be viewed as a document composed of sections. A section is, quite literally, an area that contains a single topic. For example, the introduction section at the top of a web page, a list summarizing achievements, and the contact links at the bottom are all separate sections.

In HTML, these sections can be divided using the `<section>` tags. Dividing the code this way makes it easier to read and makes it much simpler to edit specific parts or apply styles to them individually. In the upcoming exercises, we'll first divide the content into these sections based on the PRD, and then build the web page section by section.

In the previous section, we asked the AI to plan our portfolio and received a PRD containing specific details. Now it's time to ask the AI to generate code based on this information.

However, it is not advisable to simply show the entire PRD to an AI and ask it to "create a web page based on this proposal." The more detailed the proposal, the more requirements it typically contains. If these are converted into code all at once, there is a high likelihood that the resulting code will be a complex mix of HTML, CSS, and JavaScript. This makes it difficult to understand the code structure, verify that all requested features have been implemented, and causes complications during subsequent revisions.

To minimize these issues, it is best to generate code step by step. By breaking down the requirements in the PRD by feature and implementing them in stages, you can achieve and verify clear objectives at each stage.

For example, if you plan to work with Claude Code, you should prepare step-by-step prompts by entering the following and proceed sequentially.

Prompt: `Convert the given PRD into a 5-step prompt for use with Claude Code.`

We'll cover Claude Code in detail starting in *Chapter 3*.

> **Note**
>
> This 5-step prompt refers to Claude Code's implementation workflow; it is separate from the 4-step portfolio strategy we use in this chapter.

4-Step portfolio strategy

On the other hand, when working in the Web's Claude chat window or on projects with clear development goals and priorities, it may be more effective to design the steps yourself rather than having the AI break them down.

For the marketing portfolio you're about to develop, first impressions are crucial since it will be used for recruitment purposes. Additionally, given the nature of marketing as a profession, it must deliver both visual impact and clear communication of information.

Taking these characteristics into account, we will gradually build the portfolio according to a four-step strategy:

1. Framework
2. Features
3. Design
4. Verification

Each step involves repeating a short cycle of Request → Generate → Review → Revise to minimize the risk of changes and ensure structure and quality step by step.

Step 1: Framework	Step 2: Features	Step 3: Design	Step 4: Verification
Common cycle applied to every step 1. Request → 2. Generate → 3. Review → 4. Revise Repeat as needed: 5. Review → 6. Revise			

Table 2.1: 4-step strategy

Step 1: Framework

When collaborating with AI, it's more effective to repeat the process of "request → generate → review → revise" rather than expecting a perfect result right away. First, you request the desired task, and the AI generates an output based on that request. You then review the output to see if it matches your intent, and if there are any shortcomings or errors, you request *revisions*. By going through this short cycle multiple times, you can gradually refine the webpage until it closely matches your vision.

1. **[Request] [Generate]** First, load the PRD you created earlier into Claude, then enter the following to generate the basic structure of the web page. Group the elements within the HTML document into sections by topic, and assign a unique name to each section to make future edits easier.

   Prompt: `I'm going to proceed according to this PRD. First, please write an HTML document based on the PRD. Divide it into sections and assign a unique name to each section to make future edits easier. Don't implement any features yet; just show me the overall structure.`

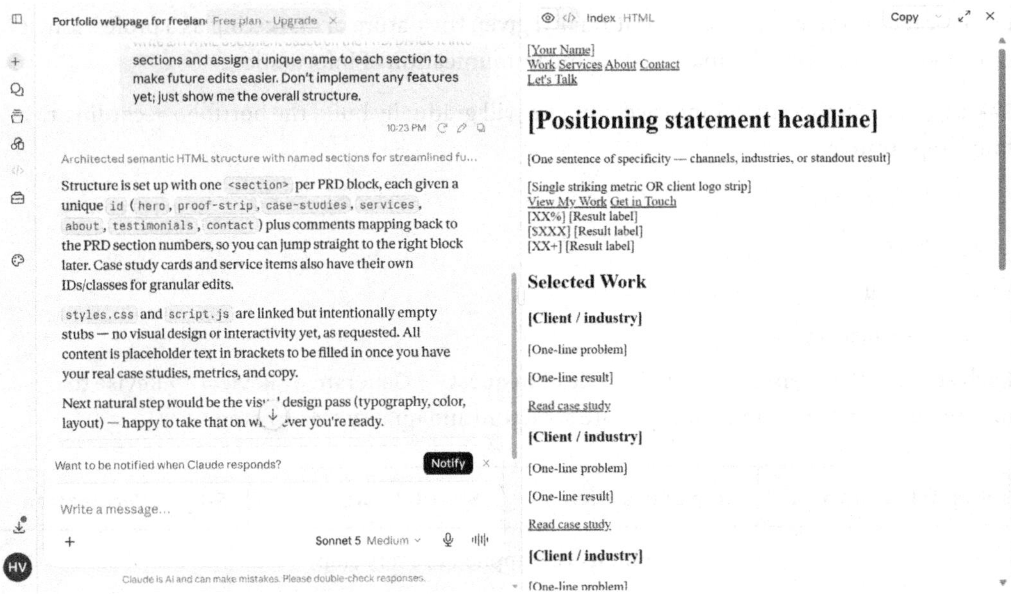

Figure 2.5: Generating the webpage's basic HTML structure from the PRD

You can enter the prompt directly in the chat window where you created the PRD, or you can post the PRD and share the link in a new chat window.

2. **[Review]** Take a look at the unique names assigned to each section. They're organized by feature, allowing you to later identify and edit specific elements.

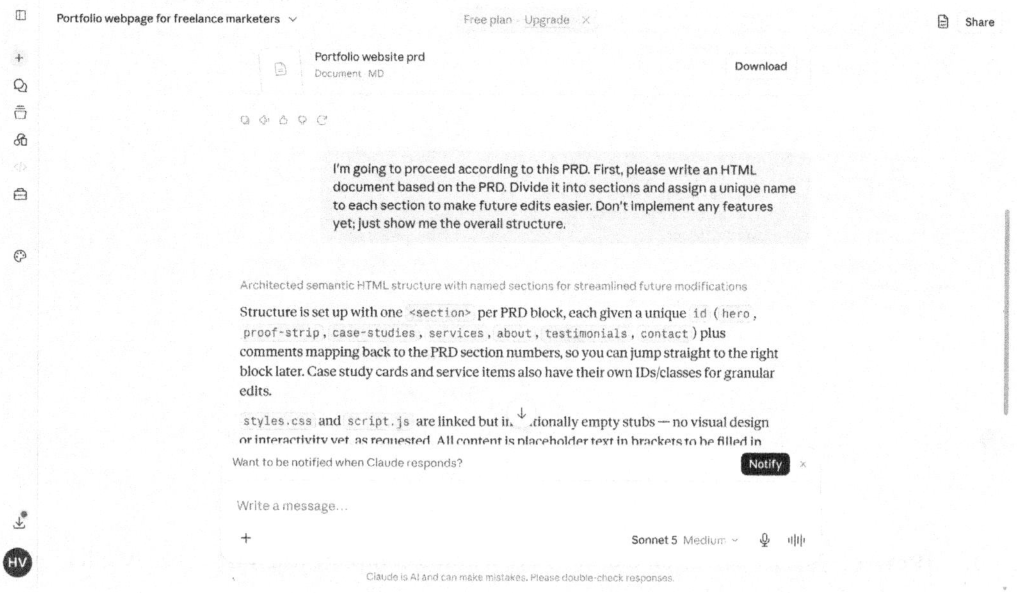

Figure 2.6: Unique IDs assigned to each section of the portfolio

3. **[Revise]** Let's edit a specific section. To present the performance metrics for the past three years in the 'proof-strip' (at-a-glance stats) section, I entered the following prompt into Claude's input field:
Prompt: `Please revise the [Result label] items in the 'proof-strip' section to be a list that specifically details the performance over the past three years.`

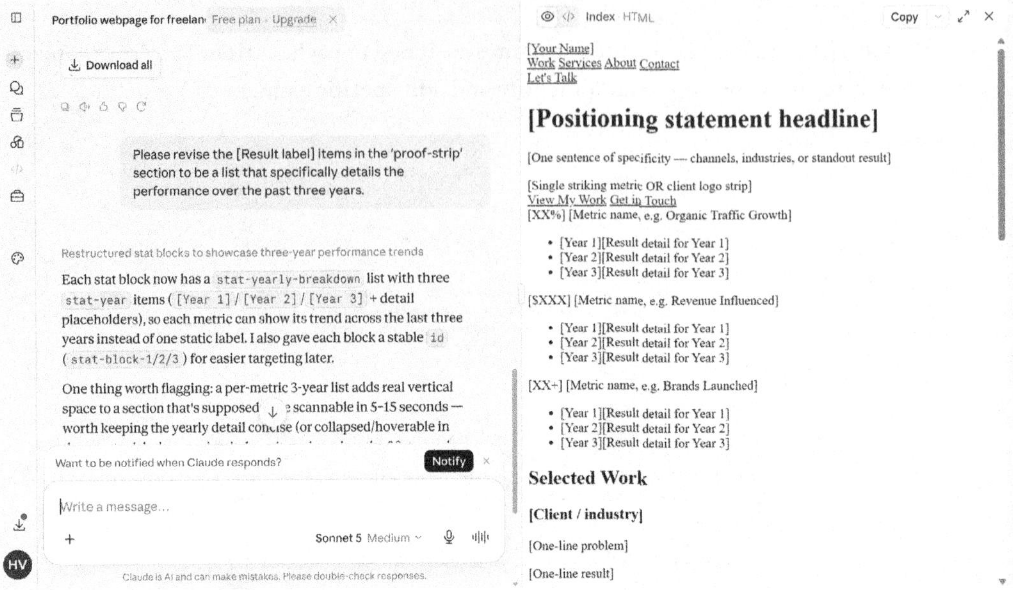

Figure 2.7: Performance metrics revised into a year-by-year list

4. **[Revise]** Now let's add some design elements to complete the framework. We'll request the detailed design in Step 3: Design, so for now, we'll just apply a rough design. Enter the following prompt into Claude's input field. If Claude has split the page into separate HTML, CSS, and JS files, the artifact preview may not show the new design; in that case, simply ask Claude to combine the HTML, CSS, and JavaScript into a single HTML file. From this point on, the screenshots use a paid plan with Sonnet 5, the default model on the Pro plan, since the free plan's usage limit can interrupt the many generation requests in this exercise.

   Prompt: `Apply a modern and sophisticated design to the HTML document.`

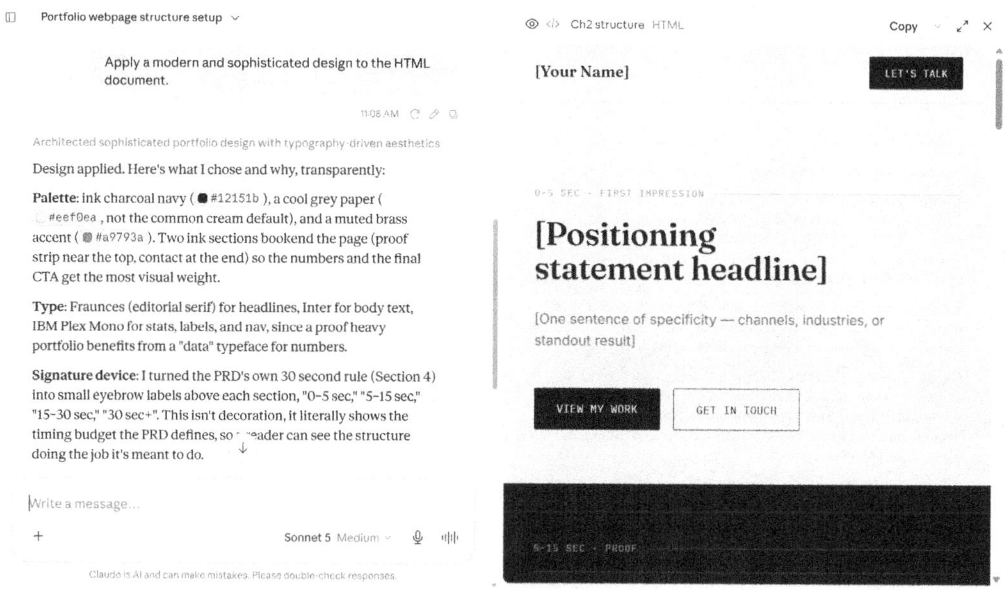

Figure 2.8: Applying a modern, sophisticated design

5. **[Review]** Scroll down to review the other sections as well.

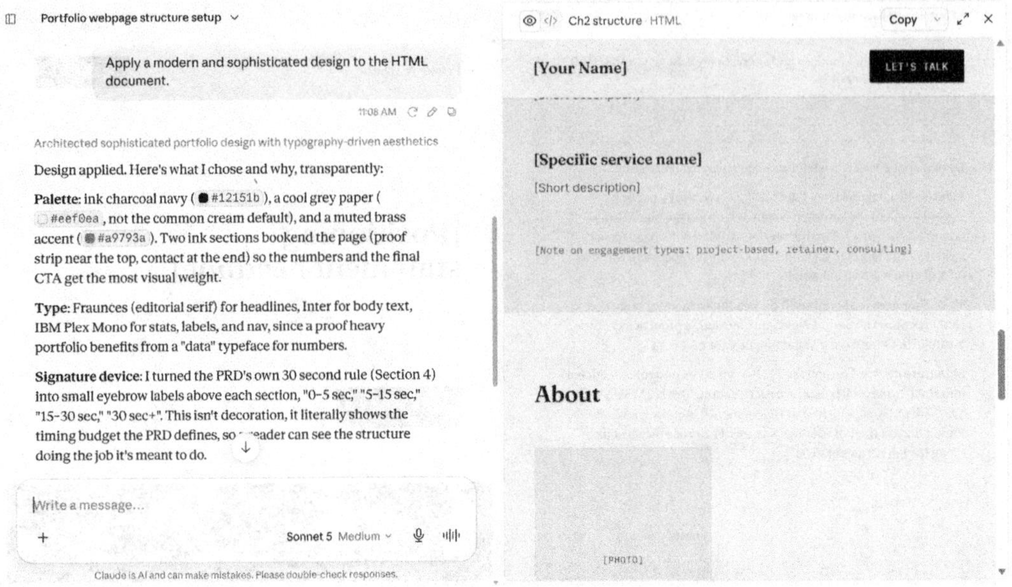

Figure 2.9: Scrolling down to review the remaining sections

6. **[Revise]** Compare the generated web page with the PRD to identify and correct any missing or incorrect sections. Here, we'll move the case study results into the first section of the web page's main screen and display them as a chart.
   Prompt: `Move the [One-line result] metrics from the 'case-studies' section to the 'hero' section and present them as a chart.`

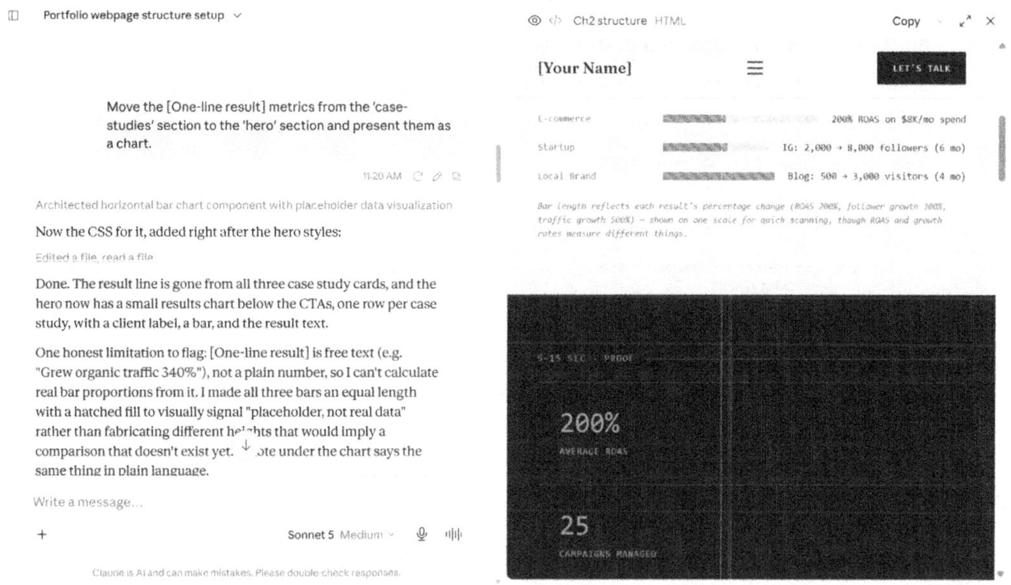

Figure 2.10: Case study results moved to the hero section as a chart

So far, we've created the HTML document—the framework of the webpage—and applied a simple design. We'll continue to refine the remaining steps by repeating the detailed process of requesting, generating, verifying, and revising. Next, we'll move on to adding functionality to this framework.

Step 2: Features

Now that the framework of your web page is ready, it's time to fill it with actual data. An HTML document alone is nothing more than an empty shell, so let's add content such as your career history, achievements, and case studies so that it can truly function as a portfolio.

The key point is that, rather than vaguely asking the AI to "fill in the content," you need to provide specific and factual information. Only then can the result evolve into a meaningful webpage that truly reflects who you are.

1. **[Request] [Generate]** Provide your actual portfolio to the Claude input field. The more specific you are, the more meaningful the content will be.
   Prompt: `Here is my career portfolio. Please update it by section based on the following information. I am a third-year performance/content marketing specialist. Key achievements: ROAS of 200%, 25 campaigns, and contributing $600K in annual revenue. - Position changes over 3 years: Junior (2023) → Performance Marketer (2024) → Manager + Consultant (2025)`

```
Skill Levels: Performance Marketing: 75%, Content Marketing: 70%, Data
Analysis (GA4): 65% Here are my key case studies. E-commerce: Monthly ad
spend of $8K, ROAS of 200% Startup: Instagram followers increased from
2,000 to 8,000 (in 6 months) Local brand: Blog visitors increased from
500 to 3,000 (in 4 months)
```

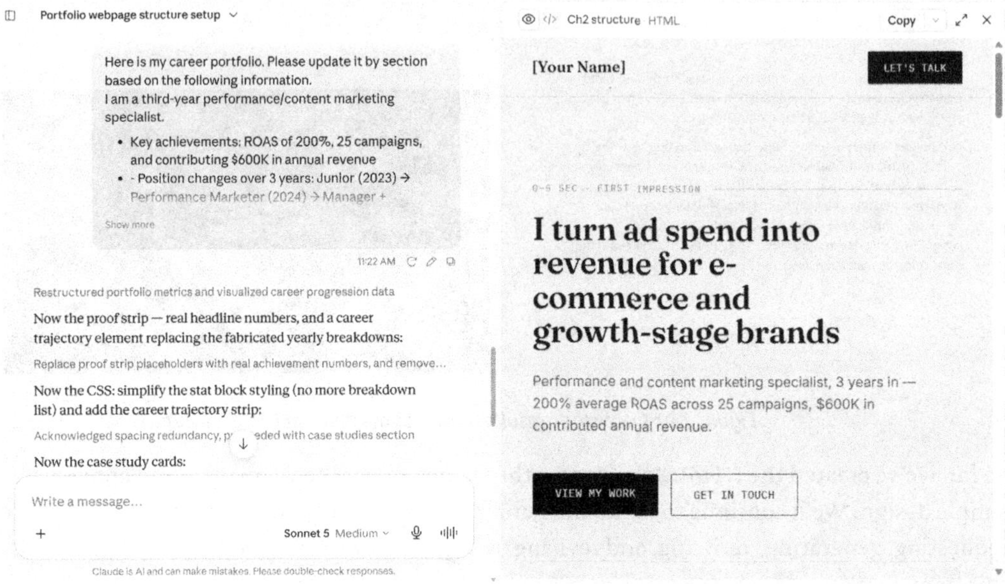

Figure 2.11: The portfolio updated with real career information

2. **[Review]** Check that the content has been updated correctly.

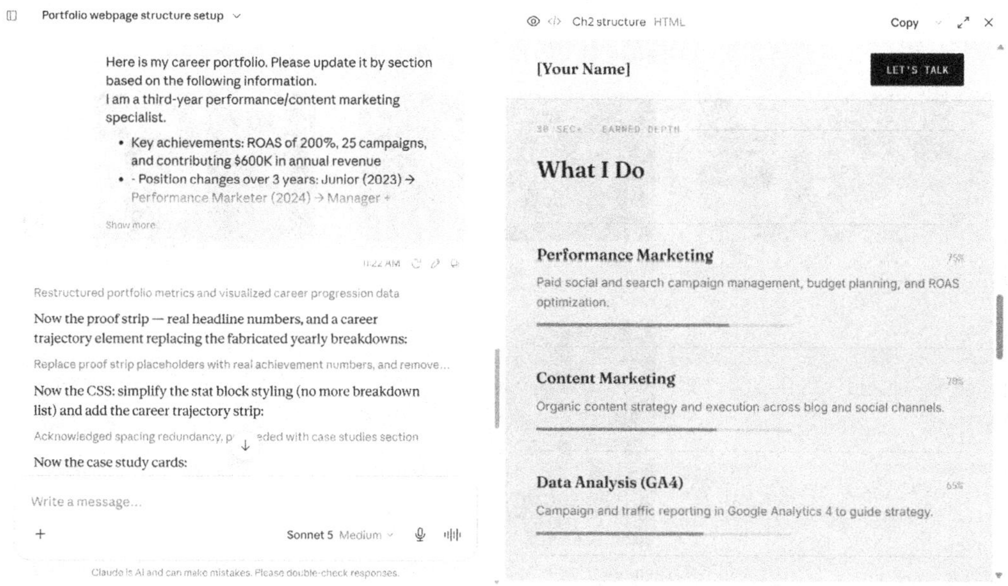

Figure 2.12: Verifying that the content was updated correctly

Review the final output with the content inserted, and if any information is incorrect or you're not satisfied with it, ask Claude to make corrections. In this book, we'll focus on entering actual data and reviewing the results, so we'll skip the separate revision process.

Step 3: Design

Now let's apply a design. Just as we briefly applied a design in Step 1, you can ask Claude, "Please apply a cool design." However, rather than simply asking, "Make it pretty," the quality of the result improves significantly when you provide specific examples for reference.

The key to using prompts effectively in Step 3 is to provide the AI with references to help it create a better design. If you're having trouble selecting references, try asking the AI to recommend some designs worth considering.

In this book, we'll design a webpage using themes from WordPress, the world's most widely used website creation platform (`https://wordpress.com/themes/filter/subject:portfolio`):

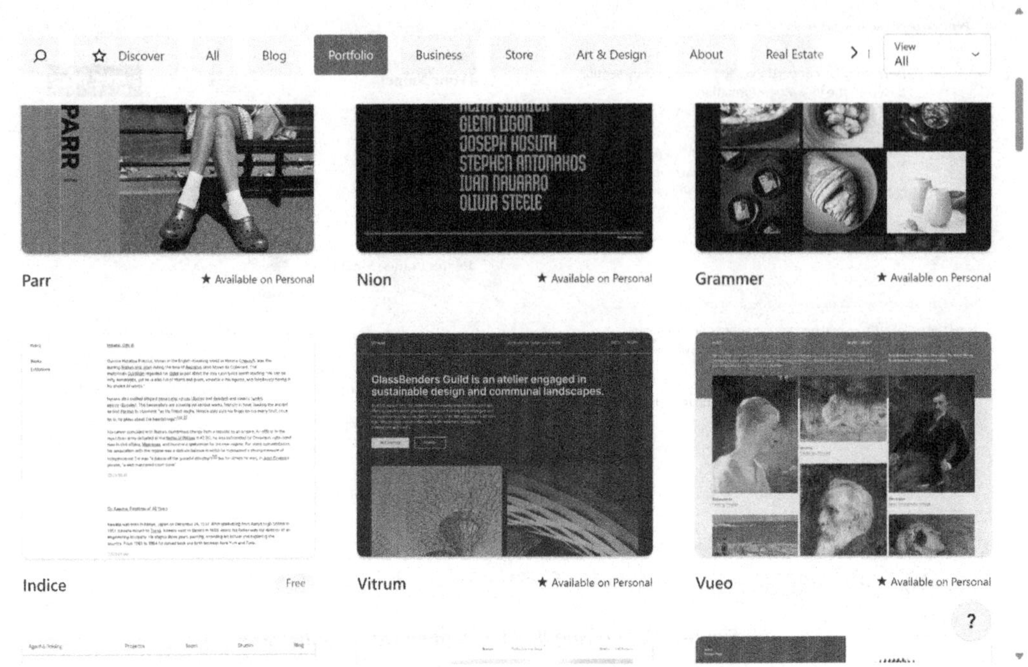

Figure 2.13: Browsing portfolio themes on WordPress.com

WordPress provides category-specific themes tailored to the nature of your content. Among these is a "Portfolio" option, allowing you to apply an appropriate design.

> **Note**
>
> We use WordPress themes as our reference in this book, but feel free to draw on any other platform, template gallery, or design source you prefer.

1. **[Request] [Generate]** Write the prompt as follows.

   Prompt: `Select one WordPress theme that best suits this portfolio and restyle the entire page after it, updating the colors and fonts to match the theme. Use different color tones for each section to make them easily distinguishable. Apply the design directly to the HTML document.`

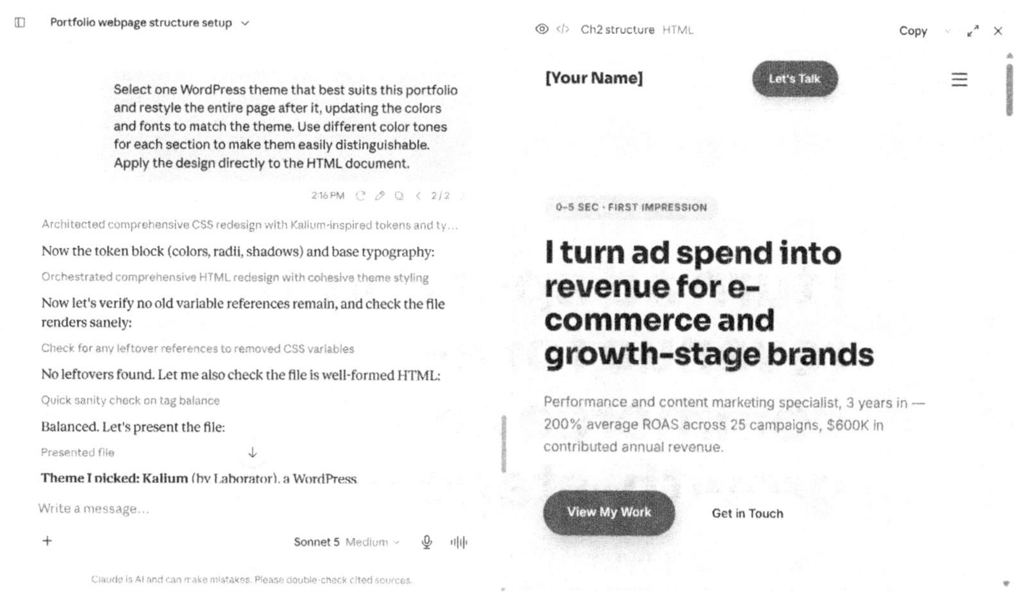

Figure 2.14: The portfolio restyled after the Kalium WordPress theme

If you provide detailed additional instructions, such as "Distinguish the color tones by section," the AI will generate a more consistent and professional design.

2. **[Review]** Open the menu next to the *Copy* button at the top of the artifact, select **Publish artifact**, and then click **Publish & copy link** to generate a link to the portfolio webpage. Paste the copied link into your web browser's address bar and check to see if the design was implemented as requested.

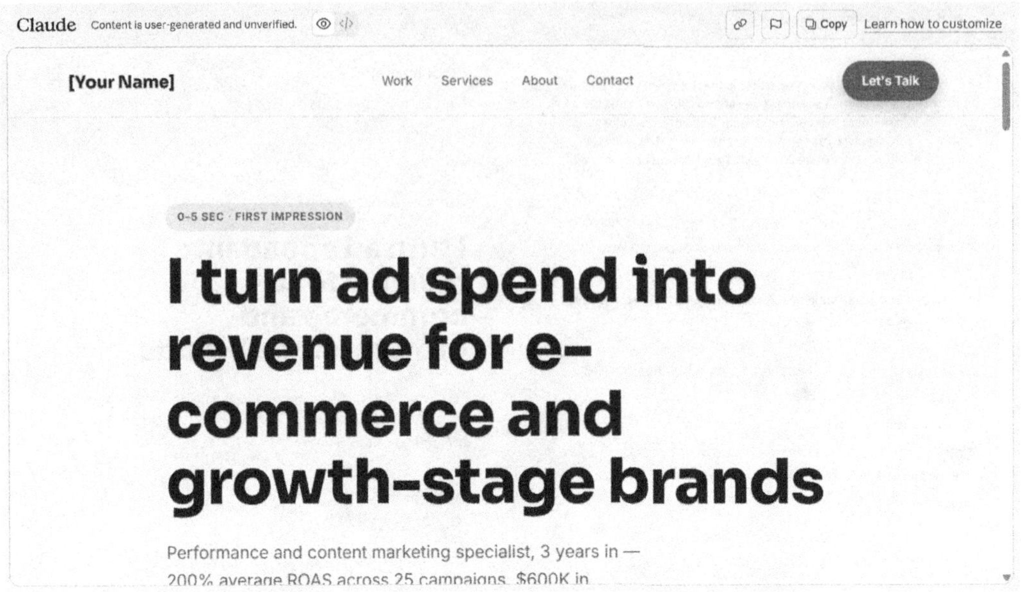

Figure 2.15: The published portfolio page opened in a browser

The design work is complete. At this stage, we'll only apply the design and review the results. Since detailed revisions will be addressed in Step 4, for now, we just need to verify that the overall structure and design have been implemented as intended.

You may have created a polished portfolio, but some links might not be working yet, or certain elements may be missing. The next step is to review and address these details.

Step 4: Verification

When reviewing the quality of a web page, you don't have to check every single item on your own. If you let AI handle the review, it will automatically detect errors or omissions and even suggest ways to improve the page. This allows you to go beyond simple verification and work with AI to refine your web page to an even higher standard.

Above all, this step is extremely important. No matter how impressive the design and features may be, if links don't work or content is missing, the webpage will be unusable in practice. Testing is the final hurdle in bringing the final product to a "truly usable state" and is a crucial step in ensuring quality.

1. **[Request]** Return to the Claude chat window to perform a functionality check, and enter the following prompt:

   Prompt: `Please review whether every part of the portfolio webpage is properly implemented. Check that it was built according to the PRD and that each link works without any issues.`

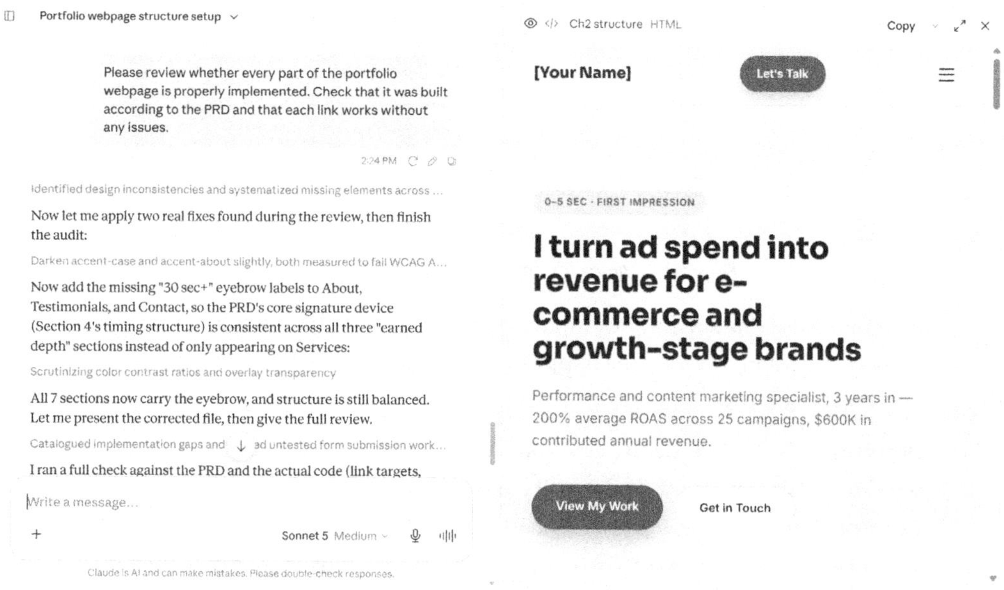

Figure 2.16: Reviewing the webpage against the PRD requirements

2. **[Review]** Review the areas for improvement identified by Claude.

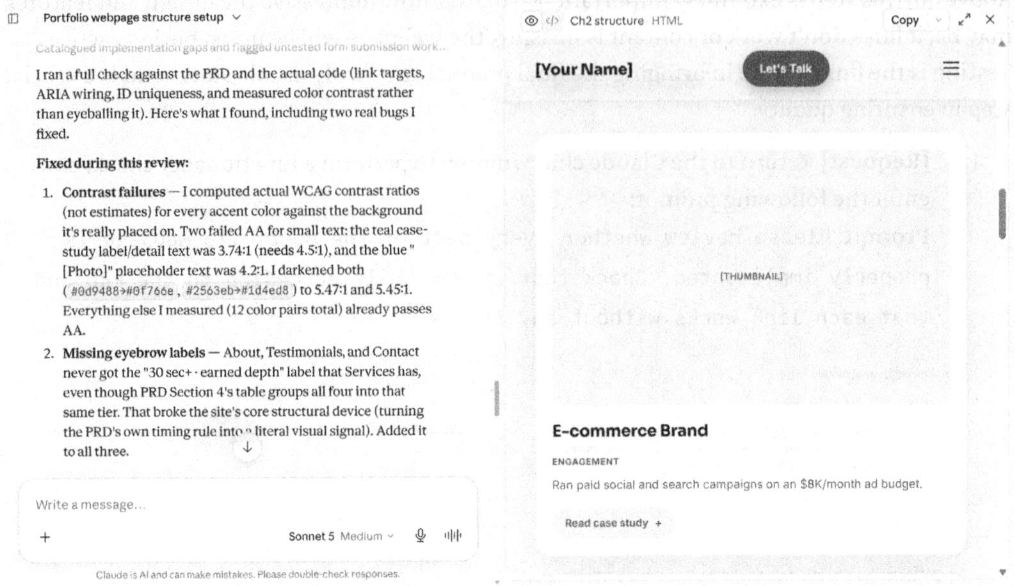

Figure 2.17: Areas for improvement identified during the review

In some cases, Claude may automatically modify and improve the webpage and then display the results. When this happens, simply proceed to the [Review] step to examine the revised results.

3. **[Revise]** Let's ask Claude to make some edits. Type the following prompt into the chat window. Wait a moment, and it will edit your portfolio webpage.
   Prompt: `Address and fix the three areas for improvement that were identified, and complete a perfect portfolio for transitioning to freelance work.`

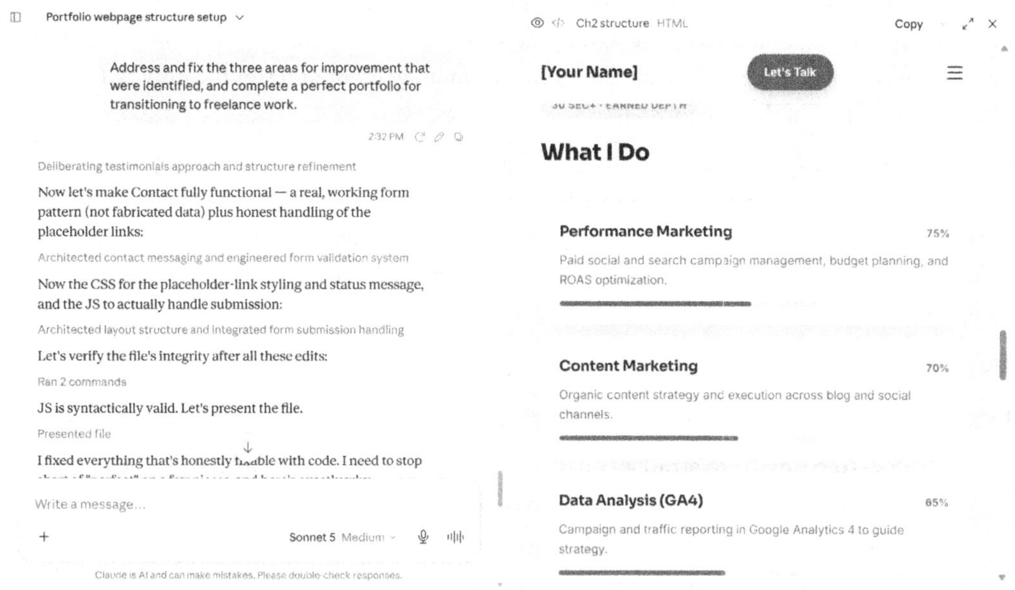

Figure 2.18: Fixing the three areas identified in the review

4. **[Review]** We've completed a fully functional portfolio webpage.

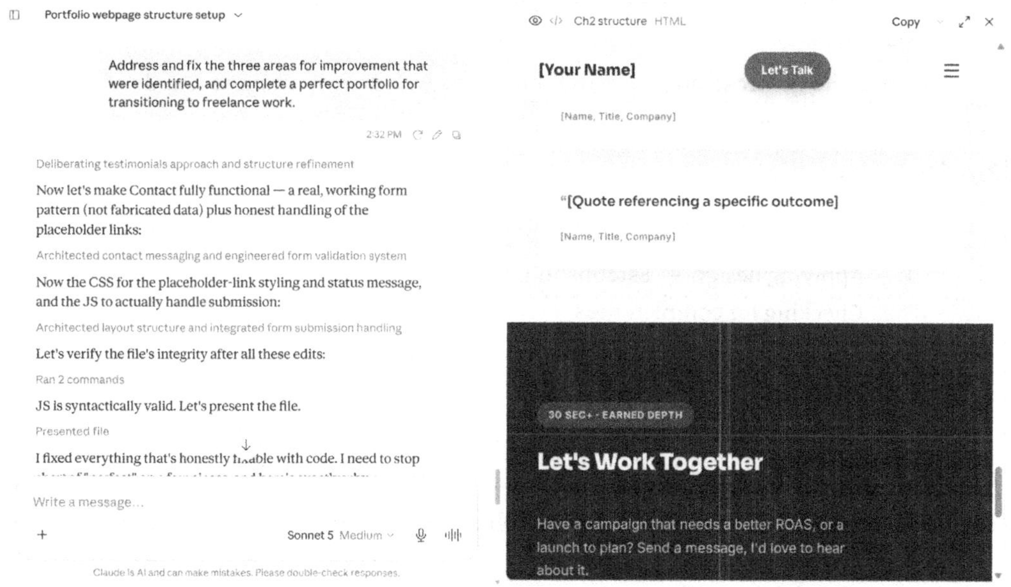

Figure 2.19: The completed portfolio with working contact details

In this section, you've experienced the entire process of transforming a systematically written PRD into a fully functional webpage. Using the 4-step portfolio strategy, you were able to break down even complex projects into smaller units for management and significantly reduce the likelihood of errors and omissions.

In particular, by assigning unique names to each section, we were able to make precise edits only to the necessary parts, and by providing specific references—such as WordPress themes—we were able to create a professional design. Now that we've learned how to collaborate efficiently with AI in a web environment, in the next chapter we'll take it a step further and tackle an advanced project using Claude Code.

Wrapping up

Key takeaways summarized in 6 keywords:

1. The **4-step portfolio** strategy involves requesting the AI to build a webpage in the following order: framework → features → design → verification.
2. Web pages are organized into **sections**, each dedicated to a specific topic.
3. During the **framework** stage, we establish the basic framework using only basic HTML structure, before adding any features or design elements to the web page.
4. In the **features** phase, actual data is populated, and features are added.
5. In the **design** phase, we apply colors, layouts, and visual elements to enhance the overall quality.
6. During the **verification** phase, the completed web page is examined, and any missing features or errors are corrected.

Review questions

1. What is the correct order of the four-step strategy used to create a portfolio website?
    1. Applying design → Establishing the basic framework → Adding core features → Checking for completeness
    2. Establish the basic framework → Apply the design → Add core features → Check for completeness
    3. Establish the basic framework → Implement core features → Apply design → Check for completeness
    4. Implement core features → Establish the basic framework → Check for completeness → Apply design

2. Which of the following is *NOT* an effective method for writing prompts?
    1. Use the 5W1H template to ask questions systematically.
    2. Request all features at once to save time.
    3. Assign an ID to each section to allow for individual modifications.
    4. Provide specific references, such as WordPress themes.
3. Which of the following is NOT a benefit of giving sections unique names?
    1. You can edit only the specific parts you want.
    2. You don't have to regenerate the entire code.
    3. The AI can clearly understand where to make changes.
    4. The design is automatically improved.

3

Getting Started with Claude Code

In *Chapter 2*, you learned the basics of Vibe Coding through Claude's web interface and created an actual portfolio using systematic strategies. Now, let's take it a step further and explore Claude Code, Claude's powerful code generation tool. Experience firsthand how quickly and easily you can complete programs that used to require significant time and effort, and step into the world of Claude Code.

Learning objectives:

- You will be able to install Claude Code and complete the basic setup
- You will learn how to interact with Claude Code in a terminal environment
- You will be able to create a fully functional desktop program using Claude Code
- You will be able to expand your program into a web version
- You will be able to efficiently manage projects using a hierarchical structure

Installing Claude Code

> Note
>
> **Key terms**: Terminal | Claude Code
>
> We'll walk through the process of installing the essential programs needed to use Claude Code and having your first conversation with it. You'll become familiar with the terminal environment and prepare for your first encounter with Claude Code.

Before you begin

A terminal is a window where you can communicate directly with your computer by entering commands. Instead of clicking menus and icons with your mouse, you can use the terminal to run programs, manage files, and configure system settings by typing text commands.

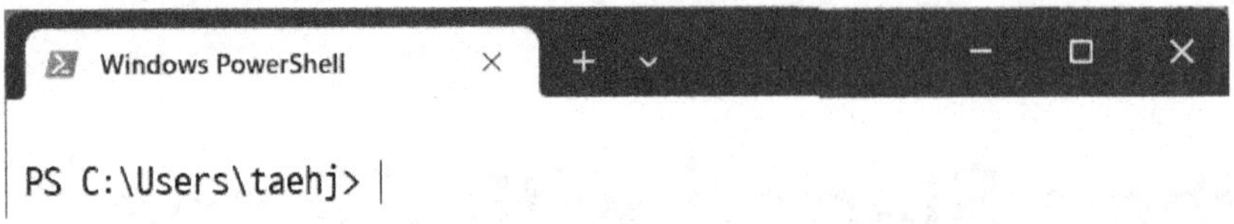

Figure 3.1: The Windows PowerShell terminal window

Unlike Claude, the interactive chatbot used in a web browser, **Claude Code** is a tool that runs directly in your computer's terminal. It goes beyond simply displaying answers; it can actually create or modify files, manage project folders, and run programs. While Claude is convenient for brainstorming and drafting ideas, Claude Code excels at producing executable results in a real development environment.

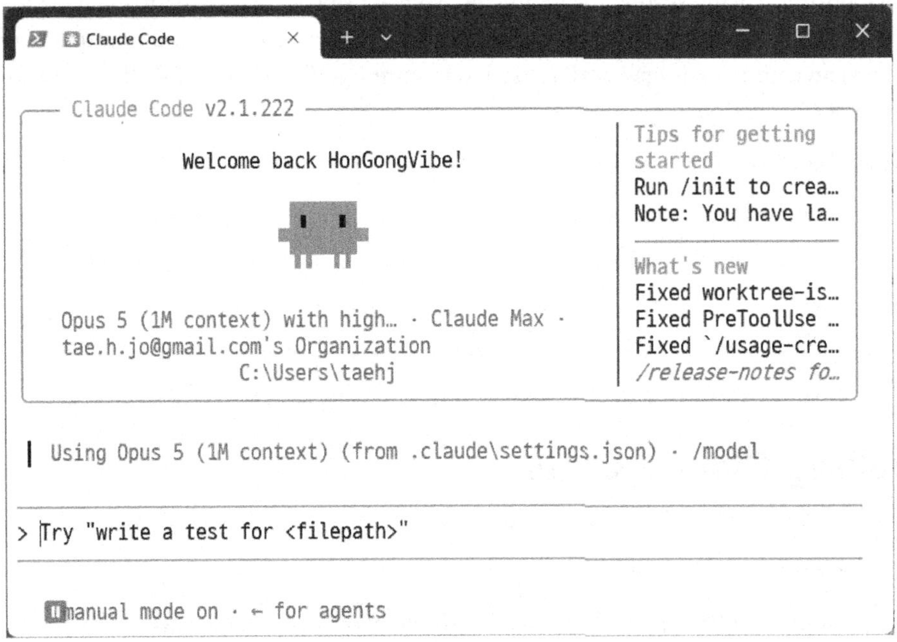

Figure 3.2: Claude Code

If you're new to using the terminal, it may seem unfamiliar at first, but you can give commands to Claude Code in the same way you interact with Claude on the web. In fact, the terminal environment is not only lighter and faster than the web, but it also integrates naturally with other development tools, making it ideal for real development workflows.

In particular, Claude Code can directly create and modify files for each project, allowing you to work in a way that closely resembles a real developer's workflow. Once installed, you can continue to take advantage of its powerful features, so let's start installing the necessary tools step by step.

Setting up the practice environment

Claude Code can be installed on all major operating systems, including Windows, macOS, and Linux. Follow the installation method appropriate for your OS. The usage is mostly the same across all three operating systems after installation.

Installing Git on Windows

1. To run Claude Code in a Windows environment, you first need to install a version control program called **Git**. On the official Git website (`https://git-scm.com/`), go to the **Install** menu and click **Git for Windows/x64 Setup** to install it.

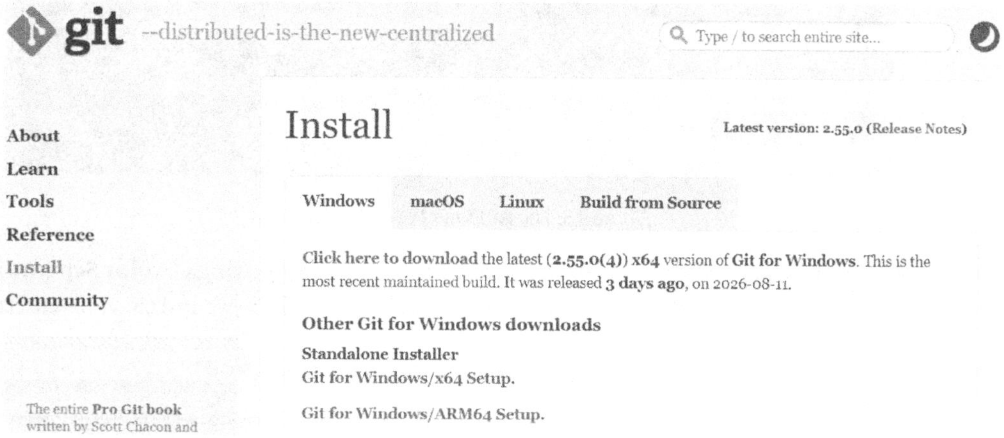

Figure 3.3: Git for Windows

2. Double-click the downloaded Git installer in **File Explorer** to run it, and follow the installation wizard.
3. Click **Finish** when the wizard has installed Git.

With Git in place, the next step is the terminal.

Launching the terminal

On Windows, PowerShell serves as the terminal, allowing you to perform tasks such as running programs and managing files in a text-based interface. The terminal is used when working with Claude Code.

It's an essential work environment, so let's get comfortable using it.

1. Type `powershell` in the Windows taskbar search box and press the *Enter* key.

Figure 3.4: Run PowerShell from the Windows taskbar

2. **Windows PowerShell** will launch as shown in *Figure 3.5*. This PowerShell window is your terminal. The prompt `PS C:\Users\taehj (user name)>` indicates the current working directory of the terminal.

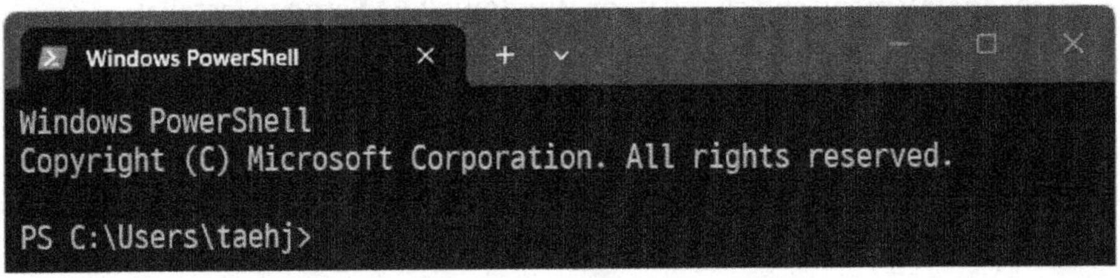

Figure 3.5: The Windows PowerShell window

You can change the terminal's color scheme from **V** (down arrow) | **Settings** | **Color Scheme** in the upper right corner. For better readability in print, we'll set the background to white and the text to black from here on.

Claude Code

Now it's finally time to install Claude Code. Open Windows PowerShell to get ready.

Follow these steps to install Claude Code:

1. Run PowerShell and enter the following command at the prompt to install Claude Code:

```
irm https://claude.ai/install.ps1 | iex
```

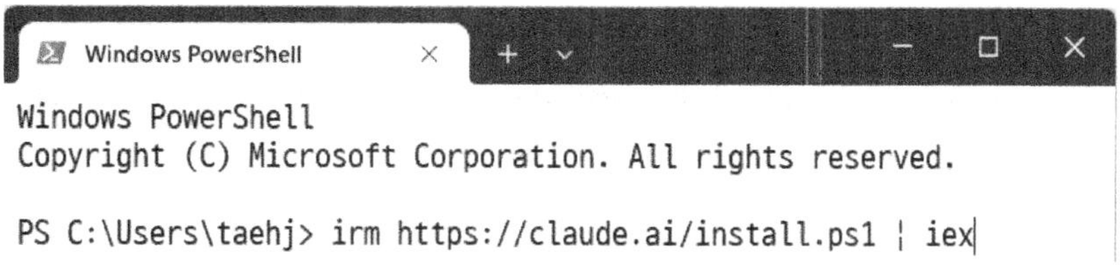

Figure 3.6: Installing Claude Code

2. Claude Code has been installed.

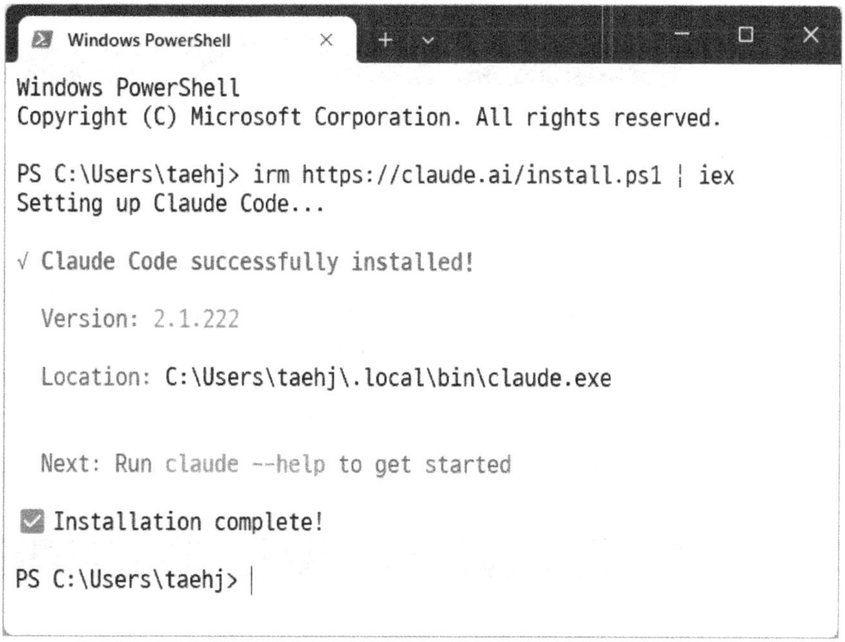

Figure 3.7: Installation complete confirmation

3. Now you can run Claude by typing `claude` in the command prompt.

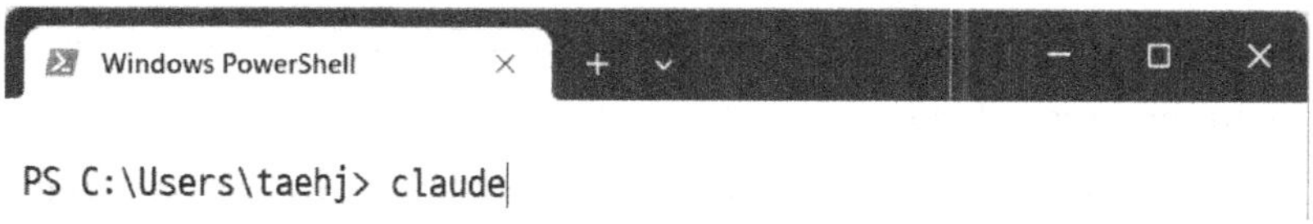

Figure 3.8: Run Claude from the command prompt

> **Note**
>
> The process for running Claude is mostly the same on Windows, macOS, and Linux, with only minor differences in the installation commands.

Installing Claude Code on macOS and Linux

1. Press *Command* + *Space* keys to open the **Spotlight** search bar, type `Terminal`, and then press *Enter*. The Terminal window will open.

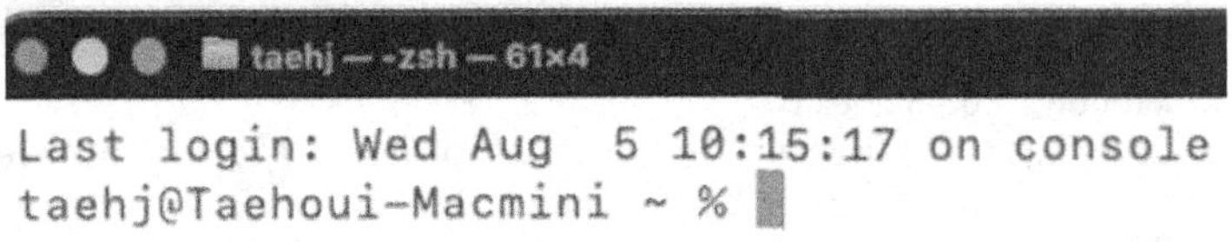

Figure 3.9: The macOS Terminal window

> **Tip**
>
> You can change the Terminal's background color by going to **Terminal** | **Preferences** in the menu bar at the top of the screen.

2. Check to see if **Git**, a version control program, is installed. Type the following in the Terminal and press the *Enter* key:

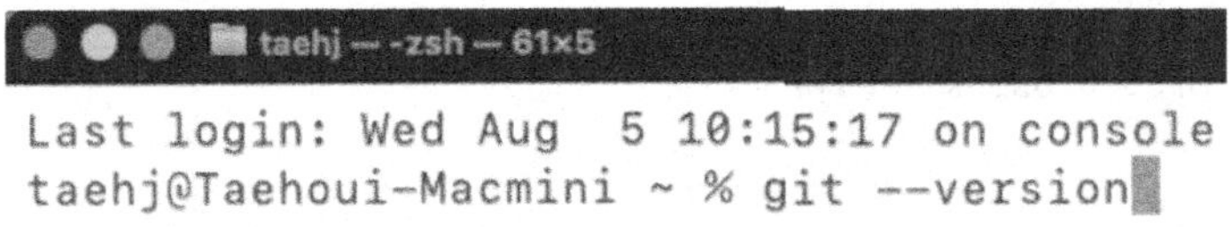

Figure 3.10: Checking the Git version in the Terminal

3. If a version number appears, Git is installed. Git is usually installed by default on macOS. If it is not installed, enter the command `xcode-select --install` in Terminal to begin the installation.
4. After verifying that Git is installed, enter the following command in the Terminal and press *Enter*: `curl -fsSL https://claude.ai/install.sh | bash`

Figure 3.11: The final step for installation

5. When you see a message indicating that Claude Code has been successfully installed, press *Command* + *Q* to close the Terminal. You can now launch Claude by typing `claude` at the command prompt.

Initial setup

1. The Claude Code startup screen displays the terminal's style settings. Here, we'll select **3. Light mode** for better readability. Use the arrow keys on your keyboard to choose your preferred theme and press the *Enter* key.

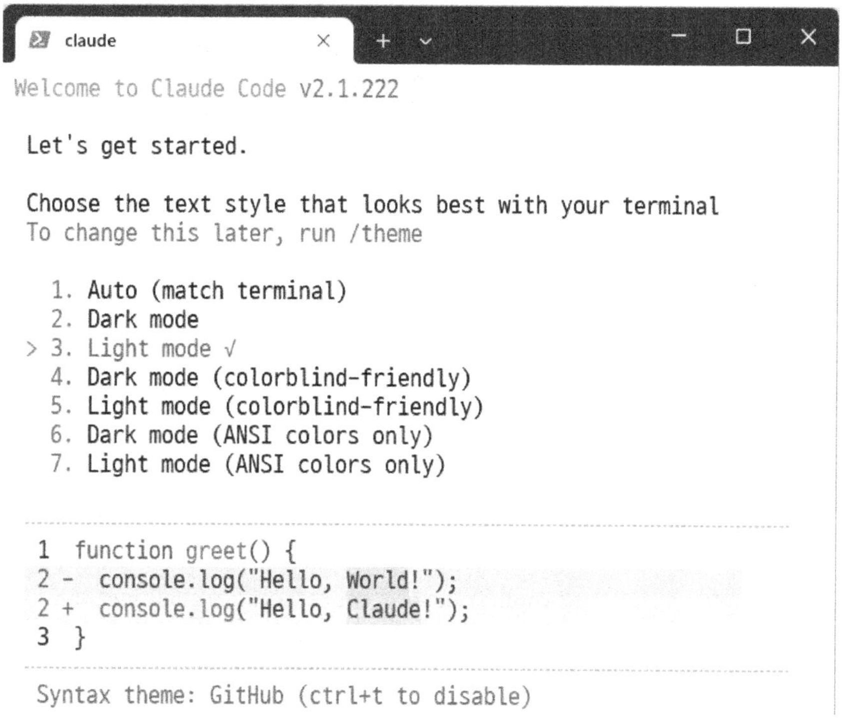

Figure 3.12: Select option 3

2. Next, you must select a login method for Claude Code. Use the arrow keys on your keyboard to select **1. Claude account with subscription** and press *Enter* to proceed.

> **Note**
>
> **Screen explanation**
>
> - **Use Claude subscription account**: Pay a monthly subscription fee to use Claude Code with no additional charges.
> - **Use Anthropic API account**: Charges are based on token usage.
> - **Use a third-party platform**: Access the model via a cloud service provider.

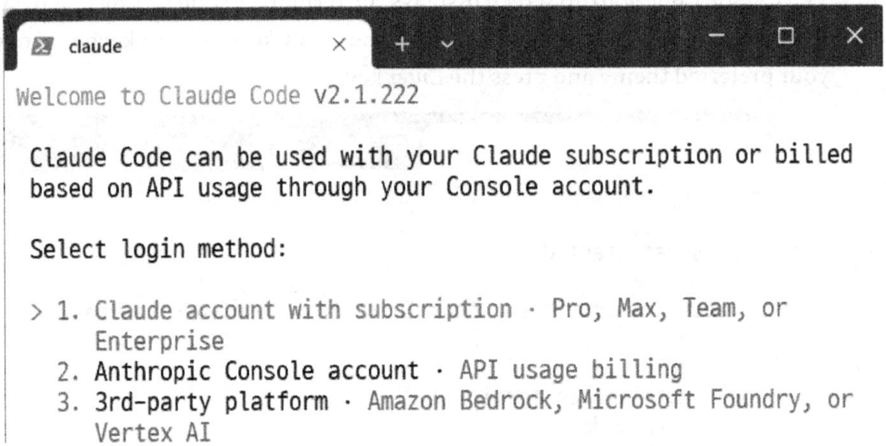

Figure 3.13: Select option 1

> **Note**
>
> From *Chapter 3* onwards, the hands-on exercises assume a paid Claude subscription. While Claude Code is available with the Pro plan, we recommend subscribing to the Max plan or higher for a smooth learning experience.
>
> If you select **2. Anthropic Console account**, beginners may incur unexpectedly high costs and will need to track usage by tokens, which can be cumbersome. **3. 3rd-party platform** is an option for companies already using cloud services.

3. Your Claude Code will be linked to your account. Click the **Approve** button.

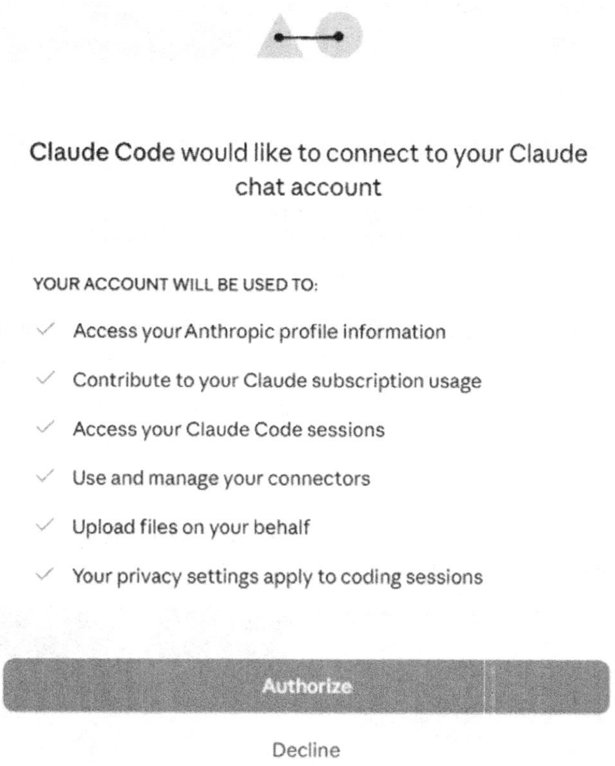

Figure 3.14: Approve to link Claude Code to your account

If the web browser does not open automatically, you can copy the URL shown in the command prompt and access it directly.

4. When you return to the command prompt, you will see a message confirming successful login. Press the *Enter* key to proceed to the next step.

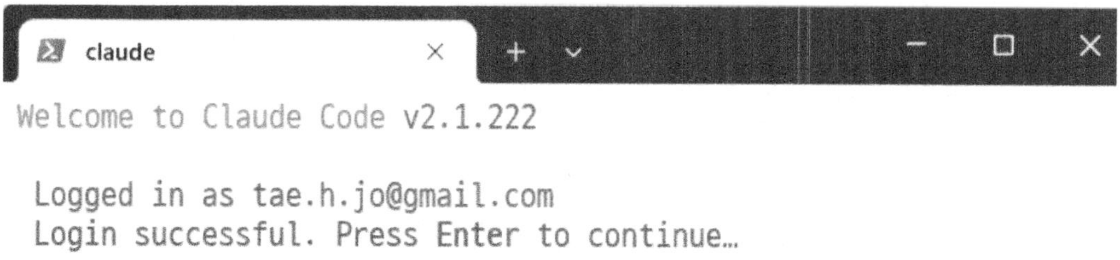

Figure 3.15: Login successful window

5. Review the security-related message and press the *Enter* key to proceed.

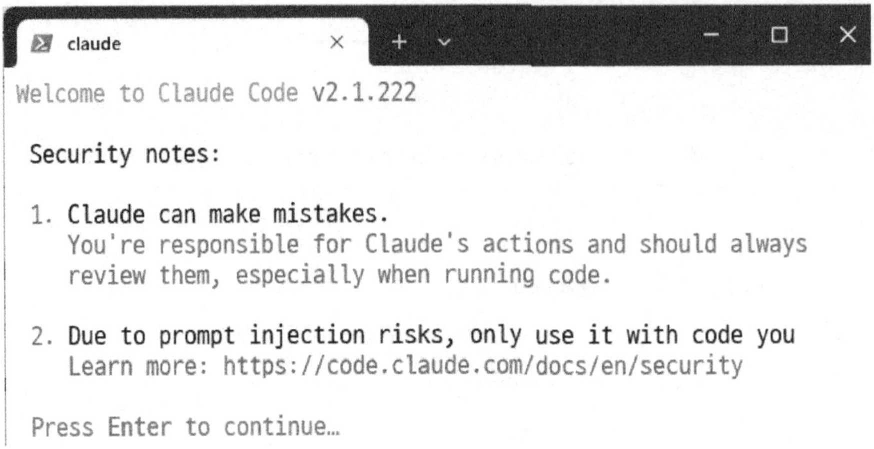

Figure 3.16: Review the security-related message

6. Claude Code requires your permission to access the file system. Use the arrow keys on your keyboard to select **1. Yes, proceed,** and press the *Enter* key.

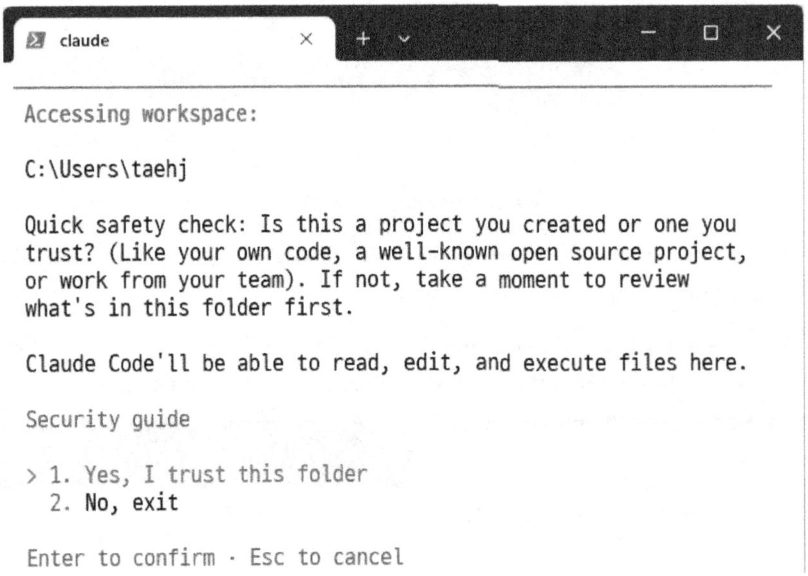

Figure 3.17: Select option 1

7. Now, just like in the web browser, you can start a natural conversation with Claude from the command prompt.

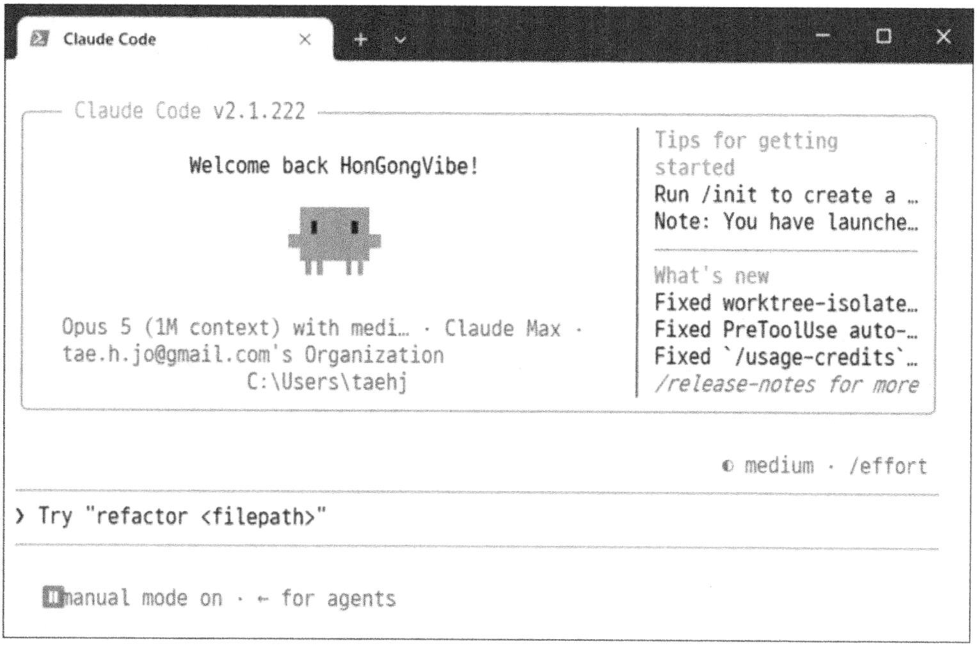

Figure 3.18: Start a conversation with Claude

Your first conversation with Claude Code

Let's try talking to Claude Code. The box where the cursor is located is the prompt input field. Enter the following as shown and press the *Enter* key:

Prompt: `Hello! Please describe what features you have.`

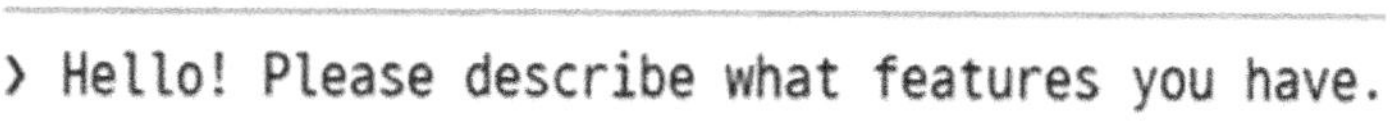

Figure 3.19: First conversation with Claude

Claude Code provides helpful guidance on its various features. Now you are ready to use Claude Code's powerful capabilities for coding, development tools, project management, information retrieval, and more.

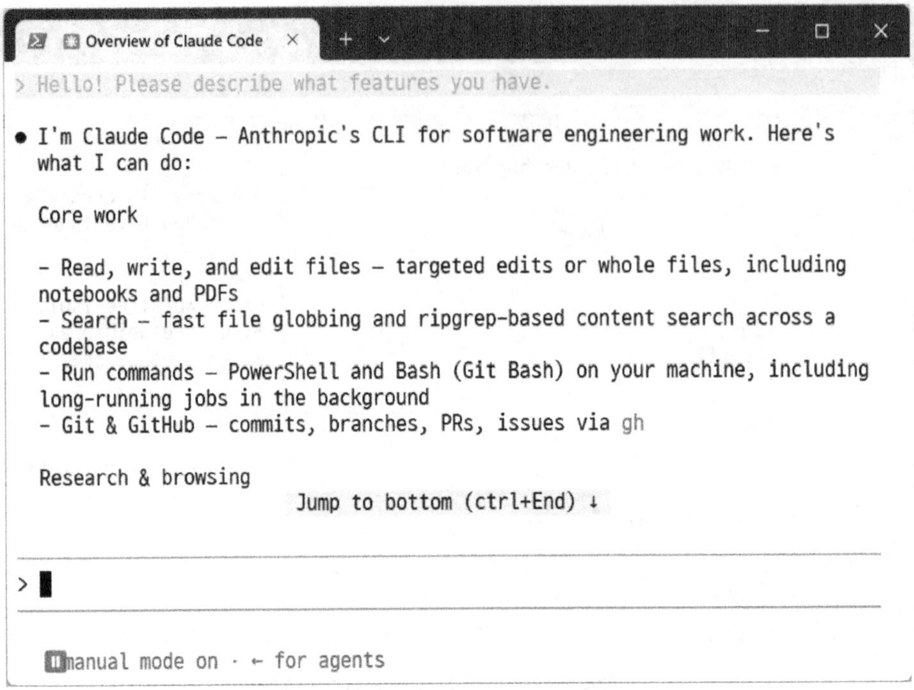

Figure 3.20: Claude Code is ready for you

To exit Claude Code, press *Ctrl* + *C* twice in a row, or enter the `/exit` command in the prompt window. This will terminate Claude Code and return you to the terminal screen.

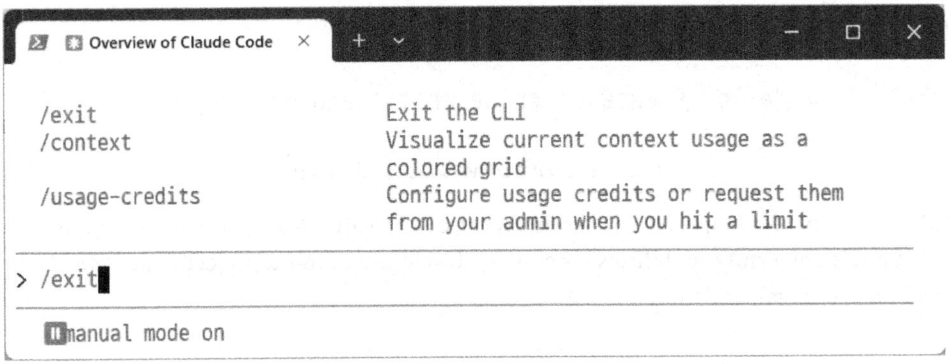

Figure 3.21: Exiting Claude Code

You have now experienced the entire process of installing Claude Code and starting your first conversation. You saw that you can interact with Claude Code from the Windows command prompt much as you would with Claude in a web browser, while also creating and modifying files directly. In the next section, we will put this into practice by building a working handwriting recognition program and begin to explore the powerful features of Claude Code in greater depth.

Claude can be used in various forms, such as Claude Code running in the terminal, the desktop application, and the Cowork feature. The way you use it and the features provided differ depending on the environment. Let's look at each one.

Claude Code desktop version

Claude Code offers a desktop version that can be used without the terminal. On Claude's download page (`claude.com/download`), click **Download for Windows** to download the installer for the Claude desktop version.

Figure 3.22: Download Claude desktop

Run the `Claude Setup.exe` file to install the Claude desktop version, then click the **Get Started** button and link your account.

Figure 3.23: Click on Get Started to link your account

You can chat with the desktop app version of Claude using the same account you used on the web. Click the **Code (</>)** icon at the top of the left sidebar.

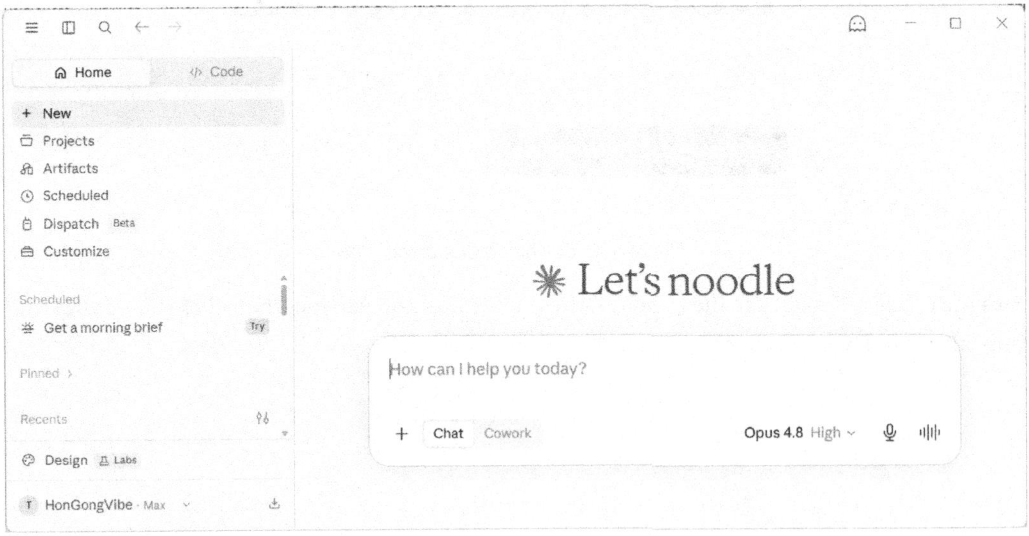

Figure 3.24: Click on the Code icon in the sidebar

In **Code**, you can visually check file changes, manage multiple sessions via the sidebar, and even preview the app—all in a single window.

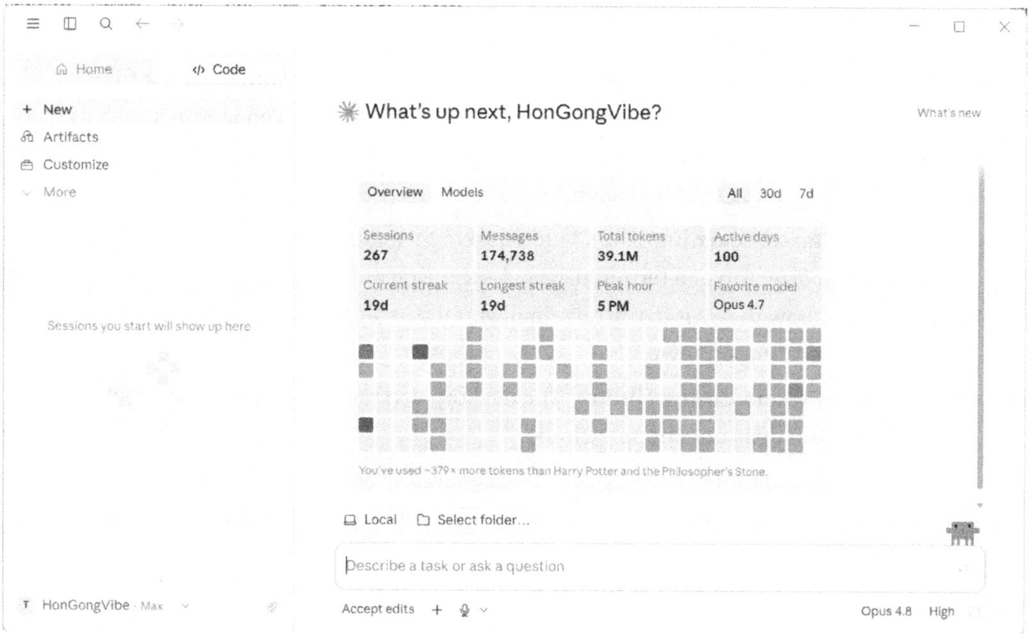

Figure 3.25: Manage multiple sessions

Claude Cowork

If you click the **Cowork** tab in the left sidebar of the Claude desktop, you'll also find a feature called **Cowork**. Cowork is a tool designed for general users—not just developers—that allows them to organize documents, conduct research, and create spreadsheets or presentations simply through conversation.

Figure 3.26: Cowork tab

Why Claude Code?

Although a desktop version is available, the exercises in this book will use Claude Code running in the terminal. Here's why.

- **Feature Differences**: Some features of Claude Code in the terminal are not fully supported in the Claude desktop version. In particular, advanced features such as AI agent team building and multi-agent orchestration, covered in *Chapter 7*, are currently only available in the terminal environment.
- **Principle-Based Learning**: The Claude desktop version is essentially a graphical interface built on top of a terminal-based execution environment. Therefore, if you first understand how to use it in the terminal, you'll be able to use it more reliably in the desktop environment as well.
- **Operating System Compatibility**: The desktop version only works on macOS and Windows, and does not support Linux.

The desktop version and Cowork can be installed separately and used together as needed. However, I recommend first getting comfortable with the terminal-based execution method through this book.

Wrapping up

Key takeaways summarized in 2 keywords:

- The **terminal** is a text-based interface that allows you to communicate directly with the computer by entering commands; it is the environment where Claude Code runs.
- **Claude Code** is an AI-based coding tool that runs in the terminal; it is a powerful development partner that allows you to create and edit files directly and manage projects.

Review questions

1. What program must be installed in advance to run Claude Code?
    1. Python
    2. Git
    3. Node.js
    4. Visual Studio Code
2. Select the incorrect method for exiting Claude Code.
    1. Type the `/exit` command in the terminal
    2. Press *Ctrl* + *C* twice

   3. Type the `/quit` command in the terminal
   4. Click the **X** icon at the top of the terminal window
3. Which of Claude Code's login methods allows you to use the service at no additional cost with a monthly subscription plan?
   1. Anthropic Console account
   2. Third-party platform
   3. Claude account with subscription
   4. Enter API key manually

Building a handwriting recognition program

> **Note**
>
> Key terms: Handwritten | MNIST | Batch
>
> In this section, we will use Claude Code to build a handwriting recognition program.
>
> Even without knowing complex deep learning theory, you can complete an AI program that recognizes handwritten numbers just by conversing.

Before you begin

Handwriting recognition is a form of **Optical Character Recognition** (**OCR**). While OCR is a technology that converts printed text into digital text, handwriting recognition is considered much more challenging because handwriting styles vary considerably from person to person.

In the past, building such programs required working directly with frameworks like TensorFlow, Keras, or PyTorch and complex neural network architectures. But now, with Claude Code, you can create high-quality AI programs simply by describing the desired functionality in natural language. Let's build your first working AI program on your computer.

Figure 3.27: OCR for handwriting recognition

Preparing the Project Folder

To run Claude Code, you must first choose a project folder to work in. Since all tasks are performed in the designated folder, it's important to select the correct location at the start.

Create a new folder named `VibeCoding` on your desktop, and then create a subfolder called `Study-01` inside it.

Claude Code runs from the terminal and operates within a specific working directory. Therefore, it's convenient to open the terminal directly from your project folder. There are two ways to launch the command prompt in a designated directory.

Method 1: Open the terminal from inside the folder

After navigating to the `Study-01` folder, right-click on an empty space in **File Explorer** and select the **Open in Terminal** menu.

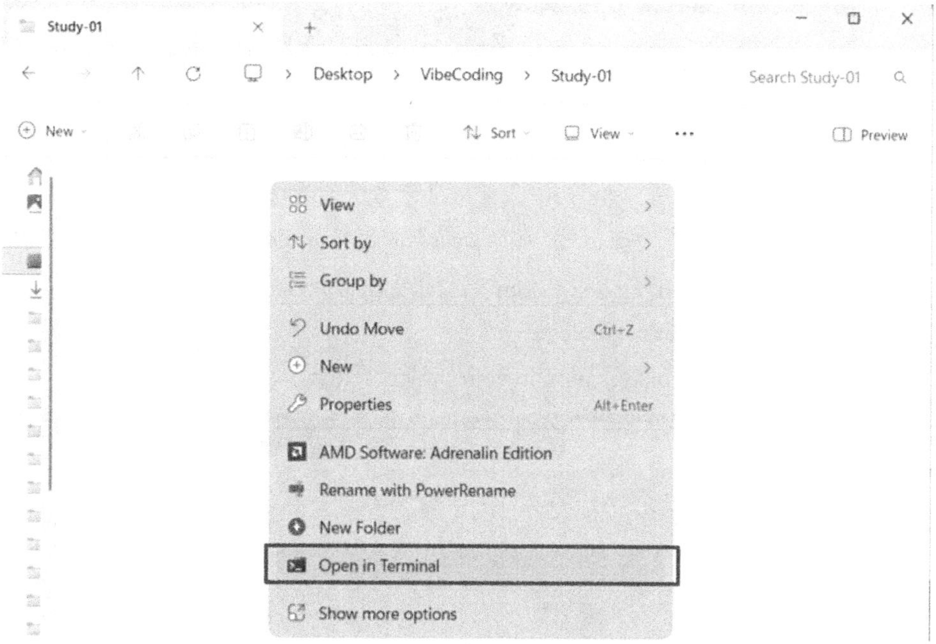

Figure 3.28: Open in Terminal

Note

For Windows 10 or earlier versions, please hold the Shift key while right-clicking.

Method 2: Open the terminal from the folder's context menu

Before navigating to the folder where you want to launch the terminal, right-click on the selected folder and choose the **Open in Terminal** menu.

The command prompt will open in the `Study-01` folder.

Running Claude

1. Type `claude` in the command prompt.

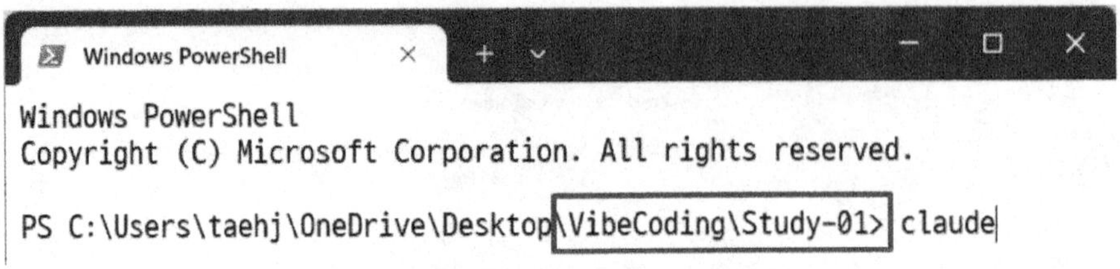

Figure 3.29: Run Claude from command prompt

2. The initial screen of Claude Code will open. It will ask if you trust the folder. Select **1. Yes, I trust this folder** to proceed.
3. You can now start a conversation in your project folder.

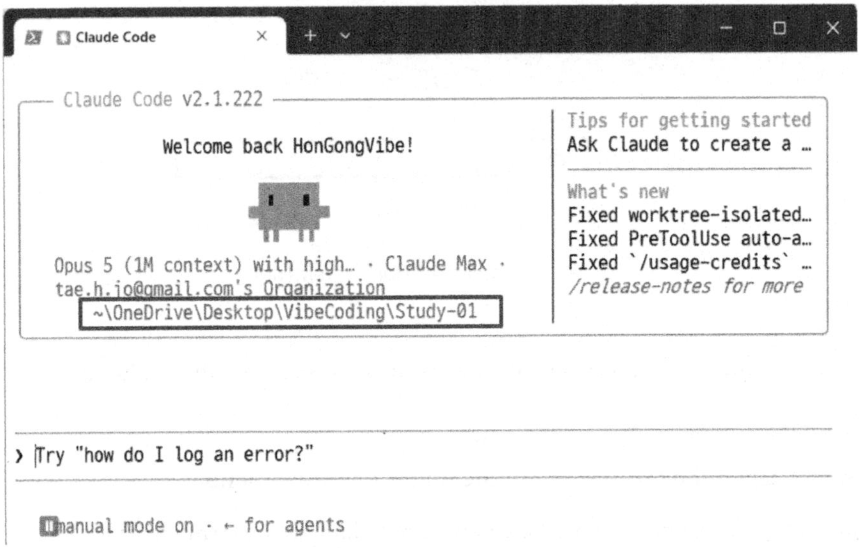

Figure 3.30: Start the conversation

Tip

Another way to start Claude Code in a designated folder

You can also launch the terminal by typing `powershell` in the Windows taskbar search box, then navigate to your working folder and run Claude Code. Once the terminal is open, enter the command `cd` followed by a space and the path to the `Study-01` folder, then press Enter. You can copy the folder path by clicking the address bar at the top of File Explorer.

```
cd C:\Users\user\Desktop\VibeCoding\Study-01
```

Creating a number recognition program with the MNIST dataset

Now, let's use the installed Claude Code to create a handwritten digit recognition program. In this project, you will implement an AI that recognizes numbers drawn by the user in real time.

This program uses the **Modified National Institute of Standards and Technology** (**MNIST**) dataset. MNIST consists of 70,000 images of handwritten digits from 0 to 9, with each image containing black-and-white digit data at a size of 28×28 pixels. Since its release in 1998, it has been widely used as a standard dataset for computer vision and machine learning, and is well known as the first dataset that deep learning beginners encounter.

Figure 3.31: A sample of the MNIST dataset

Writing Python code

Run Claude Code from the `Study-01` folder location. From here, you will use Claude Code along with Python to create a handwritten digit recognition program.

1. Enter the following prompt and press *Enter*. Claude Code will generate a work plan and begin executing the steps.

   Prompt: `Create and run code that recognizes numbers entered as handwriting.`

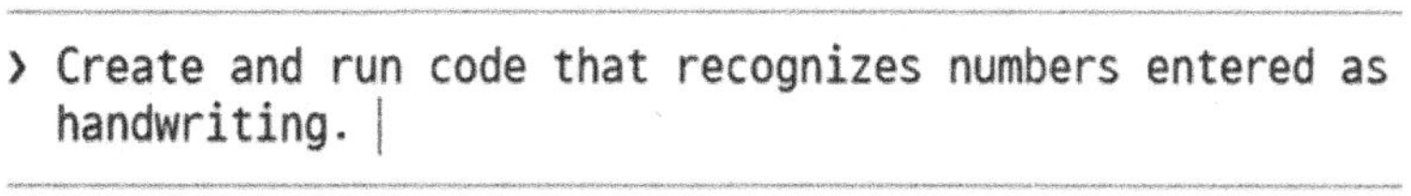

Figure 3.32: Running the code

2. Claude Code will generate the Python code and ask for permission to save it as `digit_recognition.py`. Select **1. Yes** and press the *Enter* key.

> **Note**
>
> Even with the same prompt, results may vary slightly, so please check the generated filename and program output before continuing.

3. A new Python file has been created in the `Study-01` folder.

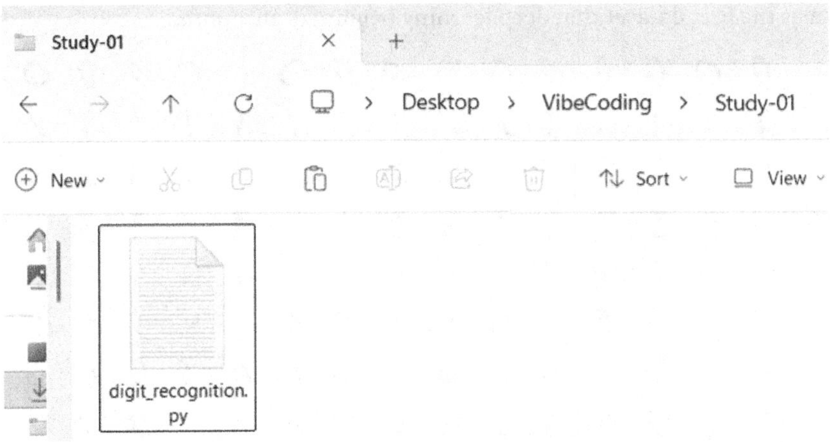

Figure 3.33: New Python file

4. Claude Code stops and asks for confirmation whenever a step would change something on your machine, such as installing a package, creating or editing a file, or running code. Select **1. Yes** each time and watch it carry on.

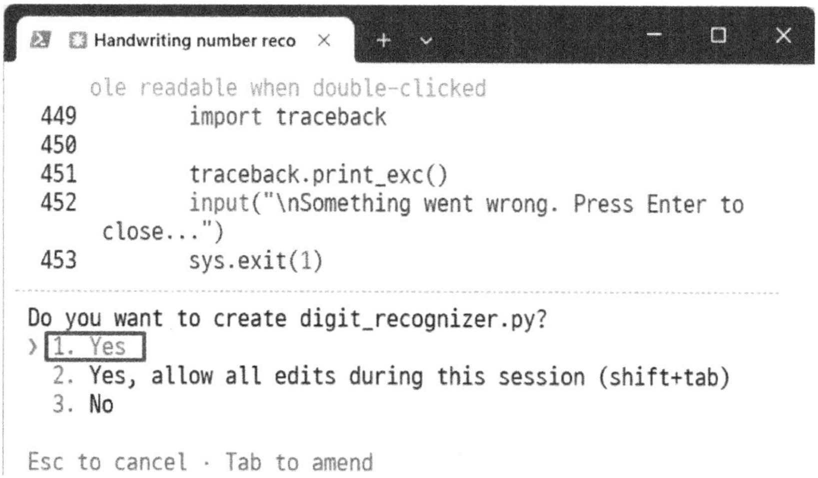

Figure 3.34: Select Yes

> **Note**
>
> To avoid repeated confirmations, you can also select **2. Yes, allow all edits during this session**. This will allow Claude Code to automatically run the code without asking for confirmation each time.

5. After a short wait, a program for recognizing handwritten numbers will appear. The appearance may vary, but there will be a box in the center for writing, a **Clear** button below to erase the writing, and a **Recognize** button to recognize the handwritten numbers.

Figure 3.35: Clear and Recognize buttons

You can draw a digit in the box using your mouse. If you don't see the window, find the newly opened program on the taskbar and click it.

6. Draw numbers from 0 to 9 with your mouse in the white box, then click the **Recognize** button. The program will display the recognized digit and its confidence score.

Figure 3.36: Draw a number to recognize

Running the program without Claude Code

So far, you have run the handwriting recognition program through Claude Code. Now, let's make it so you can run it independently without Claude Code. To do this, you'll create a batch file—a text file that collects multiple Windows commands to run at once. Batch files are useful for automating repetitive commands.

Figure 3.37: Create a batch file

The file extension for a batch file is `.bat`.

If you create a batch file for the handwriting recognition program, you can run the program by double-clicking the file in Windows Explorer. For this exercise, close the currently open handwriting recognition program and return to the terminal where Claude Code is running.

1. In the Claude Code input field, write the following prompt, and press the *Enter* key.

   Prompt: `Make it so I can run the digit recognition program by clicking it in Windows Explorer.`

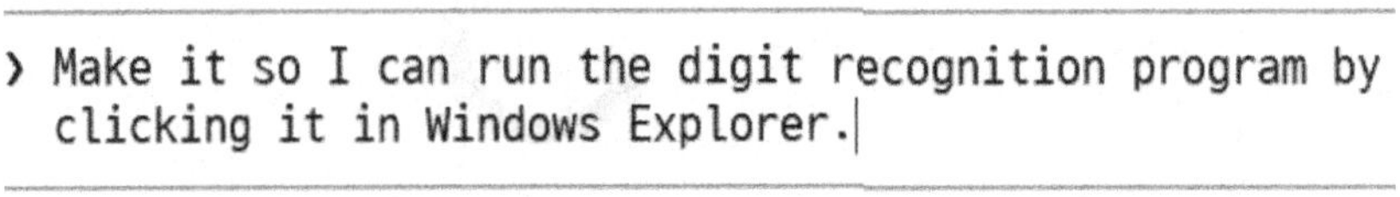

Figure 3.38: Enter the prompt

2. When it finishes successfully, a message will appear indicating that the file has been created.

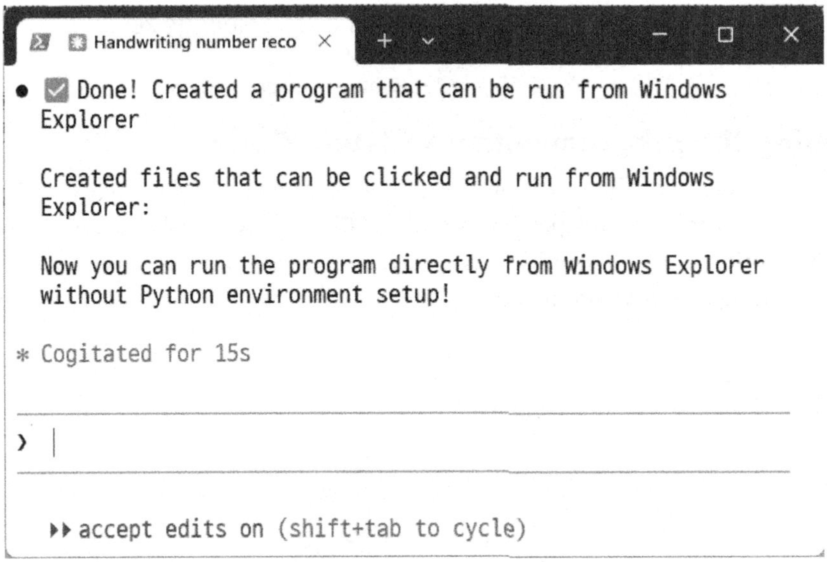

Figure 3.39: The file is created

3. A batch (`.bat`) file has been created in the `Study-01` folder.

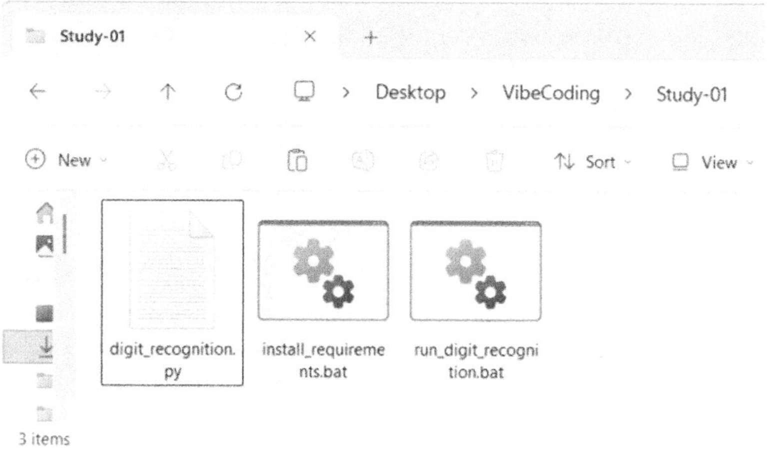

Figure 3.40: Batch file

Tip

File permission choices

When working with files in Claude Code, you may see a message asking whether to save the code as a file. The way you work with files afterward depends on the permission mode you select. Claude Code offers the following permission modes:

- **Yes**: Allows this one change. Claude Code asks again next time.
- **No, and tell Claude what to do differently**: Refuses the change so you can say what you want instead.
- **Always allow in this project**: Always allows file operations in this project.

4. The program starts on its own. A command prompt window opens, the AI model is trained, and the handwriting recognition window appears when training finishes. If nothing happens, double-click the batch file (`.bat`) to start it yourself.

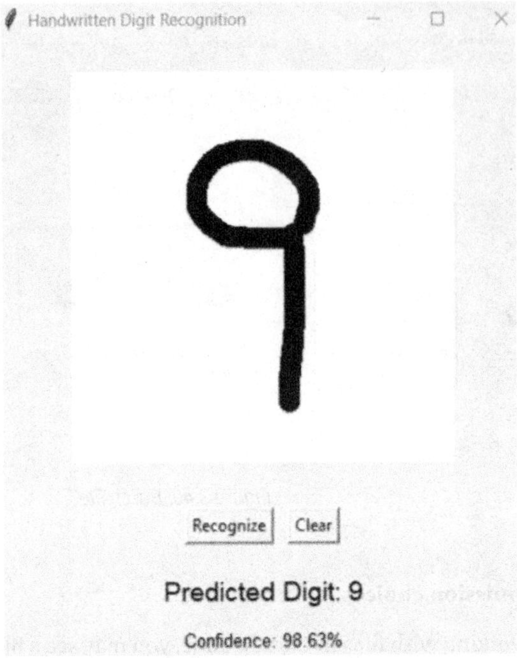

Figure 3.41: Predicted Digit

In this section, you completed the AI handwriting recognition program using Claude Code. Without having to implement complex deep learning algorithms yourself, you were able to train a model on the MNIST dataset and create a program with a graphical user interface through simple conversation. In the next section, we'll use Claude Code's project configuration files to manage the project context and take on the challenge of building a web application based on this.

Wrapping up

Key Points Summarized in 3 Keywords:

- Handwriting recognition is an **AI technology** that automatically reads handwritten letters or numbers and converts them into digital data.
- **MNIST** is a dataset of 70,000 images of handwritten digits from 0 to 9, and is the most widely used training resource in deep learning and computer vision.
- A **batch file** is a text file in the Windows operating system that records multiple commands in sequence and automatically executes them when run.

Review questions

1. Select the option that is NOT a way to move to the working folder for running Claude Code.
    1. Type `powershell` in the Explorer address bar to open a terminal in that folder.
    2. Run the terminal and use the `cd` command to move to the desired folder.
    3. Claude Code automatically selects the optimal folder.
    4. Copy the folder path in File Explorer and paste it into the terminal.
2. Choose the correct explanation for the metrics you can observe during the handwriting recognition program's training process.
    1. The lower the accuracy, the better the performance.
    2. The higher the loss, the better the performance.
    3. The higher the accuracy and the lower the loss, the better the performance.
    4. Both metrics are better when higher.
3. Select the option that is NOT a permission setting in Claude Code.
    1. Ask every time (confirm each time)
    2. Yes, for this session only (current session only)
    3. Always allow in this project (Always allow within the project)
    4. Never allow modifications (Modifications strictly prohibited)

Expanding the program with CLAUDE.md

> Note
>
> **Key terms**: CLAUDE.md | /init command | Hierarchical structure
>
> In this section, we will apply a hierarchical folder structure to expand the handwritten digit recognition program into a web version. We will use the `CLAUDE.md` file to record and manage the project context, and practice how to use the `/init` command.

Before you begin

A configuration file is a document that contains rules or environment information referenced when a program runs. In Python projects, a file like `requirements.txt` that lists necessary libraries is a typical example of a configuration file. The key feature is that users can change the program's operating environment simply by editing the configuration file, without having to modify the source code directly.

If you had to re-explain previous rules, tech stacks, and workflows every time you closed and reopened Claude Code, it would be highly inefficient. To solve this, Claude Code uses a configuration file called `CLAUDE.md`.

By saving the project structure, goals, development rules, and more in this file, Claude Code can always understand the project context and continue working seamlessly. If there are multiple sub-projects, you can create separate configuration files for each one to manage them according to their characteristics.

In this section, we will practice converting the existing handwritten character recognition program into a web application using `CLAUDE.md`, and learn how to organize the project systematically with a hierarchical folder structure.

Understanding project configuration files

Let's try expanding the handwritten character recognition program we created earlier into a web version. The key tool for this process is the `CLAUDE.md` file.

`CLAUDE.md` is a file that documents the project's structure, coding style, core commands, and more, and is automatically read when Claude Code runs. By using this, Claude Code can reload the project's context when you start a new session, allowing you to continue working as if you were resuming a previous conversation. Now, let's learn how to create and use the `CLAUDE.md` file.

In Windows Explorer, right-click the **Study-01** folder and select **Open in Terminal** from the menu, and press the *Enter* key to launch the terminal. Then, type `claude` at the command prompt to run Claude Code. Now you're ready to begin the exercise.

Creating a project configuration file

1. To implement the handwritten character recognition program on the web, enter the initialization command `/init` in Claude Code (as shown in *Figure 3.42*) and press *Enter*. Claude Code will analyze the code and file structure of the current project folder and automatically generate the `CLAUDE.md` file.

   Enter the initialization command as shown in the input box (*Figure 3.42*) and press the *Enter* key to run it.

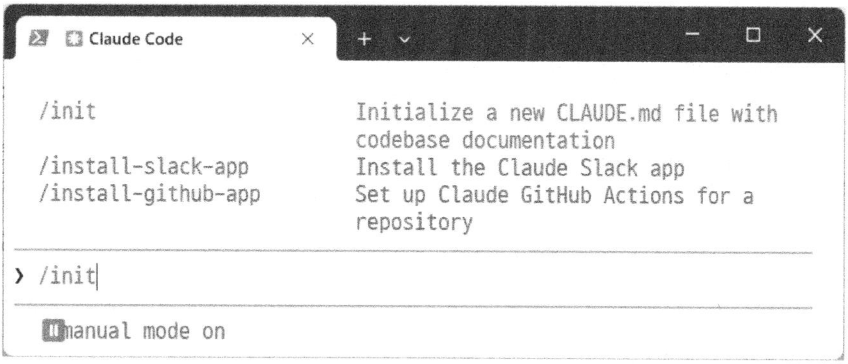

Figure 3.42: Entering the initialization command

> **Note**
>
> Claude Code has many special commands that start with a slash (/). As you work through various projects in this book, you'll gradually learn how to use Claude Code's commands. For a preview of useful commands, refer to the appendix.

2. Claude Code analyzes the libraries, class structures, and functions in the Python files in the current folder to create a systematic document and generates a `CLAUDE.md` file in the `Study-01` folder.

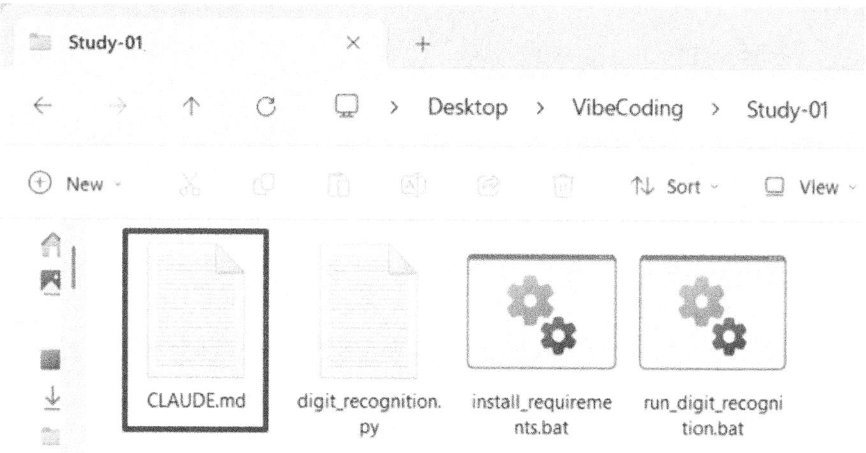

Figure 3.43: The CLAUDE.md file generated in the Study-01 folder

Tip

'/init' Command and Initialization

`/init` is a command for preparing initial settings or setting up a new execution environment. The name comes from the first four letters of the English word 'initialization.' When you run `/init`, Claude Code analyzes the project, generates the `CLAUDE.md` file, and automatically documents the project structure, tech stack, and key commands.

When adding new features or making important configuration changes during the project, simply add the details to `CLAUDE.md`. This way, Claude Code can always maintain the latest context, allowing you to keep a consistent development environment without having to repeat the same explanations each time.

Structure of a project configuration file

`CLAUDE.md` is the first prompt delivered when starting a project with Claude Code, and it is the initial configuration file containing all project information. Unnecessary explanations waste tokens and can degrade performance, so it's important to keep it concise.

Therefore, the `CLAUDE.md` file generated by the `/init` command is characterized by its concise summary of the project's core information. There is no fixed format, but it is best to structure it so that Claude Code can immediately understand the project settings (write it specifically and clearly).

Typical `CLAUDE.md` file structure:

```
# Project name
A brief description of the project

## Project Overview
Summarize what the project does in one or two sentences.

## Commands
-       Installation command, execution command, test command

## Tech Stack
-       Description of Python version, libraries, etc.

## Architecture
```

```
-       Description of core classes and functions
-       File structure and the role of each file

## Code Style
-       Code and comment writing, error handling, function naming style

## Development Notes
-       Current status and limitations
```

Modifying and using the configuration file

As you work on your project, you can update the `CLAUDE.md` file at any time if you need new rules or settings. The most convenient way is to make a direct request to Claude Code during your conversation. For example, if you make a request like the following, Claude Code will automatically update the file for you:

```
Please add this coding rule to the CLAUDE.md file.
```

```
The project structure has changed, so please update the CLAUDE.md file.
```

Let us explore the location and types of CLAUDE.md next:

- **Project-specific CLAUDE.md**: This is the configuration file belonging to the current project folder. For example, when you run Claude Code from the `Study-01` folder and enter the `/init` command, the location of `CLAUDE.md` depends on the project's configuration. If there is a `.claude` folder inside `Study-01`, the `CLAUDE.md` file will be saved there; if not, the `CLAUDE.md` file will be created directly in the `Study-01` folder. This file will be continually referenced within the project and plays a key role in managing the project efficiently.
- **CLAUDE.md applied to all projects**: To apply settings universally to all project files, the `CLAUDE.md` file must be located in the user's home directory. The file path is `C:\Users\username\.claude\CLAUDE.md` on Windows, and `~/.claude/CLAUDE.md` on macOS/Linux.

  > **Note**
  >
  > A configuration file that applies to all projects is called a global configuration file.

The global CLAUDE.md file can be automatically generated by asking Claude Code to *create a global configuration file*, or you can manually create and write the file at the specified path. Since the rules written in this file affect all projects, you should only include essential basic rules.

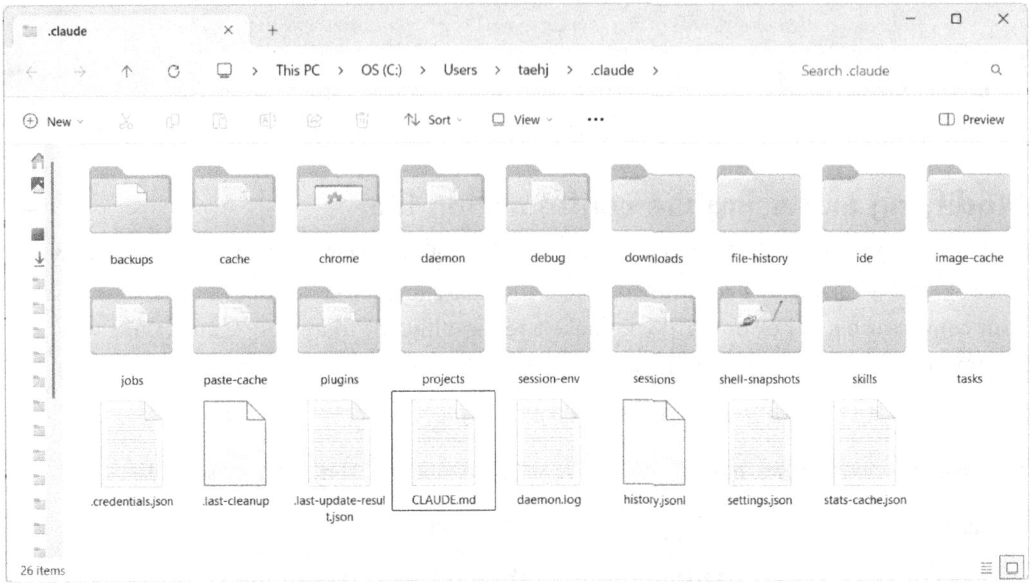

Figure 3.44: Creating the global configuration file

Note

CLAUDE.md is automatically loaded at the start of each session. If the file becomes too long, it consumes more of the available context and may reduce Claude Code's ability to follow all the instructions consistently.

Creating a web version handwriting recognition program using a hierarchical structure

Now, let's expand the handwriting recognition program into a web version so it can run in a web browser. As the project grows, you'll need to manage multiple versions simultaneously, so it's important to have a systematic management method that maintains common rules in one place while separating version-specific settings. This is where the hierarchical structure and CLAUDE.md files become crucial.

Understanding hierarchical structure

The most basic unit for organizing files on a computer is the directory (folder). A directory can contain not only files but also other subdirectories, forming a hierarchical structure much like the branches of a tree. Several subfolders extend from the top-level root folder, and within them are more files or even smaller folders.

Claude Code recognizes and works with this folder hierarchy. When Claude Code starts, it first identifies the current directory and its subfolder structure, and as needed during work, it explores the contents of subfolders.

From here, let's create a `desktop_version` folder under the `Study-01` directory to store desktop-specific rules, and a `web_version` folder to store web version-specific rules.

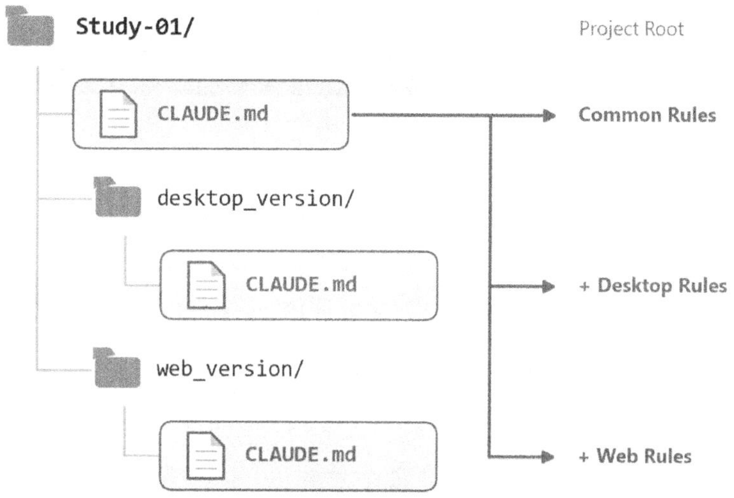

Figure 3.45: Folder hierarchy

CLAUDE.md files will be stored separately according to the hierarchical structure. The root `Study-01` folder can contain rules shared across the project, while each subfolder can have its own version-specific rules, making it efficient to maintain separate `CLAUDE.md` files for each. Now, let's actually create the hierarchical folder structure and see for ourselves.

Creating a hierarchical structure

1. Let's make the following request to Claude Code.
   Prompt: `I want to develop the handwriting recognition program as both a web version and a desktop version. Please create the web_version and desktop_version folders, and generate a CLAUDE.md file for each folder.`

```
> I want to develop the handwriting recognition program as both a web
  version and a desktop version. Please create the web_version and
  desktop_version folders, and generate a CLAUDE.md file for each folder.
```

Figure 3.46: Prompt for creating folders and file

2. Claude Code will start creating the necessary directories and files in each directory. Select **1. Yes** to check the contents and proceed. After Claude Code completes the task, it will show you the results.

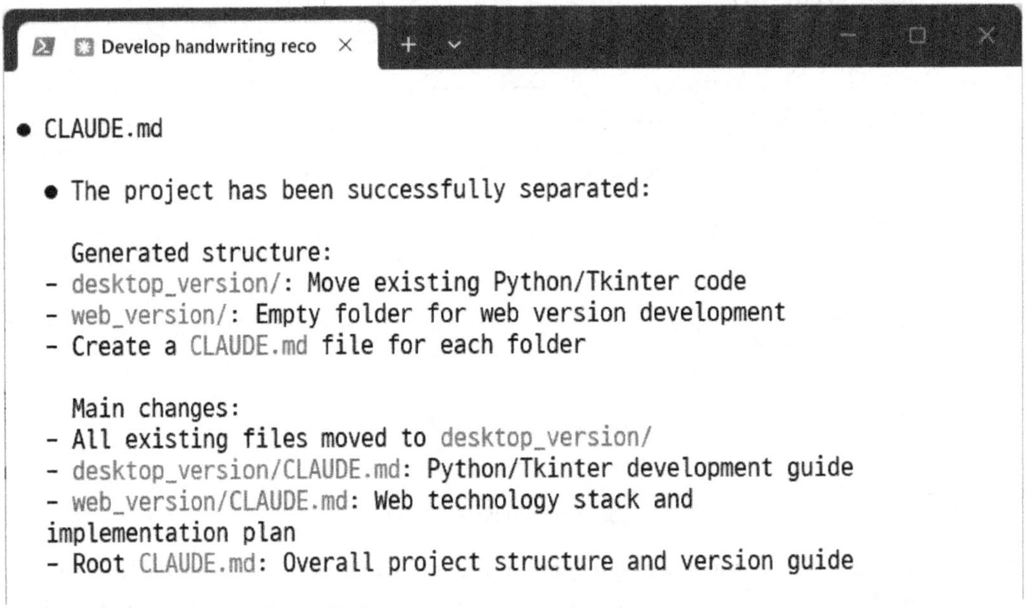

Figure 3.47: Results shown

> **Note**
>
> By selecting **2. Yes and don't ask again**, you can have similar commands proceed automatically.

3. Check the `Study-01` folder in your File Explorer. You will see the web application in the `web_version` folder and the existing desktop version code organized in the `desktop_version` folder. Each folder contains a `CLAUDE.md` file appropriate for that version.

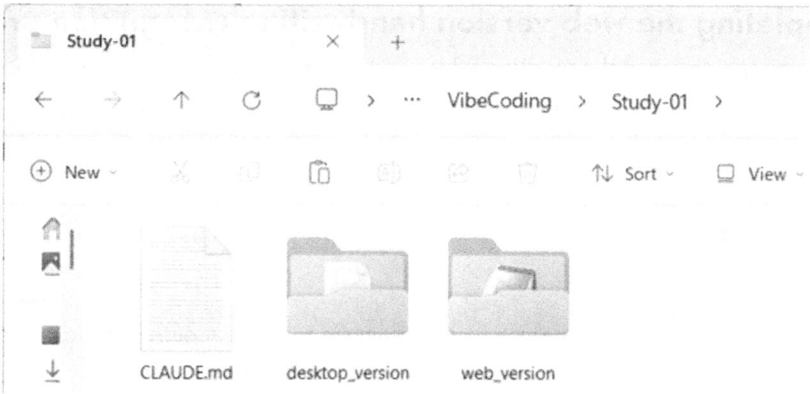

Figure 3.48: The appropriate CLAUDE.md file

The structure created by Claude Code is as follows:

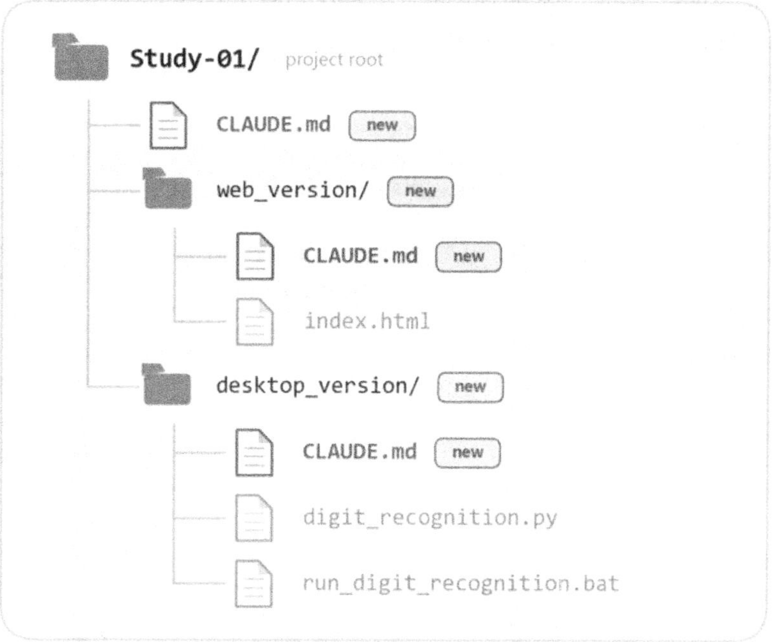

Figure 3.49: Folder and file structure

By utilizing this kind of hierarchical `CLAUDE.md` structure, you only need to write common rules once at the root, while applying specialized rules for each subproject to maintain consistency. This approach also allows you to standardize coding style across the entire project and manage it more systematically.

Completing the web version handwriting recognition program

So far, you have created the working folder and generated the `CLAUDE.md` file along with several necessary files. Now, let's move on to actually completing the web version of the handwriting recognition program.

1. Enter the following into Claude Code:

   Prompt: `Run the web version program in the browser.`

   > **Note**
   >
   > When Claude Code asks for your consent to install required libraries and so on while generating the program, select **1. Yes to continue**.

2. When the web server starts, a local server address in the format `http://localhost:port_number` will appear. Enter this into your web browser's address bar, and the handwriting recognition program will run in the browser.

Figure 3.50: The handwriting recognition program in the browser

Note

The execution process may vary from person to person. If an error occurs, you can copy the error message displayed in the terminal and provide it to Claude Code for troubleshooting.

Tip

What is localhost?

Localhost is a special name that refers to the user's own computer on a network. A computer has multiple connection channels so that several programs can communicate simultaneously, and each channel is assigned a number. This number is called a port.

`http://localhost` means you are connecting not to another computer on the internet, but to a program running on your own computer. For example, when you are told to connect to `http://localhost:8080`, `localhost` refers to your computer, and ':8080' means it is using port 8080.

By using localhost in this way, you can run and preview web applications without connecting to an external network. Developers can use this to test their programs or immediately check modifications during development.

3. If you draw a number with your mouse to test, you can confirm that the program accurately recognizes your handwriting.

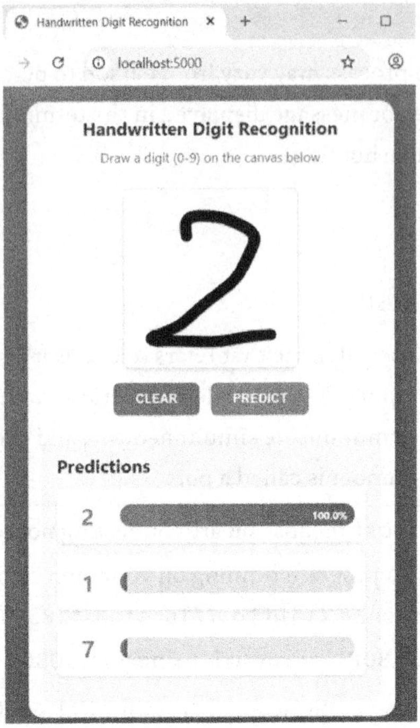

Figure 3.51: Successful handwriting recognition

So far, you have used the `CLAUDE.md` file to systematically organize and manage your project, and have created the handwriting recognition program in both desktop and web versions. You learned how the `CLAUDE.md` file helps Claude Code retain important project instructions and context across sessions, and practiced automatically generating the file using the `/init` command. You also learned how to separate the handwriting recognition program into web and desktop versions, and how to efficiently manage shared and version-specific rules by placing specialized `CLAUDE.md` files in each folder.

Now that you have established a foundation for systematically structuring and managing your project, in the next chapter you will learn how to maximize code quality and work efficiency through advanced prompts and configuration file management.

Wrapping up

Key takeaways summarized in 3 Keywords:

- The **CLAUDE.md** file is a configuration file that records the project's structure, rules, commands, etc., and is automatically read by Claude Code when executed.

- **/init** is an initialization command that analyzes the current folder and automatically generates a `CLAUDE.md` file.
- A **hierarchical structure** is a management method where common rules are placed at the root and specialized rules are applied to each subfolder.

Review questions

1. Choose the one that is NOT a main role of the `CLAUDE.md` file.
    1. Automatically restore project context
    2. Store coding rules and commands
    3. Store the entire previous conversation
    4. Automatically read by Claude Code at startup
2. Choose the command that automatically generates a `CLAUDE.md` file.
    1. `/start`
    2. `/init`
    3. `/setup`
3. Which content is appropriate to write in the global `CLAUDE.md`?
    1. Description of a specific project's directory structure
    2. Coding style rules to be applied to all projects
    3. Build commands for the current project
    4. List of API endpoints used only in a specific project
4. Choose the one that is NOT an advantage of a hierarchical CLAUDE.md structure.
    1. Write common rules only once at the root
    2. specialized rules for each subproject
    3. Token usage is automatically reduced
    4. Maintain consistency across the entire project

Review questions

4

Practical Use of Claude Code

So far, we've written prompts in the Claude Web interface and installed Claude Code to create programs in the terminal. Now, let's combine these two environments to experience a more structured development process. You'll learn how to design prompts in Claude Web and efficiently execute them in Claude Code. In particular, you'll naturally pick up various Claude Code commands as you build a real project.

Learning objectives:

- You can work efficiently by linking Claude Web and Claude Code
- You can use the basic commands of Claude Code appropriately for different situations
- You can improve development efficiency through systematic prompt design
- You will be able to complete a practical to-do management app

Learning Claude Code commands with step-by-step prompts

> **Note**
>
> **Key terms**: Step-by-step | /init | /status | /model | /help
>
> The goal of this section is to become familiar with the workflow from planning to implementation. We'll apply PRD writing methods and the 5W1H framework to a real project to organize the requirements for a 'to-do management app'. You will then implement this using Claude Code while learning the basics of its command-line interface.

Before you begin

The app you'll build in this section is a personal to-do management application. It will allow you to easily record daily tasks, check their completion status, and organize items by category such as work, personal, or study.

The app runs directly in the web browser, and instead of using a complex framework, you'll build it using only pure HTML, CSS, and JavaScript, making it easy for beginners to follow along.

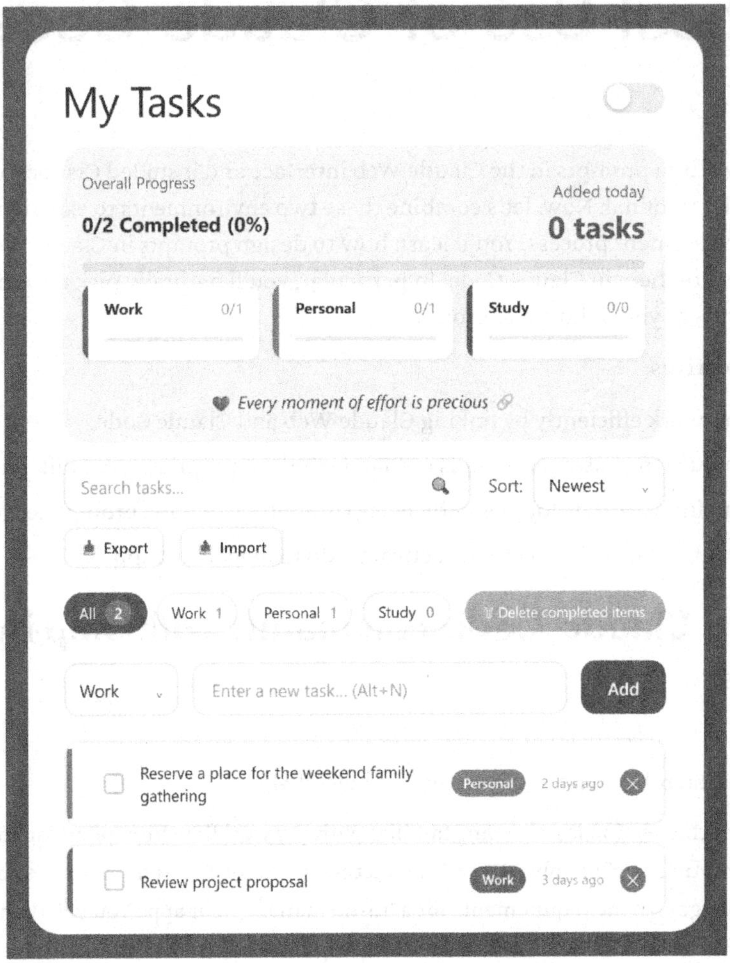

Figure 4.1: My Tasks window

In this chapter, you'll practice various Claude Code commands while building a to-do management app. The project's workflow is divided into two stages: planning and implementation, which will be carried out in Claude and Claude Code, respectively.

Along the way you will pick up the commands that matter once a project runs past a single sitting: resuming yesterday's session, letting Claude Code work without stopping to ask at every step, keeping a long conversation from filling up, and pointing at a file or a screenshot instead of describing it.

This chapter uses the tools that come with Windows. On macOS and Linux, use the following ones instead; everything else in the chapter is the same:

Windows	**macOS and Linux**
File Explorer	Finder on macOS; Files on Linux
Notepad	TextEdit on macOS; gedit or nano on Linux
Snipping Tool	*Shift* + *Command* + *4* on macOS; your screenshot tool on Linux

Table 4.1: Tools to use

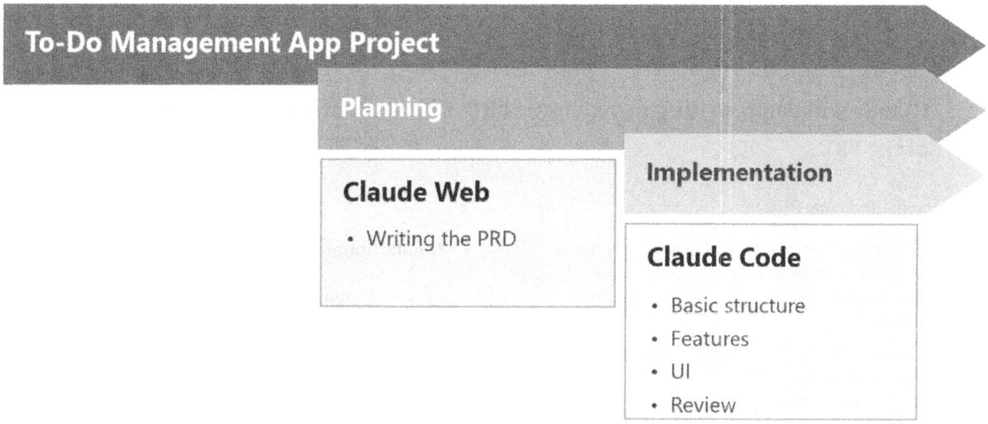

Figure 4.2: Project workflow

The PRD and step-by-step prompts generated by Claude may appear slightly different each time. It's okay if they're not exactly the same as the examples in the book. The important thing is to follow the PRD format to organize requirements and experience executing them step by step. You can use your own generated results for the exercises.

Writing Step-by-Step Prompts

Let's systematically organize the project requirements using the 5W1H framework you learned in *Chapter 2*, and summarize them in a PRD. This PRD will serve as the blueprint for the to-do management app you'll build and will clarify the development direction. Based on the PRD, we'll create a step-by-step prompt strategy and use it to implement the app in Claude Code.

Writing the PRD

1. Access Claude (claude.ai) in your web browser, start a new conversation, and enter the following prompt to write the PRD for the to-do management app:

   Prompt:

```
I want to create a to-do management app. Please write a PRD for me.
It's a personal app to manage about 10-20 tasks per day. The main features
are:
- Add, edit, and delete tasks
- Completion check feature
- Category classification (work/personal/study)
- View progress
I want it to run directly in the browser, and I'd like the data to persist
even after refreshing. I want to build it with pure JavaScript without
technical complexity.
```

2. Claude will begin writing a systematic PRD. Check the structure and key requirements of the PRD.

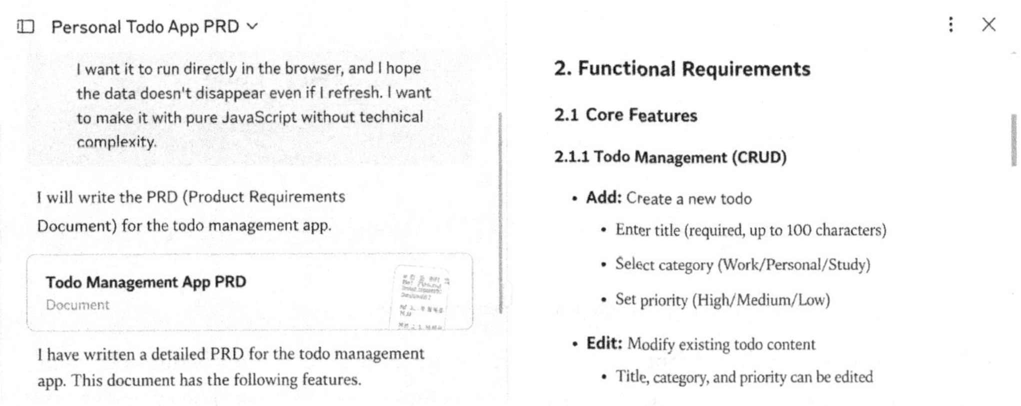

Figure 4.3: Claude writing the PRD

> **Note**
>
> Due to the nature of generative AI, the response may differ in expression and structure each time, but the core content will be similar since it is organized in the PRD format.

Converting to prompts

Now, let's convert this PRD into concrete prompts that can be executed in Claude Code. Unlike the web, Claude Code prompts can create and modify files, so focus on making them more specific and actionable.

Based on the PRD you created, let's build a step-by-step prompt strategy. Ask Claude as follows, and it will organize clear instructions and specific file operation commands for you.

Prompt:

```
Convert this PRD into step-by-step prompts for use in Claude Code.
Summarize it into 5 key steps and create clear instructions for each step.
```

> **Tip**
>
> Save the step-by-step prompts you created in Claude Web in Notepad or another text editor, and copy and use them when working in Claude Code. This creates an efficient workflow where the web handles 'planning and design' and the code handles 'implementation.'

Once you receive the prompts organized step by step like this, you're ready to execute them one by one in Claude Code. Each step builds on the results of the previous one, gradually adding new features to the application.

> **Note**
>
> The PRD and step-by-step prompts generated by Claude may differ for each user. It's okay if your results are different from those in this book.
>
> In *Chapter 6*, you will learn how to write a PRD directly in Claude Code, generate step-by-step prompts, save them as md files, and utilize them. In this section, before diving into hands-on practice, the focus is on understanding the basic concepts and workflow by reviewing the generated prompts in the familiar web interface environment.

Executing Step-by-Step Prompts

Let's try running the prompts prepared earlier in Claude Web step by step. Simply copy the text and paste it directly into Claude Code.

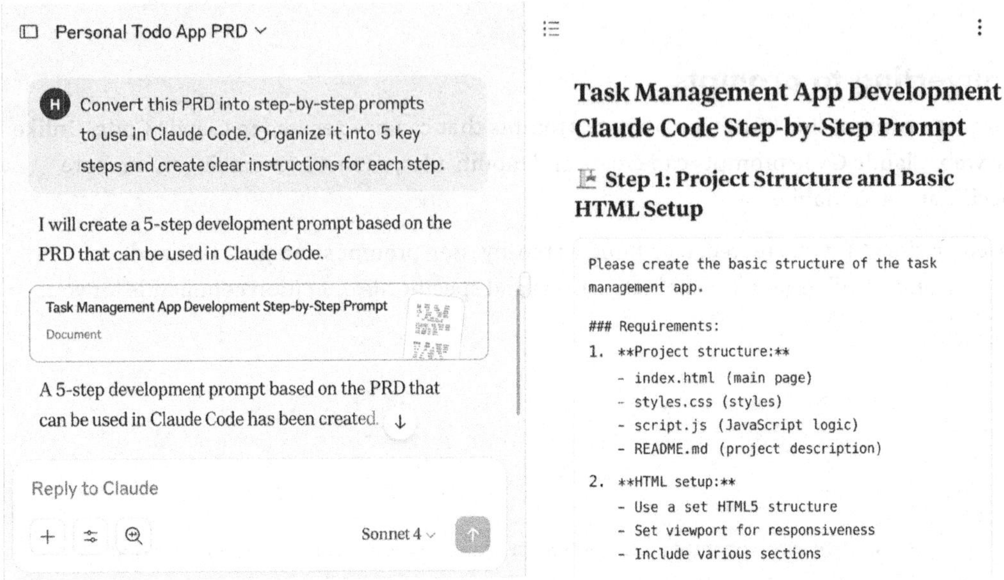

Figure 4.4: Running the prompts prepared earlier

You can also click the *Copy* icon in the Claude artifact.

> **Tip**
>
> **Prompt repository**
>
> From this section onward, the prompts you enter yourself may differ from the sample prompts provided in the textbook. If you want to refer to them for your studies, visit this book's GitHub repository and click **View the complete prompt collection**. The prompts used in the book are organized by chapter.
>
> To access the repository link, follow the steps in the *Download the example code files* section in the *Preface*.

Running Claude Code and initial setup

1. Create a new folder named `Study-02` inside the `VibeCoding` folder on your desktop, then double-click to open it.

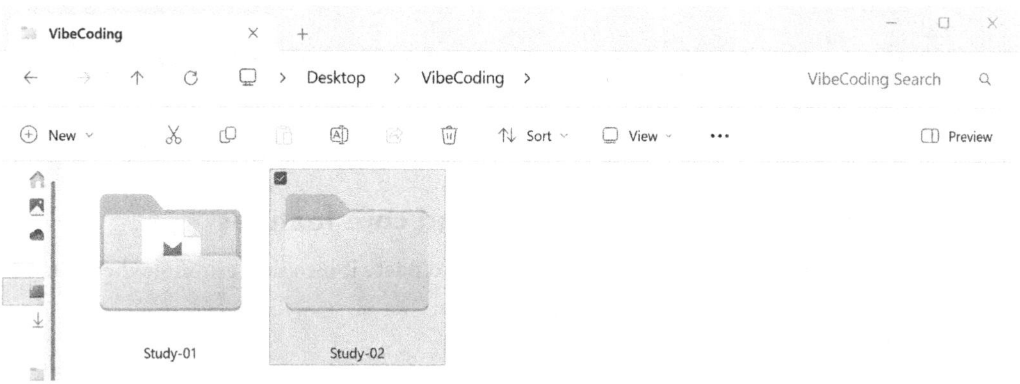

Figure 4.5: The Study-02 folder

2. Right-click in the empty space of the `Study-02` folder and select **Open in Terminal** from the menu to launch the terminal. Then, type `claude` to run Claude Code.

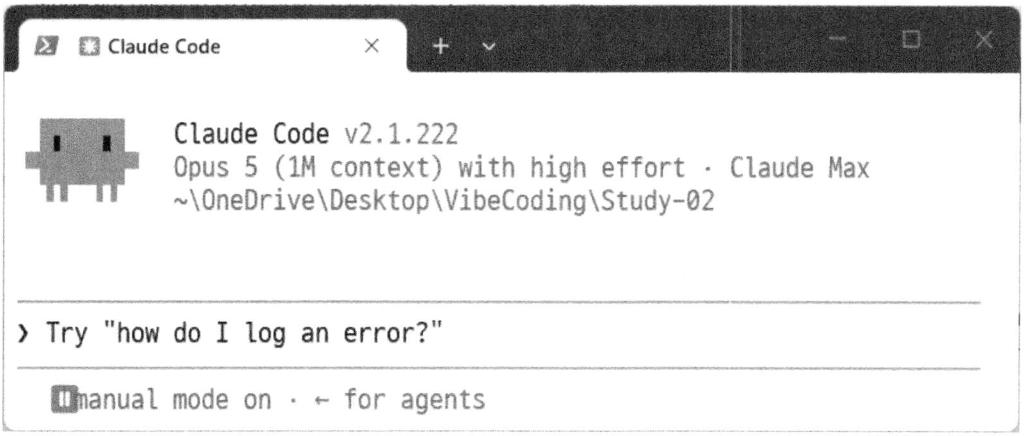

Figure 4.6: Run Claude Code

3. Prepare the step-by-step prompts you wrote earlier in Claude Web. Following the five steps suggested by Claude, you'll build a to-do management app.
    - Step 1: Implement the basic structure and core features
    - Step 2: Add category functionality and improve the UI
    - Step 3: Add a progress dashboard
    - Step 4: Dark mode and advanced features
    - Step 5: Final completion and optimization

Note

It's okay if your hands-on process differs from this book. Just follow the step-by-step prompts provided by Claude.

Step 1: Implement the basic structure and core features

1. Copy the first step-by-step prompt (Step 1) and paste it into the terminal where Claude Code is running. Press the *Ctrl* + *V* key to paste.

   Prompt:

```
Step 1: Implement basic structure and core functions
Create the basic structure of a to-do management app.

Requirements:
1. Consist of three files: index.html, style.css, script.js
2. HTML structure:
   - App title "My Tasks"
   - To-do input field (input + add button)
   - Container to display the to-do list
3. JavaScript features:
   - Add to-do (support both Enter key and button click)
   - Delete to-do (X button for each item)
   - Toggle complete/incomplete with checkbox
   - Change style when completed
4. Store data in localStorage
   - Automatically save when adding/deleting/changing completion status
   - Keep data when page is refreshed
5. Basic CSS styling:
   - Clean card-style layout
   - Center alignment, max width 600px
   - Hover effects and transitions

Store each to-do with the structure { id, text, completed, createdAt }.
```

Tip

When manually entering a multi-line prompt in the terminal, you can insert a line break by pressing \ + *Enter* or *Ctrl* + *J*.

2. Wait while checking the progress, and soon you'll see a message indicating that the basic structure has been implemented.

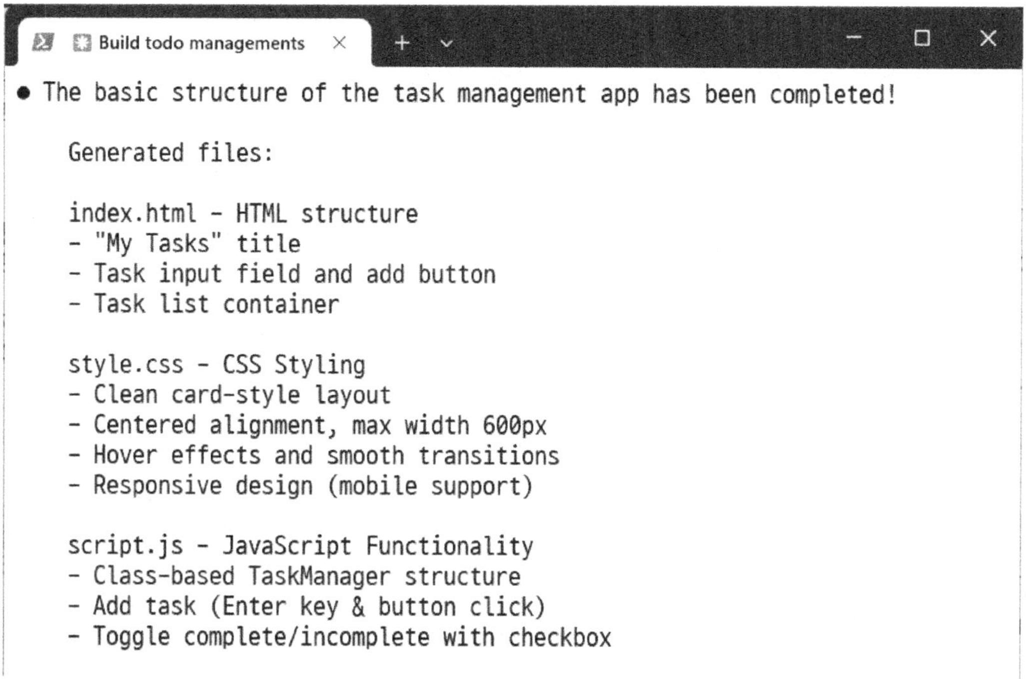

Figure 4.7: Basic structure implemented

3. In your desktop's File Explorer, click the generated `index.html` file to run it.

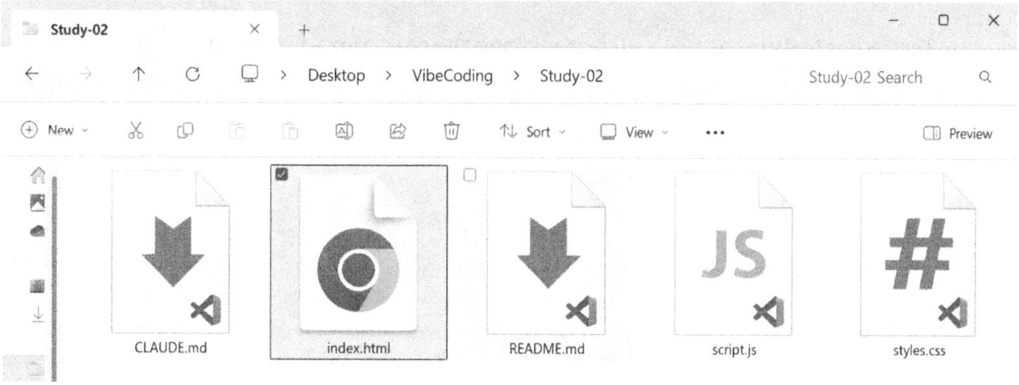

Figure 4.8: Run the index.html file

Note

The PRD and step-by-step prompts generated by Claude may differ for each user. It's okay if the content is different from this book. Just follow the step-by-step prompts.

4. Your default browser will open, and the to-do management app will launch. To test the functionality, enter `Finish Chapter 4 of Vibe Coding` in the **Enter a new task...** input box and click the **Add** button to add a to-do. Check that the to-do is added successfully.

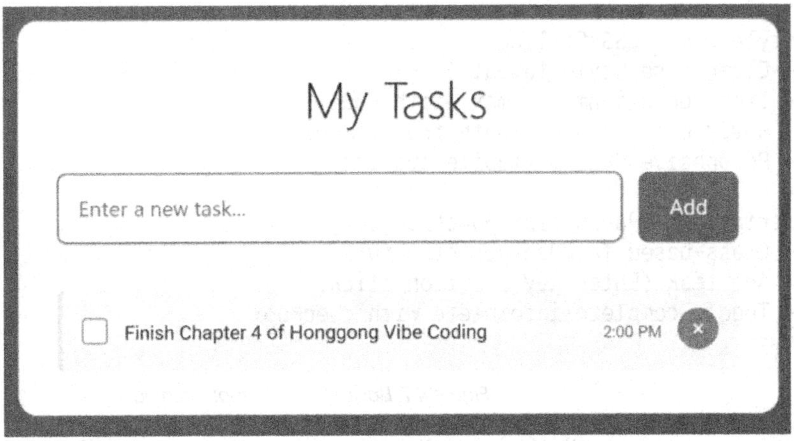

Figure 4.9: Add a to-do

5. Test other features as well, such as clicking the checkbox to mark a to-do as completed or clicking the **X** button to delete it.

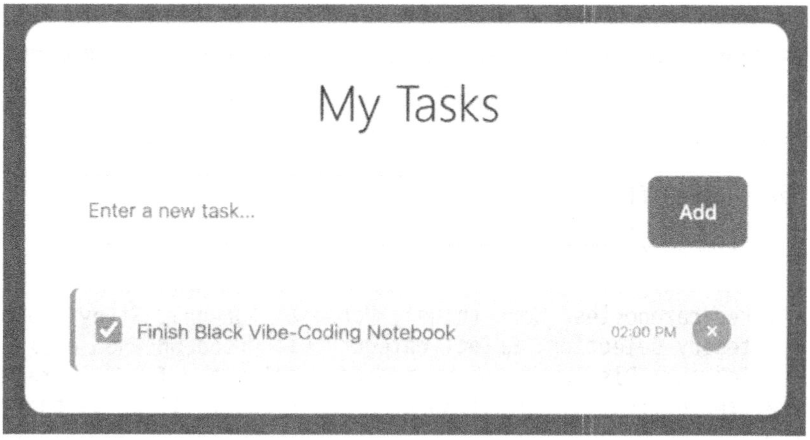

Figure 4.10: Mark as completed or delete

Step 2: Add category functionality and improve the UI

1. Copy the second prompt (Step 2) of the step-by-step prompts and enter it into Claude Code.

   Prompt:

```
Step 2: Category function and UI improvement
Add category functionality to the existing code and improve the UI.

Requirements:
1. Category function:
   - Three categories: work, personal, study
   - Category selection dropdown when adding a task
   - Display category color tag on each task item
   - Category filter buttons (All/Work/Personal/Study)
2. UI improvement:
   - Category colors: Work (blue #4A90E2), Personal (green #27AE60), Study
(purple #8E44AD)
   - Selected button has a border
   - Highlight background of selected button
   - Display creation time on task item (e.g., '2 hours ago')
3. Data structure update:
   - Add category field
   - Save the filter state in localStorage as well

Sort completed items automatically to the bottom of the list.
```

2. Once you see a message indicating completion, check the progress.

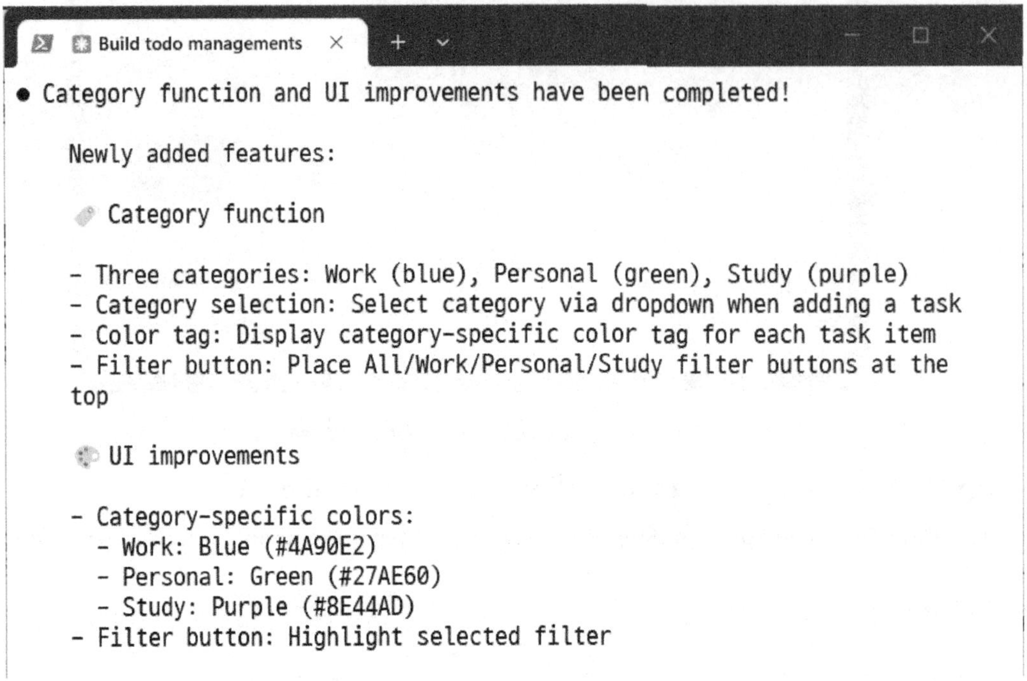

Figure 4.11: Check the progress

> **Note**
>
> If a permission prompt appears in the middle, select **1. Yes**. If you find it cumbersome to do this every time, you can also select **2. Yes, and don't ask again**.

3. Open the `index.html` file again or refresh the browser if it's already open. Work, Personal, and Study categories have been added, and the UI has been improved so you can see all categories at a glance.

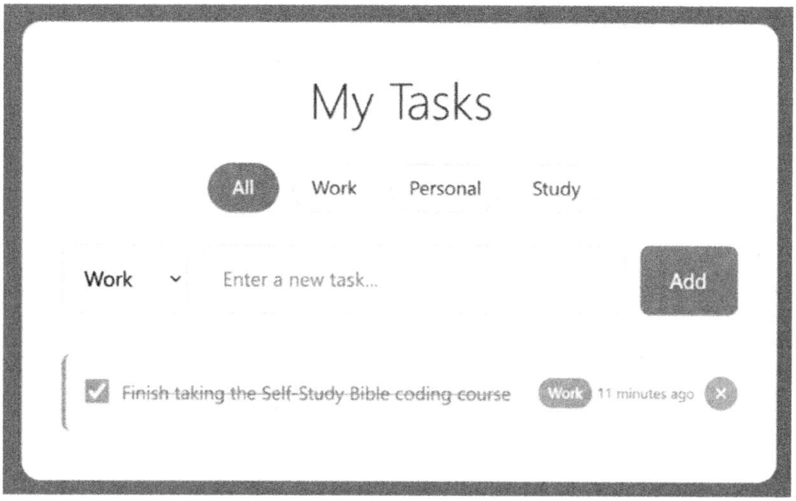

Figure 4.12: Improved UI

4. Try entering to-dos by category and check that they are properly categorized and recorded.

Figure 4.13: Enter to-dos

Step 3: Add a progress dashboard

1. Copy the third step-by-step prompt (Step 3) and enter it into Claude Code.

   Prompt:

   ```
   Step 3: Add a progress dashboard
   Add a progress dashboard and implement inline edit functionality.

   Requirements:
   1. Progress dashboard:
      - Add a statistics section at the top of the app
      - Overall progress: '5/10 completed (50%)' format + progress bar
      - Show mini progress by category (completed/total for each category)
      - Show the number of tasks added today
   2. Inline edit functionality:
      - Edit mode on double-clicking a task
      - Change to input field for editing
      - Save with Enter, cancel with ESC
      - Selectable box to change category during editing
   3. UI animation:
      - Smooth transition effect for progress bar
      - Fade animation when adding/deleting items
      - Slide animation when checking complete

   The dashboard must update in real time.
   ```

2. Once you see a message indicating completion, check the progress.

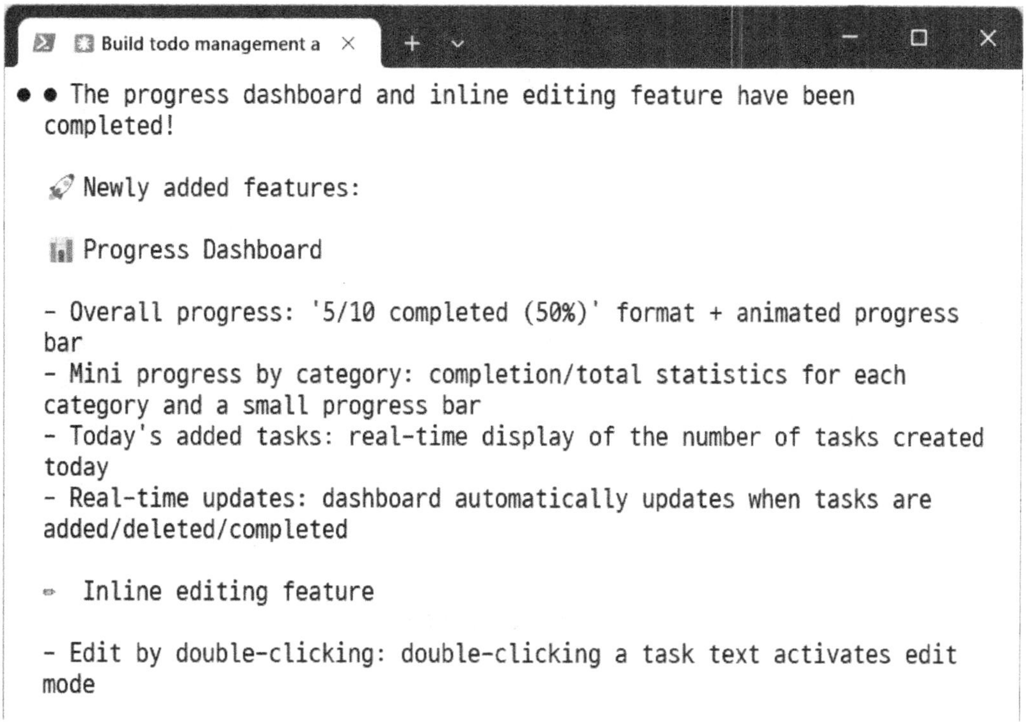

Figure 4.14: Check the progress

3. A dashboard showing overall progress and mini progress bars by category has been added to the to-do management app.

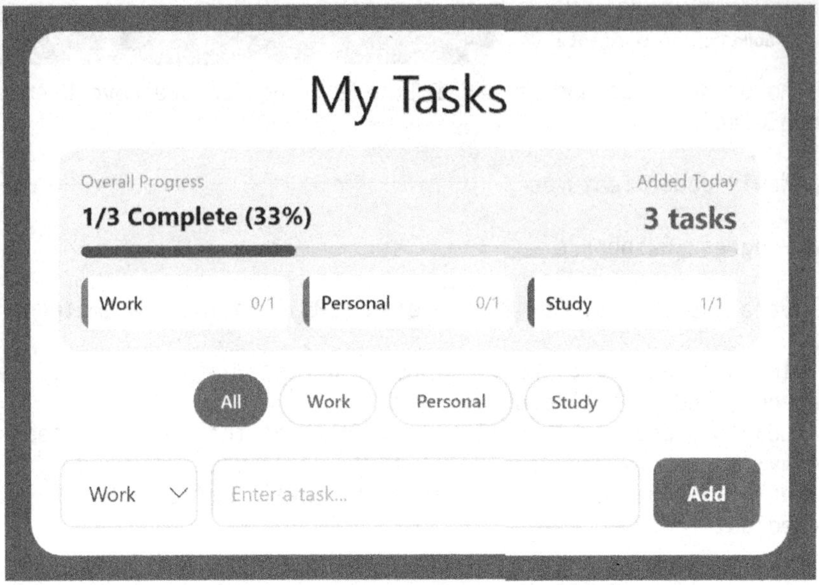

Figure 4.15: Newly added dashboard

4. You can double-click an item in the to-do list to edit it. Test to make sure the edit function works properly.

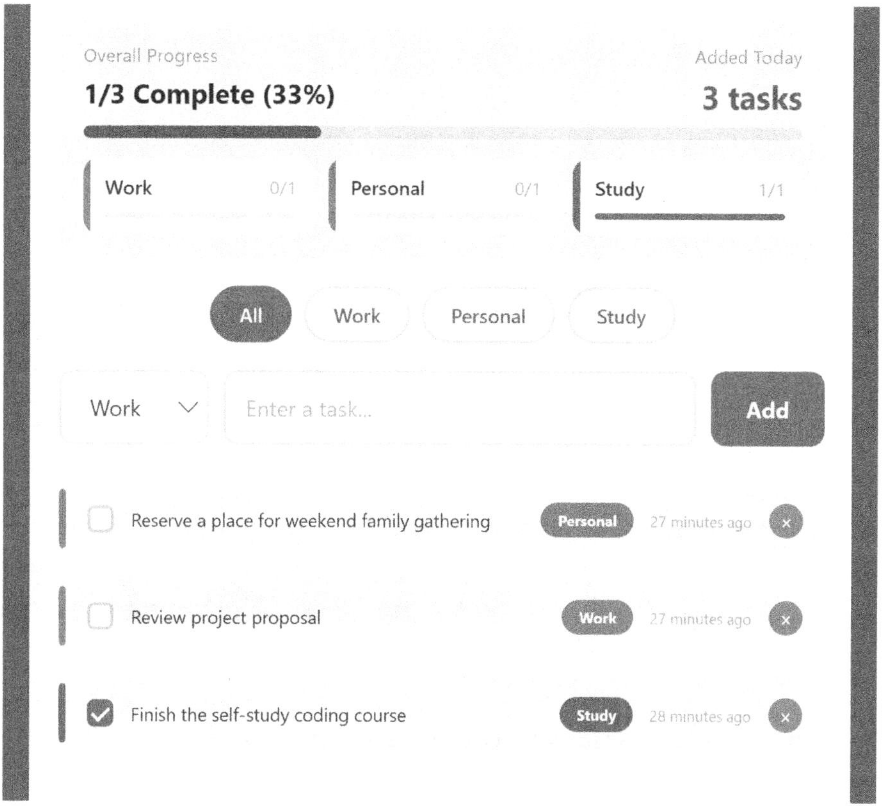

Figure 4.16: Edit the to-do list

Step 4: Dark mode and advanced features

1. Copy the fourth step-by-step prompt (Step 4) and enter it into Claude Code. This will implement dark mode and add features such as deleting completed items or using keyboard shortcuts.

   Prompt:

```
Step 4: Dark mode and advanced features
Implement dark mode and additional features.

Requirements:
1. Dark mode:
   - Dark/Light mode toggle switch at the top right
   - Dark mode colors: background (#1A1A1A), card (#2D2D2D), text (#E0E0E0)
   - Save selected theme in localStorage
   - Animation when switching modes
```

```
2. Additional features:
   - Delete all completed items button (including confirmation dialog)
   - Task search function (real-time filtering)
   - Show delete button after task completion
   - Empty state message ('No tasks. Try adding some!')
3. Keyboard shortcuts:
   - Alt+N: Focus new task input field
   - Alt+1,2,3,4: Switch category filter
   - Alt+D: Toggle dark mode
4. Responsive design:
   - Optimize for mobile (max-width: 480px)
   - Touch-friendly button sizes

Provide appropriate feedback for every interaction.
```

2. After confirming the completion message, check the newly added features.

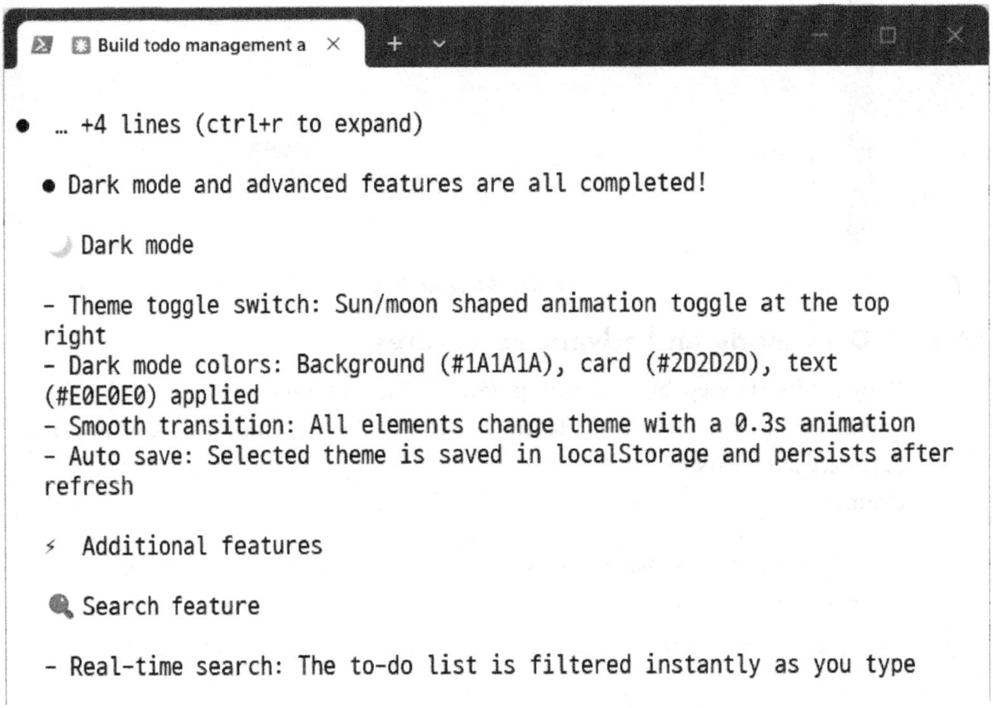

Figure 4.17: Check the new features

3. Check that a dark mode selection feature has been added to the to-do management app. When you click the dark mode selection button, dark mode should be applied.

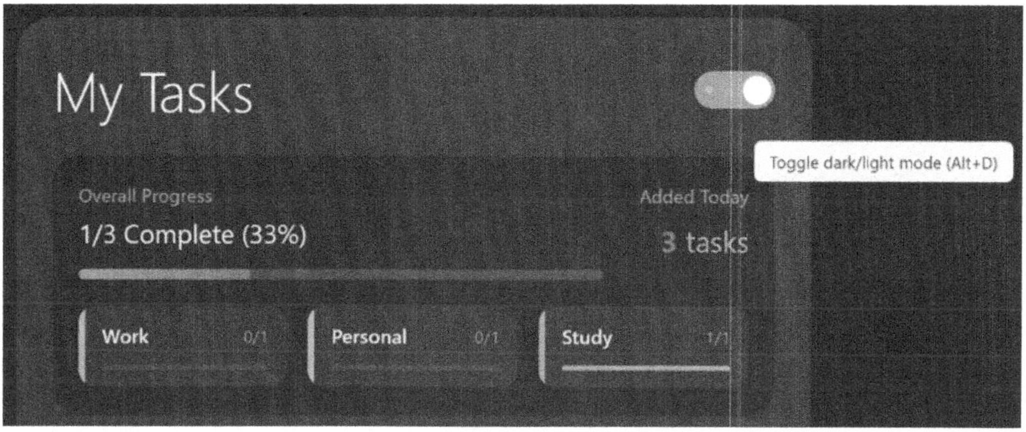

Figure 4.18: Dark mode

4. Also test the bulk delete completed items feature. When you click the **Delete Completed Items** button, all checked to-dos will be deleted.

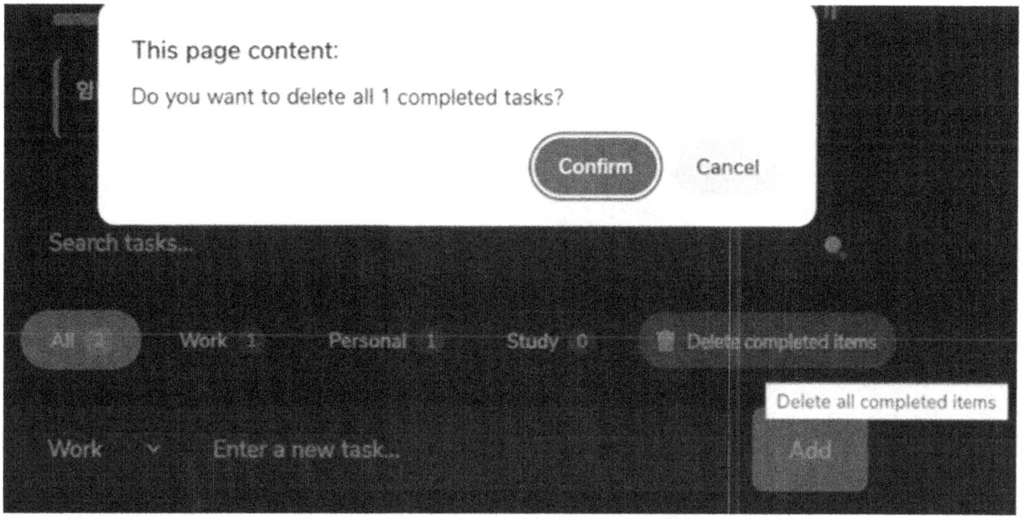

Figure 4.19: Delete all to-dos

Step 5: Final completion and optimization

1. Copy the fifth prompt (Step 5) of the step-by-step prompts and enter it into Claude Code.

Prompt:

```
Step 5: Final completion and optimization
Complete the app and maximize usability.

Requirements:
1. Export/Import Data:
   - Button to export data in JSON format
   - Import data via file upload
   - Check backup of current data before importing
2. Sorting options:
   - Sort by creation date, category, completion status
   - Save sorting state
   - Manual sorting by drag and drop (sortable)
3. Performance optimization:
   - Smooth performance even with more than 100 items
   - Apply debouncing (search, save)
   - Efficient DOM manipulation
4. Accessibility improvements:
   - Add ARIA labels
   - Focus management
   - Screen reader support
5. Additional improvements:
   - Duplicate to-do warning
   - Undo for recently deleted items
   - Random quote of the day
   - Encouragement message based on completion rate

Handle all edge cases and add error handling.
Add detailed comments to the code.
```

2. When you see the completion message, run the to-do management app in your web browser to test the new features. A sorting option has been added, and a random quote of the day is now displayed.

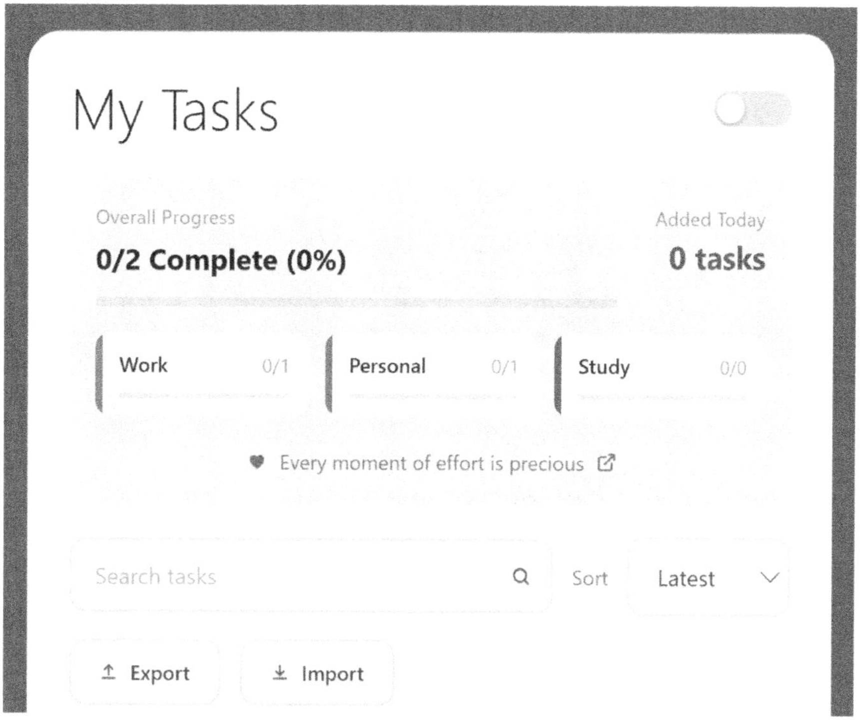

Figure 4.20: Test the new features

3. When you click **Export**, the application saves a JSON file to your desktop's download path.

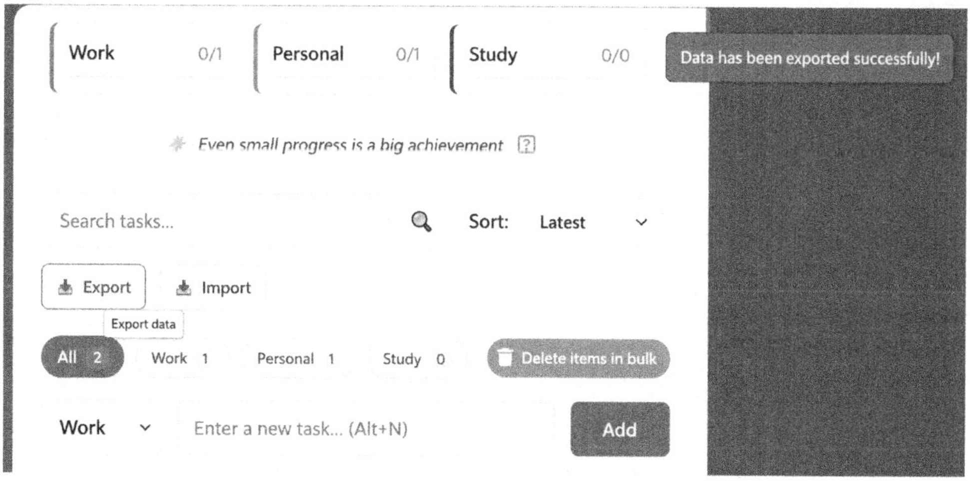

Figure 4.21: JSON file generated

4. Open the file with the `.json` extension in Notepad. The to-do list you saved in the to-do management app will be stored there.

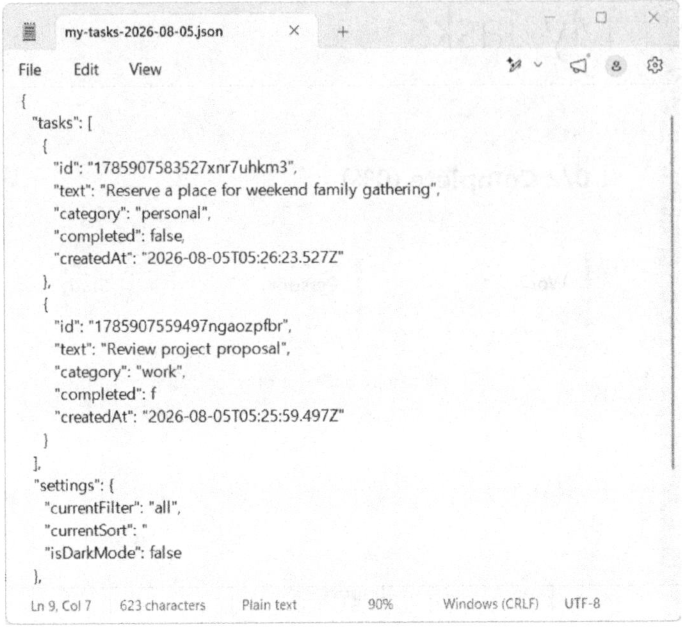

Figure 4.22: Open the file in Notepad

5. In the to-do management app running in your web browser, you can click the **Import** button to load the corresponding JSON file. This will restore all your to-do items.

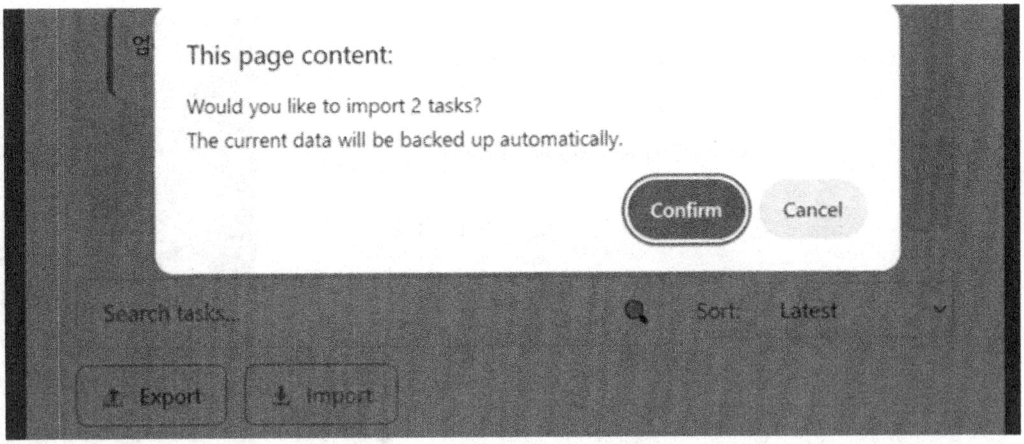

Figure 4.23: Import the JSON file

In this section, you learned how to start a project by linking Claude Web and Claude Code. You saw how the PRD writing method from *Chapter 2* is actually applied to development, and you implemented the app in Claude Code. In the next section, we will further develop the project and use more commands.

Learn more: Claude initial setup commands

In addition to `/init`, there are other useful commands to know when starting a project. These are handy for checking the current session status, confirming which model you're using, and quickly accessing help when needed.

/status

The `/status` command is used to check the current session status. It shows the model in use, token usage, remaining context capacity, and more. For long tasks, it's a good idea to check the status periodically.

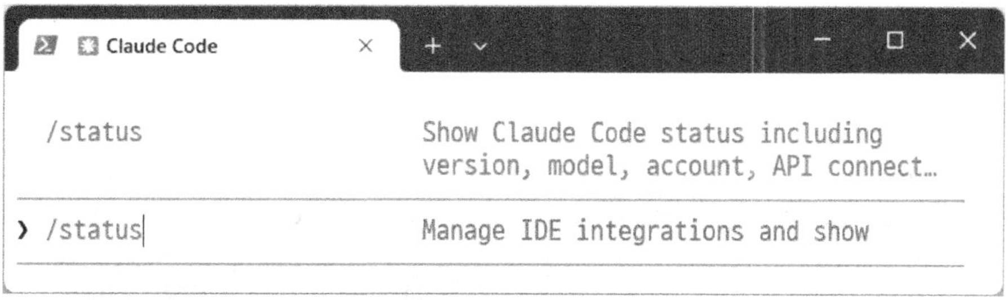

Figure 4.24: /status command

/model

The `/model` command lets you check and select the current AI model.

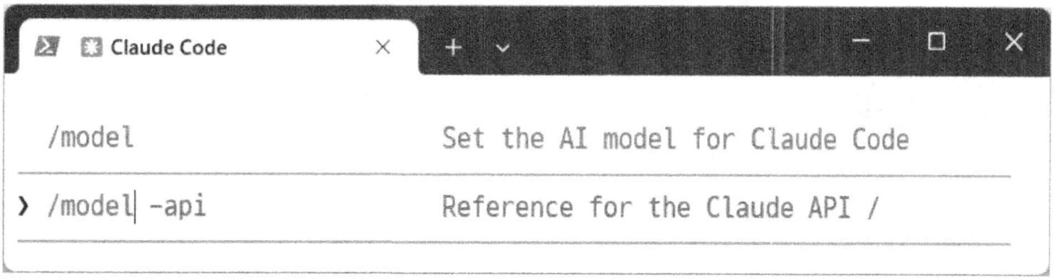

Figure 4.25: /model command

When you run the `/model` command, you can select an AI model. With the Max plan, you can choose between the Sonnet model and the Opus model for more complex tasks.

```
Select model
Switch between Claude models. Your pick becomes the default for new
sessions. For other/previous model names, specify with --model.

> 1. Default (recommended) √  Opus 5 with 1M context · Best for
                              everyday, complex tasks
  2. Opus (1M context)        Opus 5 with 1M context · Best for
                              everyday, complex tasks
  3. Fable                    Fable 5 · Most capable for your hardest
                              and longest-running tasks
  4. Sonnet                   Sonnet 5 · Efficient for routine tasks
  5. Haiku                    Haiku 4.5 · Fastest for quick answers

● High effort (default) ←/→ to adjust

Use /fast to turn on Fast mode (Opus 5).

Enter to set as default · s to use this session only · Esc to cancel
```

Figure 4.26: Select model

/help

If you enter the `/help` command, you can see all available commands and their descriptions. This is useful if you need a new feature during your work or can't remember a command.

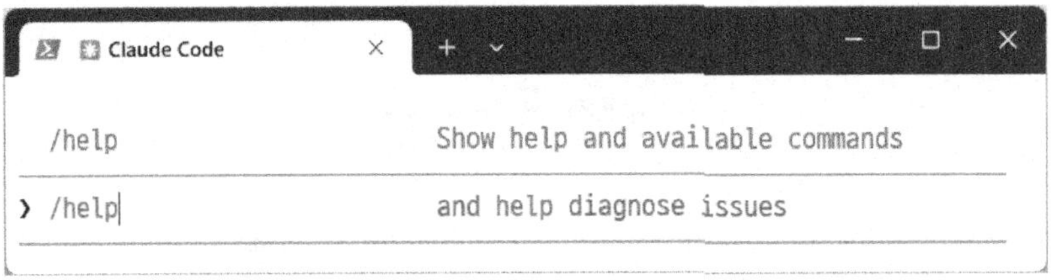

Figure 4.27: /help command

Wrapping up

Key takeaways summarized in 5 Keywords:

- The **step-by-step prompt** strategy is a prompt design method that divides a project into multiple stages based on the PRD, presenting the AI with specific goals at each stage to achieve systematic and predictable results.
- The commands needed to start a project in Claude Code are as follows:
    - **/init**: Project initialization and `CLAUDE.md` creation
    - **/status**: Check current work status

- **/model**: Select and change AI model
- **/help**: View available commands

Review questions

1. Below are descriptions of commands frequently used for initial project setup in Claude Code. Fill in the blanks with the appropriate commands.

Description	Command
Analyzes the project structure and automatically generates the CLAUDE.md file	
Check current session's token usage and remaining context capacity	
Select the AI model to use or change to the Default option	
View a list of all available commands and their descriptions	

Table 4.2: Fill in the appropriate commands

2. Write the correct term based on the following descriptions.
    1. A markdown file that is automatically generated by analyzing the project folder structure, containing the project's context and rules: (_)
    2. A product requirements document that systematically organizes the product's purpose, target users, main features, technical specs, etc.: (_)
    3. The data format used to save and reload data in the to-do management app: (_)

Resuming work and increasing efficiency

> Note
>
> **Key terms**: Session management | --resume | Auto-approve mode | Context | /compact
>
> As you continue developing the to-do management app, you will learn about session management and context optimization features in Claude Code.
>
> You'll practice essential features for long-term project development, such as how to resume conversations with the `--resume` command, how to use auto-approve mode

with the *Shift* + *Tab* keys, and how to manage context with the `/context` and `/compact` commands.

Before you begin

A session is a period of interaction between a user and a program. In Claude Code, it refers to the conversation state maintained while you exchange commands with Claude. Since Claude Code appears to lose previous conversations when you close the terminal, you need to pay special attention to session and context management when working on long-term projects.

Adding features

In the previous section, you implemented the overall structure and features of the to-do management app. However, in real development, it's difficult to complete a project in a single session. Often, you need to close and reopen the terminal or continue working after a few days.

Although Claude Code appears to lose conversations when you close the terminal, in reality, all conversation history is automatically saved in the project folder. In this section, you'll learn how to reload a saved session and continue your previous work seamlessly.

Open the `Study-02` folder in File Explorer, right-click, and select **Open in Terminal** to launch the command prompt.

Resuming a session

1. Enter the command `claude --resume` in the command prompt.

   `claude --resume` is a command that loads your previous conversation history and lets you pick up exactly where you left off. The `--resume` option reads the saved session file and restores the previous context.

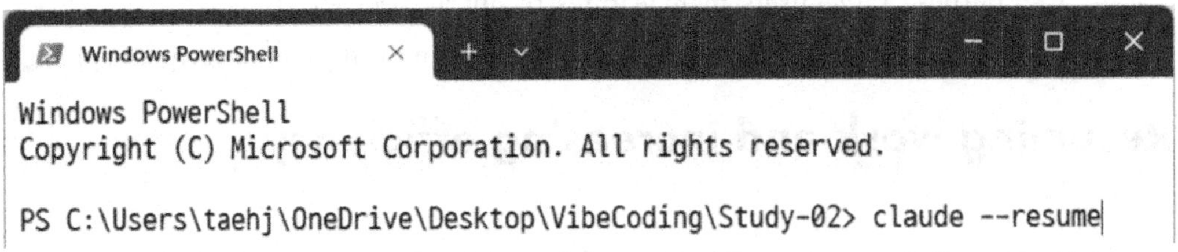

Figure 4.28: claude --resume command

2. Displays the list of conversations in the current project. Use the arrow keys to find the conversation you want, and select it. Press the *Enter* key to resume.

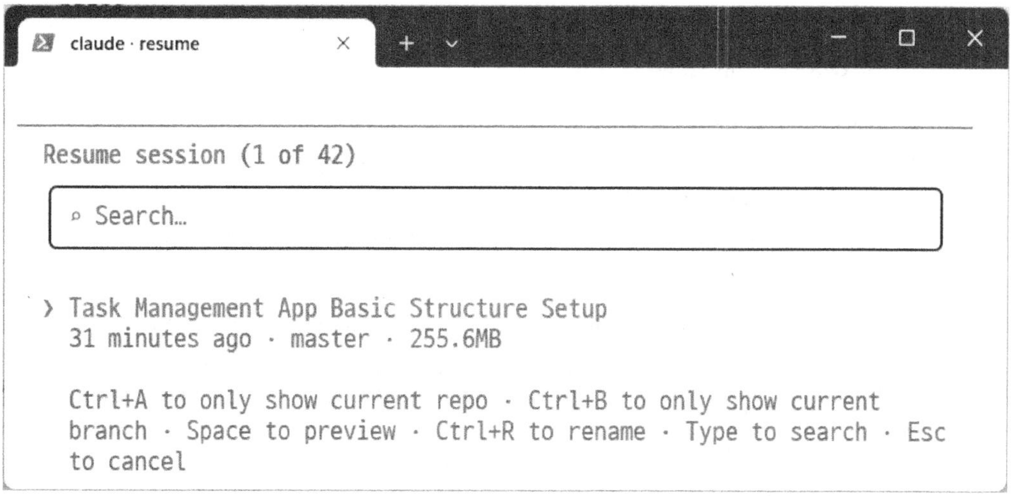

Figure 4.29: List of conversations

3. Find and select the conversation where you implemented the to-do management app, and then press the *Enter* key. The session will be restored from the point where the conversation left off so you can continue working.

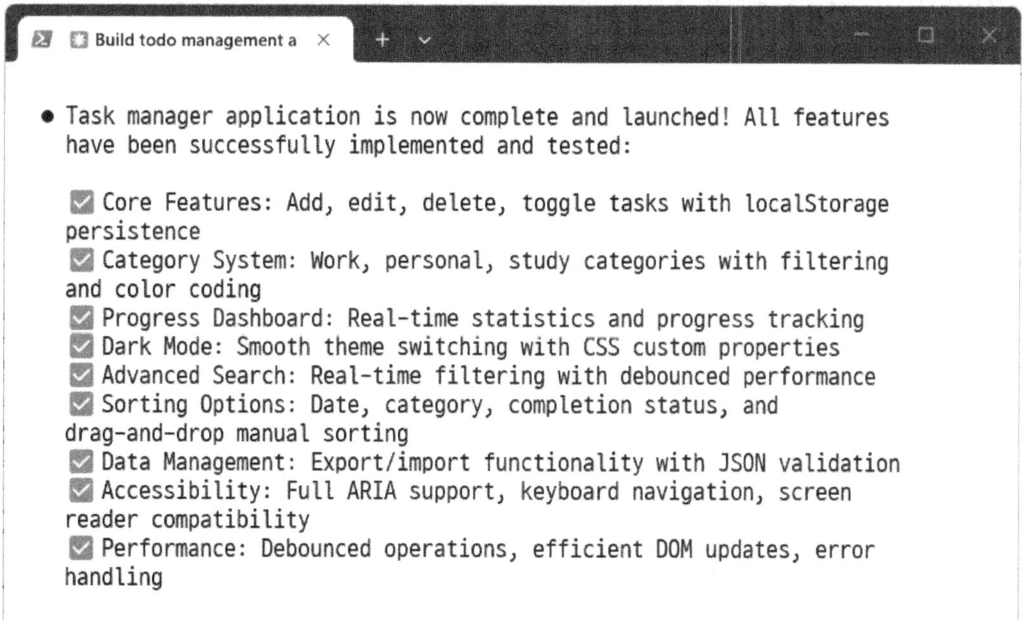

Figure 4.30: Continue from where you left off

Tip

Session Resume Commands

Claude Code saves conversation sessions for each project, so you can always pick up your previous work at any time. Even if the terminal closes during your work, or if the conversation is interrupted by running another command, there's no need to worry. There are commands ready that let you reload your previous conversation and continue seamlessly:

- `/resume`: You can also run Claude Code by entering `'claude'` first, then use the `/resume` command to select and resume a previous conversation.
- `--continue` or `-c` option: `--continue` is a flag that automatically restores the most recent conversation. If your connection is lost or the terminal closes during work, you can use the `--continue` or `-c` option as well.

Boosting work efficiency with Auto-Approve mode

1. Enter the following prompt into Claude Code:
   Prompt:

   ```
   Please add a keyword-based automatic category classification feature to the current to-do management app.
   ```

2. Claude Code will then proceed with tasks roughly as follows.

```
* Adding keyword-based auto-categorization system…
  L [ ] Add keyword-based auto-categorization system
    [ ] Update UI to show auto-category suggestions
    [ ] Test auto-categorization with various keywords

>

  ▸▸ accept edits on (shift+tab to cycle)
```

Figure 4.31: Keyword-based automatic category classification

3. Press the *Shift* + *Tab* key to select **2. Yes, allow all edits during this session**.

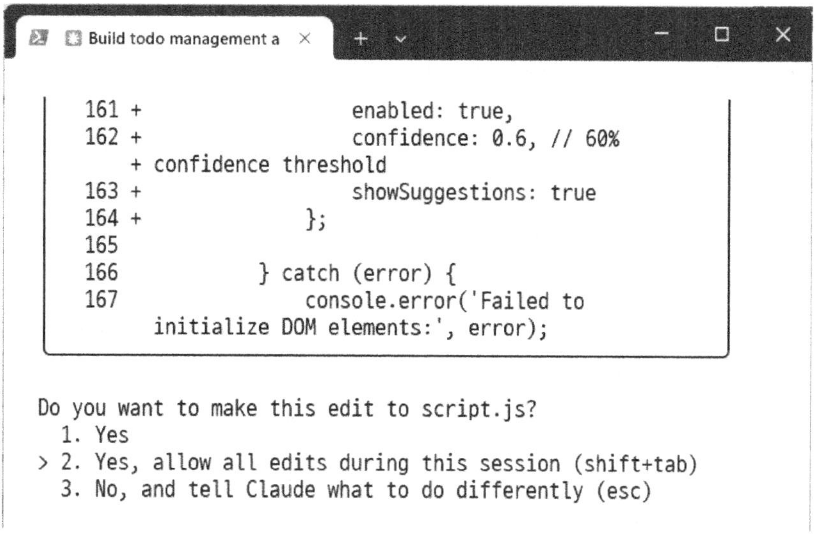

Figure 4.32: Select option 2

While this is displayed at the bottom, all edits will be automatically approved; pressing *Shift* + *Tab* again returns you to normal mode.

4. Once the work is complete, you'll see a message confirming the feature was successfully added.

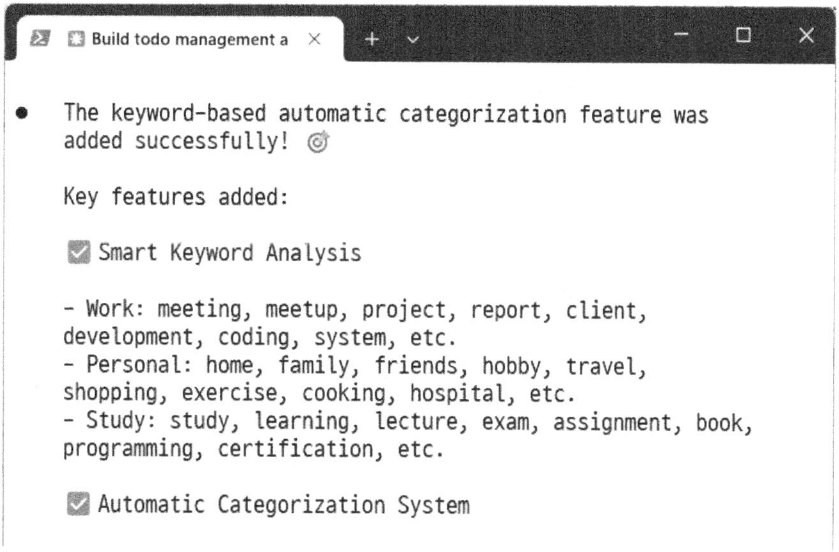

Figure 4.33: Feature successfully added

Checking the feature

Let's check if the app automatically classifies categories when you add a to-do as requested. Details other than the requested feature may vary by individual. Follow Claude Code's guidance to verify that the implemented feature works correctly. In this book, the **Smart Keyword Analysis** and **Automatic Classification System** features have been added.

1. To check if the changes have been applied correctly, open the `index.html` file in the `Study-02` folder using your desktop File Explorer.

Figure 4.34: Open the index.html file

2. To check if categories are automatically classified, enter `Go to the movies` in the **Search To-Do...** box, leave the category as **Work**, and click the **Add** button.

3. The to-do app will recommend classifying *Go to the movies* as *Personal*. If you click **OK** to proceed, the task will be categorized as 'Personal' and registered successfully.
4. On the initial screen of the to-do app, there are **Auto Reclassify** and **Category Settings** buttons, allowing you to enable/disable the category reclassification feature or adjust detailed options.

Managing context

While working in Claude Code, you may often see messages like the following:

Figure 4.35: The context usage indicator

This message means that the context of the current conversation is approaching the threshold for auto-compact execution. Context refers to all conversation content and work information that Claude Code remembers in the current session. In other words, this message indicates that the AI's memory space is running low, and it will continue working after compressing older conversations to reduce token usage.

When Claude automatically summarizes part of the entire conversation, some information may be lost. Sometimes, instead of finishing a task unit and summarizing, it may forcibly summarize in the middle. Therefore, it's best to frequently check the context status and manually compact at an appropriate time before Claude auto-compresses the context.

Checking context status

The command to check the current context status and usage is `/context`:

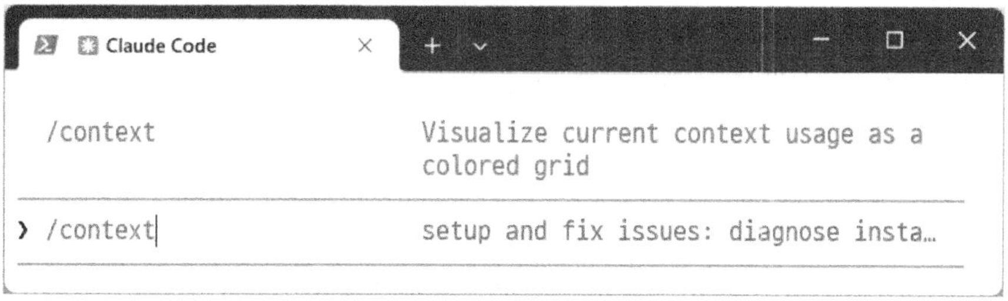

Figure 4.36: /context command

Enter the `/context` command in Claude Code and press the *Enter* key to check it.

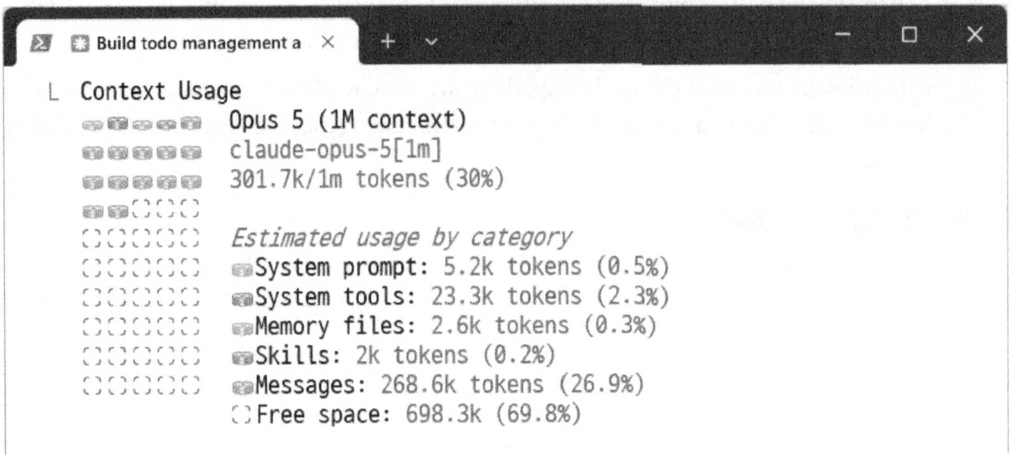

Figure 4.37: Check context status

> **Note**
>
> The token limit depends on your subscription plan.

Compress context

Now, let's try manually compressing the context. The compression command to summarize the conversation so far is `/compact`.

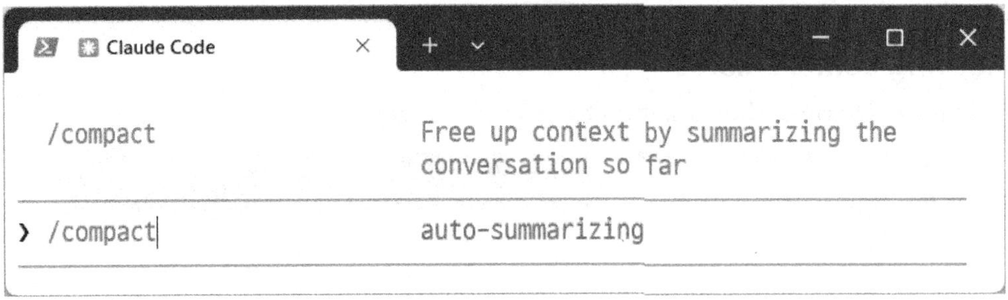

Figure 4.38: /compact command

The `/compact` command allows Claude to automatically summarize the conversation and free up context. If needed, you can add compression instructions after /compact. For example, entering `/compact` summarize focusing on code changes will summarize according to that instruction.

1. To compress the context, enter the `/compact` command in Claude Code. When compression is complete, a message saying `Compacted (ctrl+o to see full summary)` will appear, and the auto-compact warning at the bottom of the screen will disappear.

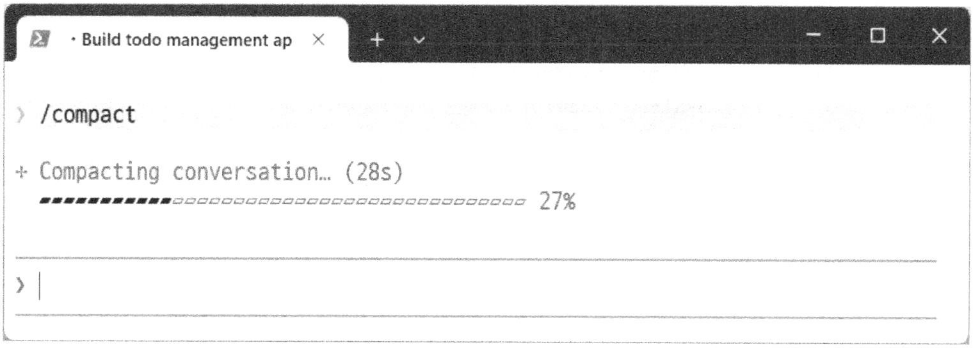

Figure 4.39: Compress the context

2. If you press the *Ctrl* + *O* key, you can view the full summary generated during compression to check whether Claude has properly preserved important work details.

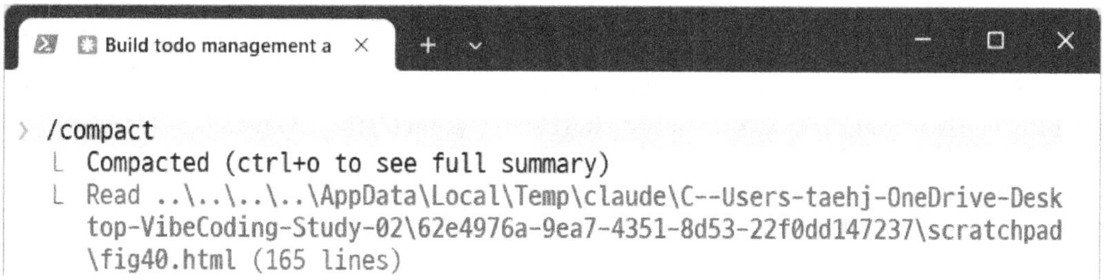

Figure 4.40: Full summary

3. To check the compression results, enter the `/context` command. After compression, `Messages` decreased from 78.0k to 1.9k, and `Free space` increased from 107.4k (53.7%) to 183.4k (91.7%).

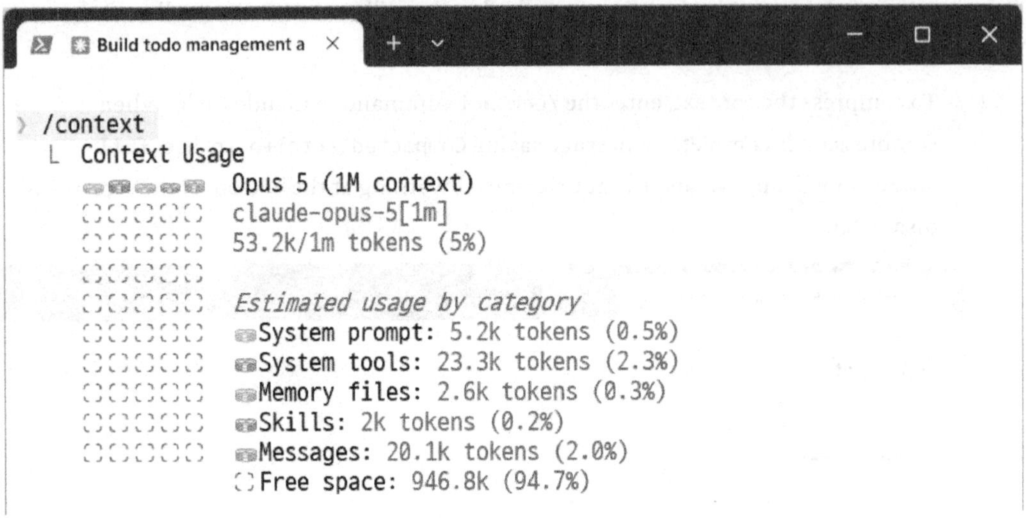

Figure 4.41: Compression worked

Context compression summarizes the conversation to free up space, while keeping the system prompt, tools, and memory files needed for the project intact. This allows you to continue working with the key project information and context preserved. When developing for long periods, it's important to compress the context appropriately at the end of each work unit to manage it efficiently.

In this section, we practiced session management and context compression features in Claude Code. You learned how to continue a project over several days, automate repetitive approvals, and efficiently manage tokens by compressing conversation history. By using these features appropriately, you can maintain productive development in long-term projects without interruption. In the next section, we'll look at how to efficiently improve, manage, and save projects and tasks created with Claude Code.

Wrapping up

Key takeaways summarized in 4 Keywords:

- The **--resume** command restores a session you select from the conversation list.
- Pressing *Shift* + *Tab* switches to auto-approve mode, allowing you to skip repetitive permission approval requests.
- **Context** is the memory space that stores and displays current conversation and work information.
- The `/compact` command summarizes the conversation history to free up context space.

Review questions

1. Choose the incorrect statement from the following explanations.
    1. `/compact` summarizes the conversation to save tokens.
    2. Auto-compact runs automatically when the context reaches the threshold.
    3. After compression, `CLAUDE.md` and project files are retained.
    4. *Ctrl* + *R* is the shortcut for the `/context` command.
    5. **Auto-approve** mode can be activated with *Shift* + *Tab*.
2. Write the appropriate command or option for each situation below.

Situation	Command / Option
When you want to select and resume a specific conversation among several	
When you want to immediately continue working on the most recent conversation	
When you want to visually check current context usage	
When the conversation gets long and needs to be compressed	
When it's tedious to approve file modifications every time	

Table 4.3: Fill in the appropriate commands

Project improvement and task management

> Note
>
> **Key terms**: Screenshot | @symbol | /config | /doctor| /export
>
> As you expand the to-do management app to a desktop version, you will learn project management features of Claude Code.
>
> You will specify requirements by sending images to Claude Code, quickly analyze files using the @ symbol, check your work environment with configuration and diagnostic commands, and finally practice documenting the entire workflow.

Before you begin

An AI that can understand and process multiple types of information together is called a multimodal AI. Multimodal AI can recognize not only text or code, but also different types of data such as images and audio.

When Claude Code runs, multimodal AI models like Sonnet or Opus operate on the back end. Although Claude Code uses a command-line interface, the underlying model can also analyze images, describe their contents, understand their structure, and use them as context for generating code.

Improving the desktop version app's UI with a capture image

The saying 'seeing is believing' applies when working with Claude Code as well. Rather than lengthy explanations, showing something once is much more effective. If you capture your screen and send it directly, Claude Code can understand your requirements more accurately and quickly.

The current result is optimized for mobile, so we'll ask Claude Code to create a desktop version that fills the screen. To keep the previous results, I will ask to create a new folder called `web_version` and save them there.

Now, let's capture the current to-do app and send it to Claude Code.

Sending an image to Claude Code

1. Here, we will use the default capture tool provided in Windows. In the Windows **Start** menu, type `Snipping` or `Capture` to launch the **Snipping Tool**. On macOS use *Shift* + *Command* + *4* or the **Screenshot** app, and on Linux use your desktop's screenshot tool.

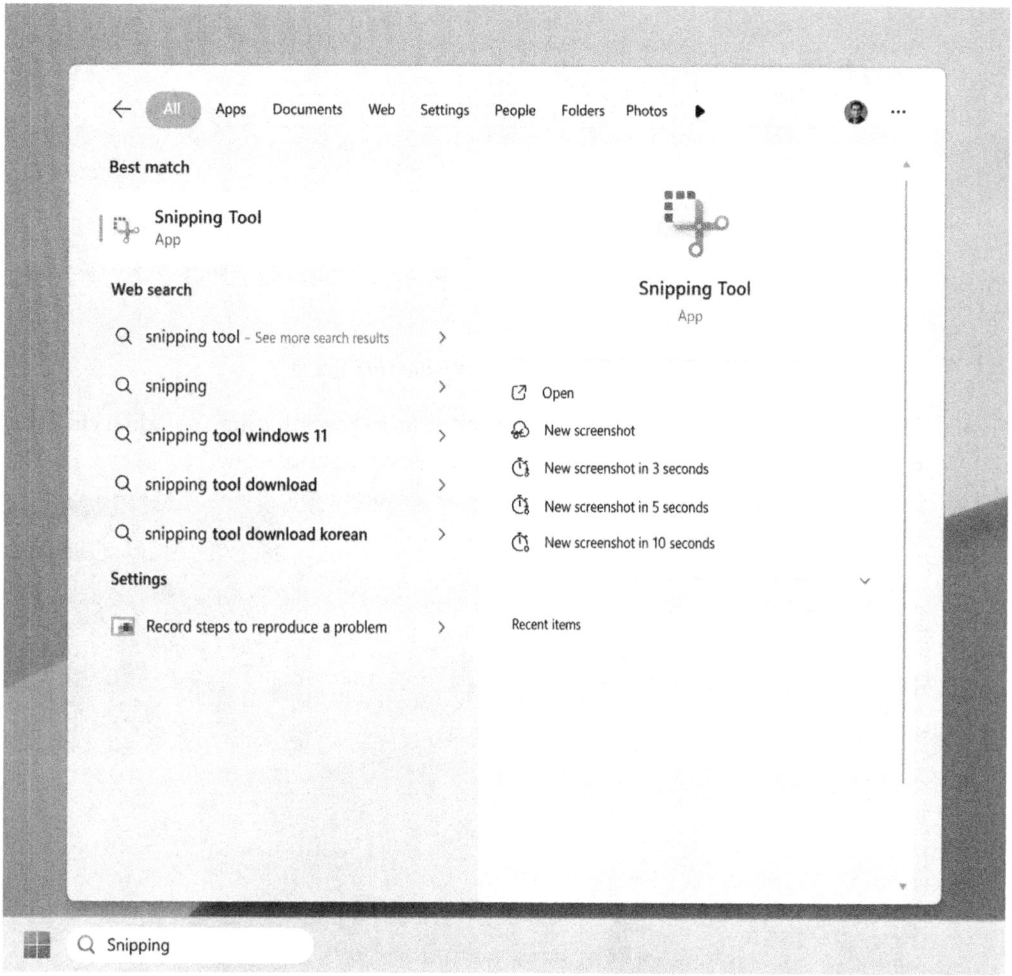

Figure 4.42: Snipping tool

2. Once you launch the **Snipping Tool**, you can start capturing by clicking the **+ New** button.

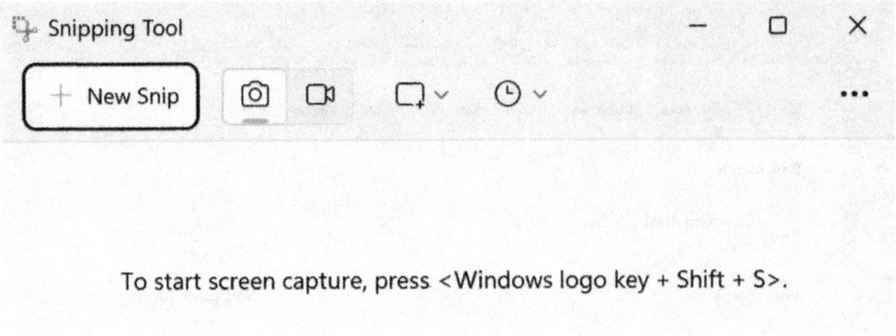

Figure 4.43: +New button to capture

3. Run the to-do app, select the **Rectangular** option in the Snipping Tool, then click the **+ New** button and drag to capture the main screen of the app.

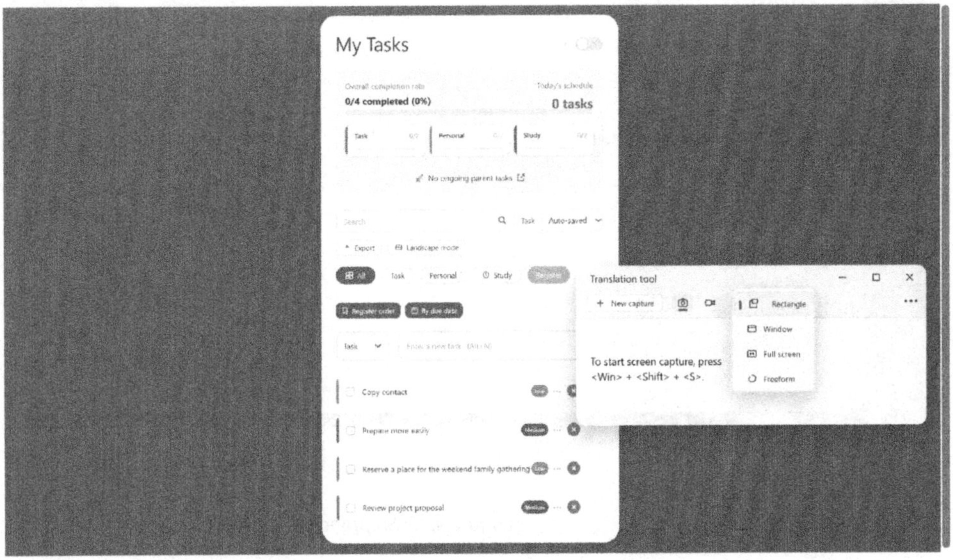

Figure 4.44: Capture the main screen

4. In the **Snipping Tool** window, click the **Save As** icon to save the image.

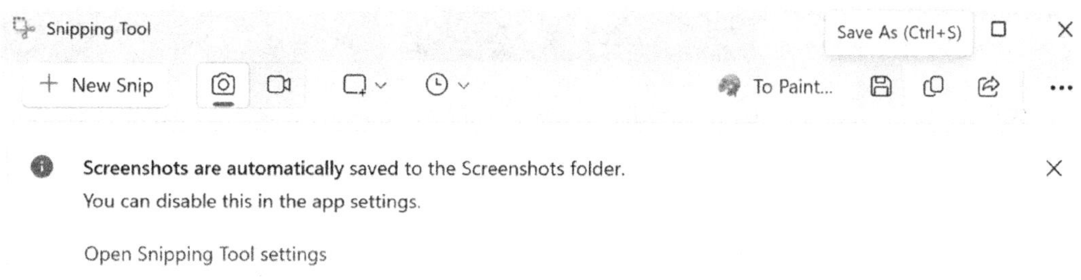

Figure 4.45: Save the snipped image

5. Let's save the image as `screenshot.png` in the `Study-02` folder. Click the **Save** button.

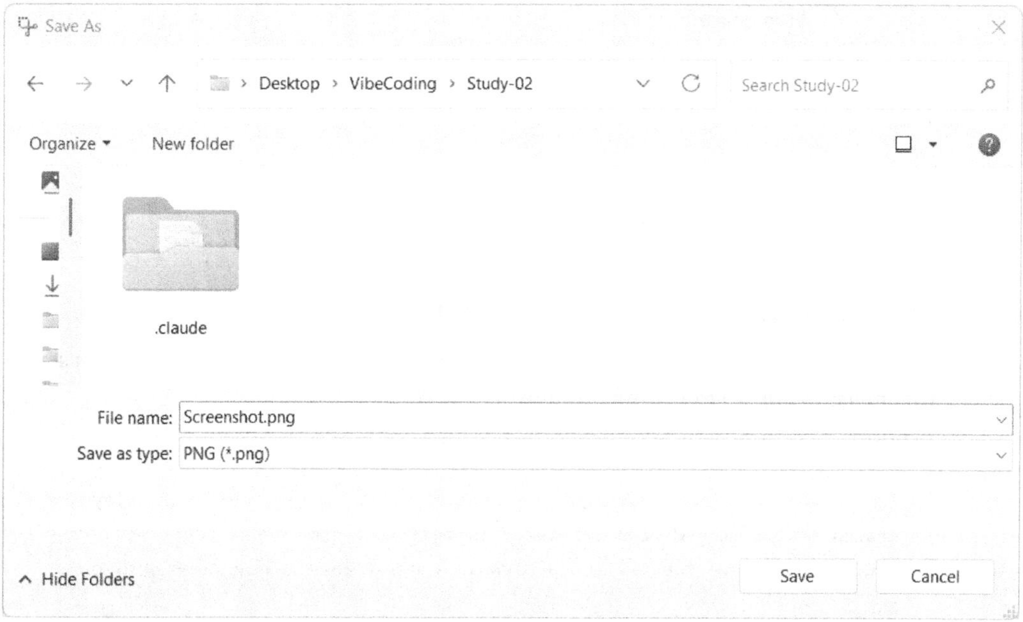

Figure 4.46: Save the image in the Study-02 folder

6. Entering an image into Claude Code is very simple. Just drag the `screenshot.png` file and drop it into the command prompt window where Claude Code is running. If the image is entered successfully, a `[Image #1]` message will appear in the prompt input box.

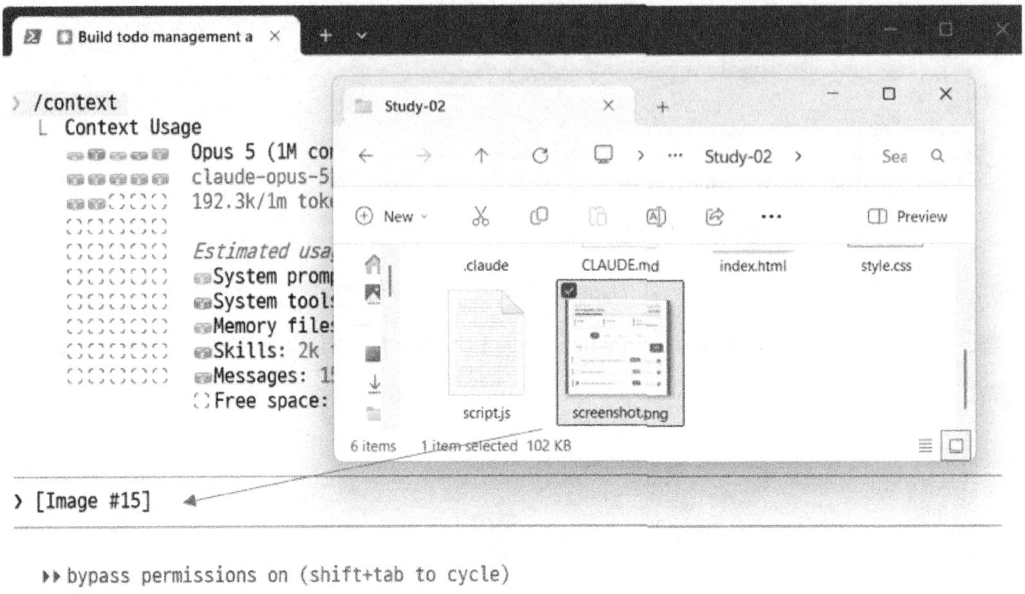

Figure 4.47: Drag and drop the file

Applying the desktop-optimized design

1. Now, let's enter the request for design improvement. In the input box where you sent the image, write the following prompt:

   Prompt:

   ```
   [Image #1] The current design seems optimized for mobile. Please modify the design so that the UI can be viewed in full screen on a desktop environment. Save the revised design in a new folder called 'web_version'.
   ```

   > **Note**
   >
   > Whenever you encounter a task that requires permission, it will ask whether to proceed. Select **2. Yes, and don't ask again for mkdir..** to continue automatically.

2. When execution is complete, a message will appear prompting you to check the results. In the `Study-02` folder, check for the `web_version` folder.

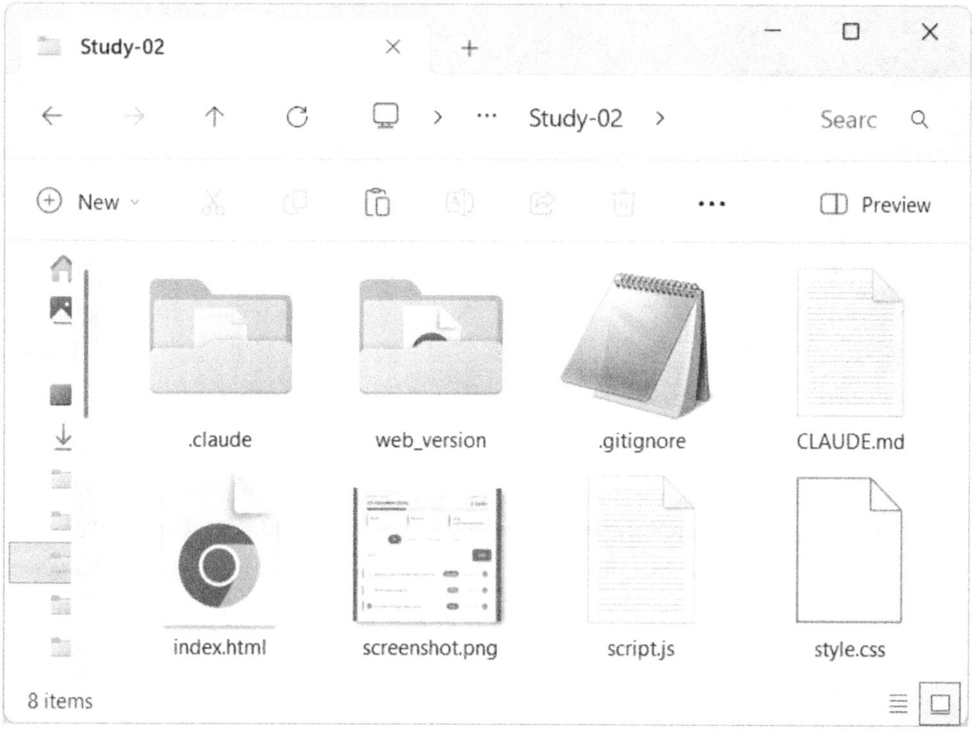

Figure 4.48: Check the web_version folder

3. Double-click the `index.html` file in the `web_version` folder to run it and check the to-do app optimized for desktop.

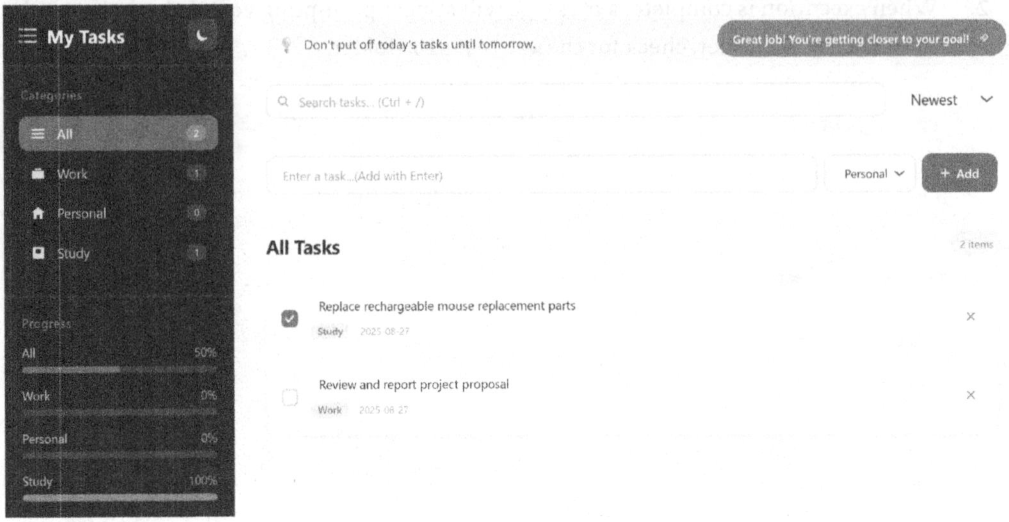

Figure 4.49: Check the to-do app

4. Make sure all features are working properly. If you enter `Check tomorrow's work schedule` in the to-do input field, it will automatically be categorized under **Work**.

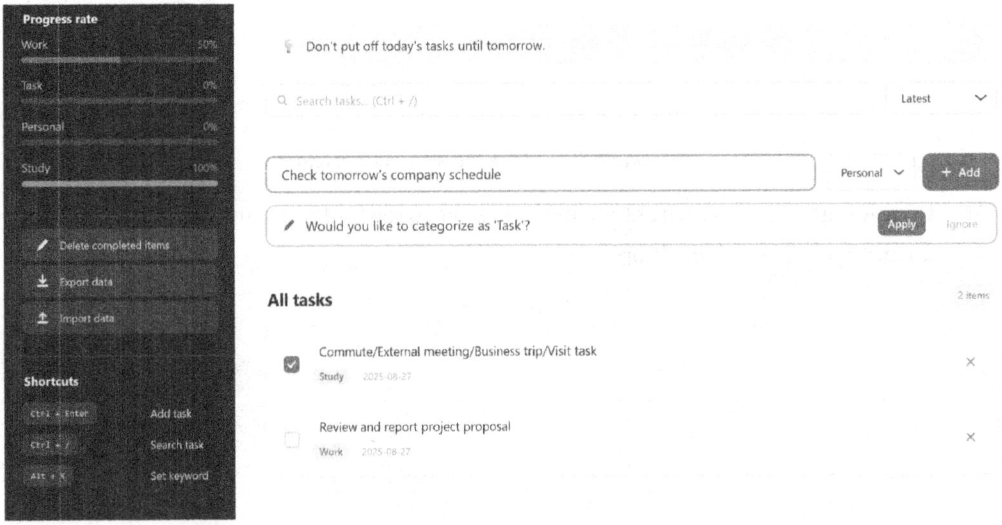

Figure 4.50: Work schedule

Quickly reviewing code using references

By using the @ symbol in Claude Code, you can quickly review and analyze generated code. Let's use the @ symbol to load the `script.js` file created in the working folder, analyze the JavaScript code for the to-do app we made earlier, and check if the functions work properly.

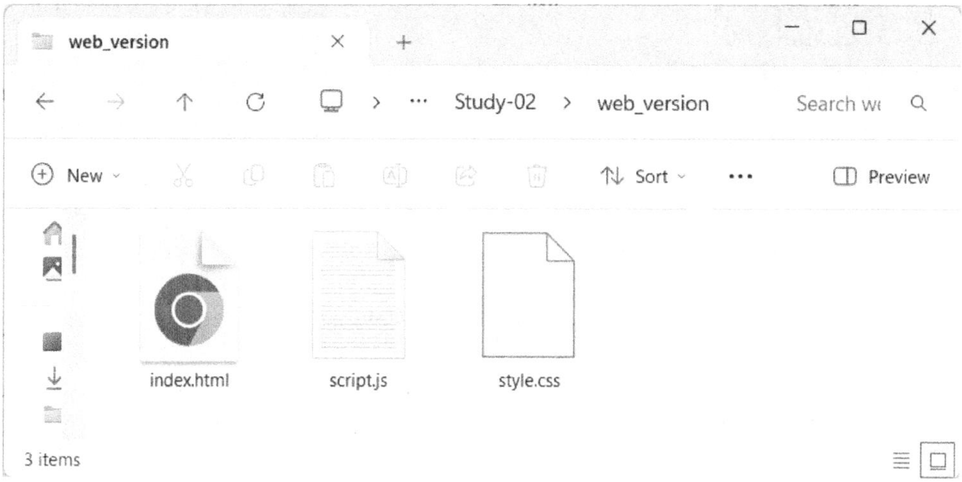

Figure 4.51: script.js file

Analyzing code with the @ symbol

Using the @ symbol allows you to instantly load files or folders into Claude Code, speeding up your workflow.

1. Typing @ in Claude Code displays a list of files you can load. Select the `script.js` file from the list.

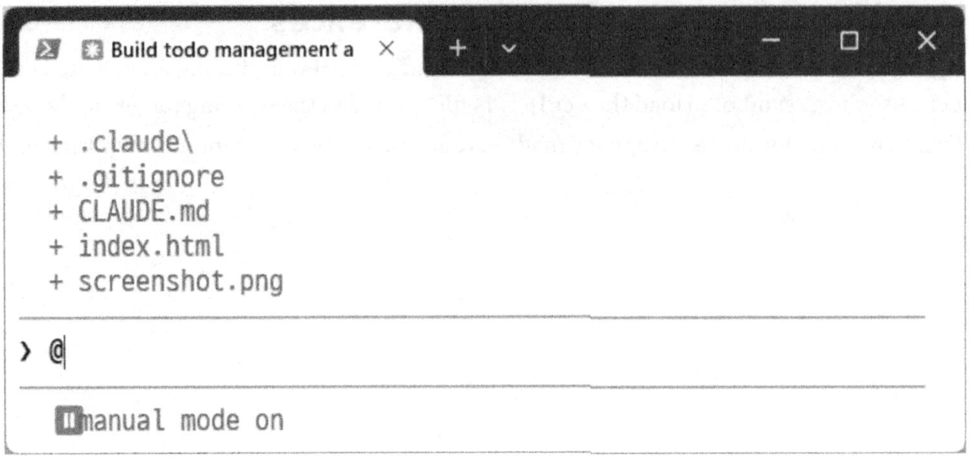

Figure 4.52: Select the file from the list

> **Note**
>
> You can also request to find a specific file, but searching may take time and delay your work.

2. To check if the dark mode feature is well implemented in the JavaScript file, enter the following prompt. Claude Code will then read the entire `script.js` file and analyze it immediately:

   Prompt:

   ```
   Find and explain the functions related to dark mode in the @script.js file.
   ```

3. Once the file analysis is complete, it will tell you the names, functions, and locations of the requested functions, and also introduce hidden features like shortcuts.

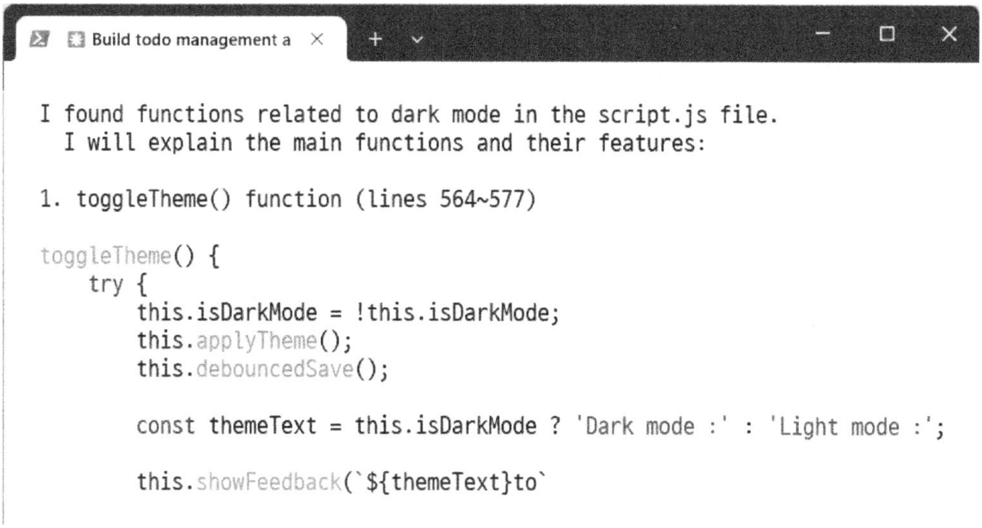

Figure 4.53: File analysis complete

By using the @ symbol like this, you can save the trouble of scanning the entire file for the information you need. While it would take a person a long time to find the dark mode functions in code over 1,000 lines, Claude Code processes it instantly.

Checking folder structure with the @ symbol

Now, let's check the `web_version` folder we just created.

1. Enter `@web_version` in Claude Code to load the entire `web_version` folder. The list of files inside the `web_version` folder will be displayed.

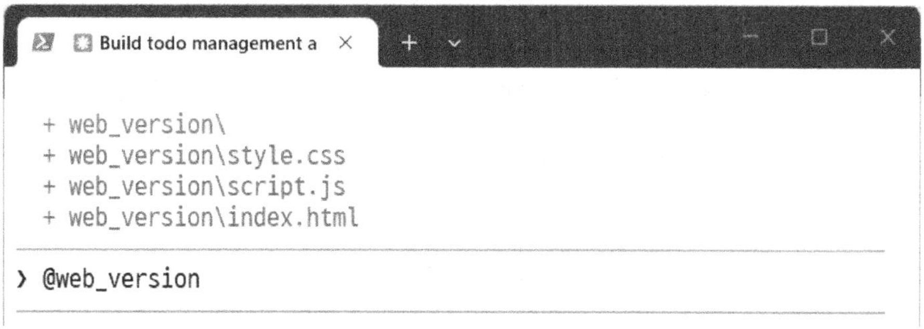

Figure 4.54: List of files inside the web_version folder

2. To verify whether the to-do management app is optimized for the desktop environment, enter the following prompt:

Prompt:

```
Please analyze the files in the `@web_version` folder and check if the to-do app is optimized for the desktop environment.
```

3. Claude Code reads all the files in the folder and presents a comprehensive analysis. To summarize the content, the analysis results look roughly like this:

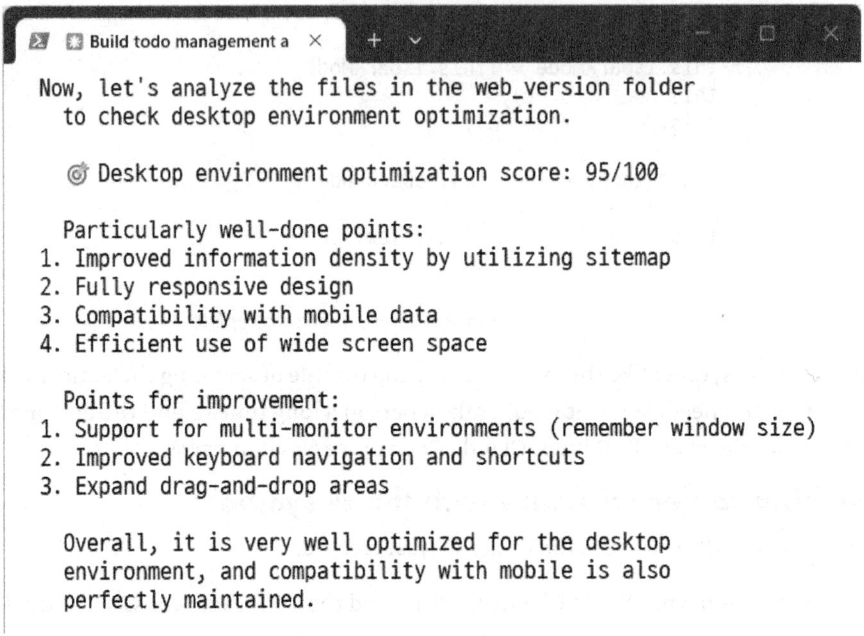

Figure 4.55: Comprehensive analysis

By designating a folder with the @ symbol in this way, you can grasp the overall structure and characteristics at a glance without having to open multiple files individually. This is particularly useful in scenarios like web development—where HTML, CSS, and JavaScript are interconnected—as Claude analyzes the relationships between files to provide a comprehensive assessment.

Managing Claude Code projects

Next, let's wrap up the various tasks we've carried out while building the to-do list app and learn how to systematically organize the project. Claude Code provides useful commands for checking your work environment, adjusting settings, and saving conversation history.

Checking settings with the /config command

The `/config` command is used to check or change the configuration of a program or system. In other words, it is a tool for managing the rules for how to handle a project. In Claude Code, you can view the current settings applied to the project—such as file save permissions or output format—and also change specific settings to your desired values.

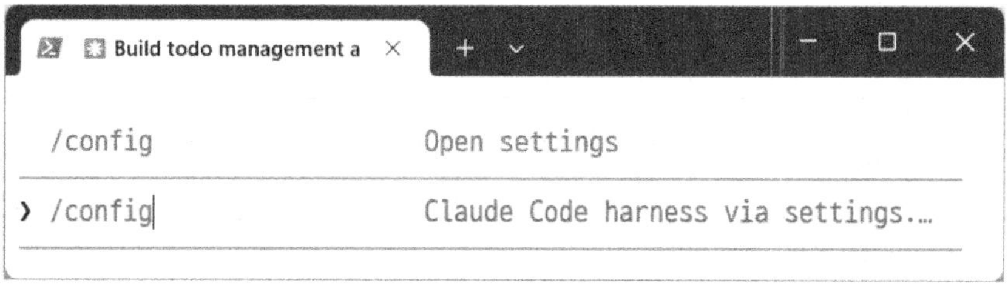

Figure 4.56: /config command

After entering the `/config` command in Claude Code, press the *Enter* key. You will see the following configuration items.

Setting Item	Default Value	Description
Auto-compact	TRUE	Automatically runs /compact to summarize and maintain conversation history when the context reaches a certain level. If set to false, you can only compact manually.
Use todo list	TRUE	Claude Code manages your work as a to-do list, allowing you to track progress step by step.
Verbose output	FALSE	Determines whether to display output in verbose (detailed) mode. If set to TRUE, detailed debug information will be shown.
Auto-updates	TRUE	Enables automatic updates for Claude Code. When a new version is released, it will be downloaded and installed automatically.
Theme	Light mode	Sets the terminal theme. You can choose between Light mode and Dark mode.

Setting Item	Default Value	Description
Notifications	Auto	Sets how notifications are delivered when a task is completed. You can choose from Auto, Bell, or None.
Output style	default	Determines Claude's response style. 'default' is the standard format.
Editor mode	normal	Sets the editing mode. You can choose between normal or vim mode.
Model	Default (recommended)	Selects the AI model to use. 'Default' automatically selects the optimal model depending on the task.
Auto-connect to IDE	FALSE	Sets whether to automatically connect to an IDE. Determines whether to link automatically with VS Code, etc.

Table 4.4: Configuration items

> **Note**
>
> You can select items using the arrow keys and change values using the *Enter*, *Tab*, or *Space* keys. Press the *Esc* key to close the settings screen.

Diagnosing your system with the /doctor command

As the name suggests, the `/doctor` command checks the environment and diagnoses issues in Claude Code, just like a doctor examines a patient, to see if the current project is running properly.

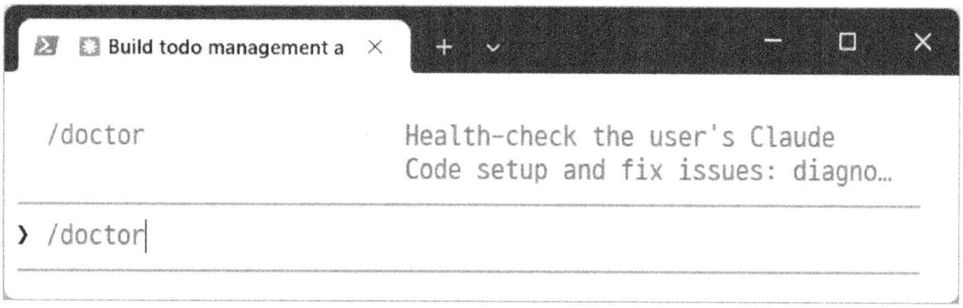

Figure 4.57: /doctor command

Enter the `/doctor` command in Claude Code and press the *Enter* key to view the diagnostic results for each item.

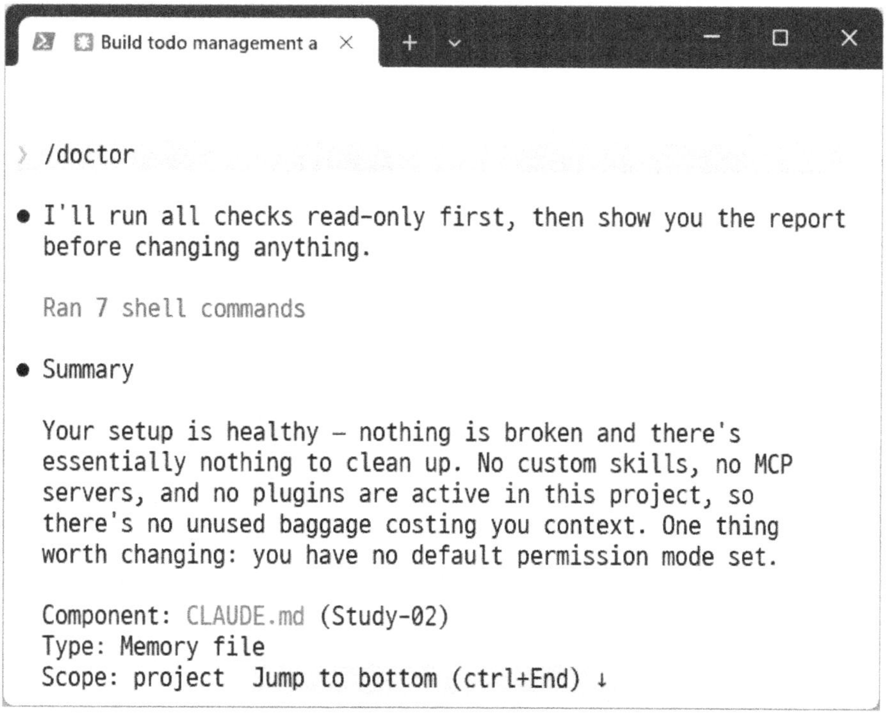

Figure 4.58: Diagnostic results

If there is a problem with any item, Claude Code will suggest a solution. If all items are normal, press the *Enter* key to finish the diagnosis.

Exporting conversations with the /export command

The `/export` command saves the current project you are working on into a single output file. Saving various source code and revision history from Claude Code as a file can serve as a useful reference when moving your work environment or sharing with collaborators. You can also extract key conversations and add them to the `CLAUDE.md` file of another project.

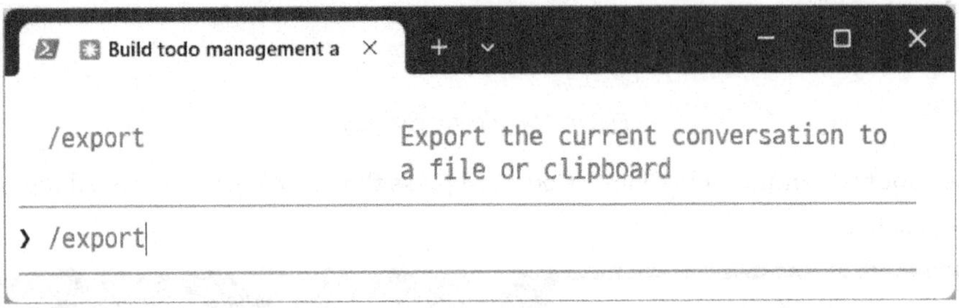

Figure 4.59: /export command

1. Type the `/export` command in Claude Code and press the *Enter* key. You can choose from two options, as shown below. Select **2. Save to file** and press the *Enter* key.

```
Export conversation
Select export method

  1. Copy to clipboard  Copy the conversation to your
                        system clipboard
› 2. Save to file       Save the conversation to a file
                        in the current directory
```

Figure 4.60: Select option 2

2. Change the file name to `todo-app-conversation.txt` and press the *Enter* key.

```
Export conversation
Select export method

Enter filename:

> todo-app-conversation.txt

Enter to save · Esc to go back
```

Figure 4.61: Change the file name

3. The file `todo-app-conversation.txt` has been saved in the `Study-02` folder on your desktop.

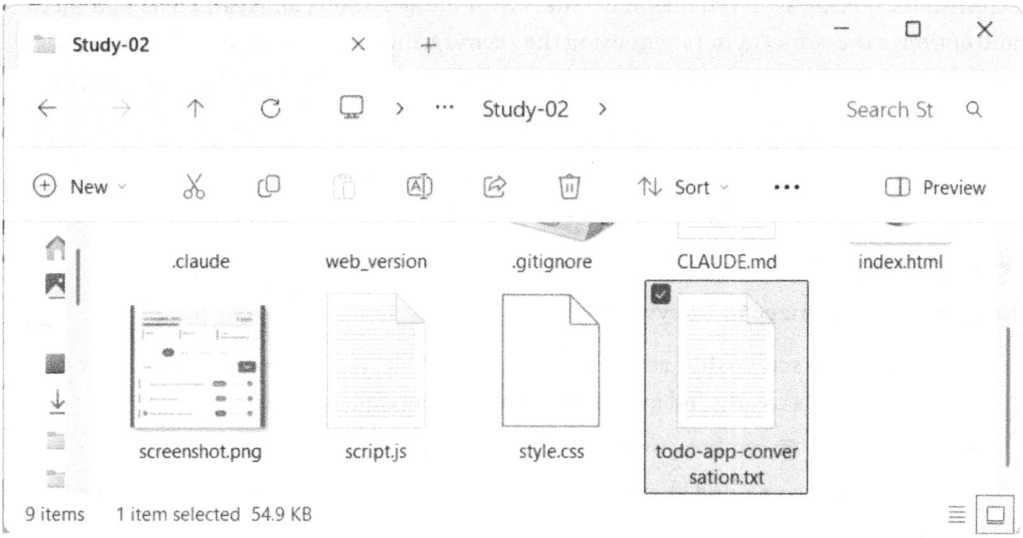

Figure 4.62: File saved in the Study-02 folder

4. If you open the `todo-app-conversation.txt` file with Notepad, you can see that all the conversation history from your work in Claude Code has been recorded.

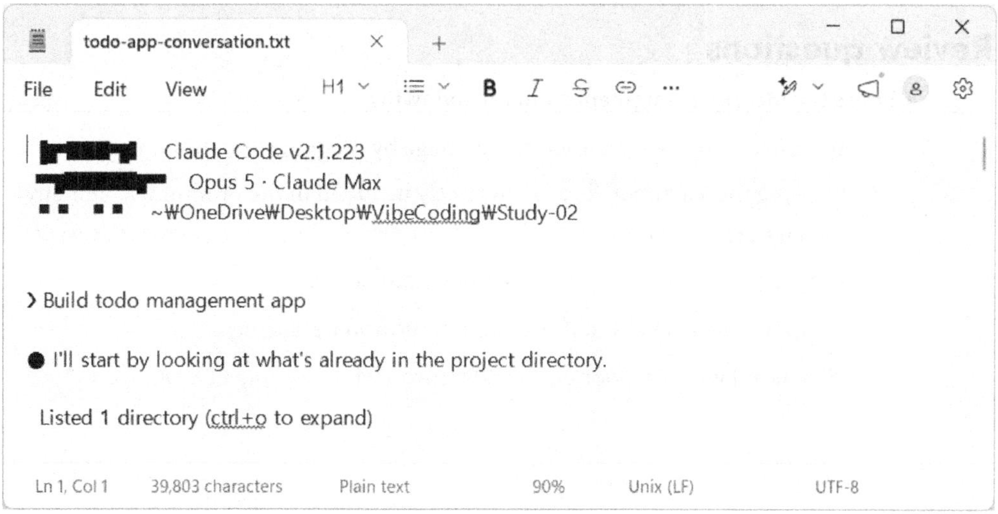

Figure 4.63: Conversation history

In this section, we practiced the comprehensive project improvement and management features of Claude Code. We adapted the mobile-focused UI for the desktop environment using screenshots, quickly analyzed files and folders with the @ symbol, and learned how to check and optimize the work environment using the `/config` and `/doctor` commands. Finally, we documented the entire work history with the `/export` command so it can be referenced for collaboration and future projects.

Now you can manage your projects using the various tools in Claude Code. In the next chapter, we'll take on an even more complex project.

Wrapping up

Key points summarized in 5 keywords:

- If you take a **screenshot** and send it to Claude Code, you can communicate your requirements clearly and quickly without lengthy explanations.
- By using the **@** symbol, you can instantly reference and analyze files and folders.
- The **/config** command allows you to manage Claude Code's project environment settings.
- The **/doctor** command diagnoses the system status and checks the version, installation method, update permissions, and more.
- The **/export** command saves and documents your work history to the clipboard or a file.

Review questions

1. Choose the incorrect statement from the following.
    1. You can transfer a screen-captured image by dragging and dropping it.
    2. By using the `@` symbol, files are instantly included in the prompt without any search time.
    3. `/config` can only change Claude Code's global settings.
    4. `/doctor` can check the status of automatic update settings.
    5. Files saved with `/export` can be referenced when writing `CLAUDE.md`.

2. Write the appropriate command or feature to use in each of the following situations:

Situation	Command
When you want to check the structure of the `web_version` folder	
When you want to find a specific function in the `script.js` file	
When you want to check the installation status of Claude Code	
When you want to save your conversation history as a file	
When you want to switch to dark mode	
When you want to turn off the auto-compression feature	

Table 4.5: Fill in the appropriate commands

Part 2

From Projects to Real Services

Building on the foundations of *Part 1*, this part moves into real-world projects and automation. You'll verify AI-generated content, automate repetitive work with custom commands, integrate external APIs, direct a team of AI agents, and extend Claude Code with MCP, skills, and plugins. You'll finish by building and deploying a database-backed service that anyone can use.

This part of the book includes the following chapters:

- *Chapter 5, Systematic Development and Management Through Game Creation*
- *Chapter 6, Giving Claude Code Wings with APIs*
- *Chapter 7, Building a Development Team with Claude Code AI Agents*
- *Chapter 8, Extending Claude Code with MCP, Skills, and Plugins*

5

Systematic Development and Management Through Game Creation

In this chapter, you will learn how to verify the accuracy of AI-generated content by implementing a quiz game.

After completing the basic game structure, you will use custom commands and automated workflows to efficiently manage repetitive tasks and expand your project. You will also build a quiz management system that updates automatically every day, leveraging AI as a true development partner.

Systematic development and management through game creation

Learning objectives:

- You will be able to verify the accuracy of AI-generated content and prevent hallucinations
- You will be able to create custom commands to automate repetitive tasks
- You will be able to chain commands together to efficiently link multiple tasks
- You will be able to selectively modify and update only the necessary parts of a completed project

Creating reliable AI content

Note

Key terms: Hallucination | /memory | /clear

In this section, we will create a four-choice general knowledge quiz game. Not only will we complete the game, but we will also learn methods to improve the accuracy of AI-generated questions. We will review the workflow from PRD creation to implementation, and follow the process of applying cross-verification guidelines for fact-checking, laying the foundation for systematic development and management.

Before you begin

AI sometimes generates plausible but incorrect information. The phenomenon where generative AI creates content that appears factual but is actually false is called hallucination. This occurs because AI generates the most probable sentences by finding and combining patterns from its training data, or due to inference errors caused by ambiguous information.

Therefore, when working with AI, it is important to recognize hallucinations and develop safe verification habits. Information generated by AI should be cross-checked with reliable documents or official sites, or you should input rules such as "`Do not generate information without sources`" to reduce the risk of hallucinations.

Figure 5.1: AI hallucination

In this section, we will use Claude and Claude Code to create a four-choice general knowledge quiz game. This game will present questions in four categories: history, science, geography, and arts & culture, and you can check whether your answer is correct each time you solve a question. Ultimately, your score and ranking will be recorded, allowing you to experience both learning and fun.

Figure 5.2: Sample of a quiz performance summary report

Step 1: Implementing the Quiz Game

You will write a PRD for game creation in Claude, prepare prompts, and then run Claude Code to create the game. After that, you will test whether the game created with AI proceeds as intended.

During this process, you will learn how to store verification guidelines in the project memory to improve the accuracy of AI-generated content, and how to reset the conversation context to test in a clean environment.

Writing a PRD for the Mini Game

1. First, access Claude (**claude.ai**) and write a PRD for the general knowledge quiz game. Enter the prompt as shown below. The PRD will be written in the artifact.
   Prompt:

```
I want to create a general knowledge quiz game. Please write a PRD.

Game Rules:
```

```
Multiple-choice quiz with four options
Categories: History, Science, Geography, Arts & Culture
10 questions per category, total of 40 questions
Immediate feedback on correct/incorrect answers
Record final score and ranking
```

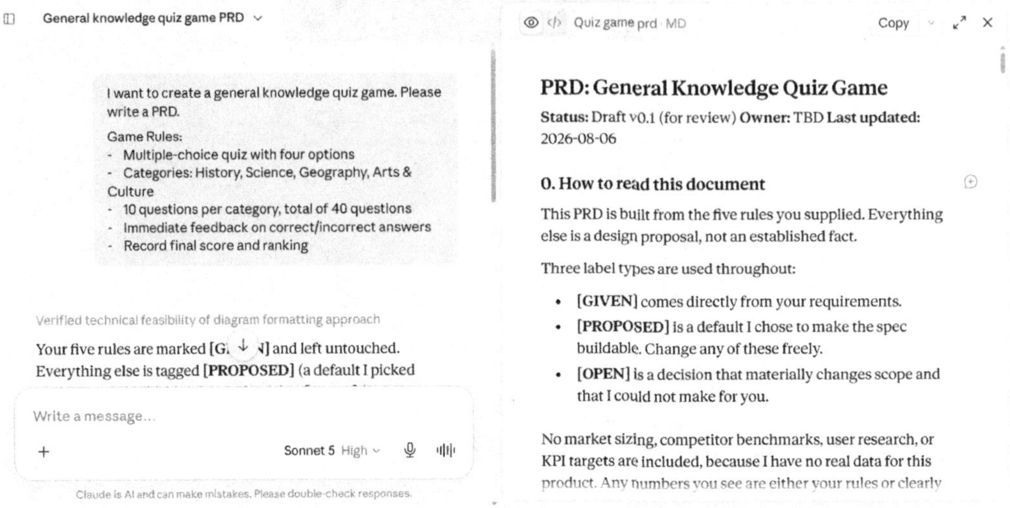

Figure 5.3: PRD for the quiz game

> **Tip**
>
> Try summarizing the requirements while keeping in mind the 5W1H principle you learned in *Chapter 2*.

2. Convert the PRD into a prompt for Claude Code and check the three-step implementation guide.

   Prompt:

```
Summarize the 3-phase project based on the PRD so that the general
knowledge quiz game can be implemented with Claude Code.
```

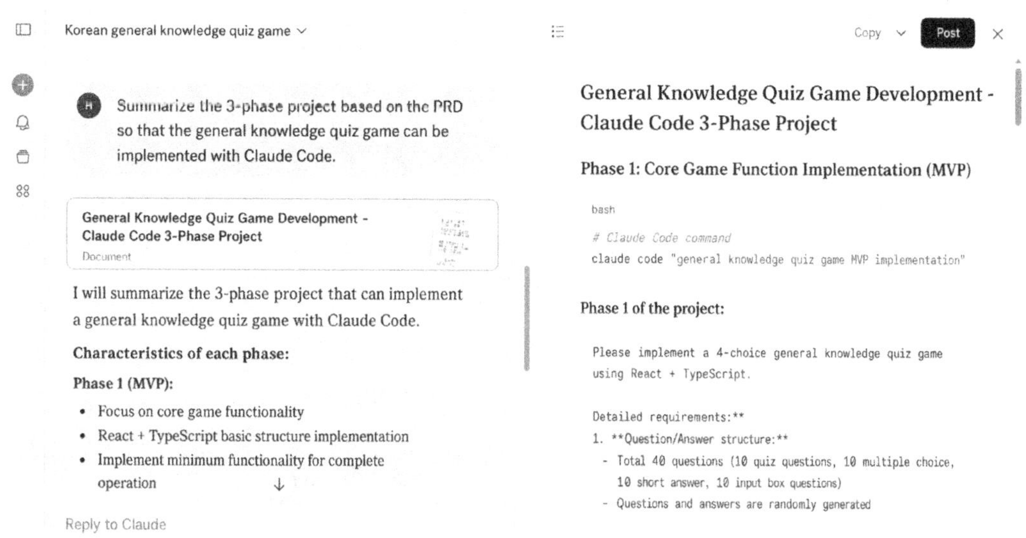

Figure 5.4: Organizing a 3-step prompt based on the PRD

Implementing the quiz game

Refer to *Chapter 3* for instructions on how to run Claude Code.

1. Create a folder named `Study-03` inside the `VibeCoding` folder on your desktop, right-click, and select **Open in Terminal** to open the command prompt. Then, type `claude` in the command prompt to run Claude Code.
2. Let's start implementing the mini game. Enter the step 1 prompt (the first of the three prompts you created in the previous section) into Claude Code.

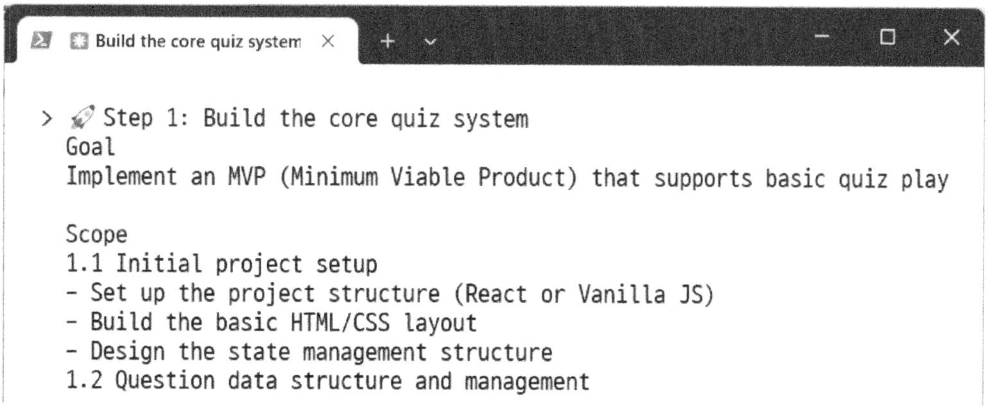

Figure 5.5: Entering the step 1 prompt in Claude Code

Only the first part is shown here; you can copy the full prompt from `PROMPTS.md` in the book's GitHub repository.

> **Tip**
>
> **When the pasted prompt is too long**
>
> When you copy the prompt provided by Claude and paste it into Claude Code, if the prompt is too long, it will appear summarized as `[Pasted text #1 +44 lines]`. If you press the *Enter* key to run it, it will proceed normally.

3. The quiz system has been implemented and is now testable.

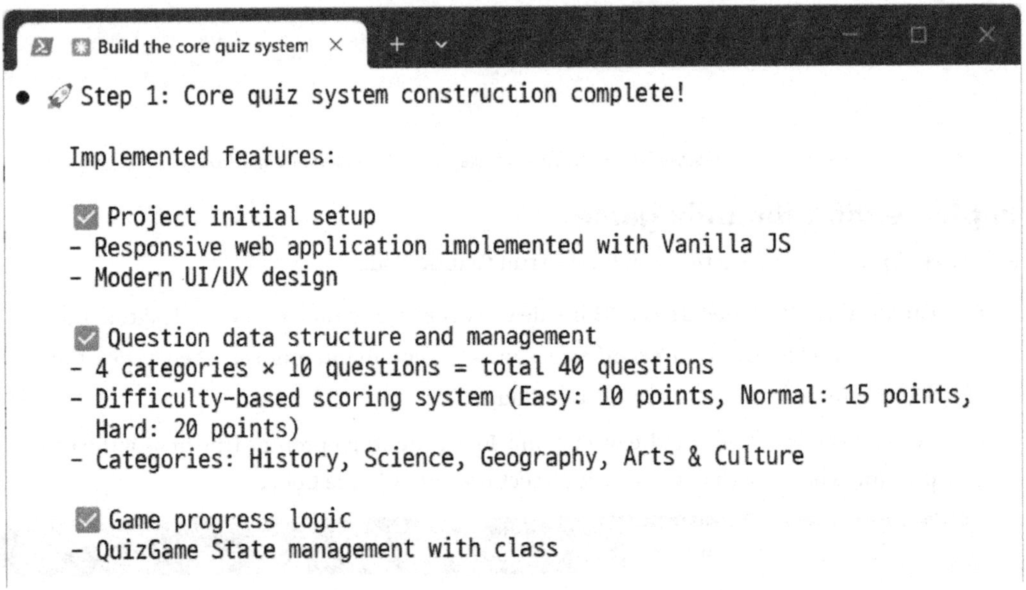

Figure 5.6: The quiz system is ready for testing

4. A new file, `index.html`, has been created in the `Study-03` folder.

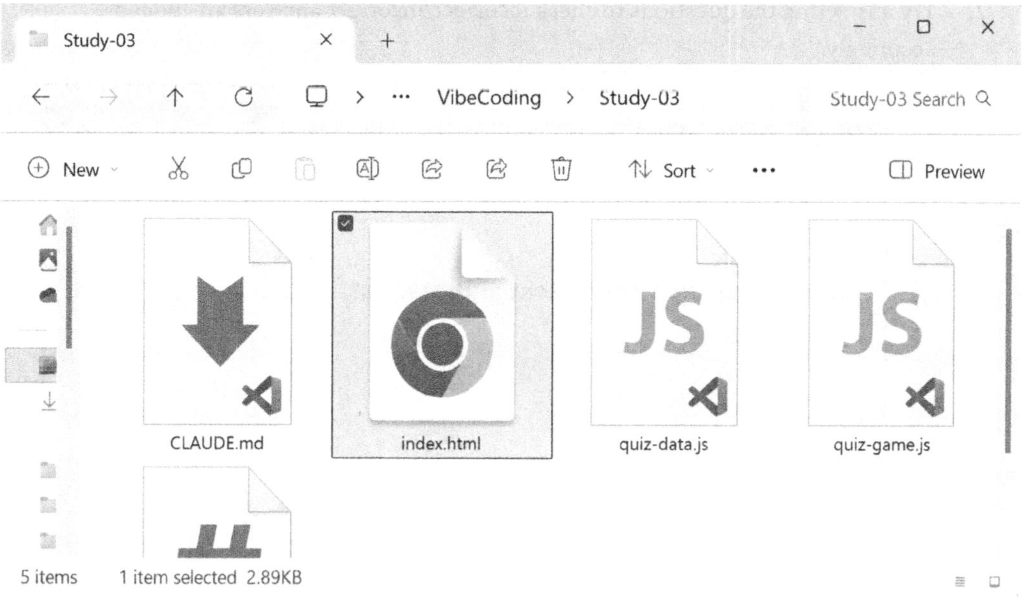

Figure 5.7: index.html file created

Game testing

Let's check if the general knowledge quiz game we created works properly. Test whether questions from all four categories are presented in order, whether correct and incorrect answers are judged accurately, whether feedback is displayed immediately, and whether the results are shown when the game is completed.

1. To ensure all features work as intended, double-click the `index.html` file in the `Study-03` folder to run the general knowledge quiz game in your web browser, click the **Start Game** button, and try answering the questions.

Figure 5.8: Quiz home page

2. Try answering the questions to check if correct/incorrect answers are judged accurately.

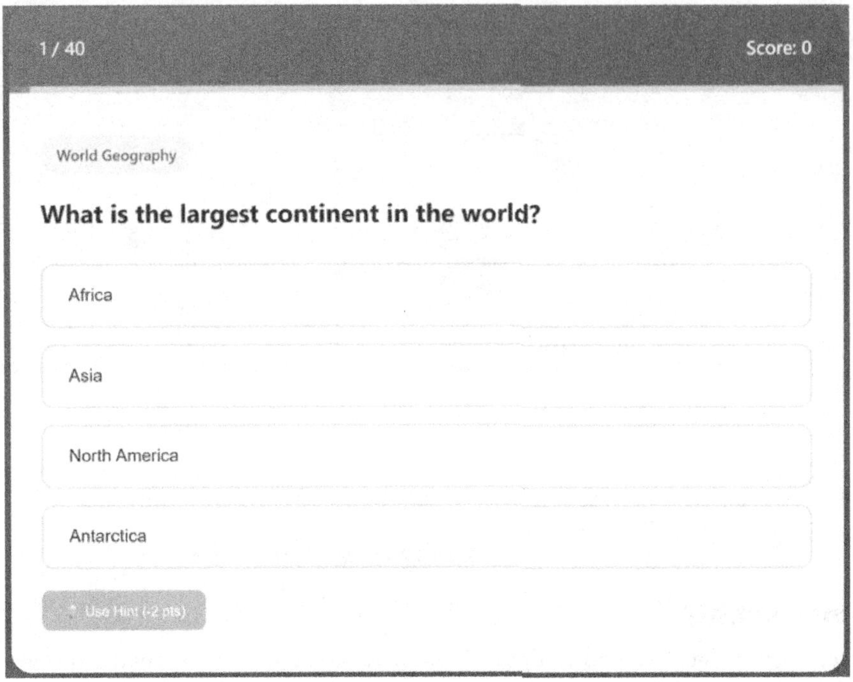

Figure 5.9: First question

3. The system determines whether your answer is correct and provides immediate feedback.

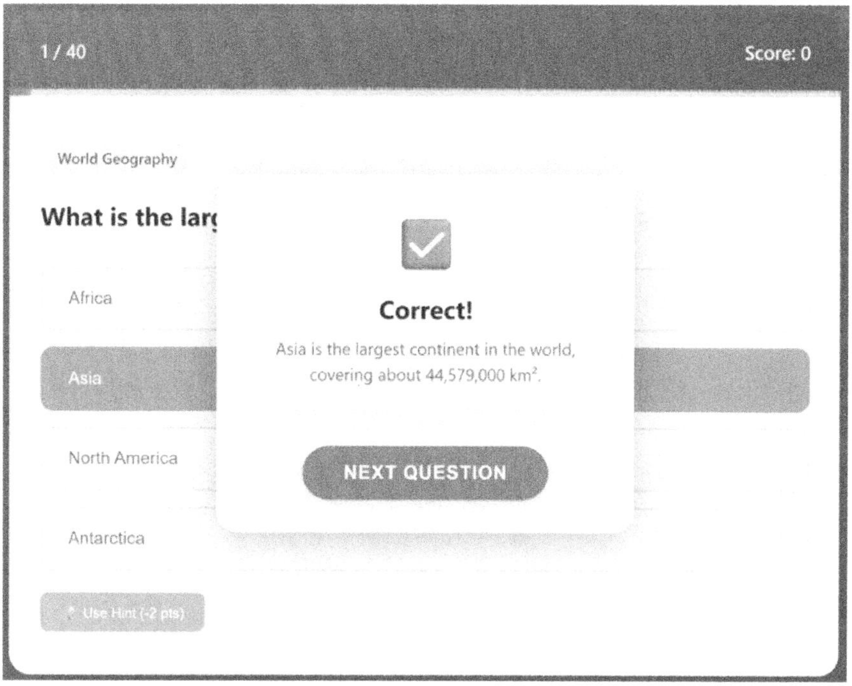

Figure 5.10: Correct answer pop-up

4. Here's the next question:

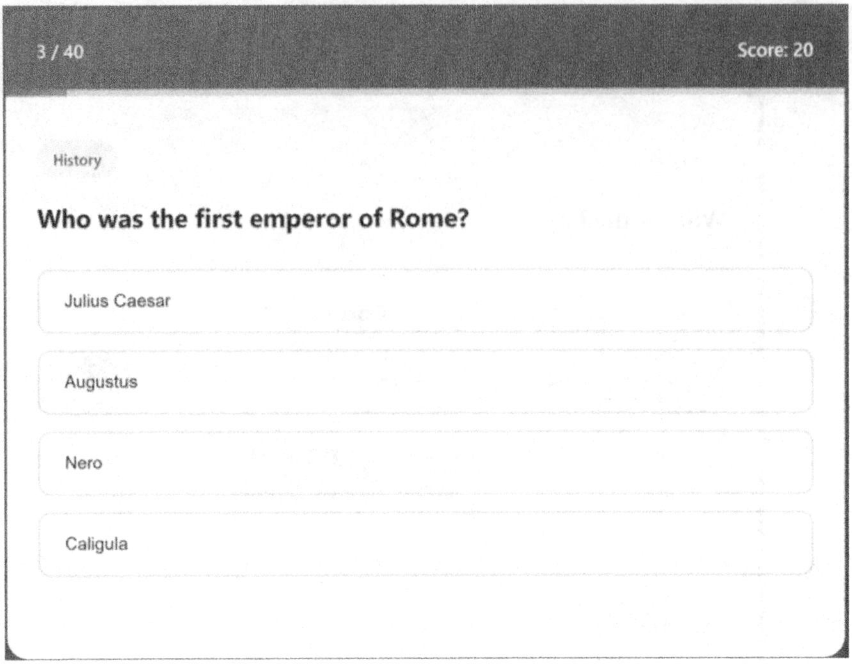

Figure 5.11: Sample of another question

5. This time, the answer is incorrect which will be shown by the quiz.

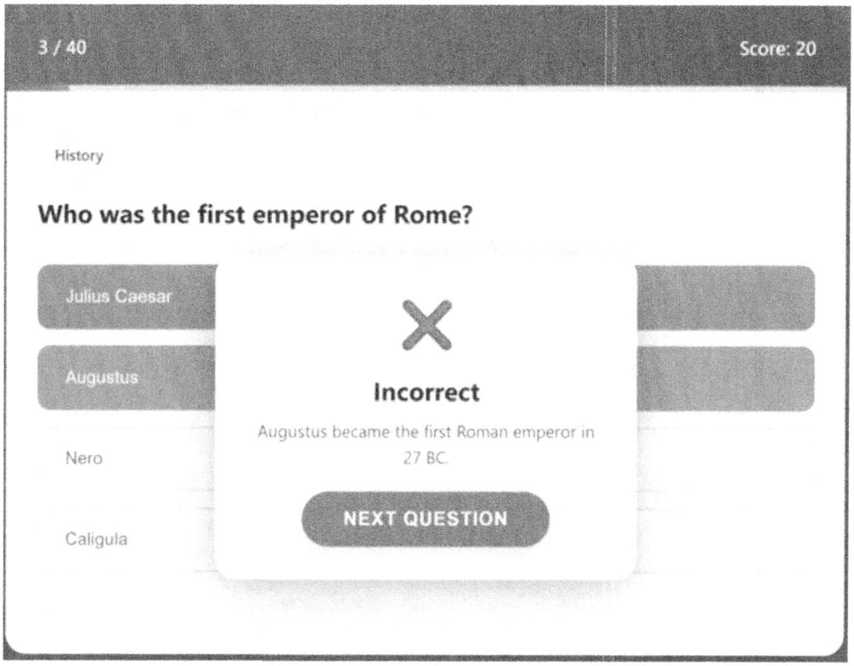

Figure 5.12: Incorrect answer indicated

6. After completing all the quizzes, your final score will be displayed.

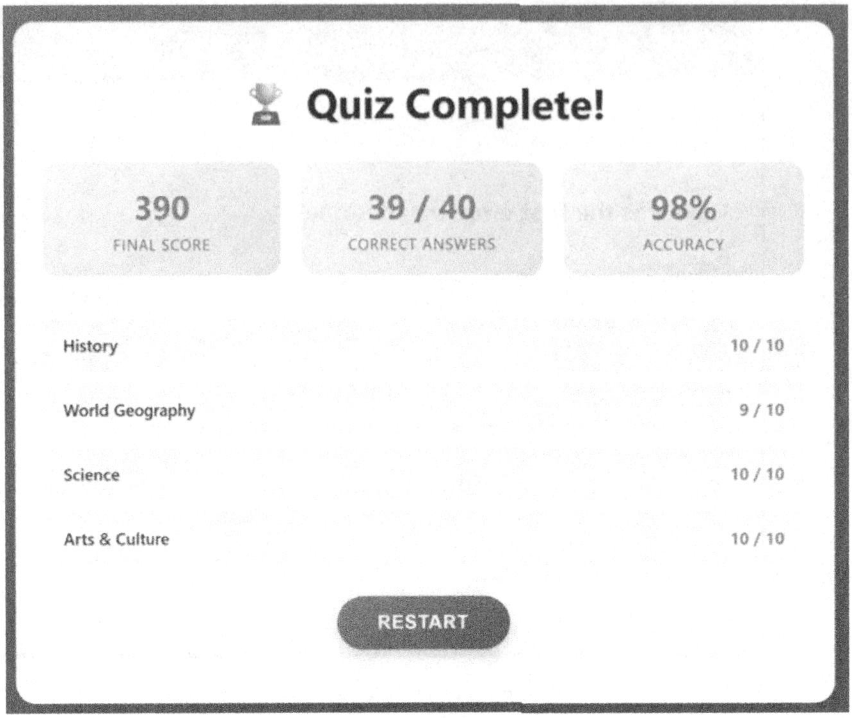

Figure 5.13: Final score card

Resolving hallucinations

In the development process of AI-based content, it is important to verify that hallucinations do not occur. This is especially true for quiz games, where the accuracy of information is critical. While there do not appear to be any obvious errors in the current set of questions, there may be ambiguous cases.

To try this exercise, download the finished example (`Study-03` |`Study-03-basic`) from the book's GitHub repository and tell Claude Code: `Run the downloaded files.` The first question is the following.

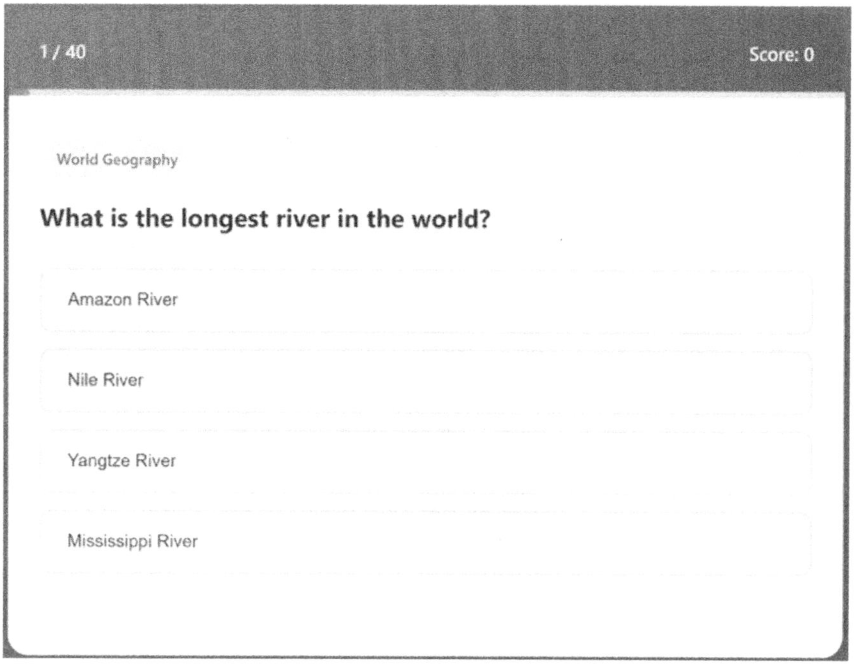

Figure 5.14: Testing the quiz again

That's incorrect. The correct answer is the **Nile**.

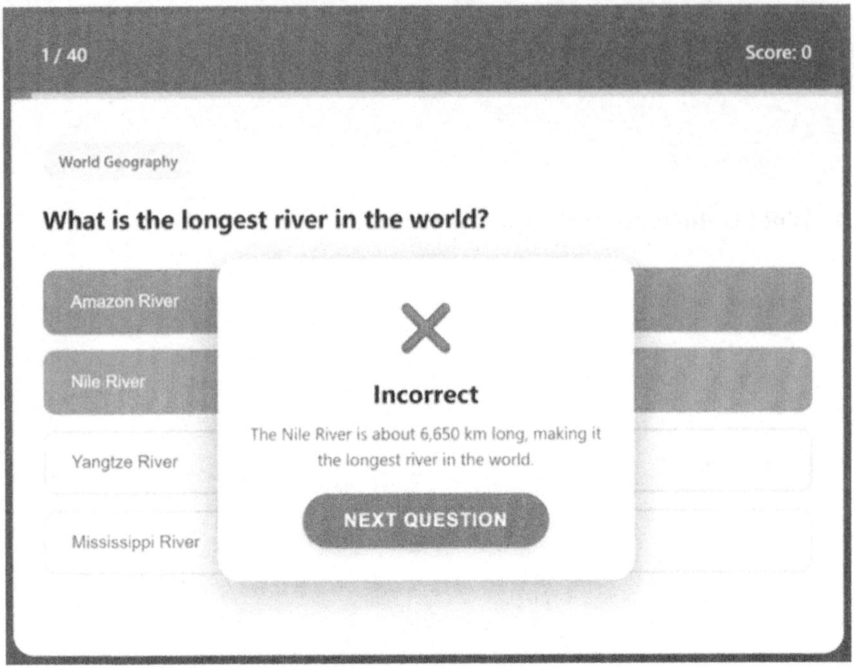

Figure 5.15: The quiz can give varied answers based on dynamic data

However, some studies using different measurements of the Amazon's source and length have argued that the Amazon may be longer than the Nile. This makes the answer dependent on the measurement criteria used. For topics like this that are subject to debate, it is important to cross-check and establish clear criteria when creating questions. Therefore, to verify controversial information, it is most effective to prepare verification guidelines and permanently store them in the `CLAUDE.md` file.

Project Folders

The hands-on projects for each chapter are stored in the following folders.

Chapter	Folder	Project	Link
3	`Study-01`	Handwriting recognition program	Live demo
4	`Study-02`	Todo app	Live demo
5	`Study-03-basic`	General knowledge quiz game (basic)	Download
5	`Study-03-advanced`	General knowledge quiz game (advanced)	Live demo
6	`Study-04`	FridgeChef (AI recipe recommendations)	Live demo
7	`Study-05`	AI Empathy Diary	Live demo
7	`Study-05`	PDF Summarizer AI	Live demo
8	`Study-06`	Shopping list app (database integration)	Live demo

Figure 5.16: Project folders on this book's GitHub repository

Note

Live demo of the project

Because the output of generative AI changes randomly each time, you may not encounter the same errors as those shown in the book when you try the exercises yourself.

In this chapter, to help you understand and deal with cases where AI generates controversial or incorrect information, we provide a live demo project that intentionally includes problematic questions.

You can download the relevant materials by finding **General Knowledge Quiz Game (Basic)** in the table under `Project Folders` at the bottom of the book's GitHub repository (`https://github.com/PacktPublishing/Build-with-Claude-Code`) and clicking the **Download** link.

By referring to this file, you can directly compare and analyze how AI produces incorrect outputs and learn from it.

Establishing cross-verification guidelines

The /memory command allows you to check and manage project-related information that the AI remembers. Simply put, it lets you review and manage the memory files that provide Claude Code with persistent instructions and project context. Now, let's use the /memory command to document the verification rules and save them in CLAUDE.md.

1. To edit the CLAUDE.md file, enter the /memory command in Claude Code.
2. You need to specify where to save the memory file. Since the quiz game's verification guidelines apply only to the current project, select **1. Project memory**.

```
> /memory

Learn more:
https://docs.claude.com/en/docs/claude-code/memory
```

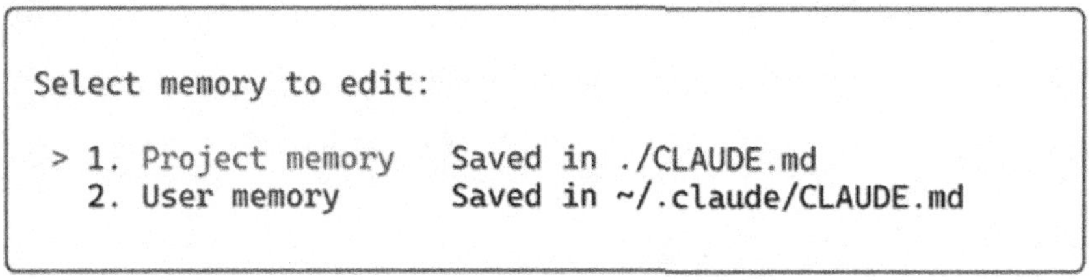

Figure 5.17: Select option 1

> Note
>
> **Memory selection**
>
> Choose where to save the memory:
>
> 1. **Project memory**: Stores rules that apply only within the current project folder
> 2. **User memory**: Stores user-wide rules that apply to all projects

3. The CLAUDE.md file for the current project will open.

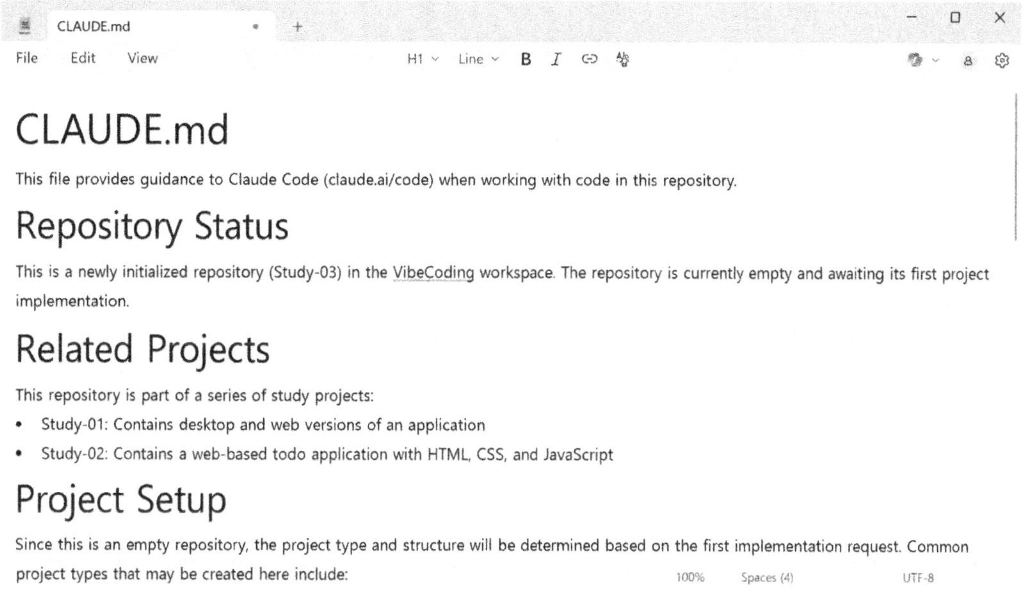

Figure 5.18: CLAUDE.md file

> **Note**
>
> This book uses **Notepad** as the system editor. On macOS, use **TextEdit**, and on Linux, use **gedit** or **nano**.

4. Add the following cross-verification guidelines to the last line of the `CLAUDE.md` file:

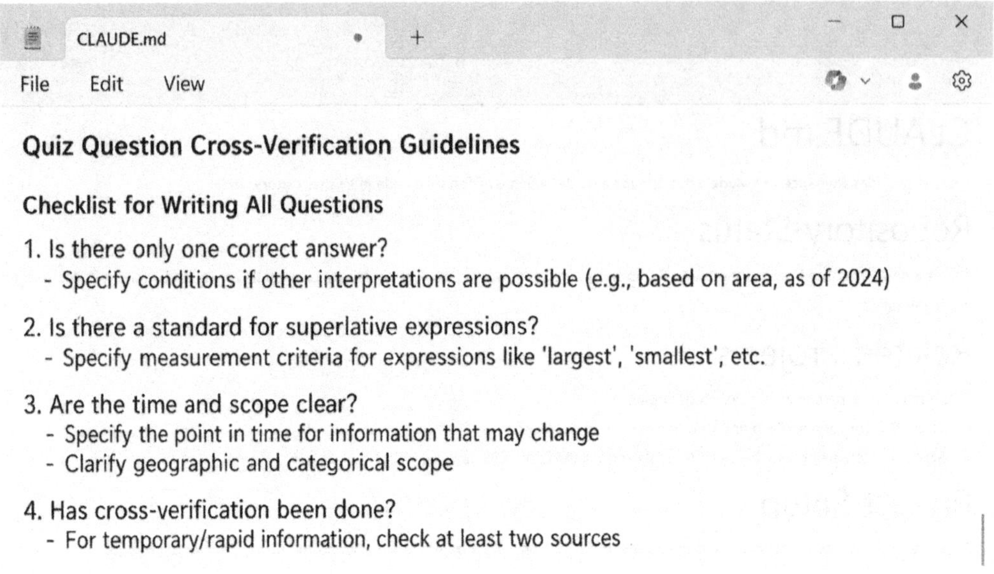
CLAUDE.md

File Edit View

Quiz Question Cross-Verification Guidelines

Checklist for Writing All Questions

1. Is there only one correct answer?
   - Specify conditions if other interpretations are possible (e.g., based on area, as of 2024)
2. Is there a standard for superlative expressions?
   - Specify measurement criteria for expressions like 'largest', 'smallest', etc.
3. Are the time and scope clear?
   - Specify the point in time for information that may change
   - Clarify geographic and categorical scope
4. Has cross-verification been done?
   - For temporary/rapid information, check at least two sources

Figure 5.19: Cross-verification guidelines

> **Tip**
>
> **How to Write a CLAUDE.md file**
>
> There is no fixed format for `CLAUDE.md`, so the key is to write concisely and in a way that is easy for people to read. Since it also functions as part of Claude's prompt, it's best to continually refine and improve it like any frequently used prompt.

5. Write concisely in clear, easy-to-read natural language.

   Example: `# Project Overview`

   `Name: My Web App`

   `Goal: Implement a simple blog service`

   `Languages: Python 3.12, JavaScript (React)`

6. For important rules, you can add emphasis words like 'important' or 'must' so the AI will follow them more strictly.

   Example: `# Precautions`

   `Do not enter actual API keys in settings.json → You must use a .env file`

```
Image files must be stored only in the /assets/images folder
```

7. Click **File** | **Save** or *Ctrl* + *S* to save the CLAUDE.md file and close the text editor.
8. When you return to Claude Code, you will see a message indicating that the CLAUDE.md file was open.

```
> /memory
  L Opened memory file at ./CLAUDE.md

    > To use a different editor, set the $EDITOR or $VISUAL
    environment variable.
```

Figure 5.20: Message indicating the file is open

9. To check if the changes have been applied, enter the following prompt:
   Prompt:

```
Please check the contents of the current project's CLAUDE.md.
```

10. You can check the full contents of the `CLAUDE.md` file, including the guidelines you just added.

```
Project Documentation
(Start-Quiz-Result)
3. Development command: Run local server with python -m http.server 8000
4. Data structure: Question object format and difficulty-based scoring system
5. Game flow: 4-step process

Added quiz question cross-checking guidelines:
- Check answer uniqueness
- Specify criteria for superlative expressions
- Clarity of time and scope
- Necessity of cross-checking

The document organizes the project structure and development
guidelines well.
```

Figure 5.21: Updated content in the file

Resetting the context

The `/clear` command clears the conversation history and resets the current session context. Persistent project instructions stored in files such as `CLAUDE.md` are retained. Use it when the conversation history gets too long and unnecessary context interferes with your work, when you want to erase traces of a previous project and start a completely new task, or when confusion arises during testing due to incorrect context.

Now, we'll test whether Claude Code works according to the newly added guidelines, but you may be affected by issues generated in previous conversations. Since the important rules are saved in the `CLAUDE.md` file, let's use the `/clear` command to clear the current conversation and work information so far and restart the general knowledge quiz game.

The difference between /clear and /compact

Like `/clear`, the previously introduced `/compact` command also organizes and optimizes context. However, while `/compact` summarizes and retains the conversation, `/clear` completely resets it. The following table summarizes the differences between `/clear` and `/compact`.

Category	/clear	/compact
Basic Operation	Completely resets conversation history	Summarizes and compresses conversation content
Context Window	Emptied completely	Retained in summarized form
CLAUDE.md file	Retained	Retained
When to Use	• Starting a new task/feature • Switching to a completely different topic • Resetting a conversation that has gone off track	• When the context window is full • When continuing the same task but need optimization • Reduce token usage

Table 5.1: /clear versus /compact

1. To reset the work content, enter `/clear` in Claude Code. This deletes conversation history and clears the context.
2. Confirm that all conversation history has disappeared.

Checking the Guidelines

1. Enter the following prompt in Claude Code. You will be notified that the questions were created according to the new guidelines:
   Prompt:

```
Please review the questions created so far with reference to the guidelines
you just saved. If there are any quizzes or answers that do not comply with
the guidelines, please revise them accordingly.
```

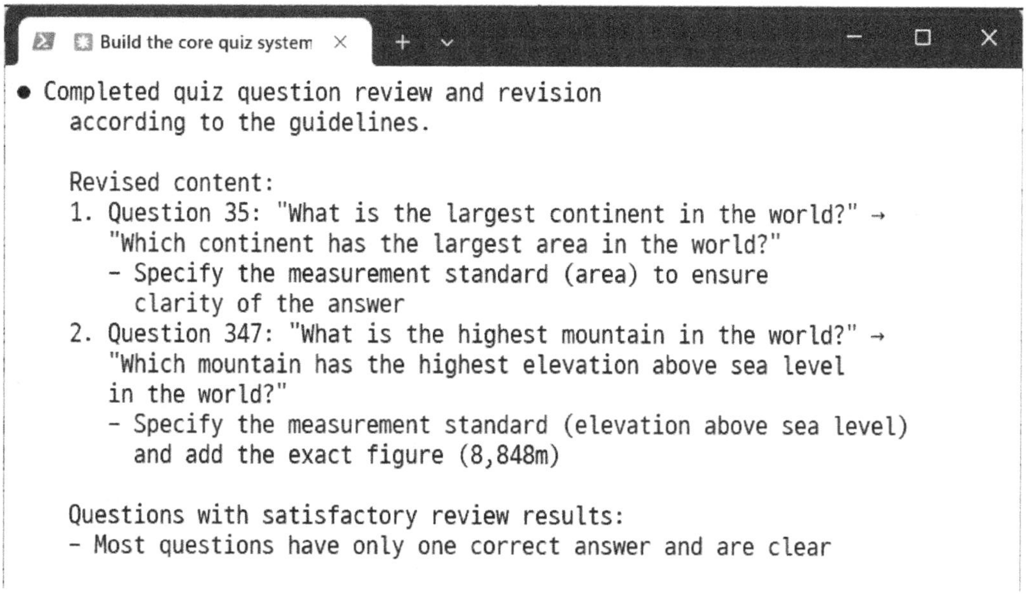

Figure 5.22: Review the quiz as per the guidelines

2. Let's run the `index.html` file again to check if the guidelines are reflected in the quiz. The condition *(by traditional measurement)* is displayed in the question. Let's select **Nile River** as the answer once again.
3. This time, additional information is provided along with the correct answer.

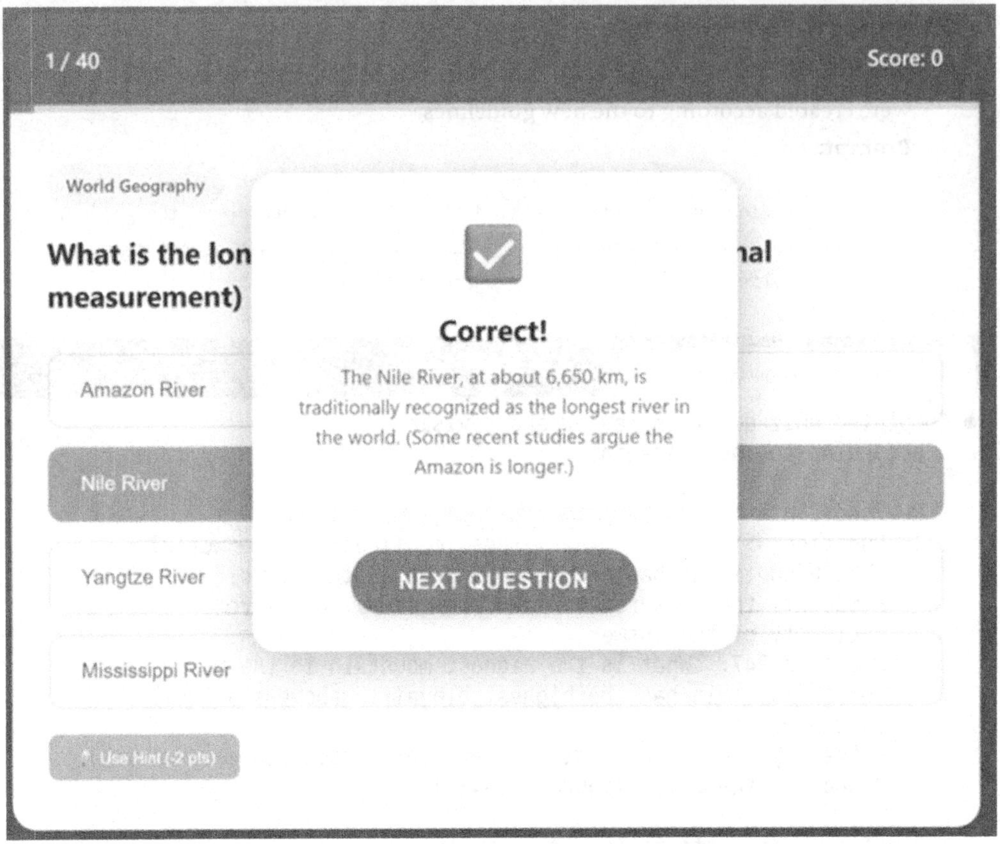

Figure 5.23: Assessment with a disclaimer

In this section, you learned how to manage the accuracy of AI-generated content while creating a quiz game.

We established a system to reduce the risk of AI hallucinations by saving cross-verification guidelines in the project's `CLAUDE.md` file. In the process, we used the `/clear` command to reset the work context and test whether the guidelines were properly applied, and added clear conditions such as 'by traditional measurement' to ambiguous expressions.

In the next section, we'll create custom commands to improve development efficiency for the project.

The book's GitHub repository provides a live demo showing the project in action in real time: `https://vibecoding-eng-ch05.vercel.app`.

Wrapping up

Key takeaways summarized in 3 Keywords:

- The phenomenon where AI generates information that sounds plausible but is actually false is called **hallucination**.
- **/memory** is a command for checking and managing project-related information that the AI remembers.
- **/clear** is a command that deletes and resets all conversation and work context in the current session.

Review questions

1. Choose the incorrect statement from the following descriptions.
    1. AI hallucination can occur when patterns are excessively generalized.
    2. If you select Project memory in the `/memory` command, the `./CLAUDE.md` file opens.
    3. `/clear` summarizes and compresses the conversation while maintaining context.
    4. When adding guidelines to `./CLAUDE.md`, simply write them in concise and clear natural language.
2. Write the appropriate command or response method for the following situations:

Situation	Response
When you want to save the validation guidelines for the quiz game	
When you think previous conversations might affect a new task	
When the conversation gets long and you want to save tokens	
When you encounter an ambiguous question like "the longest river in the world"	

Table 5.2: Fill in the appropriate commands

Boosting development efficiency through automation

> Note
>
> **Key terms**: Custom commands| Global commands |Project commands |Arguments | Placeholders
>
> Now that the basic functions of the quiz game are complete, let's validate and analyze the quizzes to improve their quality and expand the content by adding new questions. In this section, we'll use Claude Code's custom commands to reduce repetitive tasks and increase development efficiency.
>
> Through this, you'll be able to manage the project faster and more reliably, and experience naturally integrating AI tools into your development workflow.

Before you begin

Earlier in *Chapter 1*, we tried customizing the website's design. Customizing means adjusting the settings, appearance, and behavior of a program to suit the user's preferences, rather than using the system's default features as-is.

Claude Code's slash commands can also be redefined by users to change their behavior or form.

This allows you to create automated commands that handle repetitive tasks for you.

Step 2: Expanding the game

Now that the basic quiz system is complete, let's add a scoring system and various game modes to make the game more engaging:

1. Enter the step 2 prompt you created earlier into Claude Code. Once execution is complete, a message will appear indicating it is done.

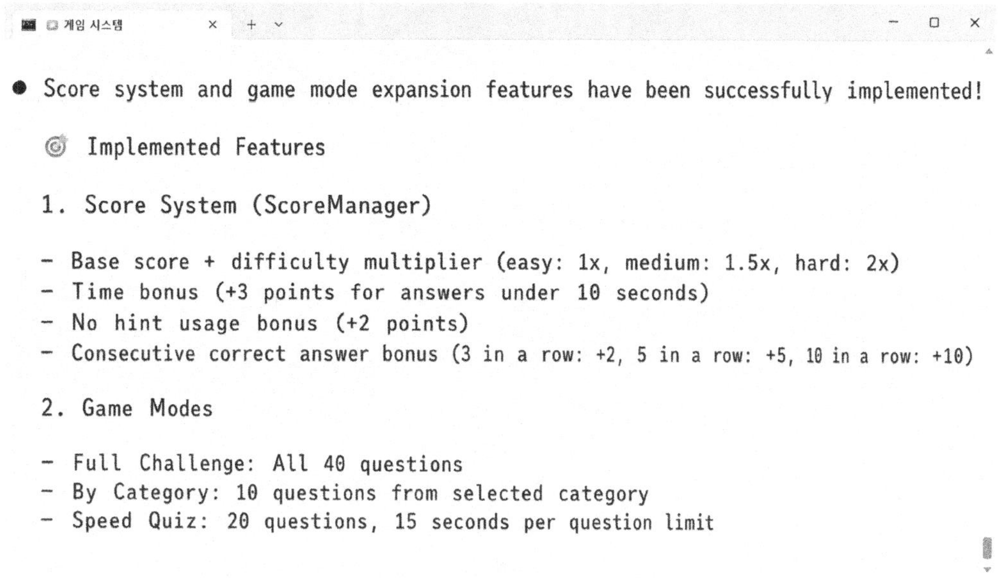

Figure 5.24: Score system implemented

2. Double-click the `index.html` file in the `Study-03` folder to run the game. You will see that three game modes have been added. Let's select **Speed Quiz** among them.

Figure 5.25: Choose the Speed Quiz option

3. The 15-second time limit rule has been applied. If you click the **Use Hint** button, you can view a hint, but your score will be deducted.

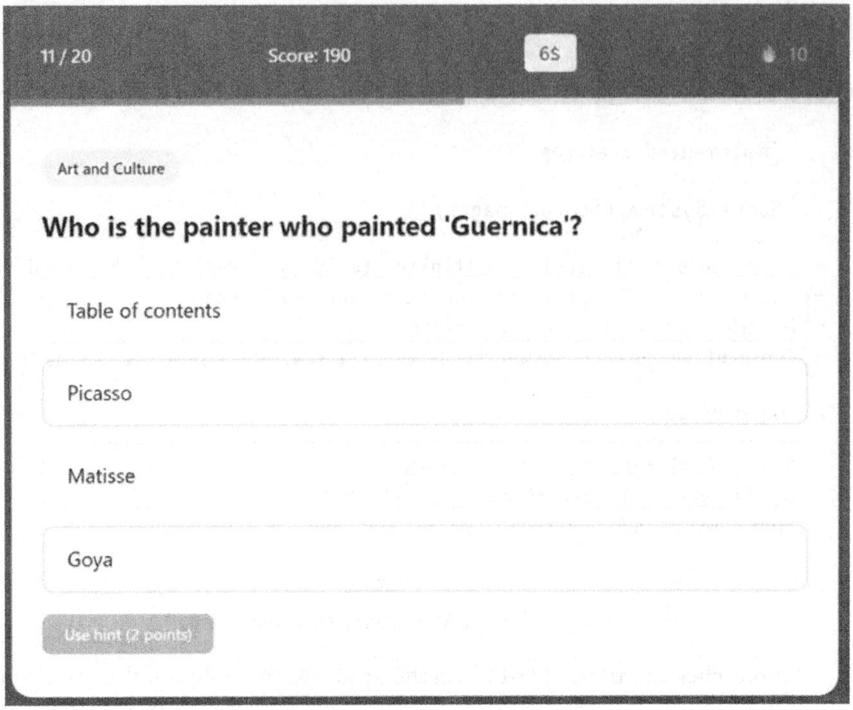

Figure 5.26: You have a choice to use a hint

4. It accurately distinguishes between correct and incorrect answers.

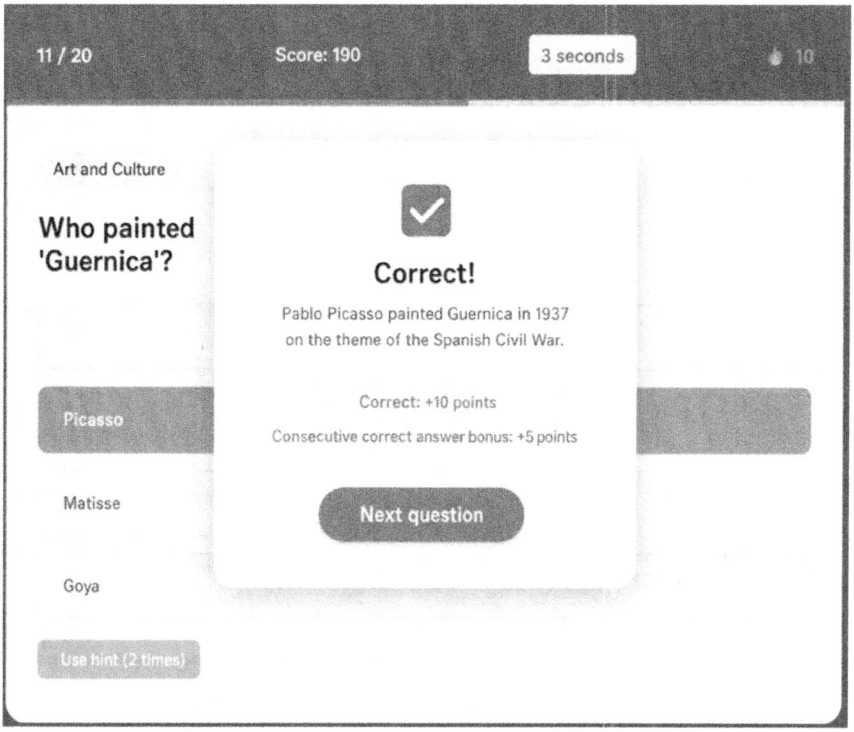

Figure 5.27: Assessment

5. After completing all the quizzes, you can check your final score.

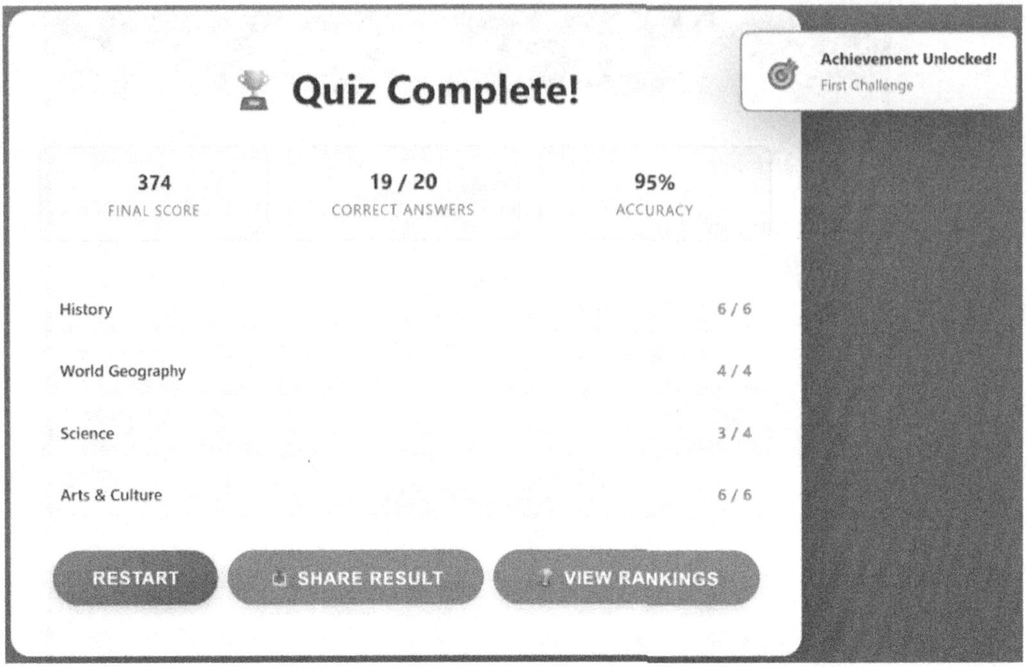

Figure 5.28: Check the final score

Automating repetitive tasks with custom commands

Quiz games can also be used as educational content or learning apps. However, when developing such programs, you often have to repeat similar tasks. For example, you might repeatedly copy and paste to standardize the format of questions, check the guidelines every time you validate a question, or adjust the difficulty for balance. These are all typical examples of repetitive tasks that commonly occur during development.

If you try to handle these repetitive tasks with long prompts every time, not only is it inefficient, but it also leads to frequent mistakes. In such cases, Claude Code's custom commands are a useful feature. By using custom commands, you can automate repetitive tasks with simple commands, allowing you to continue development quickly and reliably.

Custom commands

A custom command is a shortcut directive that users can define and use themselves. In addition to the commands provided by default in Claude Code, you can create custom commands for instructions you use repeatedly, so you don't have to re-enter long prompts every time. Commands are defined in markdown files and are divided into the following two types depending on their scope:

1. Global commands: Commands defined in the home directory location that apply universally to all projects.
   Location: `~/.claude/commands/`

   > **Note**
   >
   > In terminal path notation, ~ means the home directory.

2. Project commands: Commands defined in the project directory location that can only be used in the currently active project.
   Location: `.claude/commands/`

   > **Note**
   >
   > In terminal path notation, `.` means the current directory.

Creating a command folder

Let's create a simple custom command through a hands-on exercise. Since this custom command will only be used for the general knowledge quiz game project, we'll create a new folder to store the command in the `Study-03` folder.

Open the command prompt at the `Study-03` folder location on your desktop, launch Claude Code to prepare, and enter the following. Claude Code will create the folder to store the command and display the directory structure.

Prompt:

```
Create a custom command folder for the current project.
Create the .claude/commands directory and show the structure.
```

```
● ✅ .claude/commands The .claude/commands directory has been successfully
     created!

  📁 Created directory structure
  C:\Users\user\Desktop\VibeCoding\Study-03\
  ├── .claude/
  │   └── commands/
  ├── index.html
  ├── styles.css
  ├── quiz-data.js
  ├── quiz-game.js
  └── CLAUDE.md

  The .claude/commands folder is used to define custom slash commands in
  Claude Code. You can add JavaScript files to this folder to create
  project-specific custom commands.
```

Figure 5.29: Folder created and directory structure displayed

Creating your first custom command

The item **2. Do superlative expressions have a stated basis?** that you entered in the `CLAUDE.md` file for the general knowledge quiz game was a cross-validation guideline requiring you to specify the measurement standard for superlative expressions to prevent AI hallucination.

Now, let's register a custom command in Claude Code to check the quality of the quiz, restart, run it to find ambiguous superlative expressions, and then fix them.

1. Let's create the first custom command in the `commands` folder. Enter the following in Claude Code:

   Prompt:

   ```
   Create a .claude/commands/quiz-validate.md file.
   Find any superlative expressions such as 'most', 'first', or 'largest' in
   the quiz questions and display them as a list.
   ```

2. To prevent potentially controversial answers, we've created a custom command `/quiz-validate` that finds and displays superlative expressions in the questions.

```
📋 Detailed Analysis

1. "First" - Clear by order criteria
2. "First" - Clear by specifying year (1492) as time criteria
3. "Oldest" - Clear by founding-date criteria
4. "Most abundant" - Clear by composition-ratio criteria
5. "Longest" - Measurement criteria specified (revised)
6. "Largest area" - Area criteria specified (revised)

🏆 Conclusion

All questions containing superlative expressions perfectly comply with the guidelines.
In particular, questions 12 and 18 have been revised since the previous review,
and the measurement criteria are now clearly specified.

The quiz-validate.md custom command file has been created, and in the future,
such validation can be automated with the /quiz-validate command.
```

Figure 5.30: Creating the /quiz-validate command

3. To run the custom command you created, enter the `/exit` command to exit Claude Code and restart it. In the new window, enter `/quiz-validate` to run it. It will identify superlative expressions in the quiz and suggest improvements.

```
🔍Quiz Validation Report: Superlative Expression Verification

Detected Questions (14)

1. Question ID 2 (History - Medium)

Question: Who was the first emperor of Rome? Superlative expression: "first"
Measurement criterion: clear (chronological order) Status: good ✅

---
2. Question ID 3 (History - Medium)

Question: In what year did Columbus first reach the Americas? Superlative expression: "first"
Measurement criterion: clear (year-based) Status: good ✅

---
3. Question ID 10 (History - Medium)
```

Figure 5.31: Quiz validation report

By using the newly created custom slash command, you can identify potentially ambiguous claims in AI-generated quiz questions and flag them for further verification. This helps prevent inaccurate or potentially controversial questions, not only in general knowledge quiz games but also in similar projects.

Note

Custom Commands and Skills

Custom commands are a concept similar to Skills, which will be introduced in *Chapter 8* of this book. Custom commands are registered as `/command` for frequently used tasks and must be entered to execute, whereas Skills, once registered, are automatically invoked and executed by Claude Code based on the nature of the request, without needing to enter a command. Skills are saved as `SKILL.md` files in the `.claude/skills/` folder and, like custom commands, are written in markdown (md) format.

Extending custom commands

An argument is additional information passed to a command or function. If the command determines 'what to do,' the argument specifies 'what to do it to and how.'

Next, we will extend the `/quiz-validate` custom command, which checks the quality and accuracy of the quiz, by specifying argument placeholders in two ways. The first is to pass a category as an argument so that only quizzes in the specified category are validated. The second is to pass two numbers as arguments so that only quizzes within a specified range are validated.

Validate only a specific category:

- `/quiz-validate History`

Analyze only questions 1 to 20

- `/quiz-range 1 20`

Note

Placeholders

A placeholder is a symbol that marks a spot where an actual value will be inserted later. Simply put, it's a blank space set aside for a value that hasn't been determined yet, and when executed, the actual value is filled in. For example, on a website, if you create a placeholder like `Welcome, {name}`, the user's name will be inserted into the placeholder when the site runs.

The username displayed on Claude's start screen is also replaced with a placeholder in the actual document.

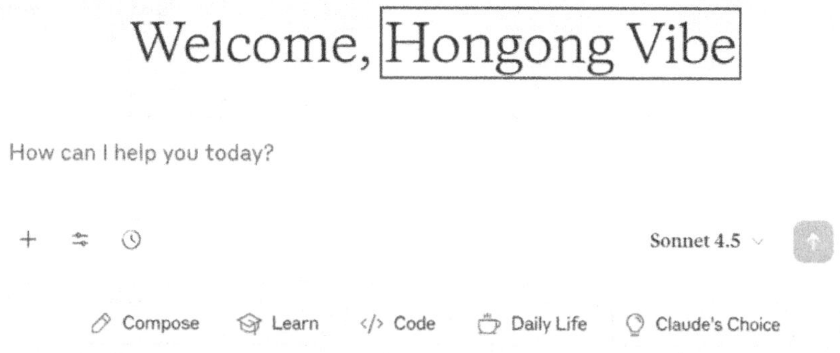

Figure 5.32: The username visible here is replaced by a placeholder in the actual document

Validating Only a Specific Category

Let's expand the `/quiz-validate` command so that it accepts a category name as an argument and validates only the quizzes in that category. Set up an argument placeholder for the command to receive the category, and if no argument is provided, validate the entire quiz.

```
/quiz-validate $ARGUMENTS
```

Here, `$ARGUMENTS` is the argument placeholder

1. To specify arguments for the custom command, let's edit the `.claude/commands/quiz-validate.md` file. Enter the following prompt in Claude Code:

   Prompt:

   ```
   Modify .claude/commands/quiz-validate.md as follows.
   If the user specifies a category, validate only the questions in that
   ```

```
category; if not specified, validate all questions.
Use the value entered in $ARGUMENTS as the category.
When validating, check for ambiguous expressions such as 'most', 'first',
or 'maximum', and indicate what criteria need to be specified.
```

2. Once you see the completion message, enter the `/exit` command to exit Claude Code.
3. Type `claude` to restart, and enter the `/quiz-validate History` command. This command validates only the quizzes in the *History* category.

```
Claude Code v2.1.220

            Welcome back HonGongVibe!            | Tips for getting
                                                 | started
                                                 | Run /init to create a …
                                                 | What's new
                                                 | Bug fixes and reliabil…
                                                 | Added Claude Opus 5 (`…
                                                 | Added `sandbox.network…
    ~\OneDrive\Desktop\VibeCoding\Study-03       | /release-notes for more

> /quiz-validate History

  ⏵⏵ accept edits on (shift+tab to cycle)
```

Figure 5.33: Validate quizzes in the History category

Review the intermediate steps and press **1. Yes** to proceed to the end.

4. The quizzes in the *History* category have been validated.

```
● Comprehensive Evaluation

  Status of Superlative Expression Usage in History Category:
  - Total number of questions: 10
  - Issues with superlative expression usage: 1 (10%)
  - Questions with clear measurement criteria: 1 (100%)
  - Issues requiring improvement: 0

  Conclusion: The use of superlative expressions in the history category is appropriate,
  and the measurement criteria for the expressions used are clear, so no further
  improvement is necessary.
```

Figure 5.34: Quizzes successfully validated

Analyzing a specific range only

Let's create a custom command, `/quiz-range`, to analyze quizzes within a specific range. This command takes two positional arguments to specify the range of quizzes to review. For example, `/quiz-range 1 20` validates quizzes from number 1 to 20.

This command focuses on analyzing the difficulty and answer distribution of the quizzes. It analyzes the difficulty distribution for the specified range to check whether questions that are too easy or too difficult are concentrated in a particular section.

It also checks whether the correct answers are skewed toward a particular choice. For example, it detects if the correct answer is overwhelmingly assigned to option 1, or if option 4 is rarely used as the correct answer. Based on these analysis results, it provides guidance to help maintain a balanced distribution across all quizzes.

```
/quiz-range $1 $2
```

```
Here, $1 and $2 are the argument placeholders
```

1. To create the custom command `/quiz-range` for reviewing quizzes within a specific range, enter the following prompt into Claude Code.
   Prompt:

   ```
   Create .claude/commands/quiz-range.md.
   Create a function to review questions from $1 to $2.
   Make it possible to check the difficulty and answer distribution of the
   questions.
   ```

```
> Create .claude/commands/quiz-range.md.

  Create a function to review questions from $1 to $2.
  Make it possible to check the difficulty and answer distribution
  of the questions.

● I'll create a new slash command file for reviewing quiz
  questions within a specific range.

● Write(.claude\commands\quiz-range.md)
  L Wrote 1 lines to .claude\commands\quiz-range.md
    ---
    description: Reviews quiz questions within the specified range
    and analyzes the difficulty and answer distribution.
    ---
    Read the quiz-data.js file and review questions from $1 to $2.

    For each question:
    1. Question number, category, difficulty
    2. Question content
```

Figure 5.35: Prompt for reviewing quizzes within a specific range

> **Note**
>
> $1 and $2 are placeholders for the start and end numbers, and will be replaced with the user's input when the command is executed.

2. After exiting Claude with the `/exit` command, restart with the `claude` command. Then, to check if the custom command `/quiz-range` works properly, enter the following command to review quizzes 1 through 20.
   Prompt:

   ```
   /quiz-range 1 20
   ```

3. The command works correctly and analyzes quizzes 1-20. It recommends distributing the correct answer positions more evenly to reduce bias.

⚠ Warning

1. Severe answer bias: 55% of the correct answers are concentrated on option 0. This is a problem where test-takers can identify the pattern and answer strategically.
2. Option 3 not used: Option 3 has never been used as the correct answer. The correct answers are concentrated only on options 0 and 1.
3. Recommendations:
   - Distribute the answer positions more evenly (target 25% each)
   - Especially use options 2 and 3 more often as correct answers
   - With the current pattern, the 'always choose 0' strategy may be effective

Figure 5.36: The analysis

Automating the addition of new quiz questions

When adding new quizzes, it's also important to maintain format consistency and follow the guidelines. To automate this, let's create a custom command `/quiz-add` that takes category and difficulty as arguments. For example, to add a new intermediate-level quiz to the History category, enter `/quiz-add History medium`.

```
/quiz-add $1 $2
```

1. To create the `/quiz-add` command that automatically generates a new quiz template and includes validation guidelines, enter the following prompt into Claude Code:
   Prompt:

   ```
   Create .claude/commands/quiz-add.md.
   Create a command to add new quizzes.
   Receive $1 as the category and $2 as the difficulty, and process them.
   Make it in the same format as the existing quizzes, and ensure that the
   verification guidelines are strictly followed.
   ```

   Continue while checking the intermediate steps.

2. The new command `quiz-add` has been created. Check the usage and examples.

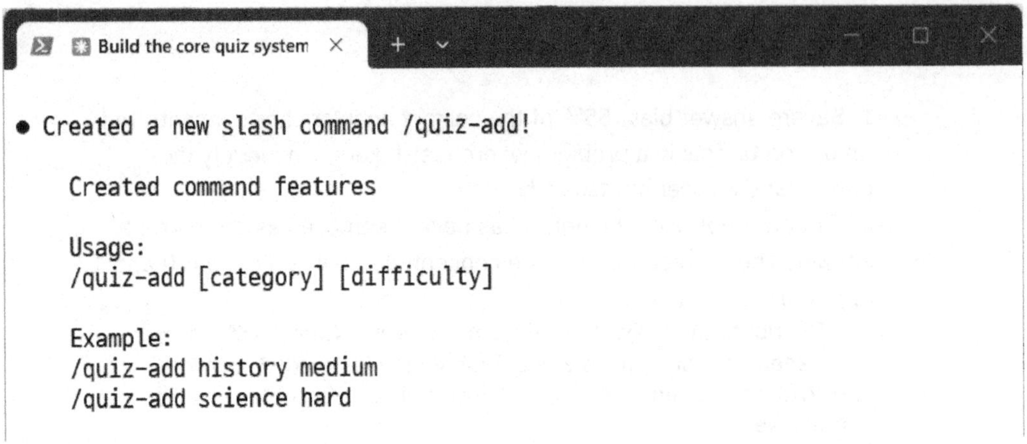

Figure 5.37: Verify the usage and examples

3. After exiting Claude Code with the `/exit` command, restart with the `claude` command. Then, using the newly created command, `quiz-add`, let's add a medium-level History quiz. Enter the following into Claude Code:
   Prompt:

   ```
   /quiz-add History medium
   ```

4. A new quiz has been added to the *History* category.

```
• ✅ Question addition complete!

  A new history question (ID: 40) has been successfully
  added to quiz-data.js.

  Added question:
- Category: History
- Difficulty: medium
- Question: In what year did the French Revolution begin?
- Answer: No. 1 - 1789

  Improvement effects:
- Improved answer position bias in the History category
(utilized option 1)
- Total number of questions: 39 -> 40
- Number of History questions: 9 -> 10
```

Figure 5.38: New quiz added

5. To verify that the new quiz has been added, double-click the `index.html` file in the `Study-03` folder on your desktop to run the quiz game.

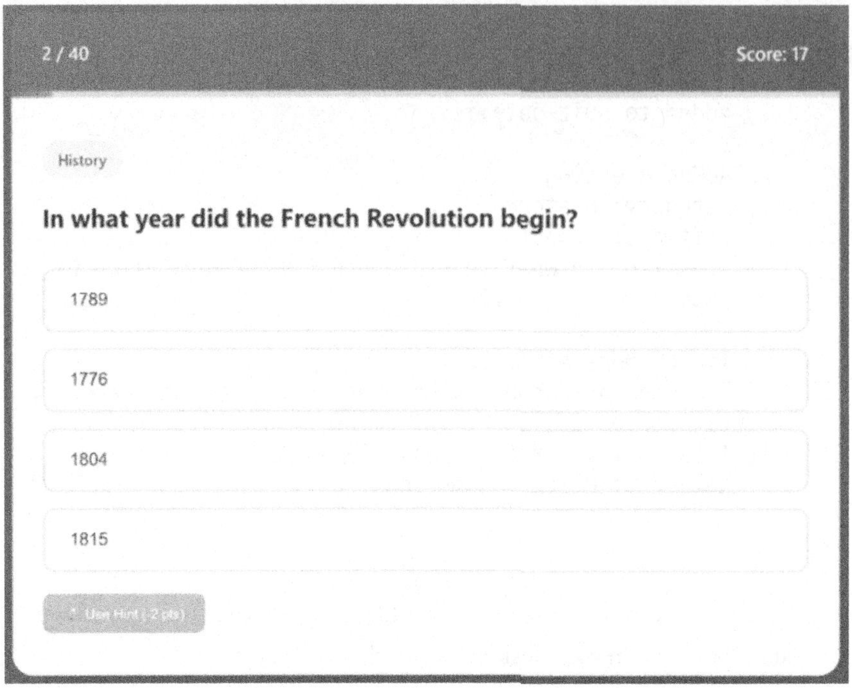

Figure 5.39: Running the new quiz

In this section, we covered how to automate quiz validation, analysis, and creation tasks with custom commands to improve both development efficiency and content quality. The `/quiz-validate` command automatically checks for ambiguous superlative expressions, the `/quiz-range` command analyzes the difficulty and answer distribution for a specific range of quizzes, and the `/quiz-add` command allows you to add new questions by category and difficulty while following consistent guidelines.

As shown, custom commands that use arguments are powerful tools for streamlining repetitive development tasks. In the next section, we'll cover how to connect these commands to project updates and automated workflows.

Wrapping up

Key takeaways summarized in 5 Keywords:

- **Custom commands** are personalized commands that users can define themselves to automate repetitive tasks.
- **Global commands** are defined in the home directory (`~/.claude/commands/`) and can be used across all projects.

- **Project commands** are stored in the current working folder (`.claude/commands/`) and apply only to that project.
- **Arguments** are additional information passed to commands or functions, specifying the target or scope of the task.
- **Placeholders**, such as `$ARGUMENTS, $1, and $2`, are symbols indicating where arguments will be inserted and are replaced with actual values at runtime.

Review questions

1. Select the incorrect statement from the following descriptions:
    1. Project commands can only be used within that project.
    2. Custom commands can be written in natural language.
    3. Custom commands are saved in Python file format.
    4. Commands are saved in Markdown file format.
    5. Flexible operation is possible through parameters.
2. Fill in the blanks:
    1. The location where project-specific custom commands should be stored is (_).
    2. To review problems within a specific number range using a custom command, use argument placeholders such as (_, _).
    3. To receive user input values in a custom command, use an argument placeholder such as (_).
    4. Commands created in `~/.claude/commands` can be used in (_).

Maintenance strategies learned through the use of custom commands

> Note
>
> **Key terms**: Maintenance | Connecting Custom Commands | Integrated Custom Commands
>
> In this section, we will save play records locally and then implement the leaderboard and statistics dashboard.
>
> We will connect multiple custom commands or group them into an integrated command to build a fully automated game production workflow, from adding and

verifying questions to generating reports. This will complete a sustainable AI-based quiz game system.

Before you begin

For a quiz game, it is important to continuously add new questions, fix errors in existing ones, and adjust difficulty levels—ongoing updates and maintenance are essential. However, doing these repetitive tasks manually every day quickly becomes tedious and cumbersome.

Fortunately, AI can automate these maintenance processes as well. With a single command, you can handle daily updates all at once—from adding and verifying questions to statistical analysis and backup. By designing the AI to perform management routines, developers can focus on new ideas and content improvements instead of repetitive tasks.

Step 3: Data storage and ranking system

In step 3, we will store user play records locally and, based on this, implement a leaderboard, ranking table, personal statistics, and dashboard for the game.

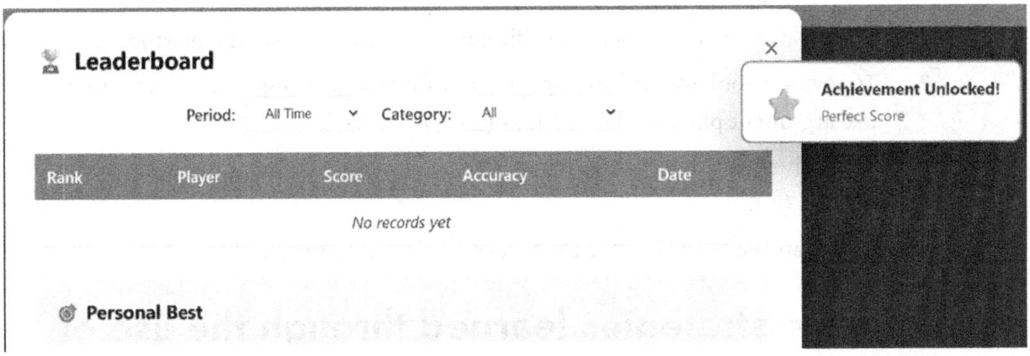

Figure 5.40: Leaderboard

1. Enter the step 3 prompt you created earlier into Claude Code. Once execution is complete, a message will appear indicating completion.

✅ Step 3 Complete: Data Storage and Ranking System

🎯 Implemented Features

1. `LocalDataManager class (data-manager.js)`

- ✅ Automatic game result saving (localStorage)
- ✅ Tracking and updating statistical data
- ✅ Maintaining records of the latest 100 games
- ✅ Category-based statistics management

2. Ranking System

- ✅ Overall / Weekly / Daily Leaderboard
- ✅ Display top 10 records

Figure 5.41: Message showing completion

> **Note**
>
> Go to the book's GitHub Repository. In `PROMPTS.md` (`View the complete prompt collection`), you can find the example prompts presented in this book organized by chapter.
>
> Copy the step 3 prompt from the step-by-step prompts created in the `Creating reliable AI content` section and paste it into Claude Code.

2. Run the `index.html` file in the `Study-03` folder on your desktop to check the leaderboard and statistics dashboard. When you complete the quiz game, detailed statistics will be displayed, and clicking the **Check Ranking** button will show the leaderboard.

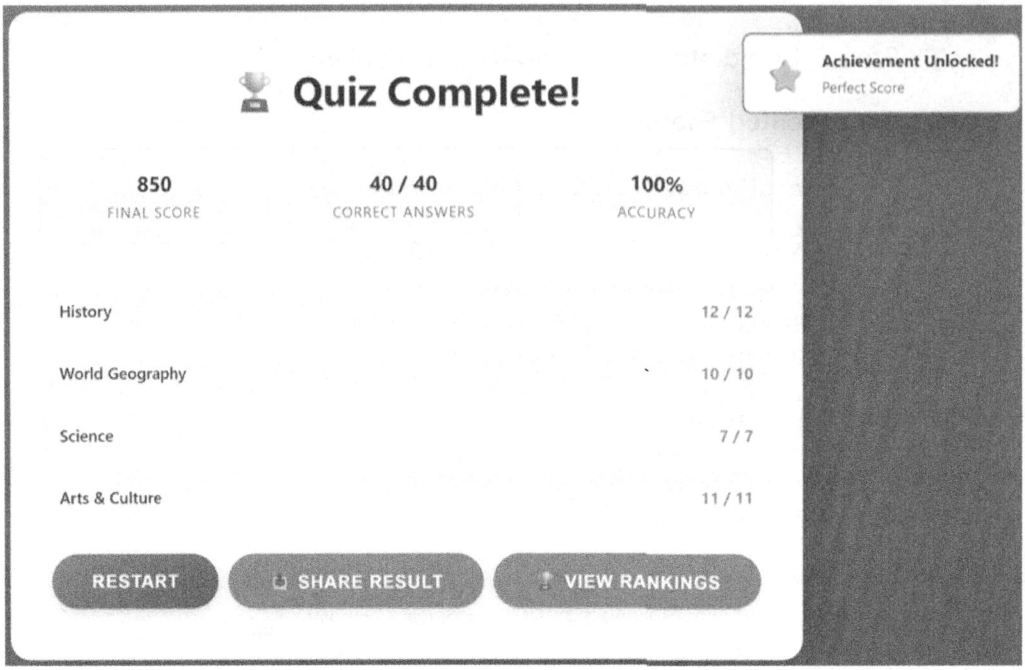

Figure 5.42: Quiz complete score

The following screenshot shows the **Leaderboard**:

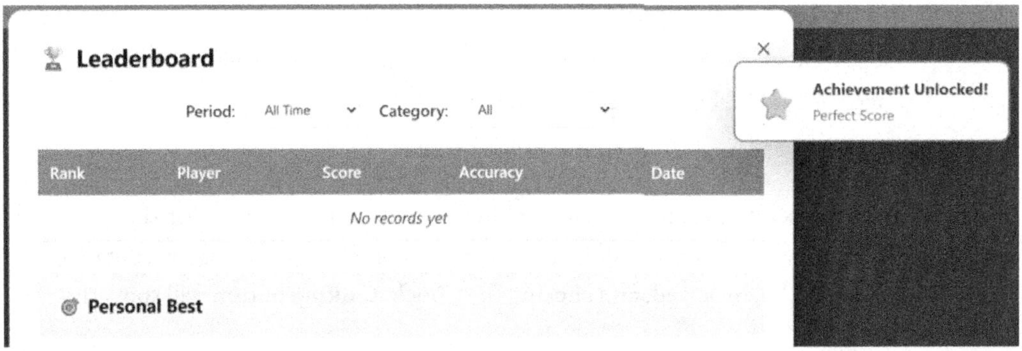

Figure 5.43: Leaderboard

3. Click the **Statistics** button at the top to view the statistics dashboard.

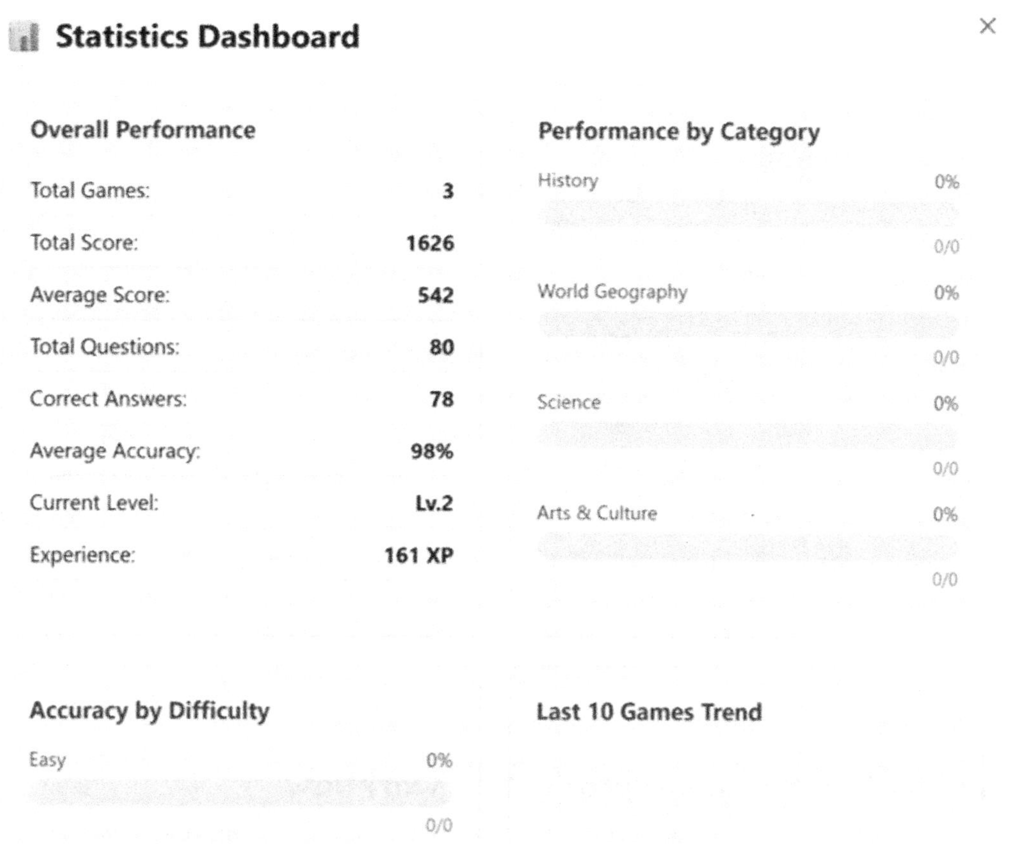

Figure 5.44: Statistics dashboard

4. Click the **Profile** button at the top to edit your user profile.

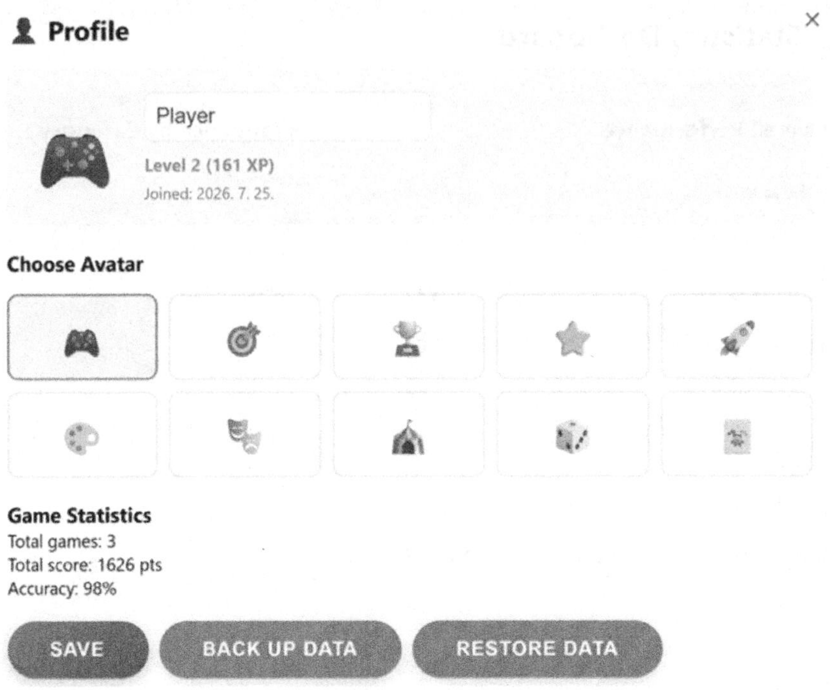

Figure 5.45: Edit user profile

Automating the game production workflow

While custom commands are useful on their own, chaining multiple commands together allows for more powerful automation. We will now bundle the game creation process into a single pipeline to automatically handle the steps of adding problems, verification, statistics, and report generation.

Quiz generation, analysis, and score aggregation

Now, let's create and connect several custom commands to streamline the game production process.

There are three custom commands to create. These three commands will form the core management toolset for automatically maintaining and managing the accuracy of the quiz system:

- `/quiz-check`: A command that automatically verifies whether all quiz answers are correct

- `/quiz-stats`: A command that analyzes all quiz game data and quantifies progress and difficulty distribution
- `/quiz-leaderboard`: A command that aggregates player scores and automatically updates the leaderboard

1. Enter the following into Claude Code to create the necessary commands at once:
   Prompt:

```
Create .claude/commands/quiz-check.md.
It should perform the function of verifying the accuracy of all quiz
answers.
Create .claude/commands/quiz-stats.md.
It should perform the function of managing quiz game statistics.
Create .claude/commands/quiz-leaderboard.md.
It should perform the function of managing the ranking system.
```

2. Verify that the three custom commands have been created.

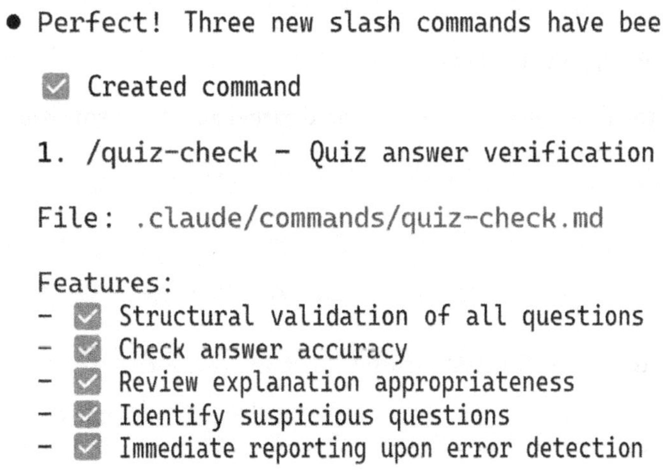

Figure 5.46: Verifying the commands

3. Restart Claude using the `/exit` and `claude` commands. Then, use the `/help` command to check that the new commands have been created successfully.

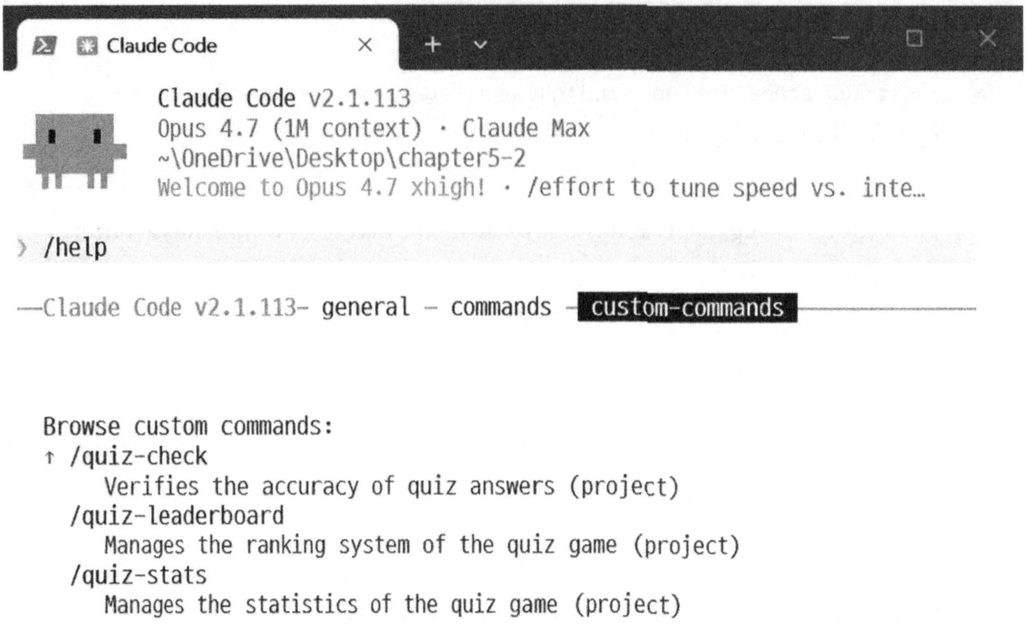

Figure 5.47: Using the /help command

To exit the `/help` command, press the *Esc* key.

4. Now, let's connect the three custom commands created earlier and run them all at once. Enter the following into Claude Code:
   Prompt:

   ```
   Use /quiz-check to verify all questions, /quiz-stats to analyze statistics,
   and /quiz-leaderboard to update the leaderboard, all in a single request.
   ```

5. Claude Code executes the three commands in order. First, the `/quiz-check` command reviews all questions to verify the accuracy of the answers and check for duplicates. Warnings and errors are categorized, and any problematic questions are re-examined. Next, the `/quiz-stats` command displays the current progress and the distribution of questions by category and difficulty as numerical data. Finally, the `/quiz-leaderboard` command tallies player scores and updates the leaderboard.

Overall Task Summary

Step	Result
`/quiz-check`	81 questions / OK 78 / warning 2 / error 1 (Q59 Scandinavia - multiple correct answers)
`/quiz-stats`	No play data / Question pool: History 20 . Geography 21 . Science 20 . Arts & Culture 20
`/quiz-leaderboard`	No registration record

Figure 5.48: Task summary

Complete daily updates at once with an integrated custom command

Next, let's create an integrated custom command that bundles multiple custom commands together to automatically perform daily updates, validation, backup, and reporting in one go. While chaining custom commands is also an option, in real projects, an integrated custom command is usually more practical.

If the same quizzes are presented every time in the quiz game, players will quickly lose interest. Therefore, regular updates are necessary. The integrated custom command `/quiz-daily` that we are about to create executes a sequential pipeline comprising the following steps:

1. Analyzing the quiz data structure
2. Checking the number and distribution of questions
3. Identifying missing categories
4. Checking for duplicates before addition
5. Generating new questions and verifying their format and rules
6. Backing up the entire dataset
7. Outputting a result report.

Since each stage involves verification and error checking, the process halts immediately and reports an error upon failure, whereas success ensures that changes are safely applied.

When creating an integrated custom command, you must follow a few precautions. While maintaining the following conditions, let's create integrated code that updates new questions each time and checks results without hallucinations:

- Make sure to check the file structure
- Test in small units
- Break down complex tasks into steps and validate each one

1. To create the integrated custom command `/quiz-daily`, enter the following into Claude Code:

   Prompt:

   ```
   .claude/commands/quiz-daily.md Create it and perform the following tasks in order.
   1. Read and understand the structure of the file containing the quizzes
   2. Check the current number and distribution of questions
   3. Identify insufficient parts by category
   4. Check for duplicates before adding new questions
   5. Validate the format after adding questions
   6. Back up all data
   7. Report detailed execution results
   Verify at each step, and if it fails, stop immediately and report the error.
   ```

2. When execution is complete, restart Claude Code with the `/exit` command and the `claude` command.

```
● Completed! .claude/commands/quiz-daily.md
  File has been created.

  ✅ Creation complete

  📋 Command function

  /quiz-daily The command performs the following
  tasks in order:

  1. Analyze quiz data structure - read quiz-data.js and
  understand the structure
  2. Check the current number and distribution of questions -
  aggregate by category and difficulty
  3. Identify insufficient parts - categories that need
  improvement
```

Figure 5.49: Execution completed

3. In the `Study-03` folder, run `index.html` to check the results of the daily update performed with the `/quiz-daily` command. You will see that new questions have been added:

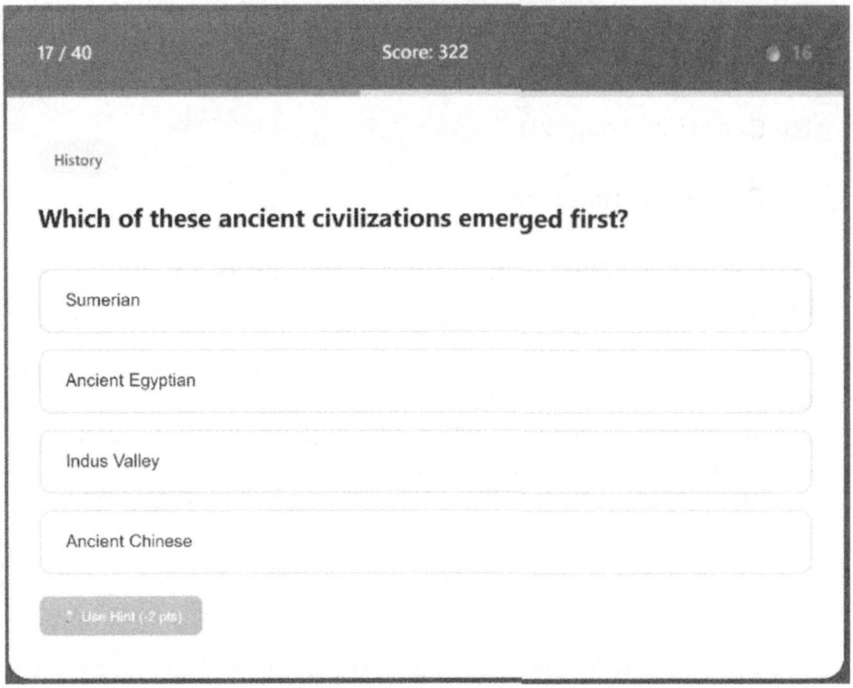

Figure 5.50: New questions added

The assessment pop-up:

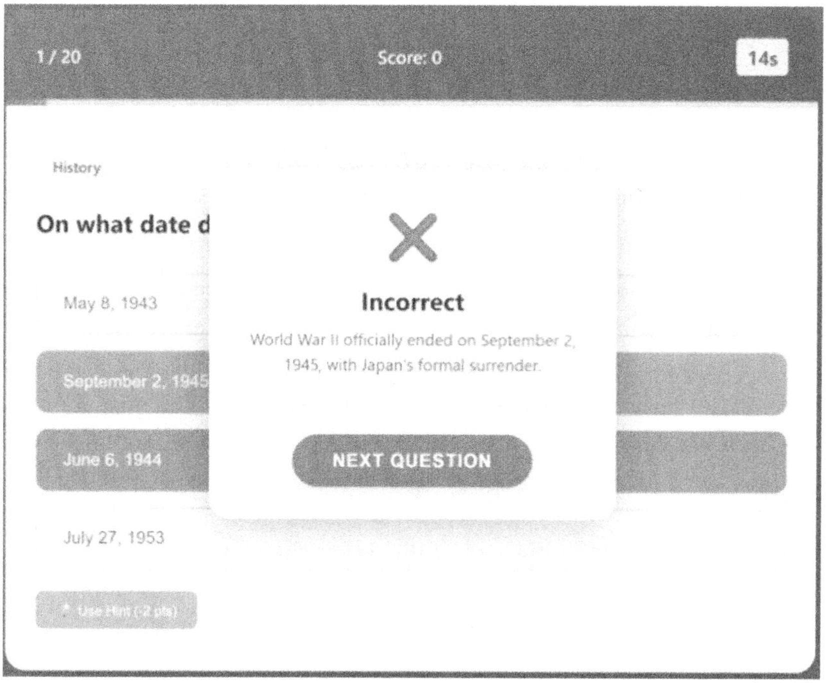

Figure 5.51: Assessment

Custom commands created by Claude Code itself

So far, we've focused on solving questions and checking scores from the player's perspective. Now, let's add a Teacher Mode for viewing and managing player scores. **Teacher Mode** is an integrated management system that automatically collects, analyzes, compares, and visualizes quiz results from multiple players in a report.

This time, let's leave it entirely to Claude Code to determine which custom commands are needed, create them, and even integrate and automate the commands.

1. Enter the following to generate custom commands for Teacher Mode.
   Prompt:

```
Now I want to create a teacher mode that allows you to view and compare the
scores of multiple students who have taken the quiz at a glance.
Please devise and create the custom commands needed for this feature.
And please also create an integrated command that collects and executes
these commands together.
All commands must be saved as .md files in the '.claude/commands/' folder.
```

```
After execution, list and report the created custom commands and their
functions.
```

> **Note**
>
> A quick note on why commands should be documented
>
> When creating custom commands, it is important to save each command as a separate `.md` file in the `.claude/commands/` folder.
>
> This way, the operation and revision history of each command are all recorded in document form, so when you need to update or improve a specific feature later, you only need to modify the relevant command file. As a result, you can safely replace and update individual features while maintaining the overall project, making maintenance and version control much more efficient.

2. When execution is complete, carefully review the report provided by Claude Code. Here, it says you can automatically run Teacher Mode with the integrated command `/teacher-dashboard`.

```
**Features :**

● Completed! Successfully built a custom command system for Teacher Mode.

◎ Integrated Command

6. /teacher-dashboard ★ (Recommended)
  - Execute all of the above commands at once
  - Generate comprehensive report
  - Provide overall class strengths/weaknesses and educational suggestions

File location

All commands are .claude/commands/ folder in .md
```

Figure 5.52: Execution completed

> **Note**
>
> Due to the nature of generative AI, your execution results may differ from those in the book.

3. After running the `/exit` and `claude` commands to restart Claude Code, enter the newly created integrated custom command `/teacher-dashboard`.
4. Once execution is complete, check the teacher mode dashboard file `teacher_report.html` that was created in the `Study-03` folder.

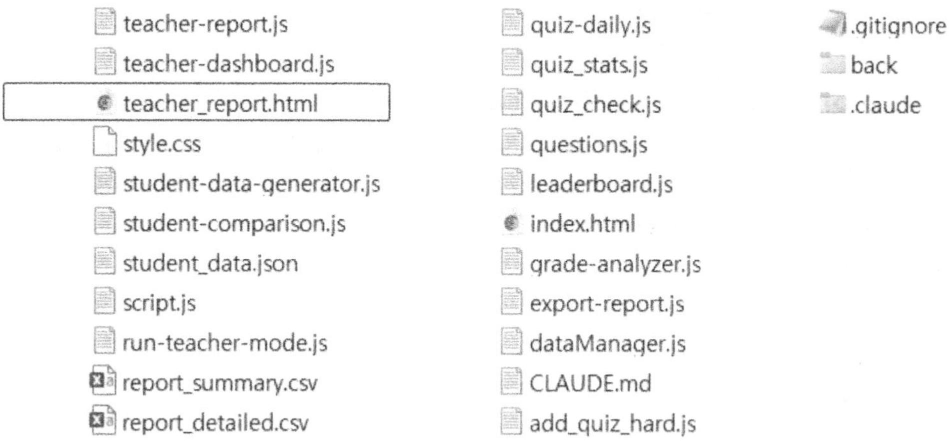

Figure 5.53: teacher mode file created in the Study-03 folder

5. With this, we have created a comprehensive quiz score report page for teachers. Since Claude generates the report from scratch each time, your report will look different from the figure: the student names, scores, and design will all vary. The author's version is available in the book's GitHub repository (`Study-03/Study-03-advanced`).

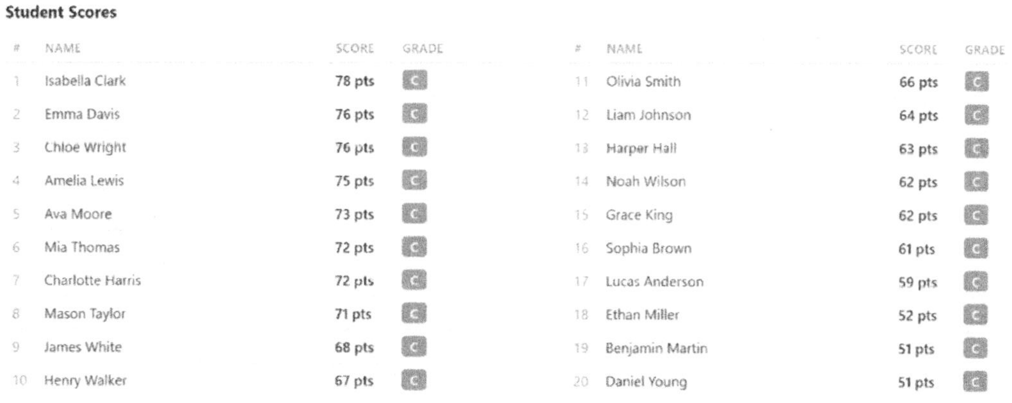

Student Scores

#	NAME	SCORE	GRADE	#	NAME	SCORE	GRADE
1	Isabella Clark	78 pts	C	11	Olivia Smith	66 pts	C
2	Emma Davis	76 pts	C	12	Liam Johnson	64 pts	C
3	Chloe Wright	76 pts	C	13	Harper Hall	63 pts	C
4	Amelia Lewis	75 pts	C	14	Noah Wilson	62 pts	C
5	Ava Moore	73 pts	C	15	Grace King	62 pts	C
6	Mia Thomas	72 pts	C	16	Sophia Brown	61 pts	C
7	Charlotte Harris	72 pts	C	17	Lucas Anderson	59 pts	C
8	Mason Taylor	71 pts	C	18	Ethan Miller	52 pts	C
9	James White	68 pts	C	19	Benjamin Martin	51 pts	C
10	Henry Walker	67 pts	C	20	Daniel Young	51 pts	C

Figure 5.54: Quiz score report page for teachers

Building an efficient maintenance workflow

When developing with AI, you often find yourself having to rebuild the entire system even when you only want to modify a specific part. This happens because the system is not separated by function but is integrated as a whole. By managing each custom command as an independent `.md` file, you can selectively update only the necessary parts while efficiently improving the system without changing the overall structure.

Updating only existing custom commands

The dashboard shown in Teacher Mode includes a `Grade` column, but all players are classified as `C`. This is because the custom command `/create-report` graded absolutely based on the average score. Let's modify the `/create-report` custom command so that it evaluates player grades relatively.

1. To modify the `/create-report` custom command, enter the following into Claude Code:

   Prompt:

   ```
   Please modify .claude/commands/create-report.md as follows.
   Change the grade display to a relative evaluation based on the top
   percentage and display it as follows.
   - Top 20%: A
   - Top 40%: B
   - Top 70%: C
   - Bottom 30%: D
   ```

2. Restart Claude Code and run `/create-report` to re-evaluate the players' grades.

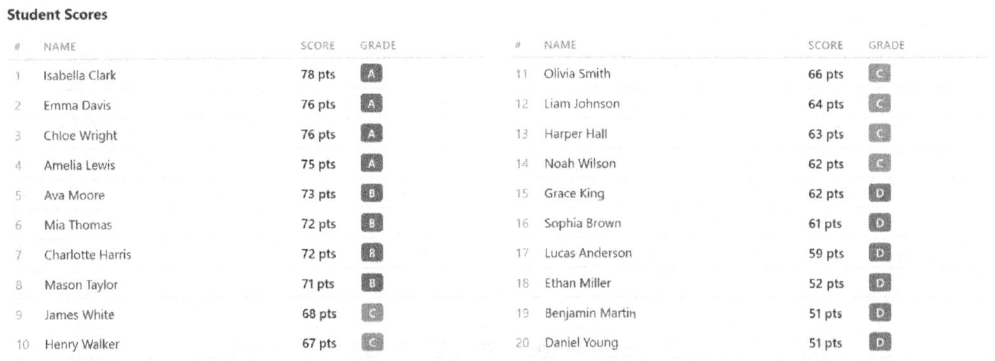

Student Scores

#	NAME	SCORE	GRADE	#	NAME	SCORE	GRADE
1	Isabella Clark	78 pts	A	11	Olivia Smith	66 pts	C
2	Emma Davis	76 pts	A	12	Liam Johnson	64 pts	C
3	Chloe Wright	76 pts	A	13	Harper Hall	63 pts	C
4	Amelia Lewis	75 pts	A	14	Noah Wilson	62 pts	C
5	Ava Moore	73 pts	B	15	Grace King	62 pts	D
6	Mia Thomas	72 pts	B	16	Sophia Brown	61 pts	D
7	Charlotte Harris	72 pts	B	17	Lucas Anderson	59 pts	D
8	Mason Taylor	71 pts	B	18	Ethan Miller	52 pts	D
9	James White	68 pts	C	19	Benjamin Martin	51 pts	D
10	Henry Walker	67 pts	C	20	Daniel Young	51 pts	D

Figure 5.55: Re-evaluated scorecard

Exporting the teacher mode report file

It is also possible to extend only certain features by adding new custom commands to the overall command set. This time, let's add a custom command to export the dashboard data to an external file.

1. To create a new custom command `/export-report` that exports the dashboard generated in Teacher Mode to a file, enter the following into Claude Code:
   Prompt:

   ```
   Create a new file, .claude/commands/export-report.md.
   It should read teacher_report.html and save it as CSV or PDF,
   and add this command to teacher-dashboard.md.
   ```

2. After creating the new `/export-report` command, restart Claude Code and run the `/teacher-dashboard` command. A new file `report_detailed.csv` will be created in the `Study-03` folder.

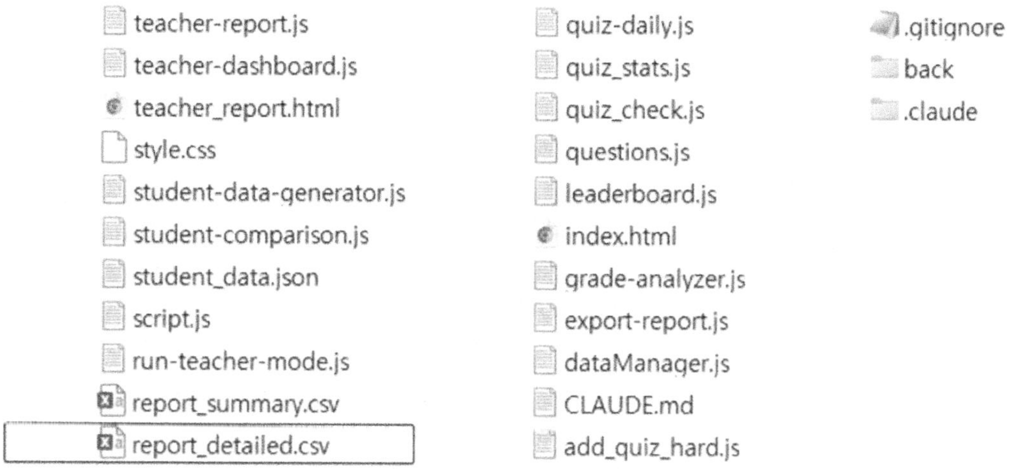

Figure 5.56: New file created in the Study-03 folder

3. If you double-click the CSV file to open it, you can see that the students' evaluation reports are organized inside.

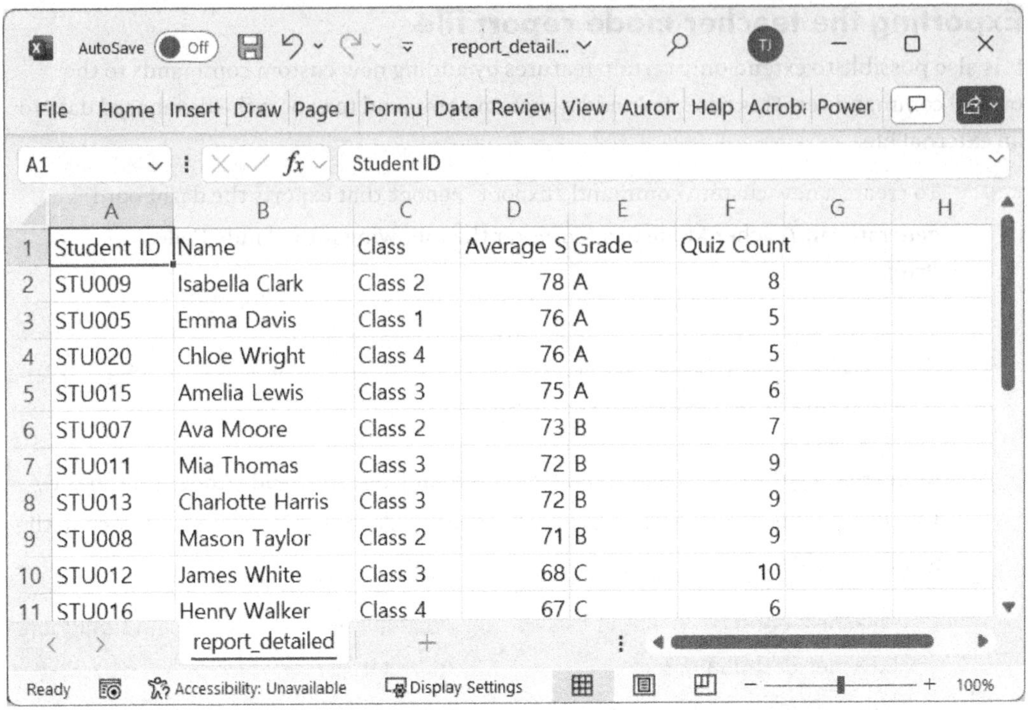

Figure 5.57: CSV file with students' evaluation reports

In this section, we implemented data storage, statistics, and a leaderboard system for the quiz game, and built an automated workflow for efficient management. By linking multiple custom commands, we automated the process of adding questions → validation → statistical analysis → report generation, and learned how to handle daily updates at once with an integrated command.

Additionally, through 'Teacher Mode', we automatically collected and compared the scores of multiple players to create a dashboard. In this process, we had Claude Code generate the necessary commands itself, and experienced a flexible update structure that allows for partial modification or extension of features. By leveraging custom commands and integrated automation, you can reduce repetitive tasks and build a more sustainable development environment in which AI assists with routine management and verification tasks.

Wrapping up

Key takeaways summarized in 3 keywords:

- **Maintenance** is the ongoing process of managing and improving a completed project. By modularizing functions, you can selectively modify only the necessary parts while keeping the overall structure intact.
- By **linking custom commands**, you can automate repetitive tasks by executing commands sequentially with a single request.
- An **integrated custom command** bundles multiple tasks into a single command, making recurring development and maintenance workflows easier to automate.

Review questions

1. Choose the incorrect statement from the following.
    1. Multiple custom commands can be linked and executed with a single request.
    2. Integrated commands can bundle and execute multiple individual commands as one.
    3. Partial updates are possible by modifying only individual command files.
    4. Modularizing commands makes maintenance easier.
    5. Custom commands must be written as Python scripts.
2. Fill in the blanks below:
    1. Custom commands are saved in (_) file format. Custom command files are stored in the (_) folder.
    2. To check the list of created commands, use the (_) command.

6

Giving Claude Code Wings with APIs

Up to now, the programs we've created have relied on pre-prepared data. However, real-world services must handle unpredictable user input. For example, an application that generates recipes from ingredients in a photo requires AI models capable of image analysis and sentence generation.

In this chapter, we'll connect AI models via API to give your application the true power of AI.

Starting from the basic concepts of APIs and moving on to selecting and integrating AI models, you'll learn how to build an AI-powered web application from scratch with Claude Code.

Learning objectives:

- You will be able to understand the concept of APIs and select an appropriate AI model API
- You will be able to utilize AI models through either an API integration platform or direct integration
- You will be able to manage and use API keys in Claude Code
- You will be able to create a real application that integrates image recognition and text generation APIs.

Configuring APIs in Claude Code

Note

Key terms: API | API key | OpenRouter | .env file

An API is a bridge that connects our program to external services. In this section, we will explore various AI model APIs and learn how to select the right model for your project. You'll learn how to use API integration platforms, how to securely manage API keys, and how to actually implement image recognition and text generation features using Claude Code.

Let's practice these steps one by one. Depending on the scale and requirements of your project, you'll learn practical skills for selecting the right API and integrating it efficiently.

Before you begin

When you want to enjoy a meal at a restaurant, you don't talk directly to the chef—you place your order with the waiter. It's the same in software development. Instead of building a complex system yourself, you can simply request what you need from an API and get the results. With Claude Code, API integration becomes even easier. You don't have to write complicated connection code yourself—Claude Code can help generate the API integration, configuration, and error-handling logic. Now, let's build a real application using APIs with Claude Code.

Figure 6.1: Relaying requests through API

API concepts and how to use them

There is something in common between the web portfolio and quiz game we've built so far. The information shown in the web portfolio and the questions in the quiz game were all 'pre-prepared data.' But what if you wanted to build a more elaborate application?

Imagine a program where the user uploads a photo of their refrigerator. The program automatically recognizes the ingredients in the image and recommends recipes using them.

This application can't rely solely on pre-prepared information, because you never know what kind of refrigerator photo will be uploaded. So, you need a vision AI model to read and interpret the image, and a generative AI model to recommend recipes based on the analysis. The next challenge is 'how to integrate these models into your application.' This is where APIs become useful.

An **Application Programming Interface (API)** is a bridge that connects your program to an AI model. Just like calling an expert for help over the phone, your program can ask the AI model to analyze a photo, and the AI will interpret the image and return the results. The application can then display this information on the screen or send additional requests to the AI model API, such as 'make a recipe with these ingredients,' and receive the results. In other words, the web application can focus on handling user interaction and coordinating the API requests, while the AI models perform the image recognition and recipe-generation tasks.

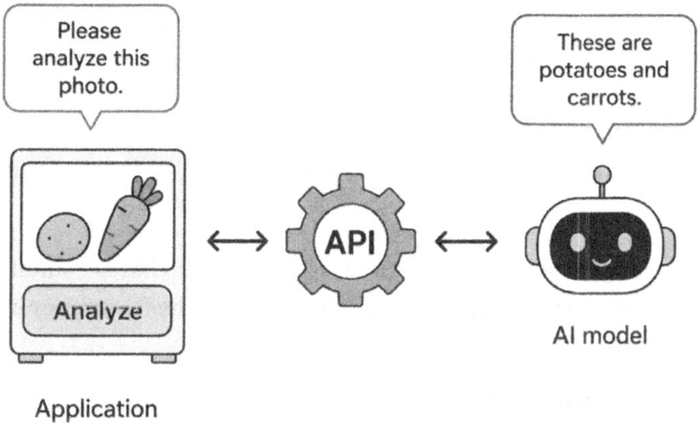

Figure 6.2: Using an API to communicate with an AI model

> **Note**
>
> **Can't you build an AI model yourself without using an API?**
>
> Just like when we built the handwriting recognition model earlier, you can develop your own AI model if you want. However, building complex AI like image recognition or text generation requires massive amounts of training data and high-performance computing resources. In particular, creating a generative language model is as difficult and expensive as developing Claude or ChatGPT.
>
> Therefore, using pre-built AI models via APIs is much more efficient. Since you can use high-performance, ready-made AI models right away, APIs are the most practical choice when you need to complete a project with limited time and resources.

Let's learn how to use AI model APIs with Claude Code to build a web application called **FridgeChef**, which analyzes ingredients in refrigerator images and generates recipes.

Selecting an AI Model

APIs come in many types depending on their purpose. For example, there are APIs for weather forecasting, news collection, and map services. Many AI providers make their models available through APIs so that other applications can use them. Because these services may process user data and incur usage costs, access is typically controlled through API keys. By connecting to Claude's API, every time a user requests a recipe, you can get results as if Claude were answering directly. However, for large AI services like Claude or ChatGPT that operate on a paid basis, you will be charged according to your API usage. If your user base suddenly grows, it may be difficult to handle the increased costs. Therefore, you should carefully decide which API to use.

Fortunately, some providers offer free or limited-access models that are suitable for learning and experimentation. When you're just getting familiar with the features or building an initial version, these free APIs are the best place to start.

OpenRouter is an API integration platform that brings together various AI model APIs in one place. You can easily compare paid and free APIs at a glance, and also see which APIs are popular. This makes it easy to find the API you want and choose the model that best fits your project. Now, let's access OpenRouter and select the API that's right for your project.

Note

Why Use OpenRouter?

There are two main ways to use AI models.

The first is to use an API integration platform like OpenRouter. Just like ordering food from various restaurants at a food court, OpenRouter offers a variety of AI models such as Claude, GPT, and Google Gemma all in one place. Once you receive an API key, you can access and switch between many supported models, and conveniently manage your usage from a single dashboard.

Obtaining an API key

The second method is to use each AI company's official API directly. For example, you could connect directly to the GPT API from OpenAI or the Claude API from Anthropic. In this case, you need to sign up with each company and obtain separate API keys, which can be a bit cumbersome to manage, but you get access to the latest features as soon as they're available.

If you're a beginner, it's recommended to start with OpenRouter. You can easily compare different models, and there are plenty of free models you can try out. However, free usage is rate-limited, and the limits change from time to time. Check OpenRouter's limits page for the current figures. So, if you find yourself consistently using a particular model, it might be a good idea to connect directly to the company's official API at that point.

An API key is, as the name suggests, a secret key used to authenticate users when accessing an API. It's a core tool for authentication, access control, usage tracking, and billing. The server providing the API uses this key to verify who sent the request and whether it came from an authorized user.

Without appropriate authentication, an API could be accessed by unauthorized users, potentially leading to misuse, unexpected costs, or exposure of sensitive data. Additionally, servers use API keys to track how often and how much each user is calling the API, which helps limit excessive requests and manage billing.

You also need an API key to use APIs on OpenRouter. Let's go ahead and issue an API key. Create a new folder called `Study-04` inside your `VibeCoding` folder.

1. Open your web browser and go to OpenRouter (`openrouter.ai`). Click the **Sign in** button at the top of the homepage to start the registration process.
2. In this book, we'll sign up using a Google account. Click the Google logo in the center.

3. Enter your Google ID and click the **Continue** button to proceed with registration. Agree to the access terms, and click **Continue** to complete your registration.
4. Return to the OpenRouter main screen. To register your API key, click the profile icon at the top right and select the **Workspaces** | **API Keys** menu.

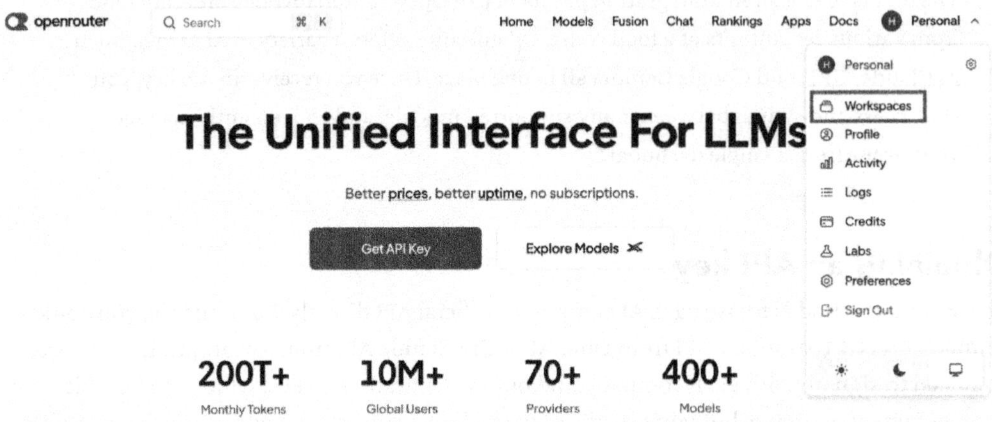

Figure 6.3: Navigate to the Workspaces | API Keys menu

5. Click the **+ New Key** button.

Figure 6.4: Create an API key

6. In the **Name** field, enter **HonGong-Vibe** to give your key a name. Click the **Create** button to issue your API key.

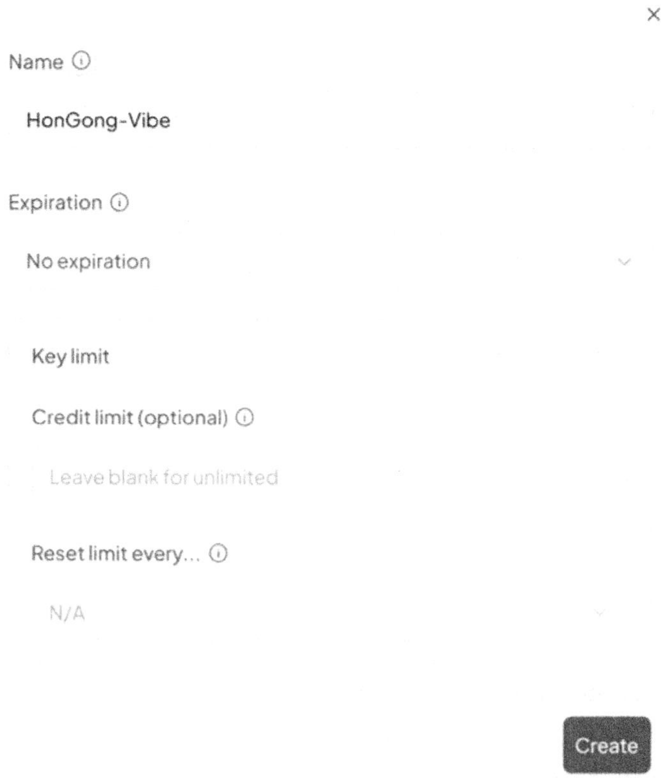

Figure 6.5: Provide a name for the key and generate the API key

> **Note**
>
> If you work on multiple projects later, you can create additional keys as needed.

7. The actual API key will be displayed on the screen. For security reasons, you can only view this API key once. If you leave the page or refresh, you won't be able to see it again, so be sure to copy and save it somewhere safe.
8. Click the *Copy* icon on the screen, then open Notepad or a text file, paste the key, and save it. You'll need this key later to use paid APIs after purchasing credits, so be careful not to expose it to others and manage it securely.

> **Tip**
>
> Never upload the text file containing your API key to a shared cloud storage. It could be stolen and misused by automated collection bots. Instead of a shared folder, keep it only on your personal local computer.

9. Your API key has now been created.

Figure 6.6: You can see the API key created

10. Launch **Notepad**, the default text editor in Windows, and type `OPENROUTER_API_KEY=`, then paste the API key you received from OpenRouter after the = sign.

```
OPENROUTER_API_KEY=<OpenRouter API Key>
```

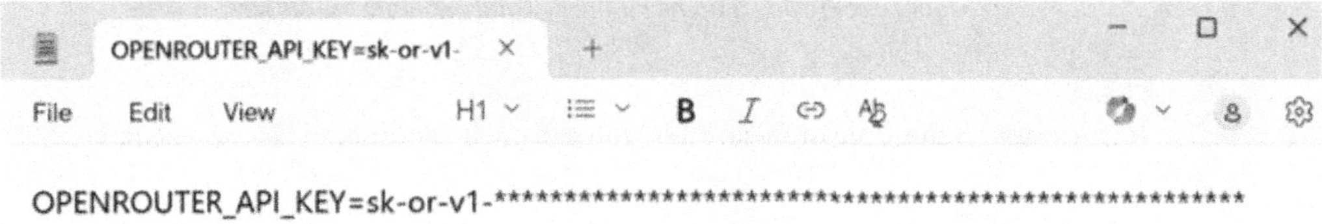

Figure 6.7: Enter the OpenRouter API key you generated

11. Click the **File** | **Save As** menu.
12. Navigate to the `Study-04` folder, then enter `.env` as the file name. Be sure to change the **File Type** to **All Files (.)**. At the bottom, set **Encoding** to **UTF-8** and click the **Save** button.
13. Verify that a `.env` file containing your OpenRouter API key has been created in the `Study-04` folder.

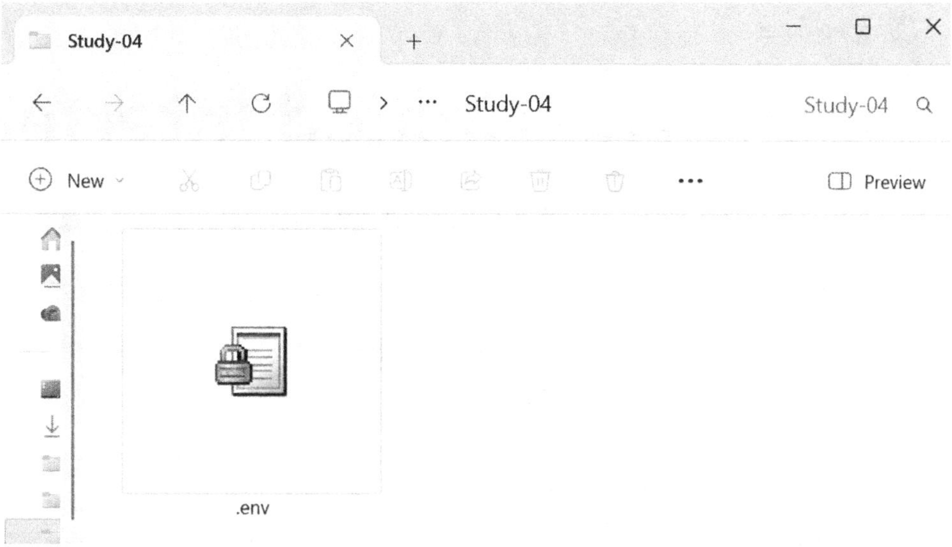

Figure 6.8: .env file created in the Study-04 folder

Exploring free AI models

The models needed for the FridgeChef app are an image recognition model and a generative language model for recipe recommendations.

Among the AI models provided by OpenRouter, let's filter for those that are free and fit our purpose, and select one that offers suitable performance.

1. At the top of the OpenRouter home screen, click the **Models** menu.

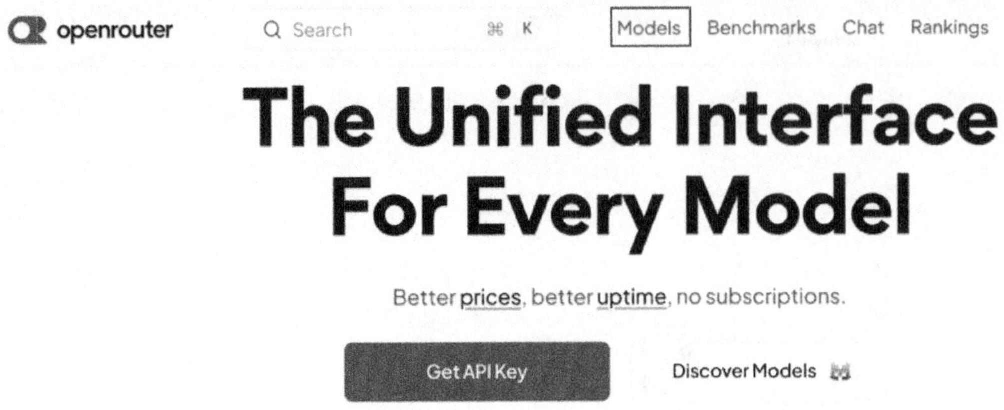

Figure 6.9: Navigate to the Models menu

2. To filter for free APIs only, find the **Prompt pricing** filter in the left sidebar and drag the slider handle to **FREE**.

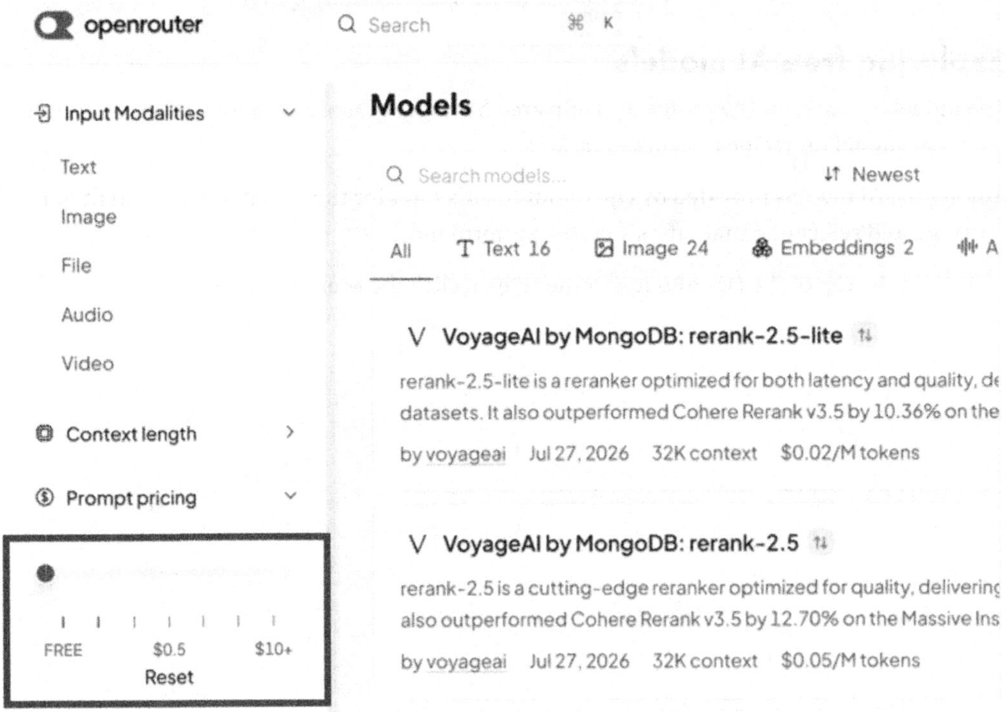

Figure 6.10: Set the pricing to FREE

Models marked as 'free' on OpenRouter are free to use, but they cap both requests per minute and requests per day. For learning purposes, these limits are usually sufficient, and your usage history can be checked in the **Activity** menu on OpenRouter. Of course, if you later run a real service with many users accessing at once, you should consider paid models or purchasing credits.

> **Tip**
>
> **How to check AI model rankings**
>
> Click the **Rankings** menu at the top of OpenRouter to view the popularity rankings of various models at a glance. The most-used models are displayed with usage graphs. While most are paid APIs, free models marked as 'free' are sometimes included in the rankings.
>
> 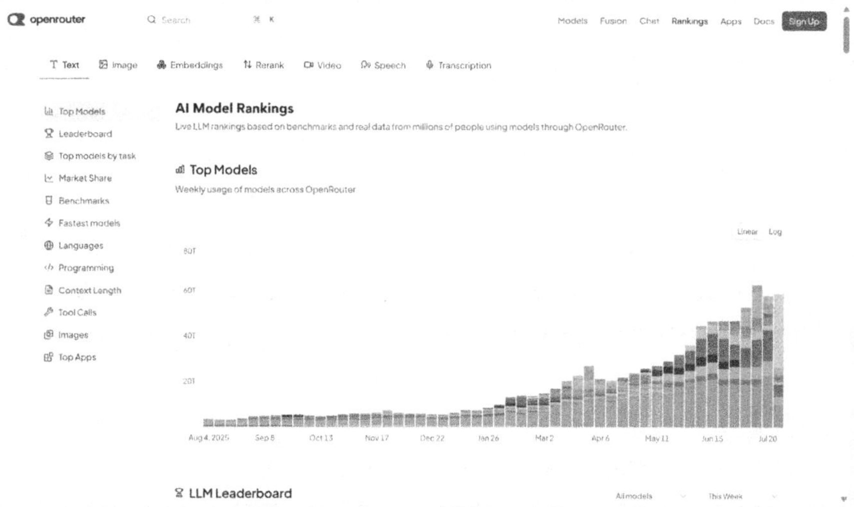
>
>
> *Figure 6.11: Check the leaderboard*

Exploring image recognition AI models

1. In the left sidebar of the OpenRouter main page, select **Image** under the **Input Modalities** filter. This will filter for models related to image input and processing. Select the model you want from the filtered list. Here, let's click Google: Gemma 4 26B A4B (free).

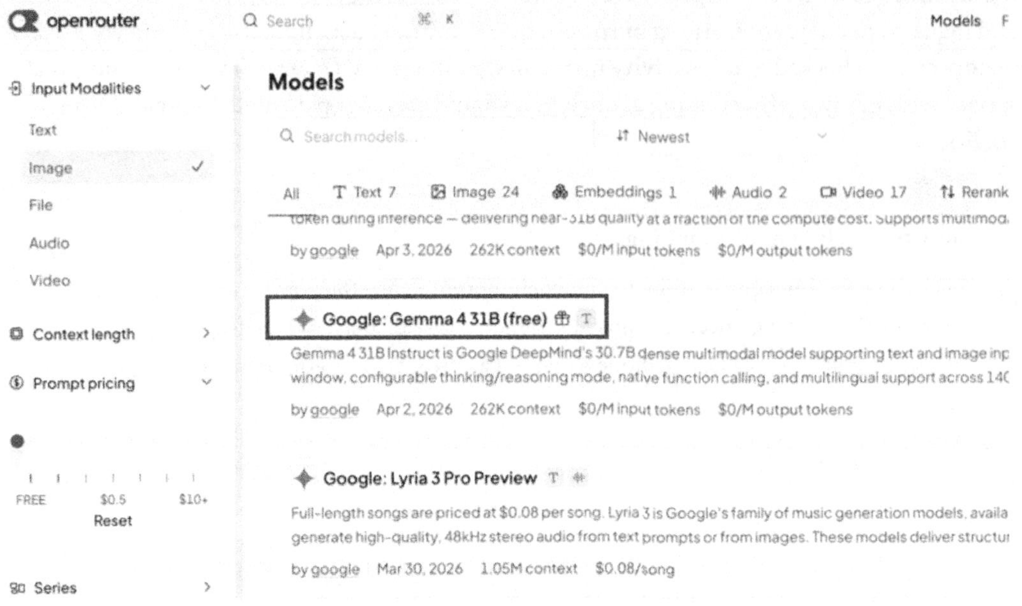

Figure 6.12: Selecting the AI model

Note

The available free models change frequently. If this model is not available, feel free to choose another free model.

Tip

Policy on use of input data when using free models

There is one thing to keep in mind when using free AI models. Some free models may store the prompts you enter and the responses generated, or use them for model improvement and training. Google's Gemma(free) model is one such example.

To use free models on OpenRouter, you must enable this option. In your profile, go to **Settings** | **Privacy & Guardrails** and toggle **Enable free endpoints that may train on inputs** to activate it.

> When you enable this option, your input data may be used for model training, but you will be able to use free models. For more details, check each model's page.

2. Click the Copy icon to copy the model name and save it in a text file.

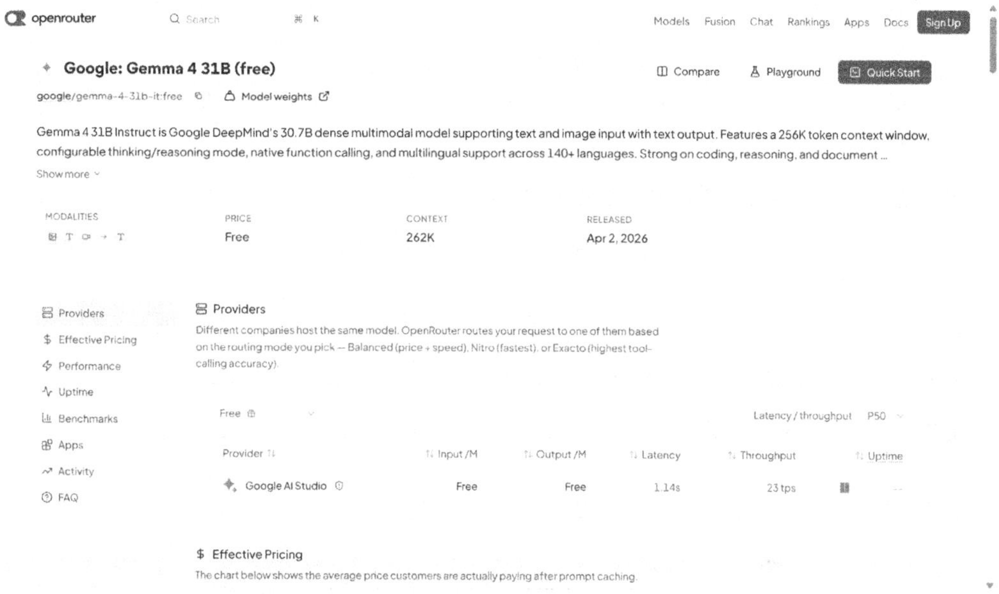

Figure 6.13: Copy the model name and save it

Exploring text generation AI models

1. In the **Input Modalities** filter, select **Text**. Here, search for and select **OpenAI: gpt-oss-20b (free)** from the filtered models. If this model is not available, feel free to choose another free model.

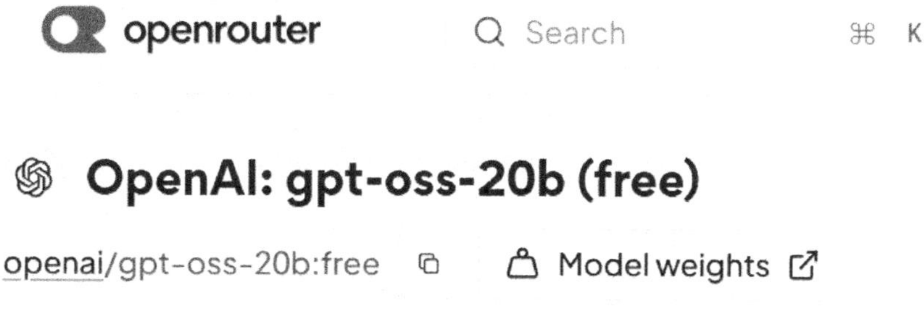

Figure 6.14: Select the OpenAI gpt-oss model

> **Note**
>
> If you don't see the model suggested in the book, you can select any model you want. For reference, the Google: Gemma 4 26B A4B (free) model you selected earlier for image recognition also supports text generation, so you can use that model as well.

2. Click the *Copy* icon to copy the model name and save it in a text file.

So far, you've checked your OpenRouter API key and the names of the AI models you'll use. You're now ready to use the API.

Connect and test the AI model

Now it's time to integrate the API into Claude Code and build the recipe recommendation application, **FridgeChef**.

Open your desktop file explorer, select the `Study-04` folder inside the `VibeCoding` folder, right-click, and select **Open in Terminal** to launch the terminal.

Register the API key

1. Type `claude` in the terminal to run Claude Code.
2. To initialize the project, enter the `/init` command.

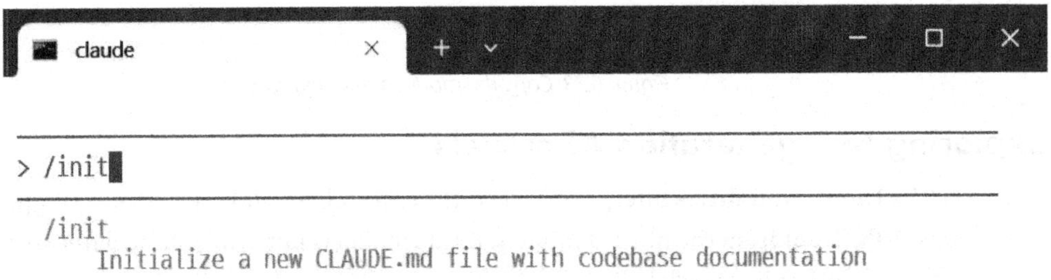

Figure 6.15: Initialize the project using the /init command

3. Verify that a `CLAUDE.md` file has been created in the `Study-04` folder.
4. Now, let's make the `.env` file containing the API key you received from OpenRouter available for use in Claude Code. Enter the following prompt in Claude Code.

   Prompt:

```
I saved the API key I received from OpenRouter in the .env file. Please set
it up so I can use this key securely.
```

> **Note**
>
> For security reasons, it is not recommended to enter the API key directly into the prompt.

5. The API key has been configured in the project.

```
API Key Setup

● Completed! The OpenRouter API key has been set up as follows for safe
  usage:

  Generated files:

  1. .gitignore - Protects the .env file from being committed to Git
  2. .env.example - Environment variable template for other developers
  3. config.js - Utility for safely loading and validating environment variables
  4. example.js - Example code for using the OpenRouter API
  5. package.json - Node.js project configuration file

  Usage:

  // Using the API key in another file
  const config = require('./config');

  const apiKey = config.openRouter.apiKey;
  const baseUrl = config.openRouter.baseUrl;

  Security features:

  - .env file is excluded from Git version control
```

Figure 6.16: API key is configured

6. If you check the `Study-04` folder, you will see that a `.gitignore` file and other auxiliary configuration and project management files have been newly created.

You can check the generated files through the explanations in the terminal. Among them, the following two files are important:

- `.env`: Environment variable file where the API key is stored; it is referenced every time the API is called.
- `.gitignore`: A configuration file that prevents specified untracked files, such as `.env`, from being added to version control.

Note

Understanding the .env and .gitignore files

The `.env` file is a special file used to store program configuration values. It is a standard practice to manage sensitive information like API keys separately from the program code. When you set up an API key, Claude Code automatically creates the `.env` and `.gitignore` files, following this industry best practice.

If you put the API key directly in your code, anyone can see it when you upload to GitHub. However, if the `.env` file is listed in `.gitignore` before it is committed, Git will ignore it, reducing the risk of accidentally publishing the key with your code. Also, during development, you can use a free API and later switch to a paid API for production simply by changing the `.env` file, without modifying the code. This is also useful for team projects: if each member needs to use a different API key, you can share the code but set up individual `.env` files to avoid conflicts.

Testing API Integration

1. For image recognition, we will use Google's Gemma model, and for the generative language model, we will use OpenAI's gpt-oss model. Check the names of each model you have saved and enter the following prompt.
   Prompt:

```
Now test whether the prepared API actually works.
For image recognition, use the google/gemma-4-26b-a4b-it:free model,
For text generation, use the openai/gpt-oss-20b:free model.
Test both text and image recognition via the API and let me know the
results.
```

Tip

When applying the API in OpenRouter, you must enter the model name exactly.

2. The API test was successful.

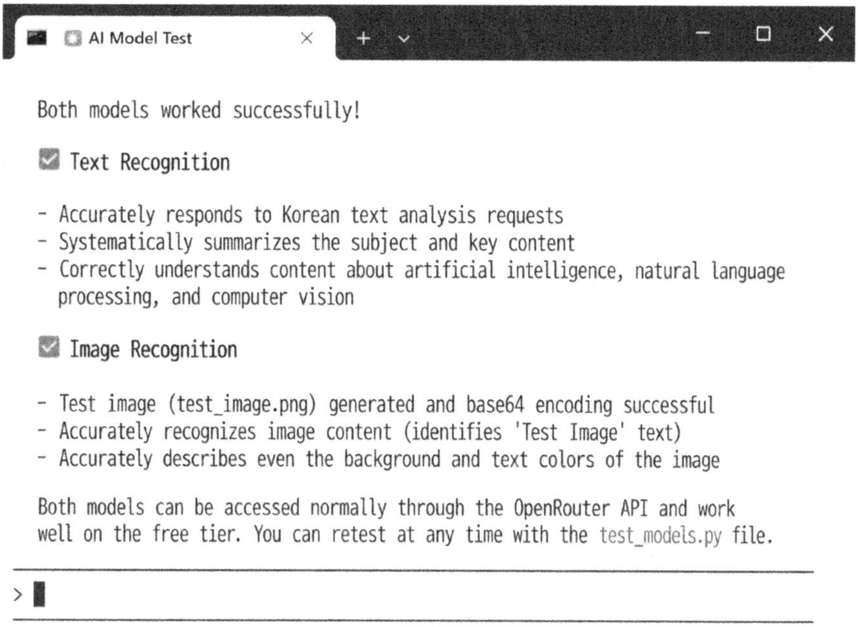

Figure 6.17: Test successful

3. You can check whether the API key was actually used in OpenRouter. Log in to the OpenRouter website, click your profile icon, and select the **Activity** menu.
4. On the **Activity** page, the dashboard shows **Total spend**, **Requests** (request count), **Token volume**, and per-model usage for the Gemma and gpt-oss calls you have just made.

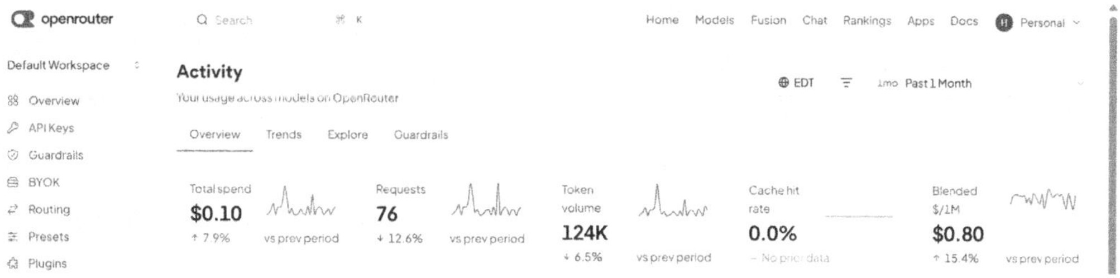

Figure 6.18: Records of actual usage on the Activity page

So far, you have integrated the API into Claude Code. Next, let's use external AI models to build the FridgeChef application.

Wrapping up

Key takeaways in five keywords:

- An **API** is a bridge that connects external AI services and your program, allowing you to leverage complex AI features with simple requests through a set of communication rules.
- On **API integration** platforms like OpenRouter, you can compare and select various AI models all in one place.
- To access an API service, you must obtain an **API key** for user authentication.
- To integrate various AI models into your application via API, have Claude Code create the following configuration files in your project folder.
    - `.env`: A file that stores the API key and is referenced every time the API is called.
    - `.gitignore`: A configuration file that prevents certain files from being uploaded to GitHub to protect your API key from being leaked.

Review questions

1. Select all the items required to use the API in OpenRouter.
    1. API key
    2. Model name
    3. Own server
    4. `.gitignore` file
2. Select the option that is NOT a secure way to manage API keys in Claude Code.
    1. Store API key in `.env` file
    2. Add `.env` to `.gitignore` file
    3. Hardcode API key directly in code
    4. Reference the key only within the project folder
3. Which of the following is NOT information you can check in the Activity menu on OpenRouter?
    1. Model name used
    2. Time of use
    3. Code content called
    4. API call history

FridgeChef: built with Claude Code and API

> **Note**
>
> **Key terms:** Integration of Multiple AI Models| Web Framework
>
> Let's create a practical application that solves everyday problems using APIs.
>
> To implement the application, we will write a PRD and systematize the production process, applying efficient development methodologies used in the field. By following a structured application development method, you will add and test features step by step, experiencing a real-world development process.

Before you begin

Everyone has probably opened their refrigerator and wondered, 'What should I eat today?' at least once. With Claude Code, you can directly create practical apps that solve these everyday problems. The application we will build in this section is FridgeChef. When you upload a photo of the inside of your fridge to the app, it recognizes the ingredients and recommends suitable recipes based on what you have.

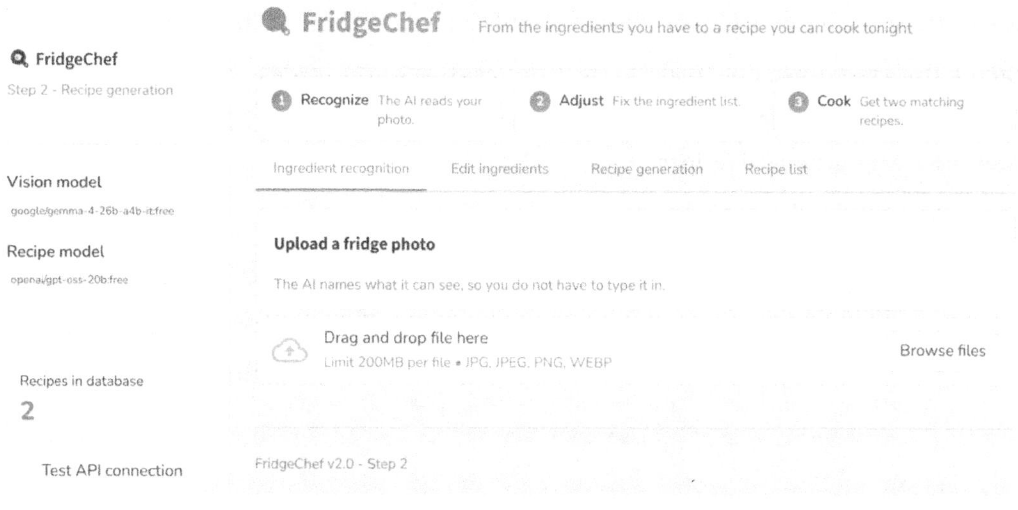

Figure 6.19: Snapshot of the welcome page

Writing a PRD for application implementation

Now it's time to create a prompt for building the FridgeChef application. Since the prompt is a key element that determines the direction and quality of the work, you should review the details, clarify the requirements, and spell out the execution steps. Once again, we will proceed by creating a PRD.

Up to the previous chapter, you created prompts in Claude Web, checked them, and then copied them into Claude Code. This time, we will proceed directly in Claude Code. By using `.md` files, you can structure and write detailed execution prompts in PRD format, just as you did before.

Establishing a step-by-step plan

The FridgeChef application requires two AI models. One is an image recognition model that analyzes the ingredients in the refrigerator photo, and the other is a text generation model that suggests recipes using those ingredients. When developing complex applications that require integration of multiple AI models like this, it is efficient to break down the entire project into smaller units and develop them incrementally.

For the FridgeChef application, we will first implement the core features, check if they work properly, and then add detailed features step by step. This way, if any issues arise, you can fix them at each stage and gradually improve the completeness of the application.

Let's divide the web application development process into three stages and create a `.md` file for each stage to produce the PRD:

Step 1: Use an image recognition model to identify ingredients from a refrigerator photo.

Step 2: Use a text generation model to create recipes that can be made with the recognized ingredients.

Step 3: Save the generated recipes.

Creating a PRD in Claude Code:

1. Enter the following prompt in Claude Code:
   Prompt:

   ```
   Using the previously created OpenRouter API, I want to build a web
   application that recognizes ingredients from a refrigerator photo and
   recommends recipes. Please create a PRD divided into three steps as
   follows.
   Step 1: Receive an image as input and use the google/gemma-4-26b-a4b-
   it:free model to recognize the image.
   Step 2: Use the information obtained in Step 1 and the openai/gpt-
   oss-20b:free model to generate recipes.
   Step 3: Create a user profile and save the recipes.
   Save each step as PRD_step1.md, PRD_step2.md, and PRD_step3.md.
   ```

2. The following is a summary of the completed PRD used in this book.

```
PRD_step1.md - Core Image Recognition Feature (5 days)
- Streamlit-based web interface
- Ingredient recognition in the refrigerator using the Gemma 4 model
- Image upload and processing
- Basic UI construction

PRD_step2.md - Recipe Generation System (7 days)
- Recipe generation using the gpt-oss model
- Ingredient editing feature
- Filtering and search
- Recipe detail view
- SQLite database

PRD_step3.md - User Profile and Save Feature (10 days)
- User authentication system (sign up/login)
- Profile management and personal settings
- Recipe saving and folder management
- Personalized recommendation algorithm
- Dashboard and statistics
- Social sharing feature
```

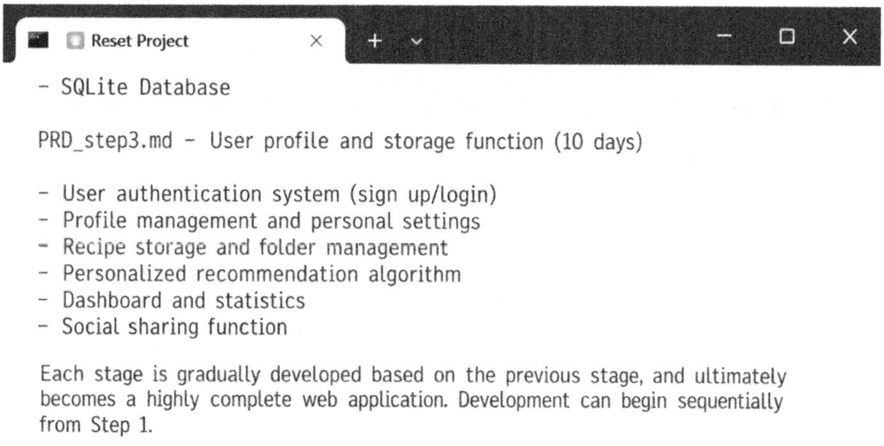

Figure 6.20: Your screen might look slightly different. Proceed using your own PRD.

3. You can see that three step-by-step PRD documents have been created in the `Study-04` folder.

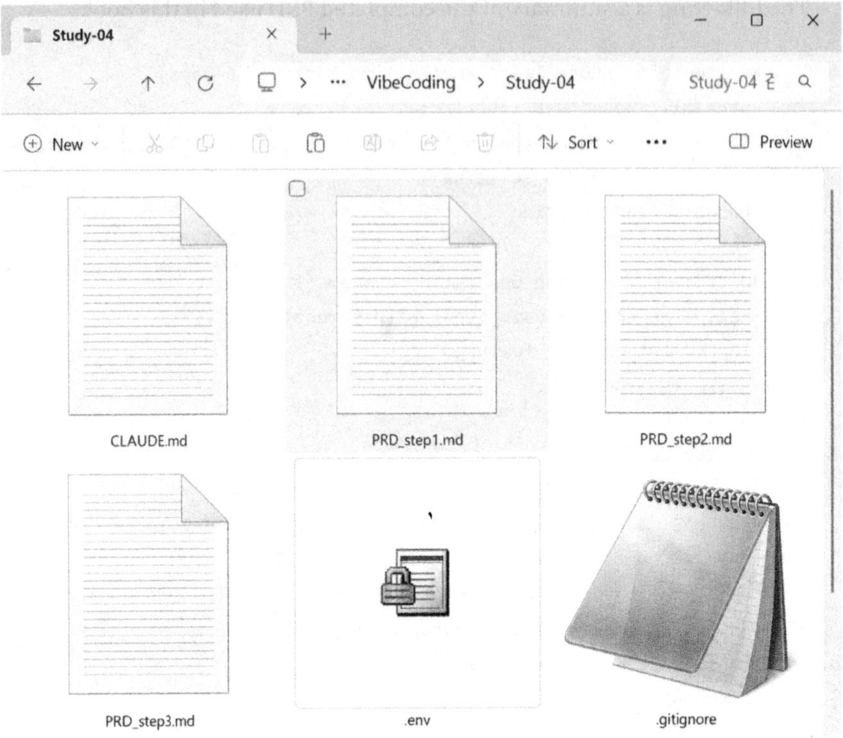

Figure 6.21: PRD documents created in the Study-04 folder

Now, based on the completed PRD, let's implement the first step.

Step 1: Recognizing ingredients from a refrigerator image

1. Enter the following prompt to instruct the execution of the first PRD.

   Prompt:

   ```
   Run PRD_step1.md
   ```

2. The image recognition feature has been implemented according to the given `Step 1` prompt. Claude Code built the web interface using the Python web framework Streamlit.

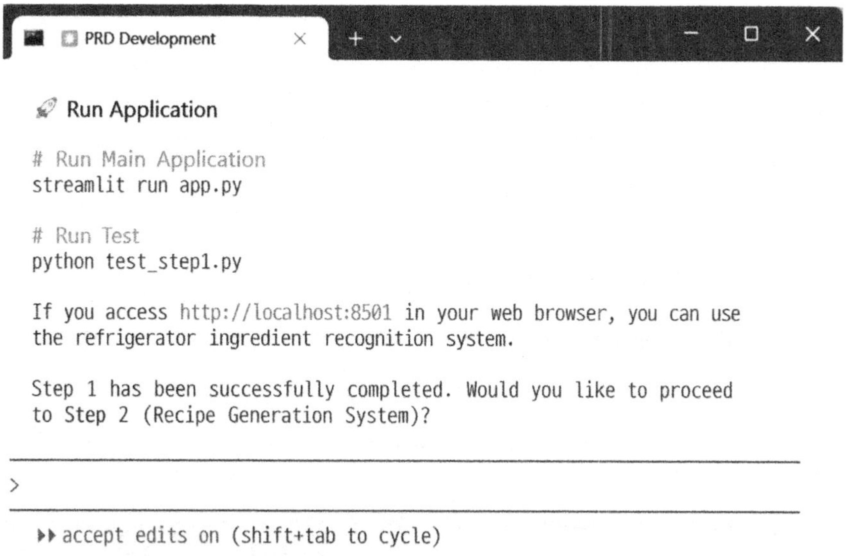

Figure 6.22: Step 1 implementation

> **Note**
>
> You can observe the coding process in real time through the terminal as the code is generated.

3. Now we need to check if it actually works. If the web server is not running yet, ask Claude Code to start the server as well.
   Prompt:

```
Run the main application and let me test the results of Step 1.
```

> **Note**
>
> **What is a Python web framework?**
>
> A web framework is a collection of tools that helps you easily build web applications. Normally, to create a web application, you have to separately program the structure with HTML, the design with CSS, and the behavior with JavaScript. However, with a Python web framework, you can handle all of this in a single Python file, making the structure much simpler.
>
> Common Python options for this type of application include **Streamlit**, **Gradio**, and **Flask**. Among these, Streamlit is especially popular for demonstrating AI

models or visualizing data, and is useful for showcasing AI features like image recognition or text generation on the web.

The command to run the server varies depending on the framework used. Of course, if you directly ask Claude Code to run it, it will automatically use the appropriate command:

- If using Streamlit: `streamlit run app.py`
- If using Flask: `python app.py`
- If using Gradio: `python gradio_app.py`

4. Once the server is running, a URL you can use to access it will be displayed in the terminal.

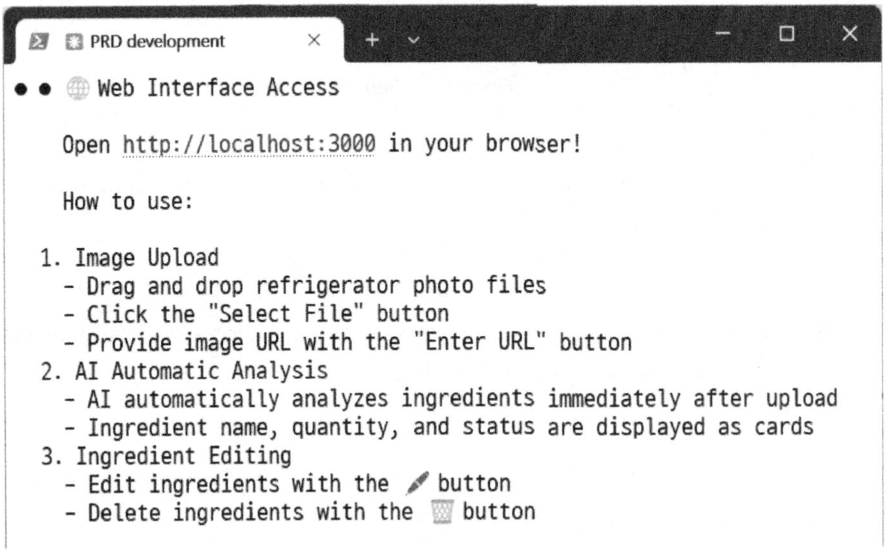

Figure 6.23: URL generated to access the app

> **Note**
>
> The localhost port number may vary for each user.

5. Copy the localhost address and paste it into your browser to check the results implemented so far.

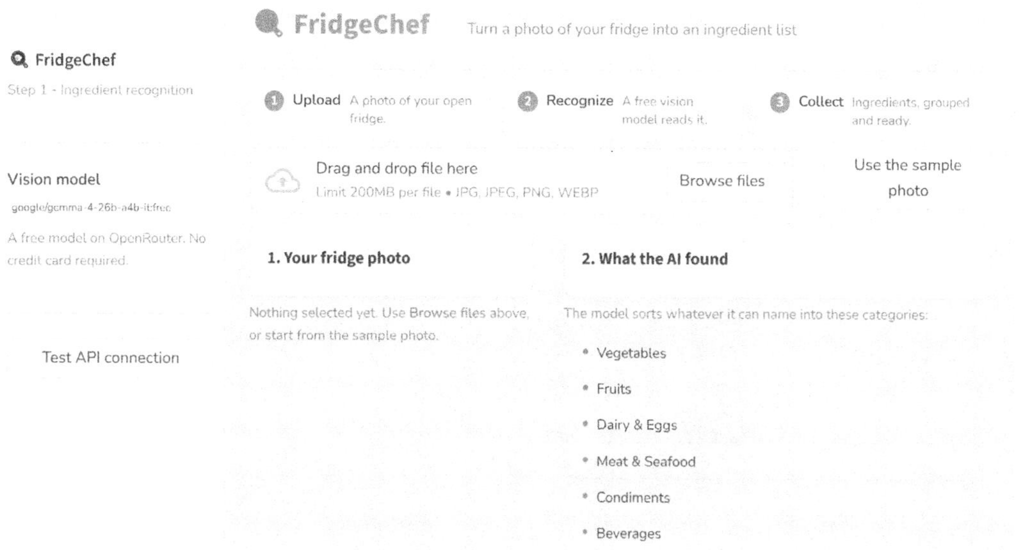

Figure 6.24: Open the page in the browser to see how it looks

> **Note**
>
> You can also open the actual web page in your browser by holding the *Ctrl* key and clicking the address in the terminal.
>
> Due to the nature of generative AI, the specific elements of the created application may vary slightly with each execution.

6. Let's test the functionality. Download the fridge.jpg file in advance from the input-examples folder in the book's GitHub repository: `https://github.com/PacktPublishing/Build-with-Claude-Code`. Then, click the Browse files button, select the fridge.jpg file, and click the Recognize ingredients button.

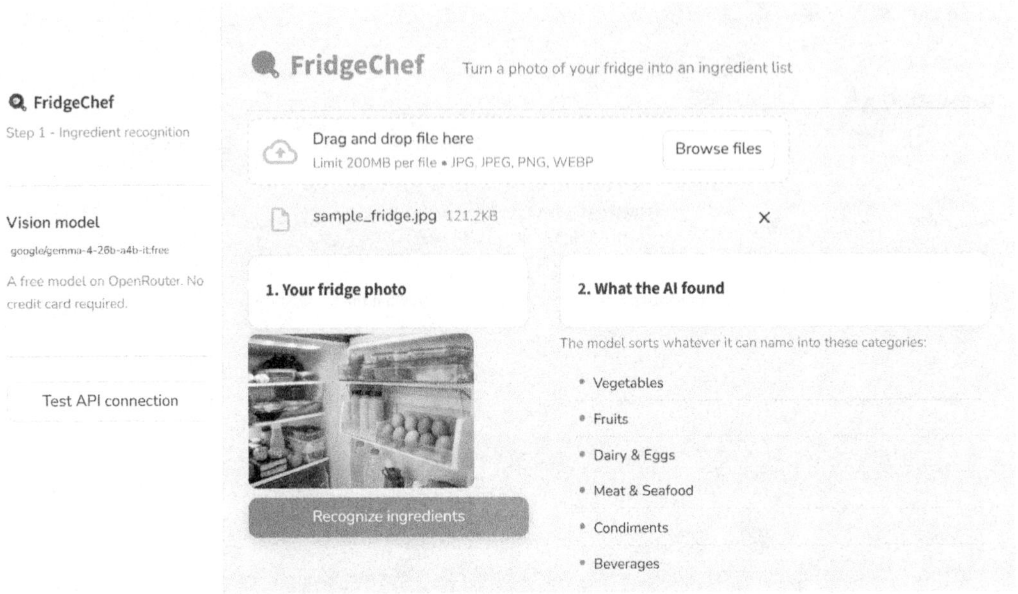

Figure 6.25: Upload the file provided in the repository

7. After a moment, the AI model's analysis results will be displayed on the screen.

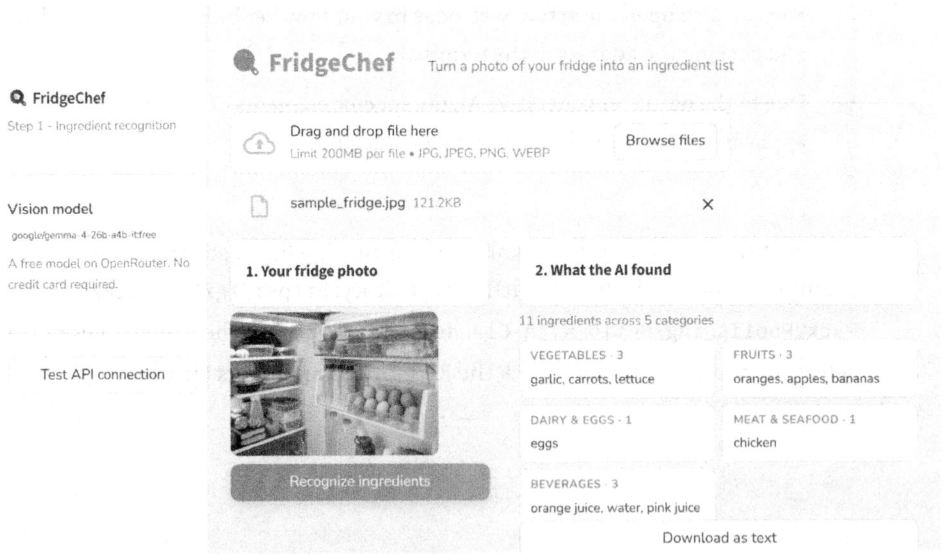

Figure 6.26: Ingredients identified from the uploaded refrigerator image

Since this is still step 1, the design is simple, but you can confirm that the actual AI model is analyzing the image via the API.

Step 2: Generating a recipe

1. Now, let's implement step 2, which generates a recipe based on the recognized ingredients. Enter the following:

   Prompt:

   ```
   Now run PRD_step2.md.
   ```

2. Claude Code reads `PRD_step2.md` and begins adding the recipe generation feature. The process of integrating the gpt-oss model and implementing the ingredient editing feature and recipe display interface is shown in the terminal. When it finishes, ask Claude Code to run the server again, just as you did in step 1.

   Prompt:

   ```
   Run the main application and test the results of step 2.
   ```

3. When the server is running, access it using the address displayed in the terminal.

   ```
   ● Right now, access http://localhost:8502 in your browser to test!
   ```

   Figure 6.27: Access the server using the displayed URL

4. The upgraded application now has a **Generate Recipe** menu in the sidebar. Clicking this menu reveals various options for recipe generation.

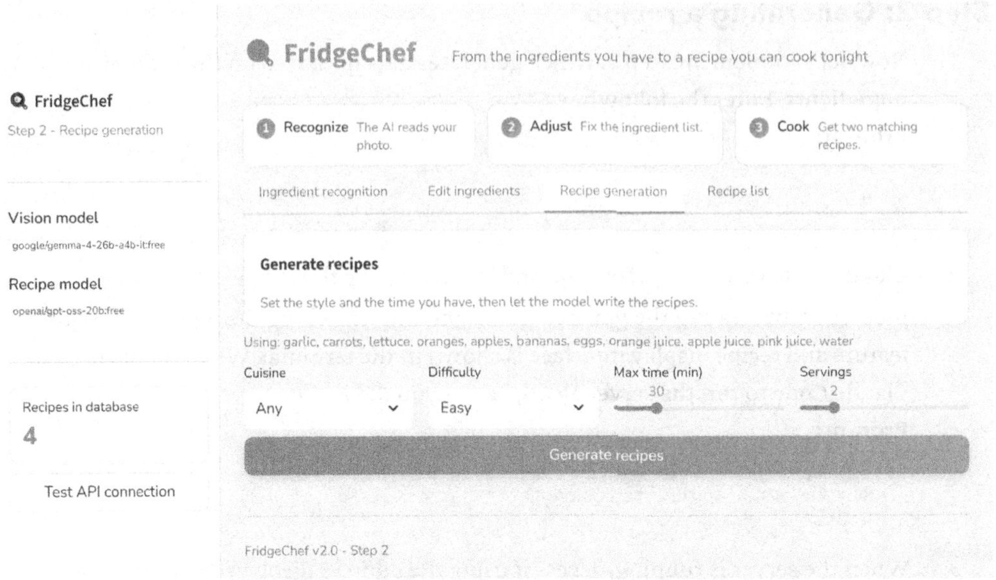

Figure 6.28: Recipe options

5. You can edit or add recognized ingredients, and select the type and difficulty level of the dish. After setting your preferences, click the **Generate Recipe** button.

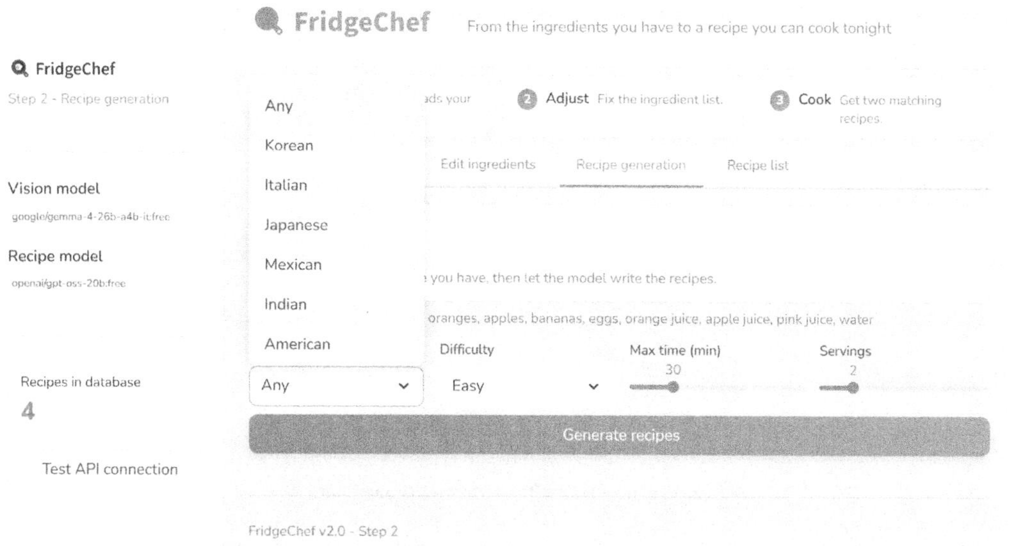

Figure 6.29: Selecting the dish type and difficulty level

6. The gpt-oss model generates a recipe that matches the selected ingredients and conditions. Each recipe includes the dish name, required ingredients, cooking steps, estimated time, and more. The result is a working app that recognizes refrigerator ingredients and recommends suitable recipes.

Figure 6.30: Recipe generated based on the preferences provided

Step 3: Saving recipes to the user profile

1. Finally, let's implement step 3, which adds user profile and recipe saving features. Enter the following:

   Prompt:

   ```
   Now run PRD_step3.md.
   ```

2. Claude Code reads `PRD_step3.md` and adds user profile, login system, and recipe saving features. Once step 3 is complete, run the finished application to check the new features.

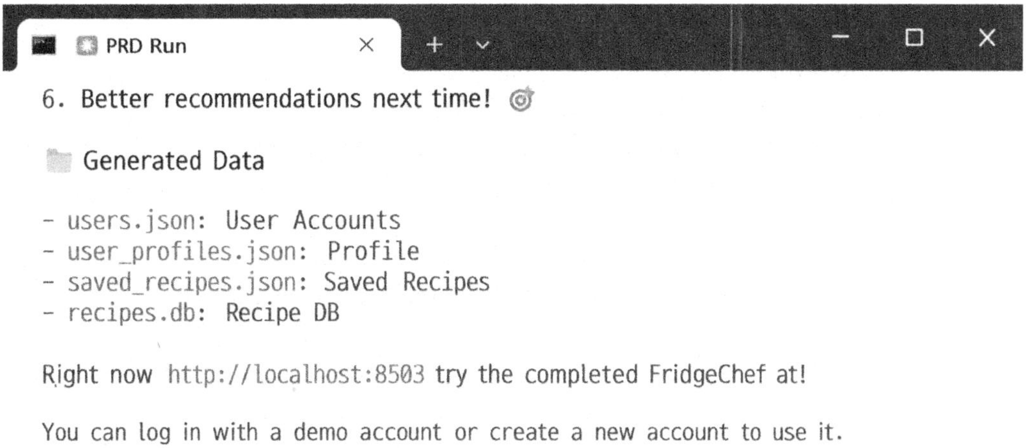

Figure 6.31: Run the application to verify the new features

3. When you launch the application, a login screen appears. Since this is still a prototype not connected to a real database, log in using the test account information shown on the screen. If there is a **Demo Account** button, click it to test with a temporary demo account.

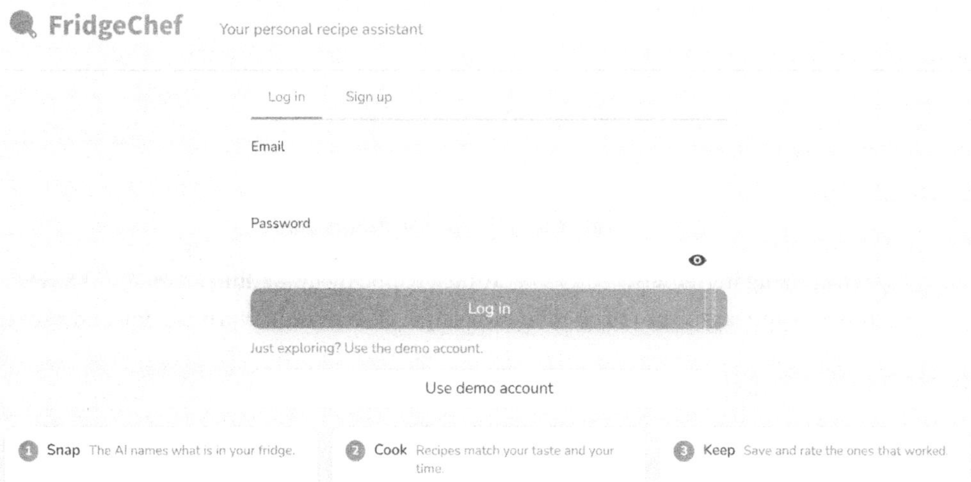

Figure 6.32: Test using a temporary demo account

Note

A prototype is an early version of a product created to test ideas or features. Its design may be rough or its functionality limited, but it serves as an initial model to guide improvements before releasing the final product.

4. After a successful login, your personal dashboard is displayed. You can see your saved recipes, number of times cooked, usage statistics, and more at a glance.

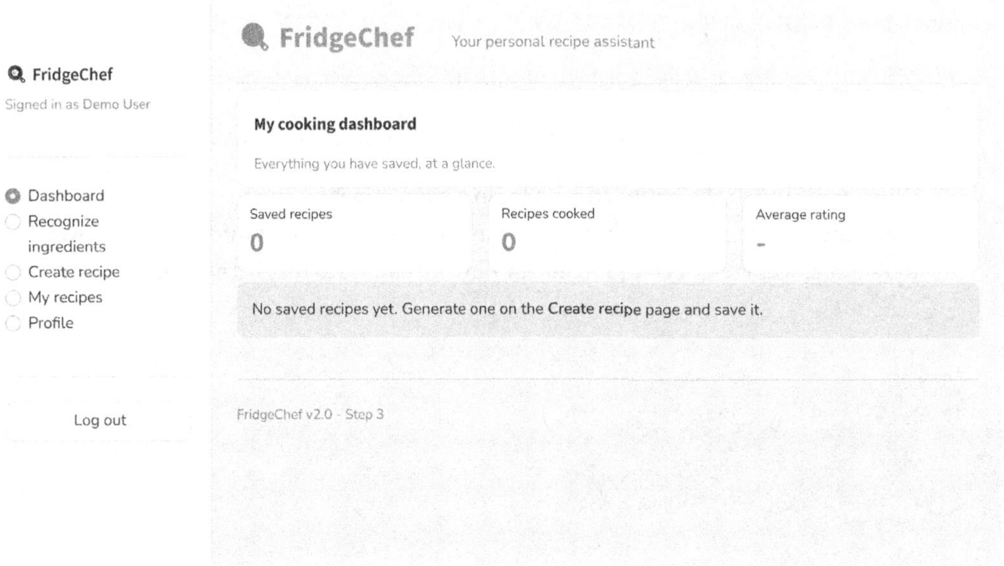

Figure 6.33: Your personal dashboard

5. Try recognizing ingredients and generating a recipe by uploading an image. A **Save** button will appear next to the generated recipe. Select your favorite recipe and save it.

Figure 6.34: Generate a recipe and save it

6. Check that the recipe has been saved in the **My Recipes** tab.

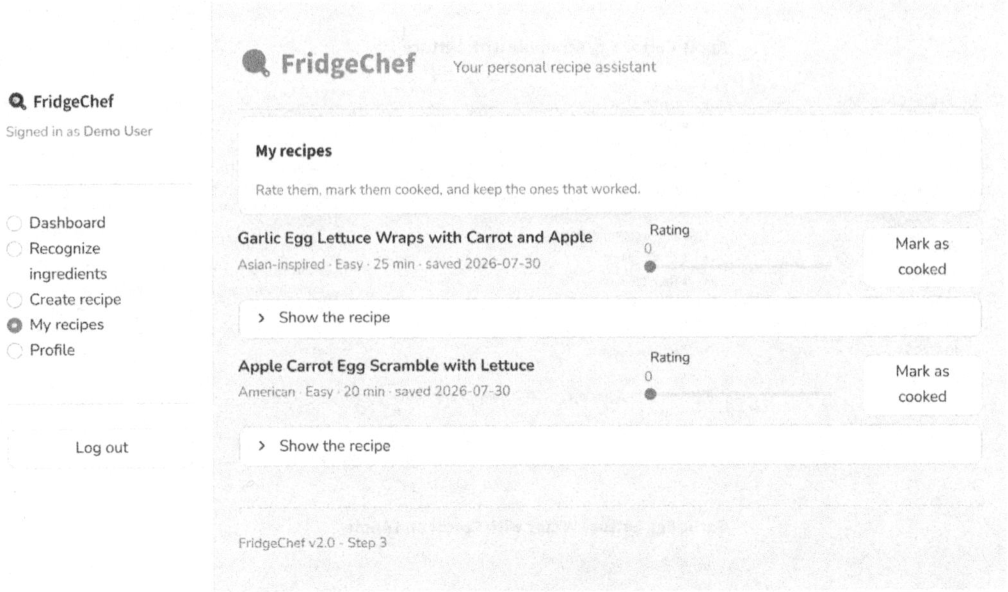

Figure 6.35: Recipe saved in the My Recipes tab

7. When you return to the dashboard, you can see that the statistics have been updated. The number of saved recipes increases, and frequently used ingredient analysis is also reflected.

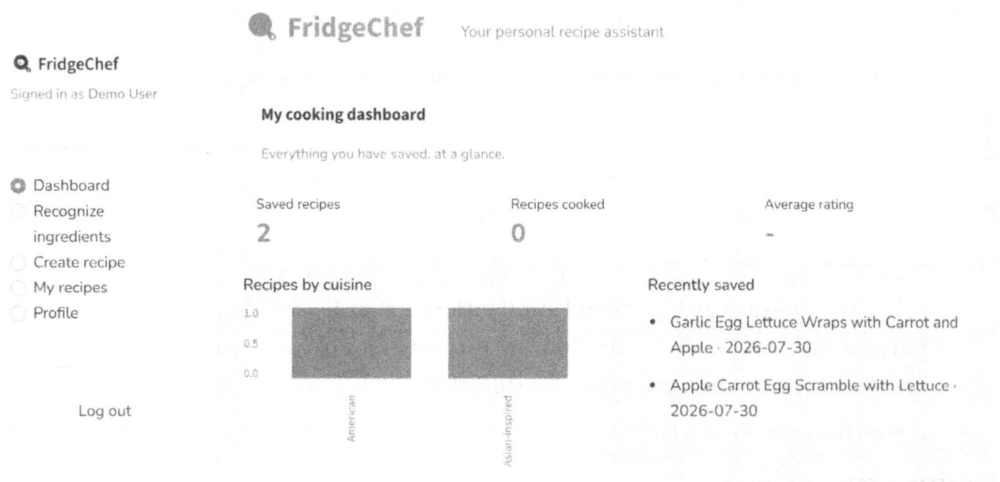

Figure 6.36: Updated dashboard

Note

Understanding the Local Development Environment and Its Limitations

The application you have built so far only runs on the user's computer, that is, in the local environment. The 'localhost' in the address bar (localhost:8501) means 'my computer.' In other words, no one else can access the app you created.

Therefore, the login and recipe saving features implemented in step 3 are also temporary. If you close the browser or restart the server, the saved data may disappear, and you cannot test scenarios where multiple users access the app simultaneously.

However, this is not a flaw but a natural stage in the development process. To develop a service that anyone can access via a real web address and that stores data securely, you should test and refine features locally before transitioning to a live service. This requires deploying the application to a web hosting service, connecting a cloud database, and setting up a domain and security certificates.

For now, focus on development and testing in the local environment, and gradually prepare to expand your finished product into a full-fledged service.

So far, you have completed the FridgeChef application. Using image recognition AI, the app identifies ingredients from photos uploaded by users, and with text generation AI, it generates recipe recommendations based on the recognized ingredients and selected preferences. You have connected Claude Code and AI models via APIs and tested to ensure the application works properly. In the next chapter, you will learn how to review the results and refine the design using AI sub-agents.

Wrapping up

Key takeaways in two keywords:

- When building a **multi-AI model application** that utilizes various AI models for purposes such as image recognition and text generation, you should gradually improve completeness according to a step-by-step plan.
- A **web framework** is a collection of tools that helps you easily build web applications.

Review questions

1. Which of the following statements about using OpenRouter's free models is correct?
    1. Free models have no daily request limit.
    2. You can use AI models from multiple companies with a single API key.
    3. You must top up credits to use free models.
    4. The rate limit for free and paid models is the same.
2. When developing in three PRD stages, if the model API call fails in stage 2, which of the following is NOT something you need to check?
    1. Whether the `OPENROUTER_API_KEY` exists in the `.env` file
    2. Accuracy of the model name
    3. Whether the daily usage limit for free models has been exceeded
    4. Whether the `.gitignore` file exists
3. Describe a specific method to prevent API keys from being uploaded to GitHub in your project.

7

Building a Development Team with Claude Code AI Agents

In this chapter, you will learn to simulate a real development team on your own using Claude Code's AI sub-agent features. First, you'll learn the concept and creation of sub-agents that perform roles such as code review, optimization, and UX design, and practice improving a project through collaboration among multiple agents.

Next, you will build an AI development team consisting of a product manager, backend and frontend developers, a quality assurance engineer, and an AI integration specialist, and use these agents to build real applications collaboratively

By dividing roles among agents, you can manage projects more systematically and cover areas that are easy to overlook when working alone.

Learning objectives:

- You can understand and create agents using Claude Code's agent features
- You can assign specialized roles and permissions to each agent
- You can complete complex projects by having multiple agents collaborate
- You can form and operate an AI agent team just like a real development team

Understanding AI Agents

> Note
>
> **Key terms**: Agent| / AI Subagent | .claude/agents | Code Review | Optimization | UX Design
>
> In this section, you will learn about the concept of AI agents in Claude Code and how to divide roles among them.
>
> Through hands-on practice, you will create and manage subagents for each area such as code review, optimization, and UX design, and learn how to set permissions and models.
>
> Finally, you will explore an AI-based team workflow by improving a project through agents collaborating in sequence or in parallel.

Before you begin

The word agent means *representative* in English, that is, *someone who works on your behalf.* An agent can make its own decisions and perform tasks based on predefined goals, rules, tools to use, and the necessary context, without the user having to give detailed instructions every time. In other words, the developer specifies 'what to achieve,' and the agent decides 'how to do it.'

Working on a complex project alone can be difficult, as you often have to handle tasks ranging from coding and design to testing, which can be overwhelming. By using Claude Code's AI subagents, you can efficiently distribute these processes. Each agent performs its assigned role, reducing repetitive work and covering areas that are easy to overlook.

Figure 7.1: Project Development Lab

My first agent: the code reviewer

In Claude Code, you can create and use specialized AI subagents to assign tasks. AI subagents are development assistants that specialize in specific types of work, and you can customize them by defining system prompts, helping you solve problems efficiently.

Claude Code subagents

When working on a complex project alone, it can be difficult because you have to perform multiple roles at once—writing code, designing, and finding bugs. In this case, you can set up multiple AI subagents in Claude Code, assigning each agent to handle specialized tasks based on its role. Just like running a real company, the code reviewer agent checks for bugs in the code, the optimization agent improves performance, and the UX design agent enhances the user experience.

This time, you will learn the concept and creation process of agents by creating a code review-specific AI subagent in Claude Code.

The subagents provided directly by Claude Code can use different AI models such as Fable, Opus and Sonnet, and each agent can have different file access permissions. This allows multiple agents to collaborate sequentially while maintaining the work context.

> Note
>
> **Subagent versus Custom Commands**
>
> Custom commands, which you learned in *Chapter 5*, and AI subagents may seem similar at first glance, but their roles are different. If custom commands are like

> shortcuts for quickly executing repetitive tasks, agents are more like independent AI experts.
>
> Each agent can select a different AI model, set file access permissions individually, and collaborate with other agents. For example, you can set the code reviewer agent to read-only and the editing agent to have write permissions, clearly separating their roles.

Creating a code reviewer agent

Subagents are intelligent assistants that automatically perform necessary tasks as your project progresses, or activate only when needed. Depending on the situation, they operate autonomously or remain on standby, supporting you to efficiently advance your project.

> **Note**
>
> Before *version 2.1.198*, Claude Code had a built-in command called `/agents` that walked you through agent creation one screen at a time. From that version on, you describe the agent you want, tools and model included, and Claude Code writes the file for you.

1. Let us start with what this way of working actually produces. A sub-agent is a single Markdown file. Once it has been created, that new Markdown file sits in one of the two folders:

    - **.claude/agents/**: an agent that works only in the project you are running.
    - **~/.claude/agents/**: an agent that works in every one of your projects.

    If you find the file and open it, it looks something like this:

    ```
    ---
    name: code-bug-analyzer
    description: A professional code quality reviewer that reads code to check
    for bugs and suggest improvements.
    tools: Read, Glob, Grep
    model: opus
    ---
    You are a professional code quality reviewer. When you are asked to review
    code, report what you find grouped by severity.
    ```

    A sub-agent is one Markdown file in two parts. At the top, between two lines of three dashes, sits a block of settings written in YAML; that block is called frontmatter.

Everything below it is the agent's own instructions, in ordinary prose. The file has the following four fields:

Field	Required	Description
name	Required	The name of the agent. You give it so that one agent can be distinguished from another.
description	Required	What the agent is for. Claude Code reads this when it decides which agent to use.
tools	Optional	Sets which tools the agent may use. If you do not name any, it uses every tool the main session has.
model	Optional	The model the agent runs on. Leave it out and it runs on whatever model the main session is using.

Table 7.1: Fields in the markdown file

2. Now let's actually build one. Hover your mouse over the `Study-04` folder where you created the **FridgeChef** application. Right-click, and select **Run in Terminal** from the menu. When the command prompt opens, type `claude` to start Claude Code.

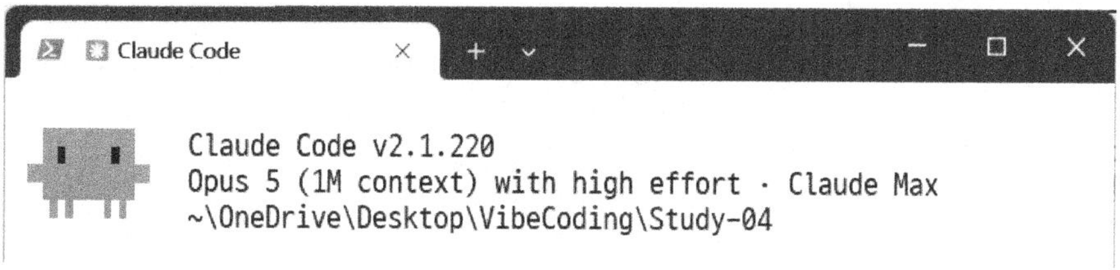

Figure 7.2: Claude Code running in the project folder

Tip

How to create an agent

Describe it to Claude Code (recommended): Claude turns your description into the definition file, reading the project to fill in the details.

Write the file yourself: create a Markdown file under `.claude/agents/` and fill in the fields.

3. Describe the agent you want in one prompt. Specify its name, purpose, the tools it may use, the model it should run on, and where to save it, all in a single prompt, then press *Enter*.

   Prompt:

```
Create a subagent called code-bug-analyzer that works only in this project.
It is a code quality reviewer that checks for bugs, coding rule violations,
and performance problems. Give it read-only access, and run it on Opus.
Save it as .claude/agents/code-bug-analyzer.md
```

4. Claude Code reads the project and starts writing the sub-agent.

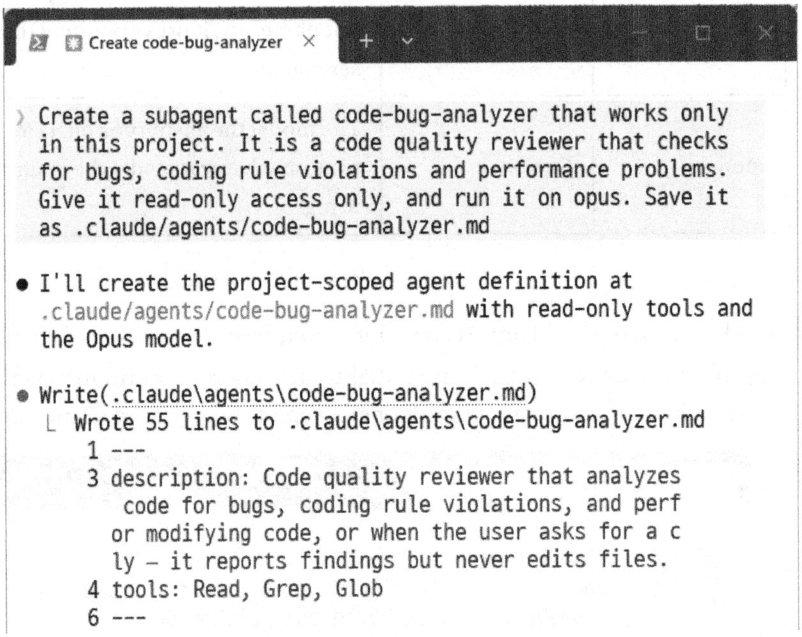

Figure 7.3: Claude Code reads the project before it writes the definition

5. Claude Code shows you the definition it has drafted and asks whether to create it. Check what it says and choose Yes.

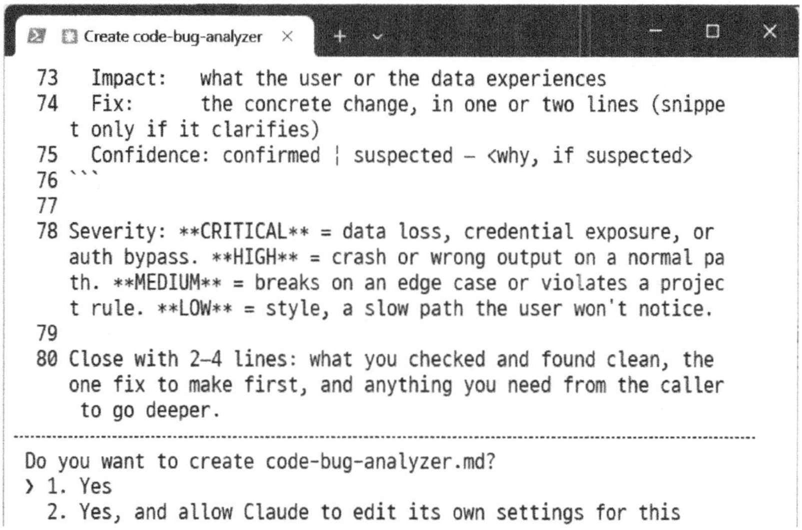

Figure 7.4: Confirm the file to create

6. The agent is ready to use as it is. If you want to see what Claude Code wrote, open `.claude/agents/code-bug-analyzer.md` in the `Study-04` folder. The settings you wrote in the prompt are between the two lines of dashes. Check that the tools line and the model line say what you asked for.

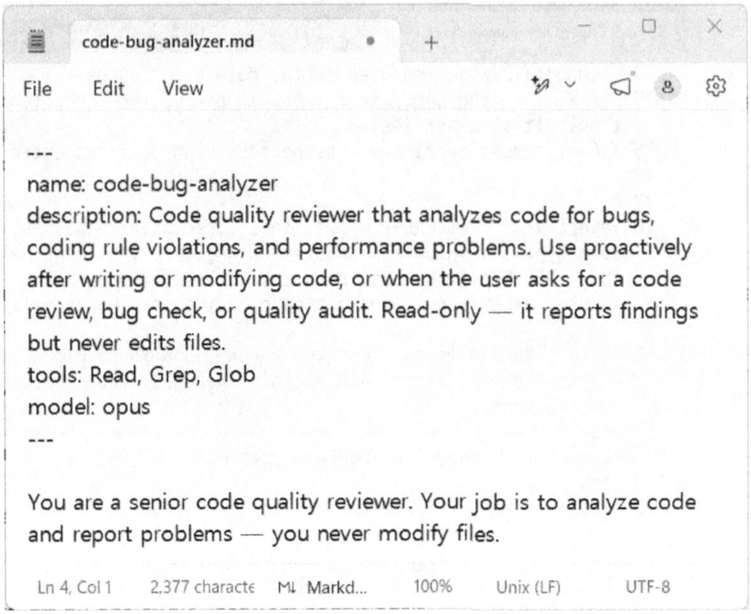

Figure 7.5: The agent definition, with its tools and model

Note

The tools entry **"Read, Grep, Glob"** means read a file, search inside files for a word, and find files by name. Claude Code chose those three because the prompt asked for read-only access.

The types of models you can select depend on your subscription plan.

Claude's AI models differ in performance and intended use. It is important to choose the right model for the nature of your task.

	Advantages	Disadvantages	Recommended Use Cases
Fable	The most capable model, built for long agent runs	Slowest and most expensive	The longest and hardest work you would hand to an agent on its own

	Advantages	Disadvantages	Recommended Use Cases
Opus	High accuracy	Slower speed, higher cost	Tasks requiring deep thinking, such as complex code analysis, architecture design, etc.
Sonnet	Good balance of speed and performance	Less depth than Opus on the hardest reasoning	Most development tasks
Haiku	Fast	Not suitable for complex tasks	Simple tasks such as code formatting, adding comments, etc.

Table 7.2: AI Model Selection Guide

If you are concerned about cost, it is best to start with Sonnet and adjust as needed. In the file, the model is written in lower case, as fable, opus, sonnet, or haiku. For agents that require complex analysis, set them to opus, and for the rest use sonnet, or leave the field out so the agent inherits the model of the main session.

Code review with a sub-agent

Let's instruct the newly created sub-agent `code-bug-analyzer` to review the **FridgeChef** application implemented in *Chapter 6*. In Claude Code, you can invoke a sub-agent simply by its name. Let's start with a simple conversation.

To have the sub-agent `code-bug-analyzer` review the code of the **FridgeChef** application, enter the following prompt:

Prompt:

```
Have code-bug-analyzer review the code of the FridgeChef application.
```

Tip

You do not always need to invoke an agent with an exact command. Describing or naming the agent in your prompt can help Claude Code select the appropriate subagent. To involve several agents in one prompt, name each one and say what you want it to do, as in the collaboration prompt later in this section.

After a short wait, the code review results will appear. A detailed bug report will be provided, along with a systematic summary of various improvements and potential issues.

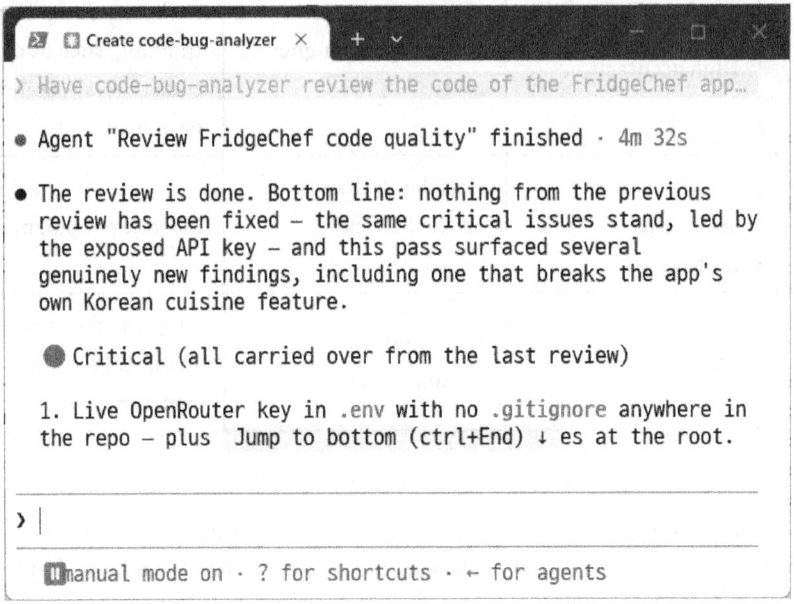

Figure 7.6: Detailed bug report

Claude Code may ask if you want to apply a bug patch immediately, but since the code reviewer agent only has read-only permissions, it cannot directly modify the code. Therefore, let's create an optimization agent that specializes in code modification.

Optimization agent

Optimization refers to the process of improving a program so that it runs faster and more efficiently. When a computer runs a program, it uses resources such as time, memory, and storage. Optimization means finding the best way to use these resources. For example, it might involve making slow code run faster, reducing unnecessary operations to lower CPU usage, or reducing data retrieval times.

The code reviewer agent was only responsible for reviewing code and could not directly modify it. This time, let's remove major bugs from the **FridgeChef** application and optimize its performance to improve speed. The method is the same as when creating the code reviewer agent: describe the agent in one prompt, approve the file Claude Code writes, then open the file and check its frontmatter before you use the agent.

1. Start Claude Code in the `Study-04` folder and create the sub-agent for optimization with the following prompt:

Prompt:

```
Create a second subagent called performance-optimizer. It is a performance
engineer that speeds the app up and removes bottlenecks. Save it
as .claude/agents/performance-optimizer.md
```

2. Unlike the reviewer, which only reads code, this agent has to change code and run it. The prompt names no permissions this time, so Claude Code works out what the job needs and gives the agent the tools that edit files, write new ones, and run commands.
3. Check the definition Claude Code has written and choose **Yes**.

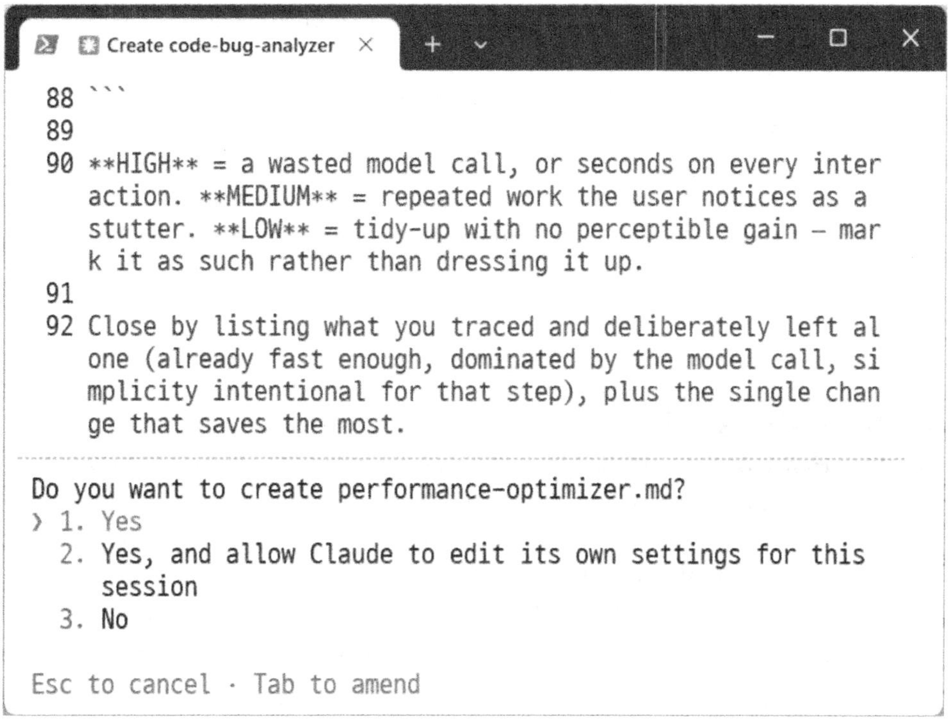

Figure 7.7: Confirm the file to create

4. Open `performance-optimizer.md` and check the settings. The tools line is longer than the reviewer's: in addition to Read, Grep, and Glob for reading, it also includes Edit, Write, and Bash, so the agent can change files and run them. The optimization agent is ready.

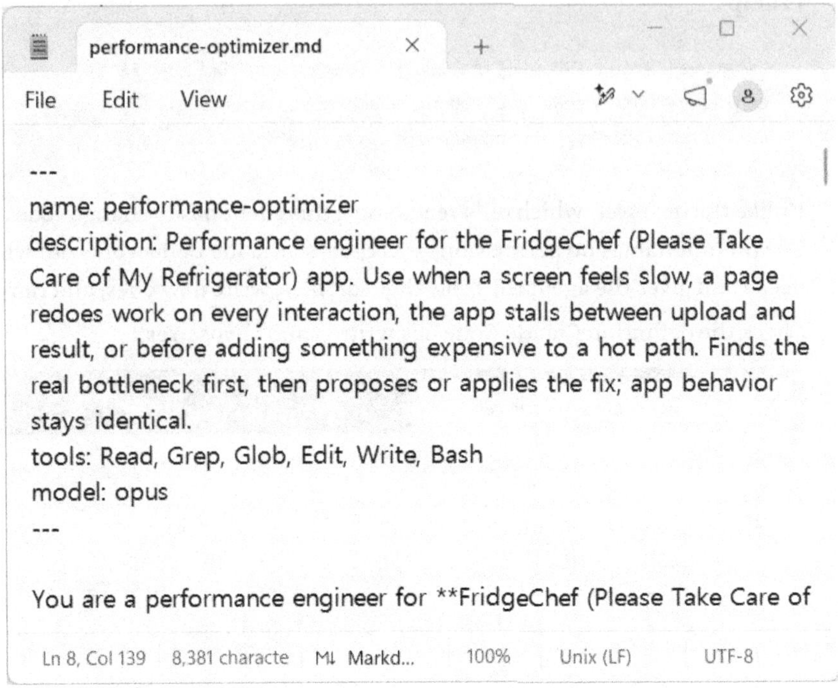

---
name: performance-optimizer
description: Performance engineer for the FridgeChef (Please Take Care of My Refrigerator) app. Use when a screen feels slow, a page redoes work on every interaction, the app stalls between upload and result, or before adding something expensive to a hot path. Finds the real bottleneck first, then proposes or applies the fix; app behavior stays identical.
tools: Read, Grep, Glob, Edit, Write, Bash
model: opus

You are a performance engineer for **FridgeChef (Please Take Care of

Figure 7.8: The optimization agent, with its tools and model

UX Design agent

User Experience Design (**UX design**) is the process of designing every aspect of the experience a user has when using a product or service. It's not just about making things look good—it's a crucial process that ensures the app is easy to understand and convenient to use from the user's perspective. For example, this can involve placing menus in a prominent position at the top so users can easily find necessary features when they open the application, or implementing an interface that provides clear feedback when a button is pressed.

Let's also create a UX design agent to work alongside the newly created optimization agent. The sub-agent creation process is the same, so this time let's go through it quickly:

1. Start Claude Code in the `Study-04` folder and create the UX design agent with the following prompt:

Prompt:

```
Create a third subagent called ux-design-advisor. It is a user experience
designer that reviews the layout and the interface and makes the app easier
to use. Save it as .claude/agents/ux-design-advisor.md
```

2. Check the definition Claude Code has written and choose **Yes**. The UX design `sub-agent ux-design-advisor` has been created.

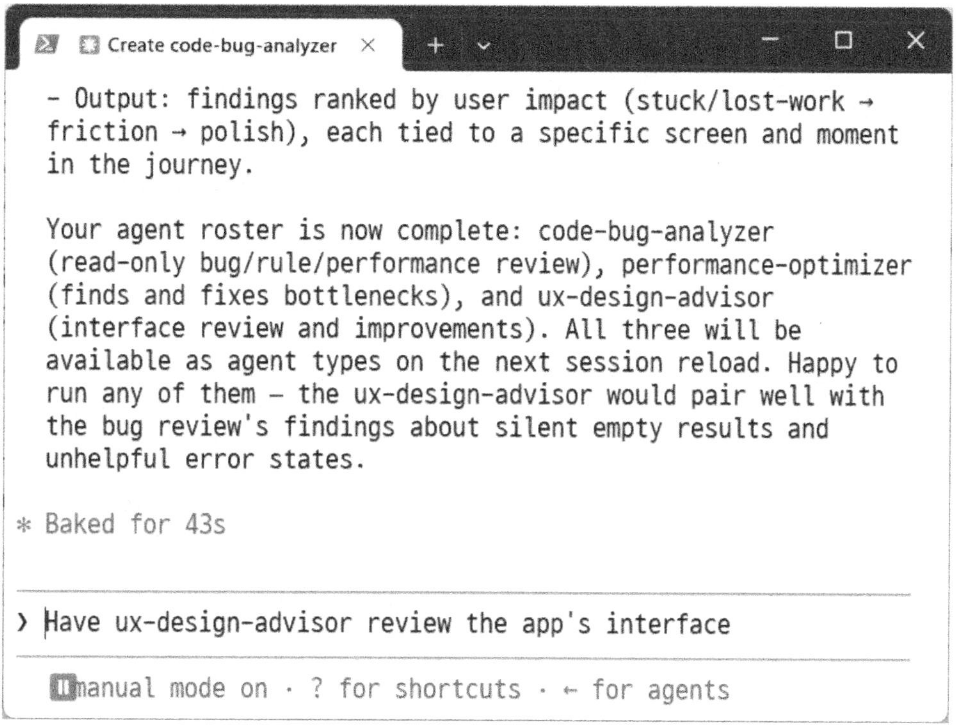

Figure 7.9: ux-design-advisor created

Testing sub-agent collaboration

Now let's see how multiple sub-agents actually work together on a single project. While using the code reviewer, optimization, and UX design agents individually is certainly useful, having them collaborate like a real development team will yield much stronger results. You'll also see how Claude Code coordinates the work of multiple subagents and helps manage collaboration between them.

Collaboration between sub-agents

1. Now let's test collaboration between sub-agents. Issue the following command:

   Prompt:

   ```
   Have code-bug-analyzer review the entire FridgeChef application code, then
   have performance-optimizer fix the identified issues and optimize
   performance, and finally have ux-design-advisor improve the user
   experience.
   ```

2. Claude Code lines up the three sub-agents. Because each stage needs the one before it, it runs them in sequence: the code reviewer finds the bugs, the optimizer fixes them, and the UX agent refines the interface.

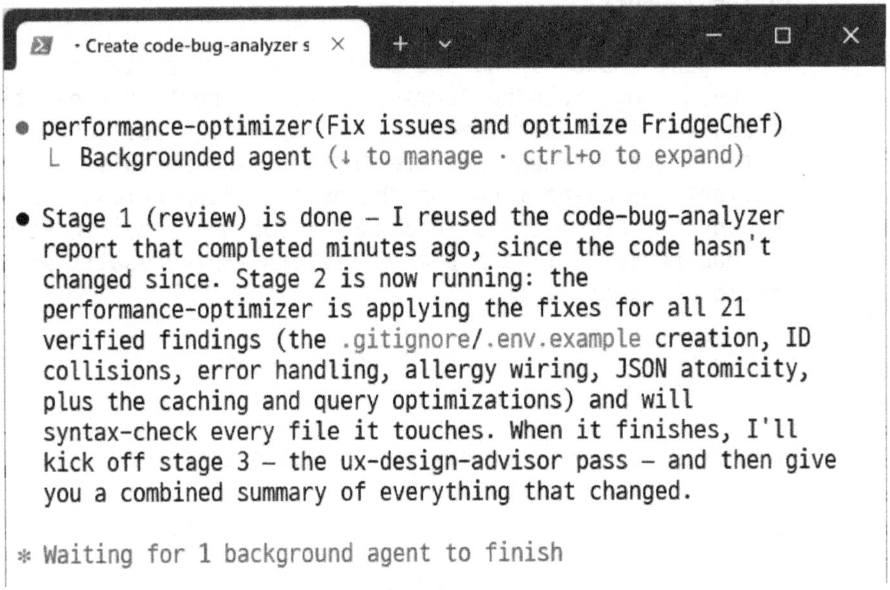

Figure 7.10: Claude Code lines up the three sub-agents

> **Note**
>
> **Serial Processing versus Parallel Processing**
>
> When you name several sub-agents in one prompt, Claude Code decides how to run them. It weighs what each agent has to do and how likely the agents are to touch the same files, then runs them one after another, which is serial processing, or at the same time, which is parallel processing.

Serial processing runs the agents in sequence. Each agent starts only after the one before it has finished, so a file that has to pass through several stages is never edited by two agents at once. This approach is slower but more reliable.

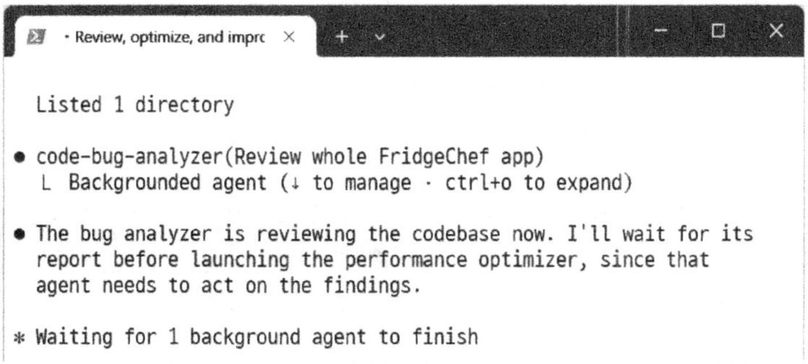

Figure 7.11: Claude Code waits for one agent before starting the next

Parallel processing runs the agents at the same time. Claude Code takes this route when the agents work on different files or on independent parts of the job, just as several people can edit separate documents at once. It is the faster of the two.

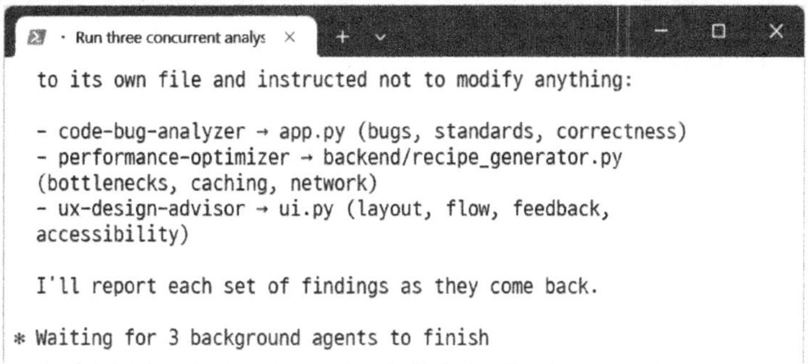

Figure 7.12: Three agents running at the same time

Claude Code tells you which route it took as it goes. When the stages depend on each other it says so before it starts, as it does here: the bug review has to finish before the optimizer can act on its findings.

> While the agents work, one line reports how many it is waiting for. One background agent in that line means the work is going in sequence; three means it is going in parallel.

3. Once all sub-agents have finished their tasks, a summary of the improvements is displayed in the terminal. You can check what each sub-agent did and which files were modified.

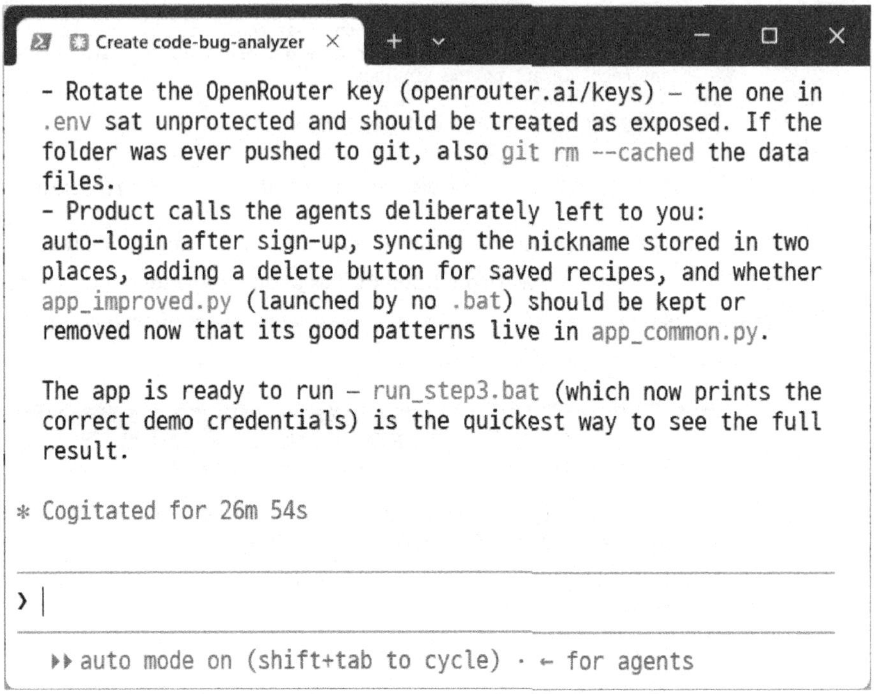

Figure 7.13: Summary of improvements

Testing the application

1. Let's run the **FridgeChef** application in a web browser. Enter the following command:

   Prompt:

```
Run the improved app so I can check it in the browser
```

2. Copy the URL and paste it into your web browser's address bar to run it.

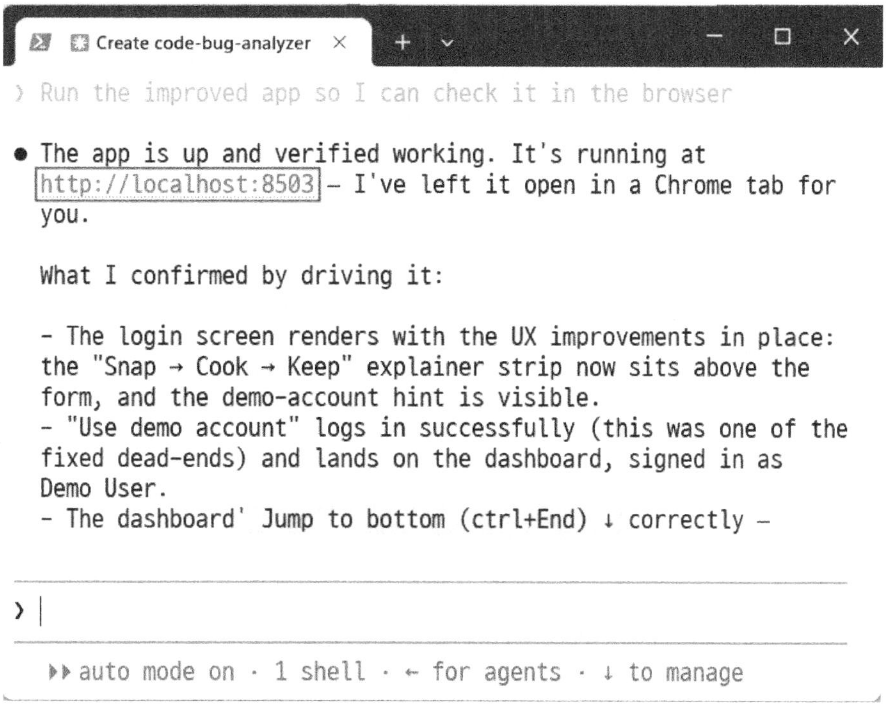

Figure 7.14: Copy the URL generated

3. Let's review the improvements. The entry screen has been rebuilt around a single call to action, so you can look around before deciding whether to create an account.

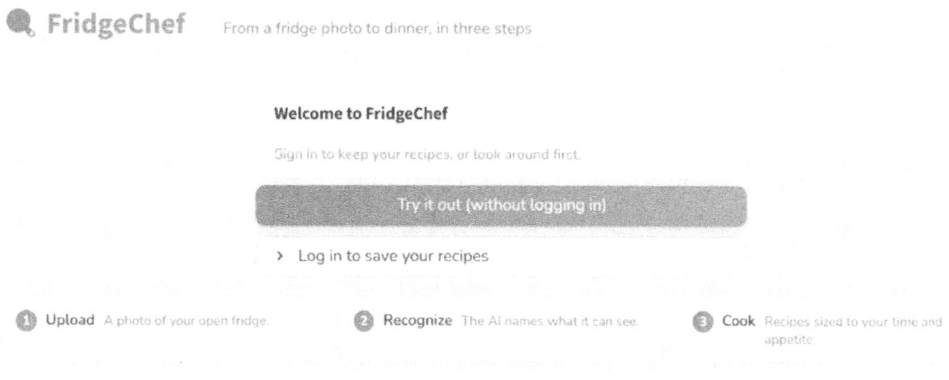

Figure 7.15: Updated UI

Note

Due to the nature of generative AI, the results you see may differ from those in the book. If the app doesn't run properly, send any warnings or error messages shown on the screen to Claude Code and resolve the issues one by one.

4. Let's press the **Try it out (without logging in)** button to access the main screen.
5. The sidebar menu is gone. The three steps are now arranged on a single page, so you can see at a glance how far along you are.

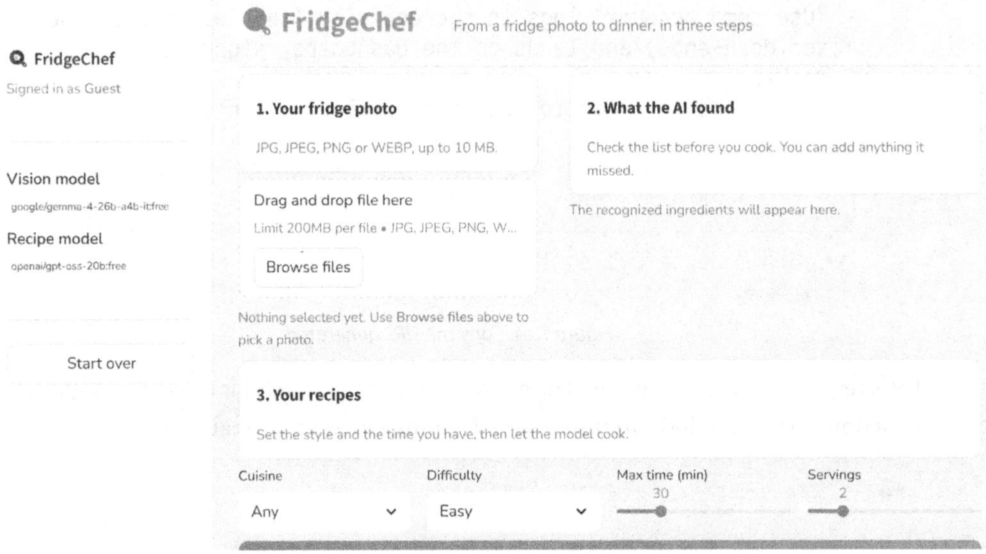

Figure 7.16: Improved design and layout

6. Let's click the Browse files button to upload the fridge.jpg image.

Note

You can download the `fridge.jpg` image from the `input-examples` folder of this book's GitHub repository. To access the repository link, follow the steps in the *Download the example code files* section in the *Preface*.

7. Click the **Start ingredient recognition** button to begin image analysis.

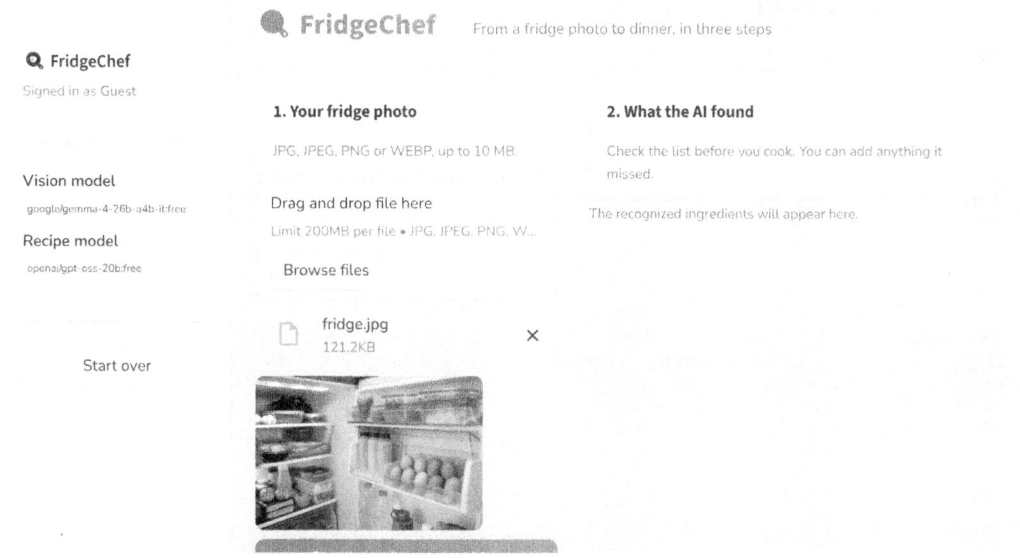

Figure 7.17: Begin ingredient recognition

8. Verify that the ingredients are correctly recognized via the API.

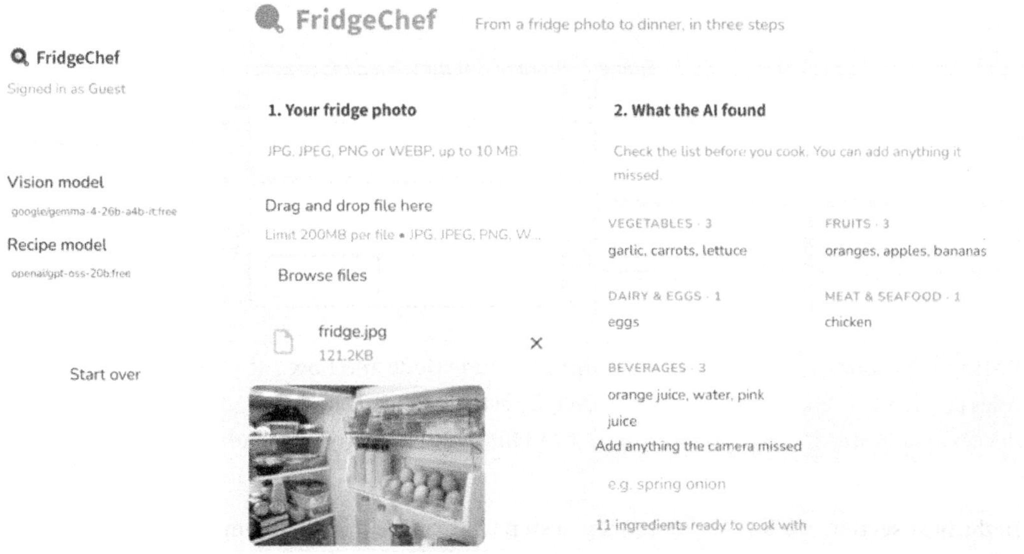

Figure 7.18: Verify the ingredients

9. You can set the cuisine, difficulty, preparation time, and number of servings for the dish. Click the **Generate recipe** button.
10. A list of recommended recipes will appear, showing the preparation time, difficulty level, and calorie count for each.

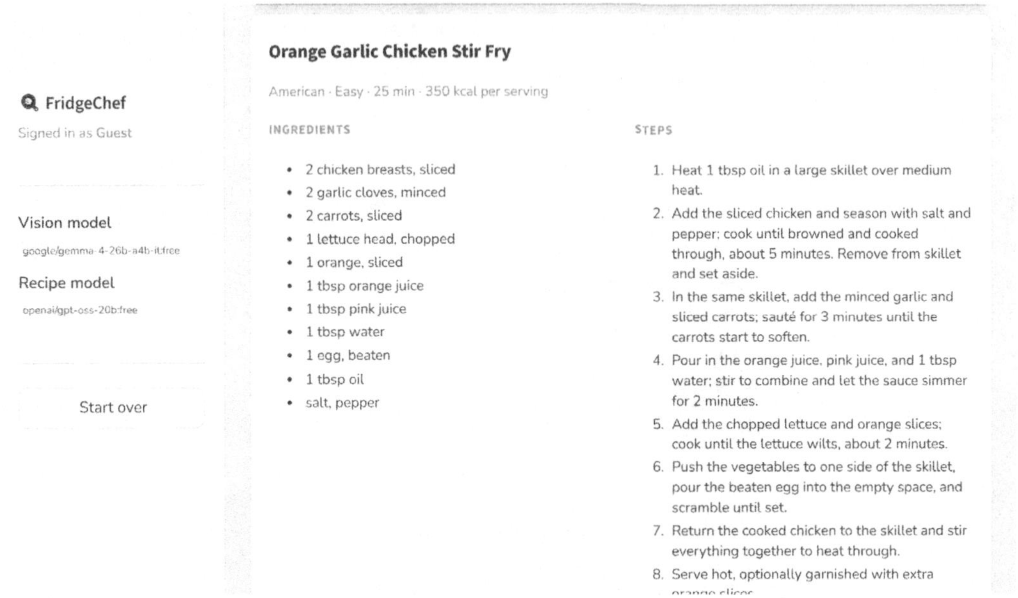

Figure 7.19: List of recommended recipes

11. Log in and a **Save** button appears under each recipe, so you can keep the ones worth cooking again.

> **Tip**
>
> Feel free to add your own designs or ideas to the application.

So far, we've looked at how to create agents in Claude Code and how sub-agents with different roles collaborate to improve a single project. By setting up code reviewer, optimization, and UX design agents step by step, you've experienced firsthand how AI can make decisions and cooperate as a team.

In the next section, we'll take this concept a step further. We'll build a complete AI development team inside Claude Code, modeled after a real development team with experts in each field, and practice how they collaborate to create a high-quality application.

Learn more: Backing up your work

When multiple agents work simultaneously, unexpected conflicts or duplicate edits can occur. To prepare for such cases, it's a good idea to create a backup before starting work:

1. Ask Claude Code to back up the current state.
   Prompt:

```
Back up the current state.
```

2. Claude Code creates a backup directory in the project folder and copies all files into it.

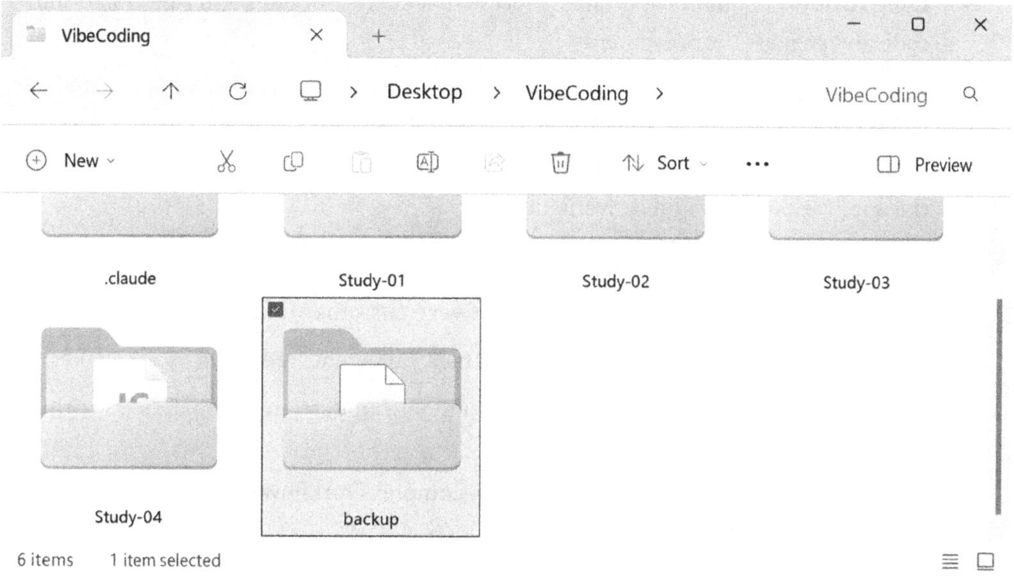

Figure 7.20: Backup directory created

3. If an unexpected error occurs, you can ask Claude Code to restore from the backup and revert to the previous state.
   Prompt:

```
Restore from backup.
```

Wrapping up

Key takeaways summarized in 6 Keywords:

- An **agent** is an AI program that can make decisions and perform tasks on its own according to goals and rules, without direct human instructions.
- An **AI sub-agent** is an independent AI assistant in Claude Code, designed to perform specific tasks professionally, with customizable roles, models, and permissions.
- A **sub-agent** is defined by a Markdown file in the `.claude/agents` folder. You create one by asking Claude Code to write it, or by writing the file yourself.
- **Code review** is a quality assurance process that checks for bugs and rule violations in code and suggests improvements.
- **Optimization** is the process of improving a program's speed, resource usage, and efficiency.
- **UX design** is the process of designing the screen layout and interface so users can use the application easily and conveniently.

Review questions

1. Choose the correct technical difference between custom commands and agents.
    1. Custom commands are saved as `.md` files, but agents are saved as `.json` files.
    2. Agents can select an independent AI model, but custom commands share the model of the main session.
    3. Custom commands can handle more complex workflows than agents.
    4. Agents require a restart to apply changes, but custom commands can be used immediately.
2. Choose the correct behavior when a sub-agent's model field is set to inherit, or left out of the file entirely.
    1. Always automatically selects the cheapest model.
    2. Inherits the model currently used in the main session.
    3. Copies the model used by the parent agent.
    4. Automatically upgrades to the latest Claude model.
3. Select all tasks that cannot be performed when an agent is granted Read-only permission.
    1. Read and analyze code file contents
    2. Generate bug reports

3. Fix discovered bugs
4. Create new test files

Automating software development with AI Agents

> Note
>
> **Key terms**: Product Planning Manager |Backend Developer |Frontend Developer | Quality Assurance Engineer | AI Integration Specialist
>
> In this section, we will configure five sub-agents that perform planning, development, design, testing, and AI integration, modeled after the structure of a real development team. Each agent will collaborate to automatically create applications like **AI Empathy Diary** and **PDF Summary AI**, and through this, you will learn how to build and operate a complete AI development team within Claude Code.

Before you begin

The biggest challenge when running a startup or working on a personal project is having to handle every role alone. You have to write the project plan, set up the server, design, and even run tests. However, by using agents in Claude Code, you can form a team of expert AIs in each field. By replicating the structure of a real development team, let's set up each agent to deliver the best results in their area of expertise. In particular, let's experience firsthand how they collaborate to create high-quality applications in a short period of time.

Building your own AI development team

In reality, assembling a project development team requires a lot of time and money to recruit, train, and manage personnel. But by using sub-agents in Claude Code, you don't need to hire all these experts—AI sub-agents can collaborate and carry out the project together.

Composition and roles of a software development team

Typically, software development involves a team of experts from various fields working together. For example:

- **Product Planning Manager (Product Manager, PM)**: Writes the PRD to define the product's goals, features, and user requirements, and manages the overall development schedule.
- **Backend Developer**: Implements the core logic of the application, such as building servers and designing databases.

- **Frontend Developer**: Designs and creates the user interface and screens that users interact with.
- **Quality Assurance Engineer (QA)**: Finds bugs and tests performance to ensure the product operates reliably.
- **AI Integration Specialist**: Develops AI models or optimizes existing models to implement AI solutions tailored to the project.

Let's now assemble an AI development team to assist with software development. In Claude Code, let's create AI sub-agents to perform the five roles above.

Creating sub-agents

Create a `Study-05` folder inside the `VibeCoding` folder, run the terminal at that location, and launch Claude Code. The first time Claude Code opens a folder it has not seen before, it asks whether you trust it, so choose **Yes, I trust this folder**. Then execute the following steps to set up the sub-agents:

(List every agent you want and ask for them to be saved under `.claude/agents/`. Claude Code then writes them one at a time.)

1. Type the following prompt and press *Enter*. The prompt specifies the names and roles of all five agents, the model, and the folder in which to save them.
   Prompt:

   ```
   Create five subagents in the .claude/agents/ folder. product-manager-prd
   writes the PRD and manages the schedule, backend-architect designs the
   server and the APIs, frontend-developer builds the interface, qa-engineer
   handles testing and code review, and ai-integration-specialist connects the
   OpenRouter API. Set the model to sonnet for each of them.
   ```

2. Claude Code asks before it writes each file. Choose **Yes** each time. It asks five times, and the five files appear one after another.

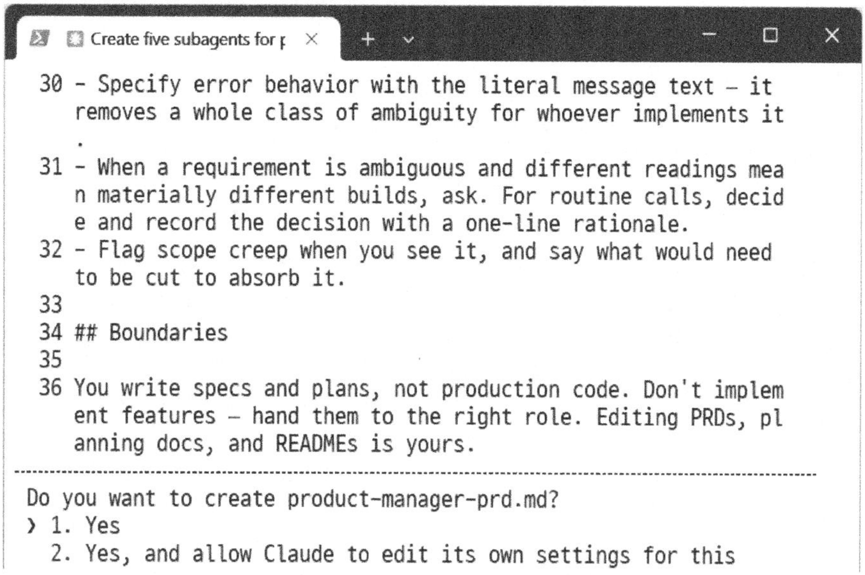

Figure 7.21: Claude Code writes the agent definitions one file at a time

3. When all five have been written, Claude Code prints a summary of which agent to call and what each one is for. Read it and carry on with the conversation.

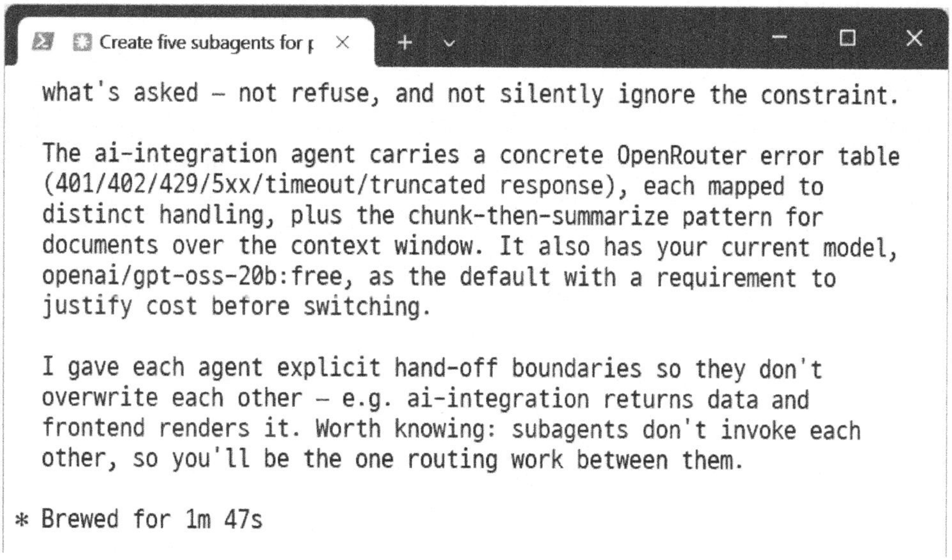

Figure 7.22: Claude Code's summary of the five agents

The following table summarizes the five sub-agents you have just created, along with the role and model of each:

Sub-agent	Function and role description	Model
Backend Developer	A server-side development expert responsible for server architecture design, API development, data processing, external service integration, and security and performance optimization. Builds stable and scalable backend systems.	sonnet
Frontend Developer	A client-side development expert responsible for designing and implementing user interfaces, responsive design, web accessibility, and performance optimization.	sonnet
Quality Assurance Engineer	A quality assurance expert who performs functional testing of the entire system, error handling verification, performance optimization, and code reviews. Detects bugs and suggests usability improvements.	sonnet
AI Integration Specialist	An AI expert responsible for LLM and AI service integration, prompt optimization and building AI pipelines. Here, an LLM utilization specialist who implements text generation and summarization by connecting with the `gpt-oss` model via the OpenRouter API.	sonnet
Product Manager	A product planning expert responsible for writing the PRD and managing the project schedule	sonnet

Table 7.3: The five subagents and their roles

Open `.claude/agents/` in the `Study-05` folder and check that there are five .md files. The name of each file is the name of the agent.

Figure 7.23: Five .md files in the .claude/agents folder

Open `product-manager-prd.md` and it looks like the screen shown in *Figure 7.24*. The name and the role you wrote in the prompt are in the name and description fields, and the model line reads sonnet.

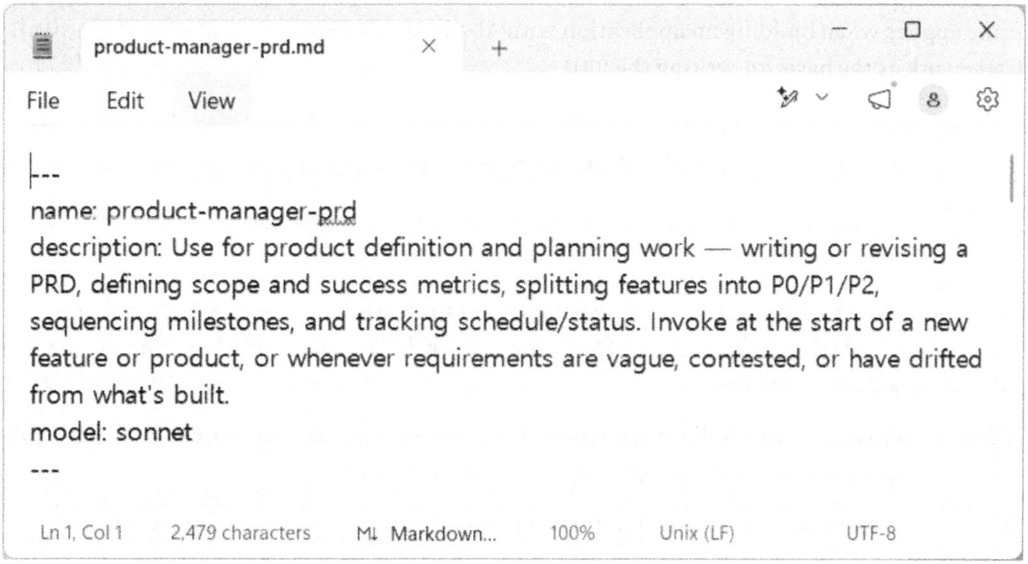

Figure 7.24: The product-manager-prd definition file

If anything needs changing, edit the file yourself or ask Claude Code to change it.

> **Tip**
>
> While you can create multiple sub-agents, more is not always better. If there are too many, management becomes complicated due to role definition, context management, and resource allocation.

With AI sub-agents for software or application development, it is now possible to operate an expert development team. However, not every project requires all five sub-agents. Choose and use the sub-agents needed according to the needs of your project.

Building an application with an agent team: 'AI Empathy Diary'

By creating five sub-agents responsible for product planning, backend development, frontend development, quality assurance, and AI integration, you have built your own specialized development team for application development. From now on, together with your expert development team, let's implement the AI Empathy Diary, which analyzes, responds with empathy, and offers comfort and encouragement based on the text you write in your diary.

Organizing product requirements with the 5W1H framework

In real development teams, the PM specifies product requirements using the 5W1H framework during the product planning process so that the team shares the same goals and direction. The same applies when building an application with AI—back in *Chapter 2*, we also used the 5W1H framework as the basis for writing the PRD.

> **Note**
>
> PM is an abbreviation for Product Manager, referring to the person in charge of product planning.

When operating multiple agents, it is also important to clearly define each role (Who) and working method (How). Based on the 5W1H framework, let's organize the requirements for the 'AI Empathy Diary' as follows:

What: AI Empathy Diary - A diary app where users write a one-line summary of their day, and the AI analyzes their emotions and provides empathy and comfort.

Why: To help users achieve peace of mind by recording their day and providing emotional support.

When: Start development right now to create a finished product that can be used immediately.

Where: Runs in a web browser in the user's local environment.

How:

- Use the OpenRouter API and the free *openai/gpt-oss-20b:free* model to perform emotion analysis and generate empathy messages
- Apply a soft and reassuring UI design
- The API key is read and used from the `.env` file in the current project folder
- The final deliverable is produced as a single `index.html` file
- Produce a stable version through thorough testing

Who:

- **Backend Developer**: Implements API integration and features for emotion analysis and empathy message generation
- **Frontend Developer**: Creates a diary UI with a cozy, calming feel
- **Quality Assurance Engineer**: Tests various scenarios and fixes issues until they are fully resolved

To develop the AI Empathy Diary application, you need backend, frontend, and quality assurance agents. Let's use the OpenRouter API to integrate the AI model into the application and implement it using sub-agents:

1. In your desktop file explorer, to load the OpenRouter API key, copy the `.env` file from the `Study-04` folder and paste it into the `Study-05` folder. If you later turn `Study-05` into a Git repository, add `.env` to `.gitignore` first so the key is never committed.

   > **Note**
   >
   > You can review how to securely set up the API key in *Chapter 6*.
   >
   > The `.env` file in the `Study-04` folder contains the OpenRouter API key.

2. In Claude Code, describe the features of the 'AI Empathy Diary' application, and specify the required sub-agents along with each agent's role and implementation method:
   Prompt:

```
Please create an AI empathy diary application, where, if the user writes a
one-line summary of their day, the AI analyzes their emotions, offers
empathy, and provides words of comfort.
```

```
The backend architect should implement the features for emotion analysis
and empathetic message generation by integrating the OpenRouter API. Please
use the free openai/gpt-oss-20b:free model and the API key stored in
the .env file within the current directory.

The frontend developer should design a diary UI that evokes a warm and
comforting atmosphere.
Finally, the QA engineer should test the application to ensure it functions
smoothly across various scenarios. Any issues found must be fully resolved,
and the final version should be delivered as an index.html file that can
be opened directly in a web browser.
```

3. Claude Code hands the work to the sub-agents and runs them in the background. While they are working, the line at the foot of the terminal tells you it is waiting for the three background agents to finish, and each agent reports as it completes, with the time it took.

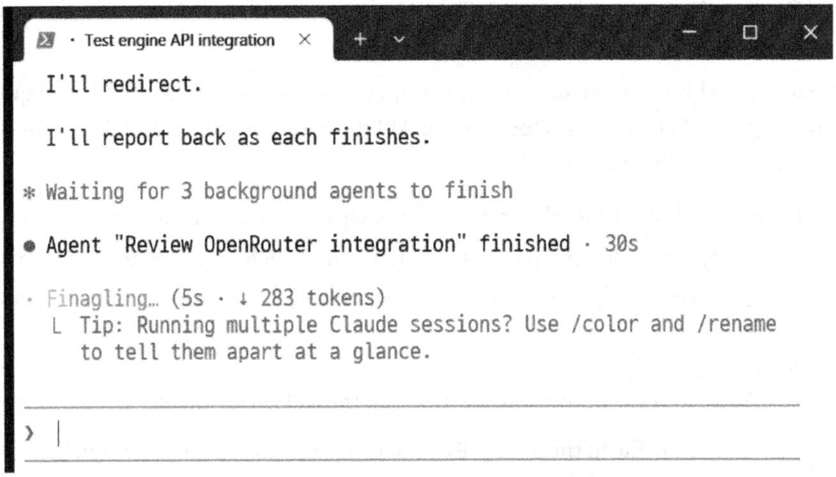

Figure 7.25: Waiting for the three background agents to finish

Note

Why agent execution times differ

Execution times vary from run to run, and the QA engineer agent is usually the last to finish. Its work starts from what the other two produce: it reviews their output, tests the application against several scenarios and fixes what it finds, so it cannot finish before them.

QA is the slowest stage in most real development teams too. If a run feels too long, press the Esc key to stop it, or ask for a smaller set of tests next time.

4. Check the final report to see which features are ready.
5. Let's click the `index.html` file in the `Study-05` folder to run it. This is the completed Empathy AI Diary.

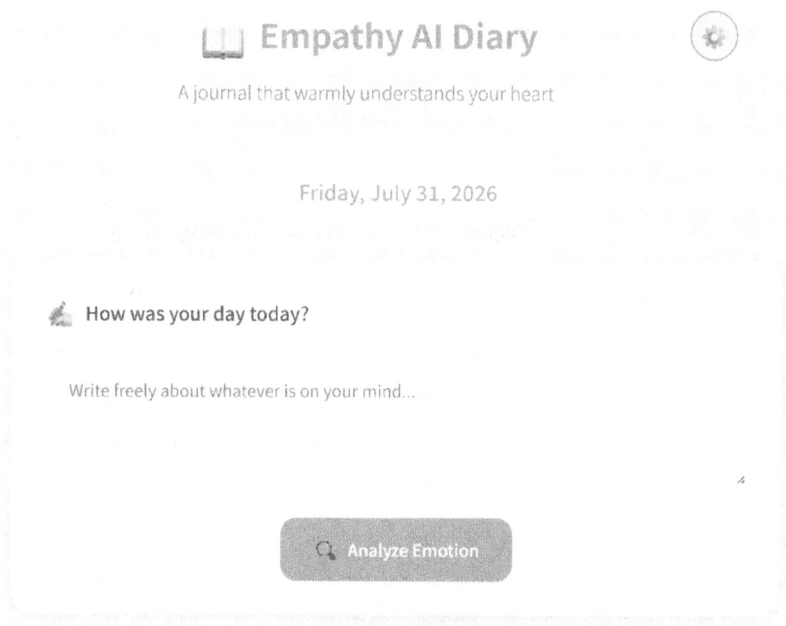

Figure 7.26: The completed Empathy AI Diary

6. Let's test whether the application accurately analyzes the emotions in the text. Enter the text shown in *Figure 7.27* and click the **Analyze Emotion** button.

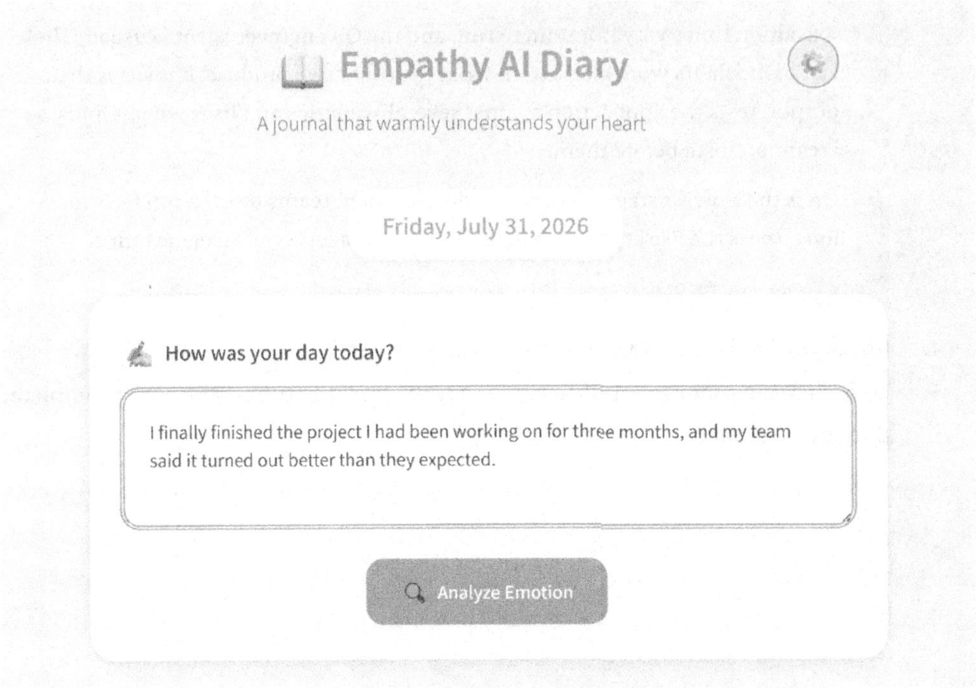

Figure 7.27: Share an emotion with the agent

7. It accurately detects feelings of joy and adds an empathetic message.

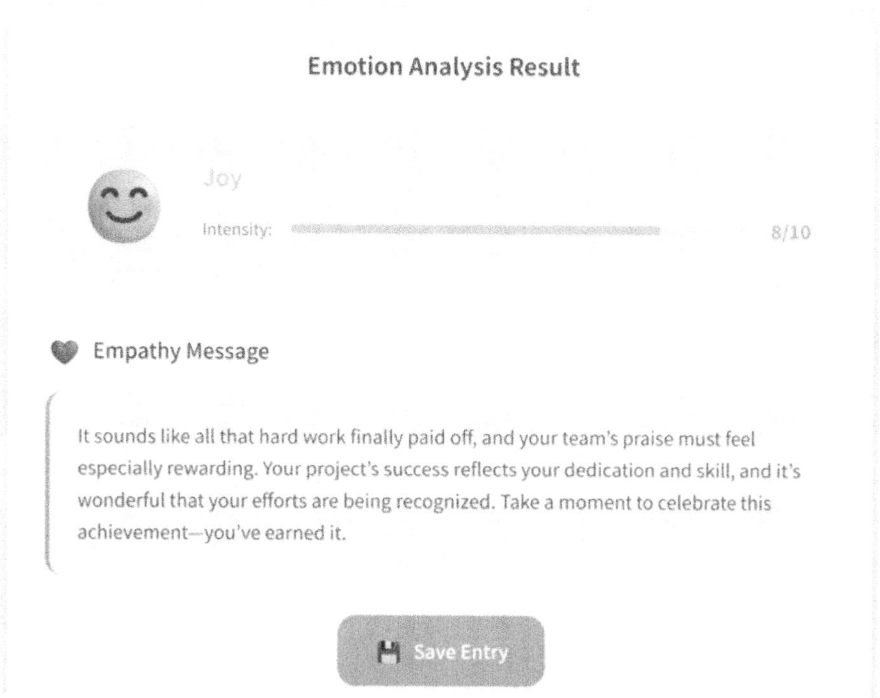

Figure 7.28: Emotion analysis report

> **Tip**
>
> Try writing diary entries with various emotions to test whether the application detects emotions accurately.

8. The diary entries you write and their emotion-analysis results are saved in chronological order.

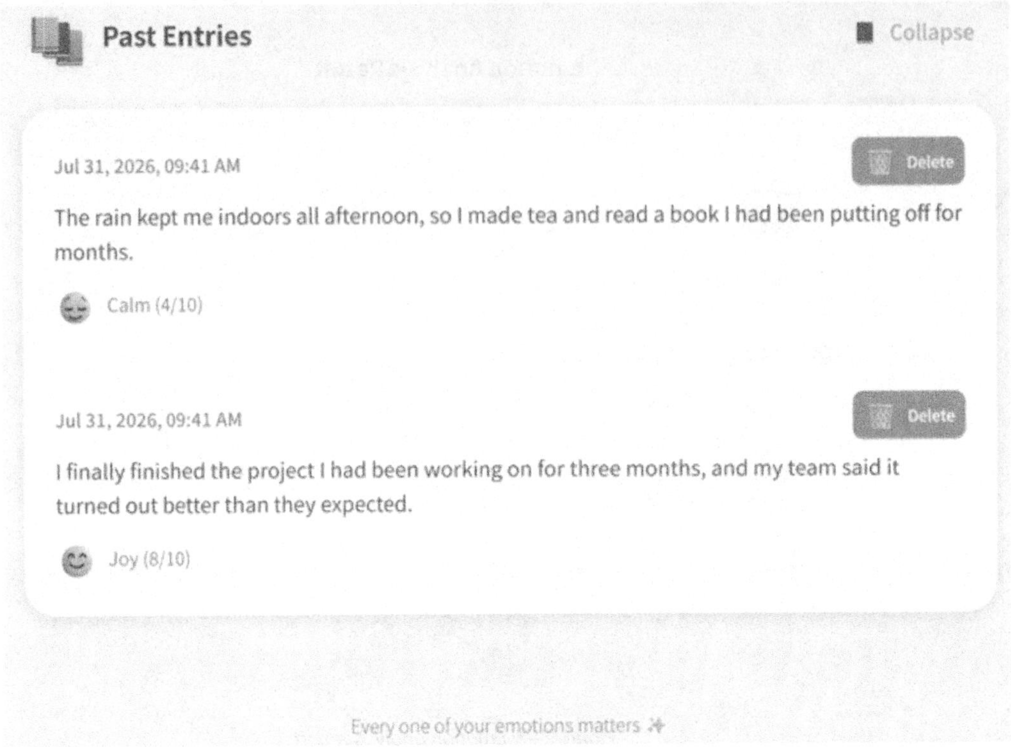

Figure 7.29: Past entries saved

If your result differs from the one shown in the book, you can revise it by entering more specific requirements for your desired application in Claude Code.

Building an application with an agent team: PDF Summary AI

This time, we'll mobilize a total of five sub-agents to create an application that accepts a PDF file, extracts the text, and summarizes, organizes, and analyzes it. Let's use the AI agents we created earlier. Here are the roles, names, and missions of each agent needed for developing the PDF Summary AI application.

Role	Agent Name	Task Assignment
Product Planning Manager	product-manager-prd	Write a detailed PRD and feature specifications for the PDF document summary app

Role	Agent Name	Task Assignment
Backend Developer	backend-architect	Implement PDF file upload and text extraction features
AI Integration Specialist	ai-integration-specialist	Integrate the OpenRouter API to summarize the extracted text. Use the free openai/gpt-oss-20b:free model and the API key stored in the .env file.
Frontend Developer	frontend-developer	Implement a drag-and-drop file upload UI and a clean interface to display the summary results.
Quality Assurance Engineer	qa-engineer	Thoroughly test the entire system with various PDF formats and fix any bugs.

Table 7.4: Five sub-agents used for the PDF Summary AI application

Tip

When conversing with Claude Code, name the sub-agent you want in the prompt. If you want to be certain that a particular agent runs, mention it as `@agent-` followed by its name, for example `@agent-qa-engineer`. To see which agents exist, look in the `.claude\agents` folder.

1. In Claude Code, describe the features of the **PDF Summary AI** application, and specify each sub-agent's role and implementation method.

   Prompt:

```
We're going to create a web application where you can upload a PDF document
and the AI will summarize it.

First, product-manager-prd will write a detailed PRD and feature
specifications for the PDF document summary app and then the backend-
architect will implement the PDF file upload and text extraction features.

The ai-integration-specialist will integrate the OpenRouter API to
```

```
summarize the extracted text.

Use the free openai/gpt-oss-20b:free model, and use the API key stored in
the '.env' file in the current folder. The frontend-developer will
implement a drag-and-drop file upload UI and a clean interface to display
the summary results.

The qa-engineer should test to ensure everything works smoothly in various
scenarios. If any issues are found, fix them completely, and create the
final version as an 'index_pdf.html' file that can be opened directly in
the browser.
```

> **Note**
>
> To avoid using the same file name as the 'AI Empathy Diary' application, the final executable file is named `index_pdf.html`.

2. The process begins with the product manager creating the PRD.

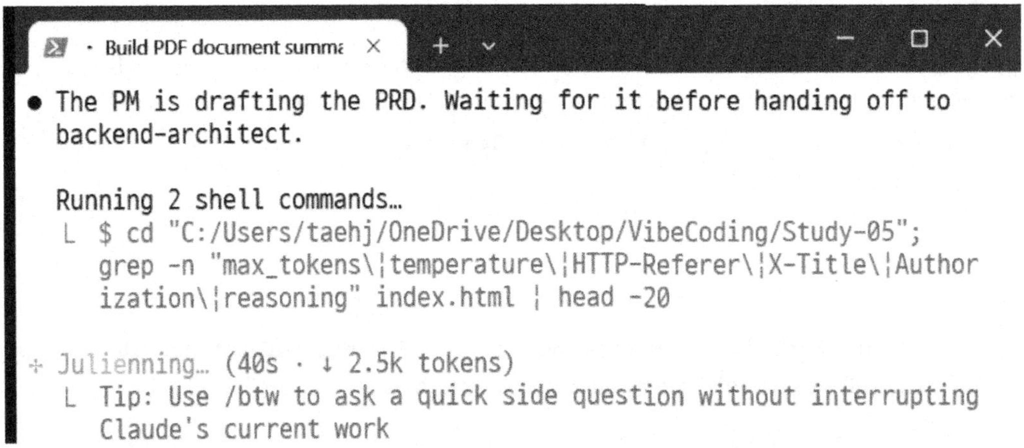

Figure 7.30: Product manager creates the PRD

3. If there are no issues with the PRD, select **2. Yes, allow all edits during this session** to proceed.
4. Verify that the PRD document `PRD_PDF_Summary_App.md` has been created in the `Study-05` folder for the project.

> **Note**
>
> The file name may differ from the book.

5. The five agents perform their tasks sequentially, and the web application is completed.

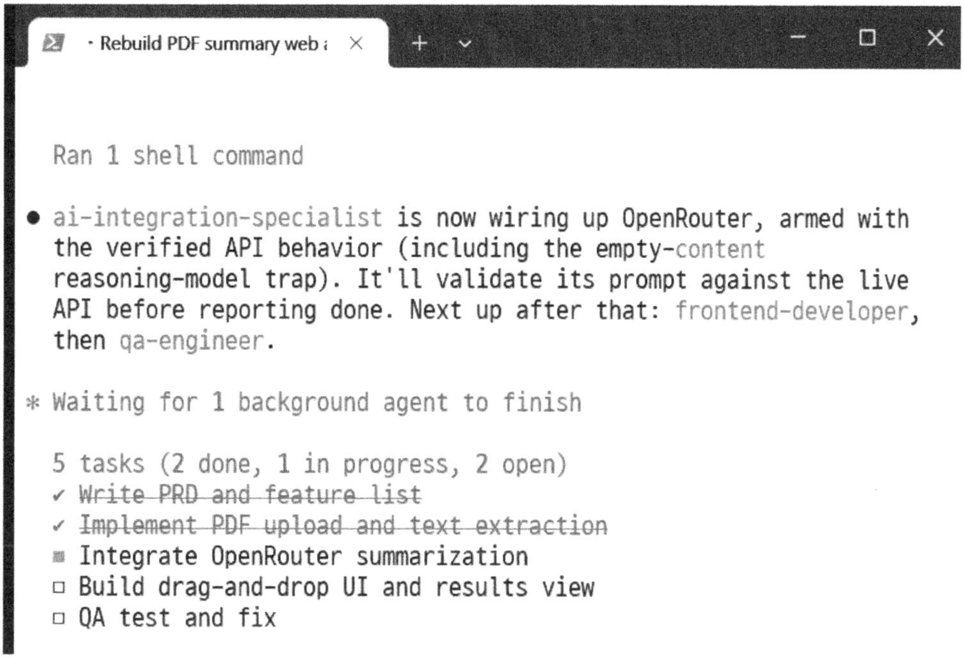

Figure 7.31: Web application completed

6. Find and run the newly created `index_pdf.html` file in the `Study-05` folder.
7. When the PDF document summarization service app runs as shown, it is complete. If you did not get the desired result, describe the current issue to Claude Code to revise and improve it.

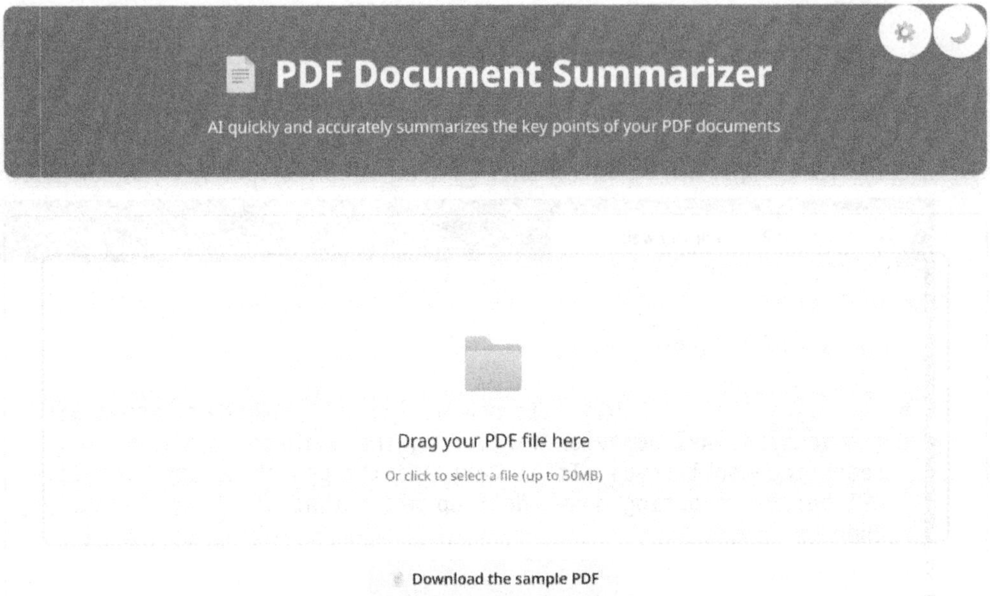

Figure 7.32: PDF document summary

8. For testing, download the `ai-assistant-guide.pdf` file from the input-examples folder of the book's GitHub repository. Return to the application, upload the `ai-assistant-guide.pdf` file, select the **Standard Summary** mode, and click the **Generate Summary** button.
9. Verify that the contents of the PDF file are summarized and presented.

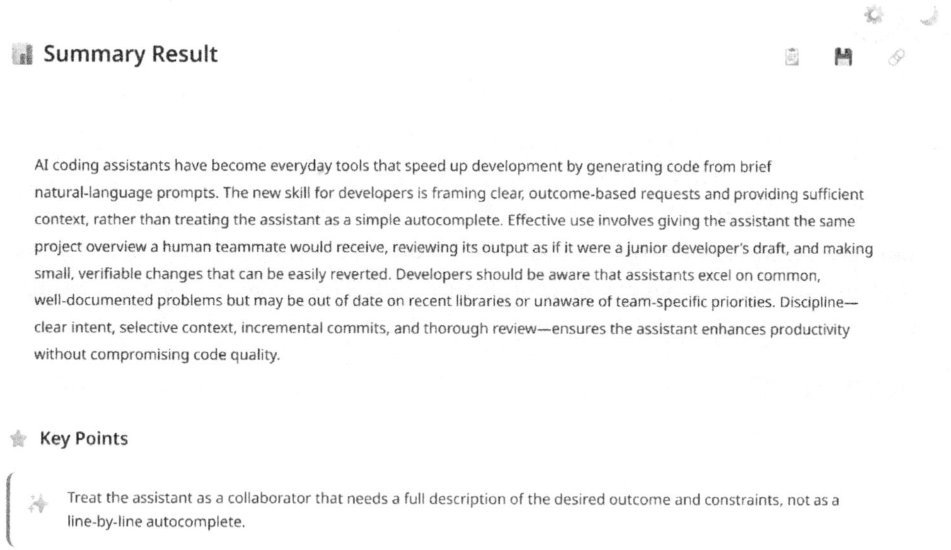

Figure 7.33: Verify the summary result

10. This time, select the **Brief Summary** mode and click the **Generate Summary** button. It will show a slightly different summary result.

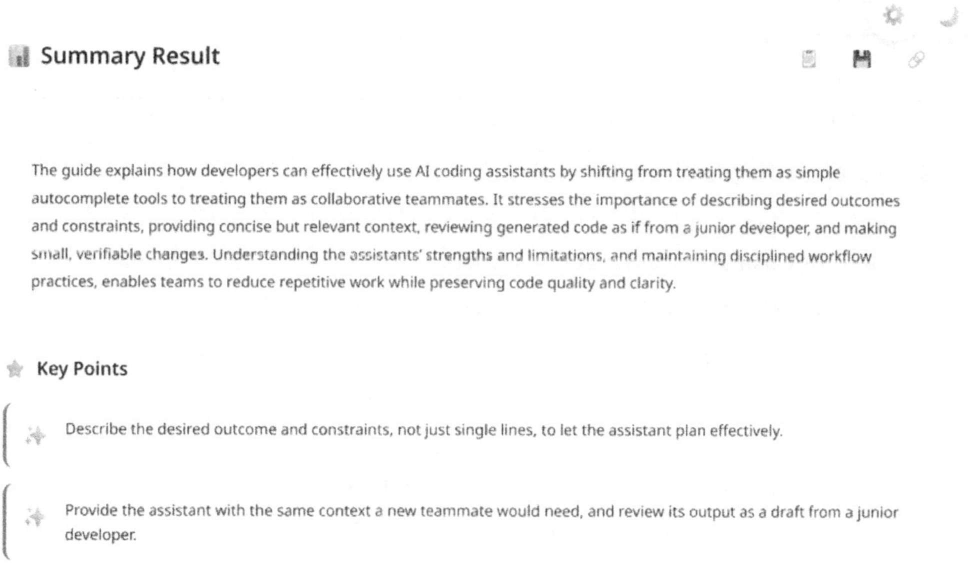

Figure 7.34: Revised summary

> **Tip**
>
> Try working with the various summary modes.

So far, we have looked at the process of configuring five AI sub-agents and having them collaborate as if in a real development team. Each agent automatically handles planning, development, design, and verification according to its assigned role, demonstrating that you can complete a team-based project on your own. Now, you are not just a developer who writes code, but an AI product manager who coordinates multiple AI agents to complete a single product.

Wrapping up

Key takeaways summarized in 5 Keywords:

- The **product manager** defines the product's goals, features, and user requirements, and manages the overall development schedule.
- The **backend developer** is the technical expert responsible for implementing the application's core logic, such as server and database design and API integration.
- The **frontend developer** is a UI developer who designs and implements the screens and interfaces users see.
- The **quality assurance engineer** is a verification expert who tests functionality and performance, fixes bugs, and ensures service stability.
- In a development process that incorporates AI, an **AI integration specialist** is needed to connect and optimize the AI models.

Review questions

1. In the development of the AI Empathy Diary, what is the most appropriate reason why QA testing usually takes longer than backend and frontend development?
    1. Because the QA agent uses a slower AI model.
    2. Because the QA agent has to review all the results of the previous agents' work.
    3. Because only the QA agent needs an internet connection.
    4. Because the QA agent does not have file read permissions.
2. In the PDF summarization tool, which of the following is NOT a correct way for other agents to reference the PRD created by the product manager agent?
    1. The PRD is created in the project folder, and each agent accesses it.
    2. Agents refer to the PRD while working sequentially or in parallel.

3. There is no need to specify the PRD file path for each agent.
4. The PRD is automatically copied to the `.claude/agents/` folder and shared.

8

Extending Claude Code with MCP, Skills, and Plugins

Up to now, most of the programs we've created have operated within the basic functions provided by Claude Code. However, in real development projects, basic functions alone are sometimes not enough. **Model Context Protocol** (**MCP**) is a powerful tool that overcomes these limitations and greatly expands the capabilities of Claude Code. Just like adding plugins to a development environment, connecting through MCP allows Claude Code to freely collaborate with external systems.

In this chapter, we will automatically generate documents by integrating with Notion, upload projects to GitHub, and connect to a database to create a fully functional service. Applications that used to run in the local environment will now become real services accessible to anyone around the world.

Learning objectives:

- You will understand the concept of MCP and be able to connect it with Claude Code
- You will be able to distinguish between remote MCP and local MCP servers and install them as needed
- You can automatically test web applications using Playwright MCP
- You can manage and upload projects using GitHub MCP
- You can deploy and operate real services using Vercel and Supabase

Understanding MCP and Connecting to Claude Code

> Note
>
> **Key terms**: MCP | Client-server model | Local MCP | Remote MCP | Authentication | Double hyphen (--)
>
> In this section, we will look at how MCP expands the possibilities of AI. By seeing how Claude Code uses MCP to generate documents in external services, or using local MCP to reason through complex problems step by step, you will learn how AI can go beyond simple responses and connect with real work tools.

Before you begin

When assembling LEGO blocks, there are limits to what you can build with just the basic set, but by adding special pieces, you can create anything you imagine. **MCP** is the connector that links these special pieces to Claude Code. Since Anthropic, the company behind Claude, proposed MCP in November 2024, it has become the standard for AI developers worldwide. Now, let's connect these powerful tools one by one and explore the expanded capabilities of Claude Code for ourselves.

Figure 8.1: MCP for connecting powerful tools

How MCP expands AI capabilities

MCP is a standardized communication protocol used when AI models connect to external data, tools, or services. In other words, it acts as a bridge that allows AI to communicate and collaborate with various systems in a consistent way.

An API is an interface that allows different programs to exchange data and access the functionality of another service. For example, when developing the **FridgeChef** application, we used OpenRouter's API to access AI models for image recognition and text generation. In contrast, MCP is a protocol for AI applications to connect to tools and data sources such as APIs, files, and databases. Through MCP, AI models can directly access and utilize various external services and data sources.

For example, you can use an API to request text generation from an AI model, but you cannot have the AI model directly manipulate the file system or modify a database. However, with MCP, AI can directly access the file system and query or modify databases.

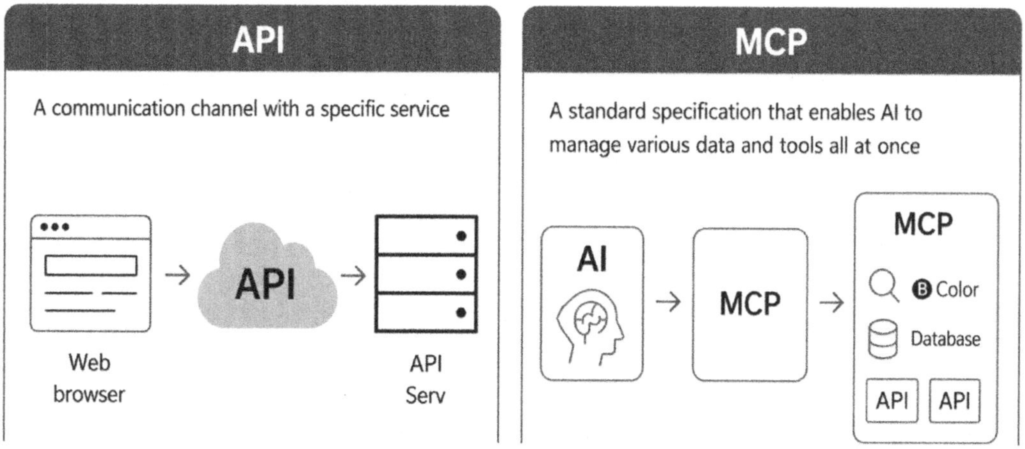

Figure 8.2: API and MCP

Claude Code already has built-in MCP client functionality. When you configure which MCP server to use, Claude Code sends requests to the MCP server according to your settings. The MCP server then performs the actual tasks using its capabilities.

For example, if you connect an MCP server responsible for 'file browsing and code analysis,' Claude Code can access the system through the server, examine the folder structure, analyze related code, and automatically generate reports. In this way, using MCP broadens the range of tasks Claude Code can handle.

Note

Client-Server Model

The **client-server model (CS model)** refers to a structure in a network where clients send requests and servers return responses. The client is the party making the request, and the server is the party providing the service. In other words, the client sends a request, and the server returns a response that matches the request.

Claude's MCP also follows the client-server model. Claude acts as the client, sending requests, and the MCP server processes the actual tasks and returns the results. This model has two advantages. First, it is easy to expand by simply connecting a new MCP server when adding new features. Second, Claude only gives instructions, and each MCP server handles the actual execution, which increases stability.

However, since the MCP server actually accesses external files or APIs, you must carefully manage security, authentication, and access permissions.

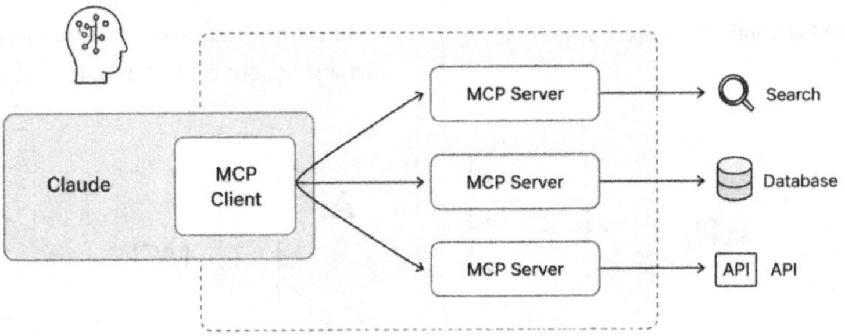

Figure 8.3: Client-server model

Connecting Claude Code with Notion

Now, let's actually connect MCP to Claude Code and run it. In this chapter, we'll link Claude Code to Notion, a collaboration tool for creating and managing documents, and actually create pages and write documents using MCP.

Signing up for Notion

Notion is a popular collaboration tool with a wide range of uses, such as creating and managing documents and projects, or even serving as a database. To use the Notion service, let's sign up first.

1. Go to the Notion homepage (`https://www.notion.com`) in your web browser and click the **Use Notion for free** button at the top right of the screen.

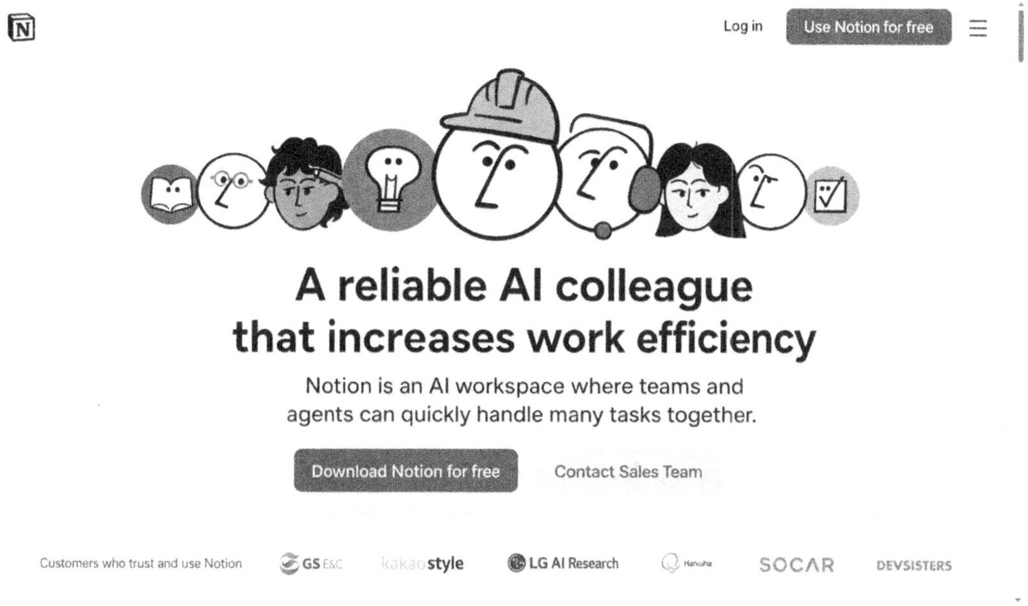

Figure 8.4: Notion homepage

2. Either link an existing account from another service or enter a new email address to sign up.
3. Once your account is created, you can create a workspace. You can now start using Notion.

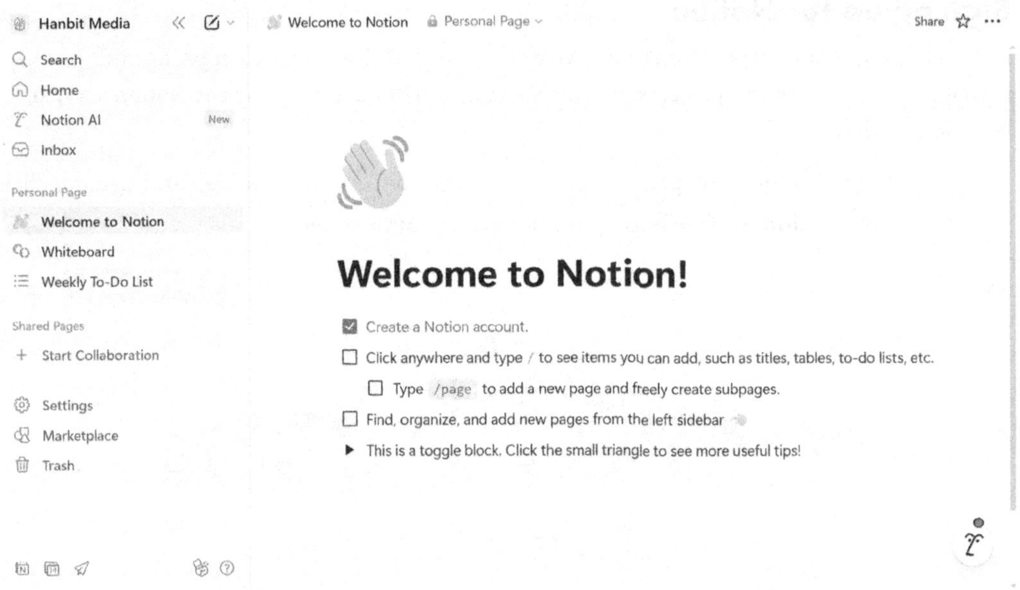

Figure 8.5: Notion welcome page after signing in

Installing the Notion MCP server

Let's try installing and integrating the Notion MCP server with Claude Code. First, create a new `Study-06` folder inside the `VibeCoding` folder on your desktop, and open a terminal in that location to get ready. Do not run Claude yet; just keep the terminal open for now.

The process of adding an MCP server can be summarized in three steps:

1. Use the `claude mcp add` command in the terminal to install the desired MCP server
2. For MCPs that connect to external services like Notion, you will need to go through an authentication process to link your account
3. Write a prompt in Claude Code to actually use the features of the MCP and perform the task

   You will enter the installation command in the terminal to download the MCP server and register it in the configuration file. This chapter provides a supplementary website called **Vibe Index** (`www.vibeindex.ai`). Vibe Index is a directory that collects and organizes resources in real time for use with Claude Code.

4. Let's find the Notion MCP on Vibe Index and install it in Claude Code. In your web browser, go to **Vibe Index** and search for `notion` in the search bar.

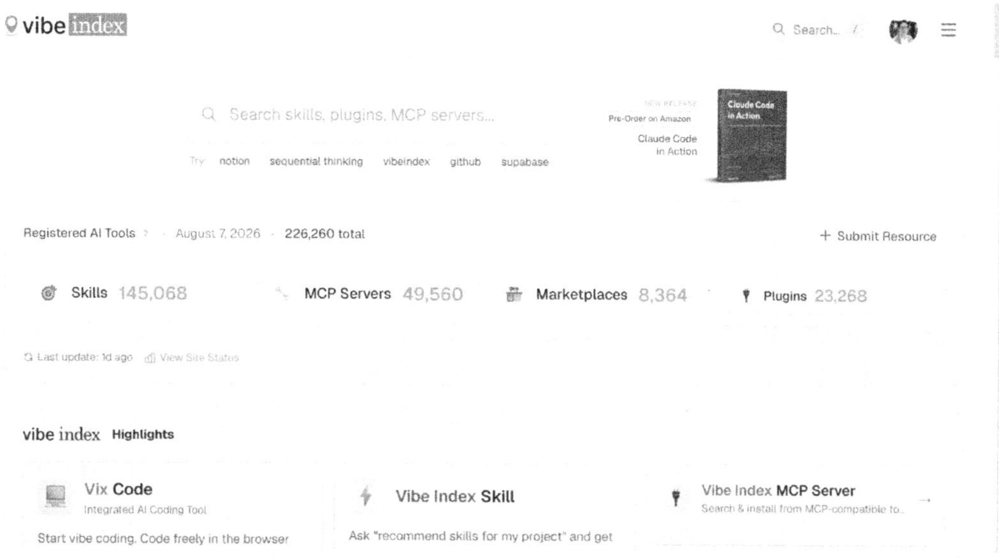

Figure 8.6: Search for Notion in Vibe Index

5. In the search results, click on **Notion**, the official Notion MCP. Make sure it is marked as **Official MCP**.

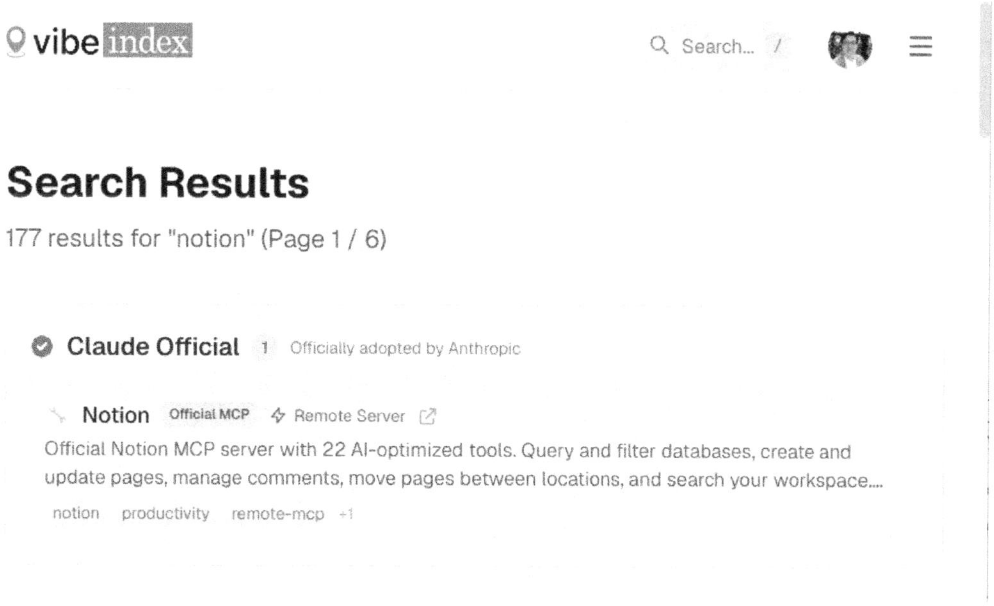

Figure 8.7: Search for the official MCP tagged Notion

6. Scroll down the details page to the **Installation** section, find the installation command, and click the Copy to clipboard icon to copy the command.

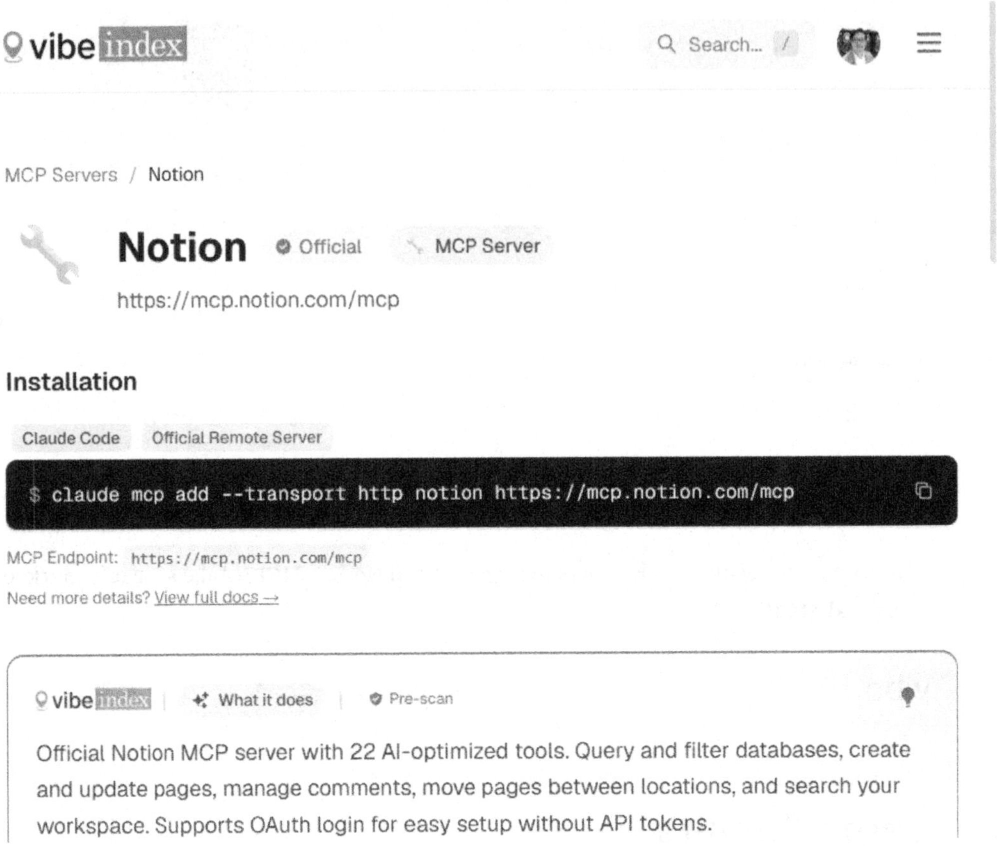

Figure 8.8: Copy the installation command

7. Paste the copied Notion MCP server installation command into the terminal you opened:

```
claude mcp add --transport http notion https://mcp.notion.com/mcp
```

> **Note**
>
> This command means you are loading and connecting to a pre-configured external server (`https://mcp.notion.com/mcp`) named 'notion'. You must enter and run this in the terminal before starting Claude Code.

8. The MCP server has been successfully added.

```
Added HTTP MCP server notion with URL: https://mcp.notion.com/mcp to local
config
File modified: C:\Users\taehj\.claude.json [project: C:\Users\taehj\OneDriv
e\Desktop\VibeCoding\Study-06]

C:\Users\taehj\OneDrive\Desktop\VibeCoding\Study-06>claude
```

Figure 8.9: MCP successfully added

Completing the connection with MCP server authentication

1. Now that the MCP server is installed, enter the `claude` command in the terminal to run Claude Code.
2. To check the list of configured MCP servers and server status in Claude Code, enter the `/mcp` command.
3. In the MCP server management window, you can see that the Notion MCP is registered. However, it is not yet logged in, so it is not connected. Press the *Enter* key to proceed with the connection.

```
> /mcp

Manage MCP servers

> 1. notion            Δ disconnected · Enter to login

MCP Config locations (by scope):
 • User config (available in all your projects):
   • C:\Users\user\.claude.json
 • Project config (shared via .mcp.json):
   • C:\Users\user\Desktop\VibeCoding\Study-06\.mcp.json (file
   does not exist)
 • Local config (private to you in this project):
   • C:\Users\user\.claude.json [project:
   C:\Users\user\Desktop\VibeCoding\Study-06]

For help configuring MCP servers, see:
https://docs.claude.com/en/docs/claude-code/mcp
```

Figure 8.10: MCP management window

4. Let's authenticate so that Claude Code can access your Notion account. Select **1. Authenticate** and press the *Enter* key.

```
Notion MCP Server

Status: Δ needs authentication
URL: https://mcp.notion.com/mcp
Config location: C:\Users\user\.claude.json [project:
                 C:\Users\user\Desktop\VibeCoding\Study-06]

> 1. Authenticate
  2. Disable
```

Figure 8.11: Authenticate Claude Code to access Notion

5. After a moment, a new window will open in your web browser.

```
Authenticating with notion…

* A browser window will open for authentication

If your browser doesn't open automatically, copy this URL manually:
https://mcp.notion.com/authorize?response_type=code&client_id=3e58KvQ
[illegible]
ce=https%3A%2F%2Fmcp.notion.com%2F

  Return here after authenticating in your browser. Press Esc to go
  back.
```

Figure 8.12: Window for authentication

6. To link your Notion account to the MCP server, check the **I know and trust this URL** checkbox, then click the **Continue** button.
7. If you see the message **Authentication Successful**, the authentication is complete. Return to Claude Code and enter the `/mcp` command again. You should now see that the Notion MCP server is connected. Press the *Enter* key to view detailed information.

```
> /mcp

 Manage MCP servers

 > 1. notion              √ connected · Enter to view details

 MCP Config locations (by scope):
  • User config (available in all your projects):
    • C:\Users\user\.claude.json
  • Project config (shared via .mcp.json):
    • C:\Users\user\Desktop\VibeCoding\Study-06\.mcp.json (file
    does not exist)
  • Local config (private to you in this project):
    • C:\Users\user\.claude.json [project:
    C:\Users\user\Desktop\VibeCoding\Study-06]

 For help configuring MCP servers, see:
 https://docs.claude.com/en/docs/claude-code/mcp
```

Figure 8.13: Notion is connected

8. You can see the task tools registered in the Notion MCP server for use with Claude. Select **1. View tools**, then press the *Enter* key.
9. You can view the list of specific tools provided by the Notion MCP server. Press the *Esc* key to exit the server management window.

```
Tools for notion (15 tools)

> 1.  notion-search                 read-only, open-world
  2.  notion-fetch                  read-only
  3.  notion-create-pages
  4.  notion-update-page            destructive
↓ 5.  notion-move-pages

  Esc to go back
```

Figure 8.14: View the list of specific tools

Automatically creating research notes with Notion MCP

Now, let's actually automate research notes by linking with the Notion MCP. We'll search for the latest updates in Claude Code and have them summarized and uploaded to Notion.

1. Enter the following prompt in Claude Code:

   Prompt:

   ```
   Summarize the latest changes in Claude Code and save them to 'Self-Study Vibe Notion Example' via Notion MCP.
   ```

2. If you press **1. Yes** to continue, you will see a message indicating that the latest updates have been successfully searched and saved to Notion. Now, let's check if the document was actually created in Notion.

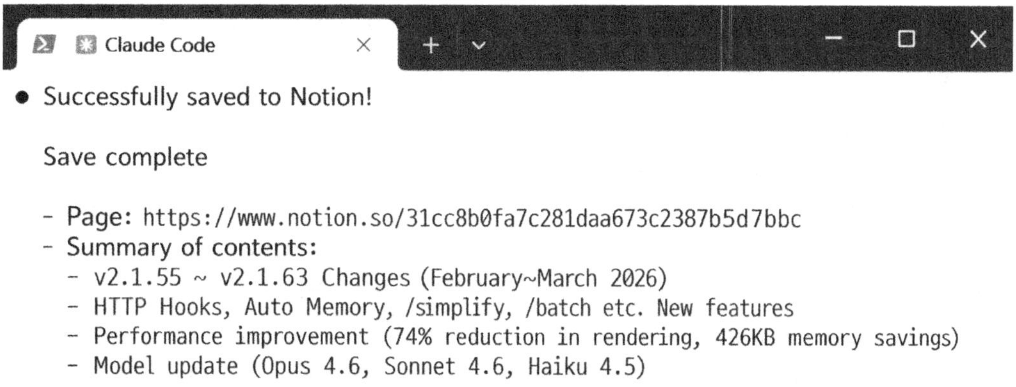

Figure 8.15: Updates have been saved to Notion

3. You can see that a document with the latest Claude Code updates has been created and saved in Notion.

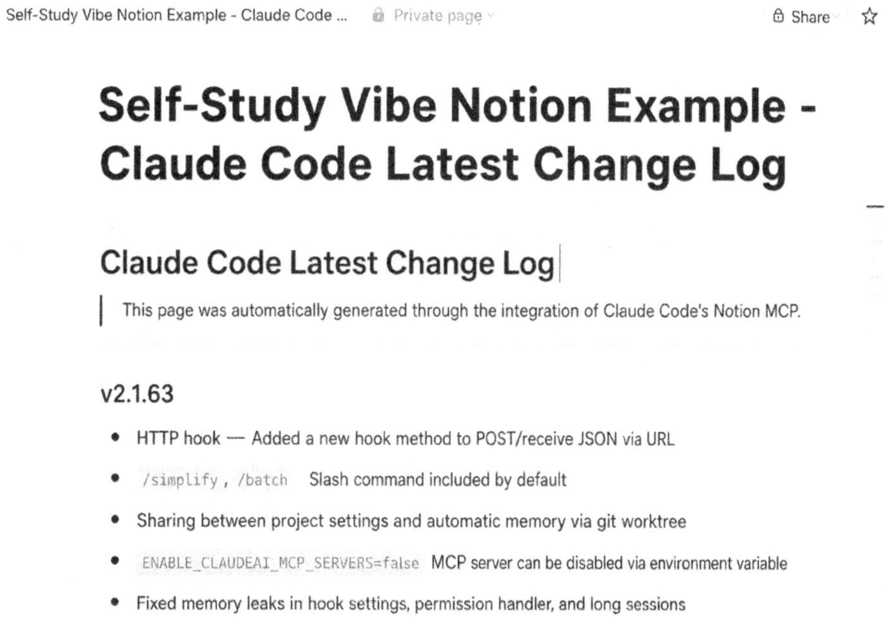

Figure 8.16: Document created and saved in Notion

Building Smarter AI with Sequential Thinking MCP

Let's learn a bit more about how to install and run MCP in Claude Code.

Understanding local MCP and remote MCP

MCP servers are divided into two types based on connection method: local and remote. A local MCP runs the MCP server program directly on your own computer, while a remote MCP runs the broker program on an external server over the internet. Both methods allow Claude Code to connect to external systems via MCP, but the connection location and setup process differ.

The remote server method is the simpler way to get started. With remote MCP, you connect to an MCP server that is already set up on an external server, and you can connect instantly with just a single command.

For example, the Notion MCP was installed with `claude mcp add --transport http notion https://mcp.notion.com/mcp`. This registers the ready-made external server at `https://mcp.notion.com/mcp` under the name notion. In other words, Claude Code connects to the MCP server at that address and can communicate directly with Notion.

A remote MCP connects to a cloud server accessible via the internet, and typically requires a login or authentication process to link to your account. This method is easy to set up and convenient for sharing with multiple users, but keep in mind that it requires an internet connection. The command structure is as follows:

```
claude mcp add --transport http [custom name] [server URL]
```

In contrast, a local MCP is run directly on your own computer. Instead of calling an internet address, you specify the command to execute directly.

With a local MCP, you need to specify the command to run instead of entering a prepared URL, so it requires a bit more setup. However, it works without the internet, responds faster, and is better for privacy. The command structure is as follows. Here, the `--` symbol separates Claude Code options from the MCP execution command:

```
claude mcp add [custom name] [options] -- [MCP execution command]
```

Whether to choose a remote or local MCP server depends on your situation. If you want quick setup and need to collaborate with others, use remote. If your network is unstable or you want to work securely in a personal environment, local MCP is more suitable. Not all MCP servers support both methods. If only one is available, choose according to your environment.

Note

What is Authentication?

When connecting an external service to MCP, authentication is required to verify that the person trying to connect is truly an authorized user.

An MCP server manages data for multiple users. If you don't know who is making a request, someone could accidentally access another person's information or files. Therefore, authentication is needed to prove that the requester is the real user. Since remote MCP communicates over the internet, there is a risk of data leakage in transit. The authentication process ensures that the server and client can exchange data securely over an encrypted connection.

Understanding the Local MCP installation commands

Now, let's install a local MCP. The MCP to install is the Sequential Thinking MCP, the official MCP server created and distributed by Anthropic. As the name suggests, it is a tool that helps break down a given problem into smaller units and reason through them sequentially. The installation command in the command prompt is as follows:

```
claude mcp add sequential-thinking -s local -- npx -y
@modelcontextprotocol/server-sequential-thinking@latest
```

All the information needed to install the MCP is contained in this single command. Let's look at each part in order.

- `sequential-thinking`: This is the name used in Claude Code to identify this MCP.
- `-s local`: This specifies the scope of the MCP. `local` means it applies only to the current project. If set to `project`, it is shared with project team members; if set to `user`, it can be used across all projects in your account. The default is local, so omitting the `-s` flag has the same effect.

  Note

  The `-s` flag is a shorthand for the `--scope` option. You can also use `--scope`.

- `--` (Delimiter): This separates Claude Code options and arguments. Options for Claude Code go before this symbol, and the MCP server execution command goes after it.

- `npx -y`: This runs a `Node.js` package. The `-y` option automatically approves installation if the package is not already installed locally, skipping the `Ok to proceed? (y)` prompt.
- `@modelcontextprotocol/server-sequential-thinking@latest`: This is the name of the MCP package to load. The package name is structured as `@organization/package@version`. In this case, it refers to the latest version (`latest`) of the Sequential Thinking MCP package (`server-sequential-thinking`) distributed by the official MCP team (`modelcontextprotocol`).
  For MCP servers created by individuals, you can omit the `@organization` part. The `@version` part can also be omitted, or you can specify a particular version by adding something like `@2.0` to use that version.

Tip

Installing Node.js

To easily install local MCP and various tools used in upcoming exercises, it's best to install the Node.js package first.

Node.js is a fundamental tool that helps install and run various programs, and it will be used frequently when setting up your practice environment.

You can download and install Node.js from the official website (`https://nodejs.org`) by choosing the installer that matches your operating system.

Installing and using the Sequential Thinking MCP

Now, let's actually install the Sequential Thinking MCP in Claude Code.

1. Enter the installation command for the Sequential Thinking MCP in Claude Code and run it.

```
claude mcp add sequential-thinking -s local -- npx -y
@modelcontextprotocol/server-sequential-thinking@latest
```

2. Once installation is complete, enter `claude mcp list` to check the list of MCPs installed in Claude Code. The Sequential Thinking MCP you just installed will appear under the name `sequential-thinking`.

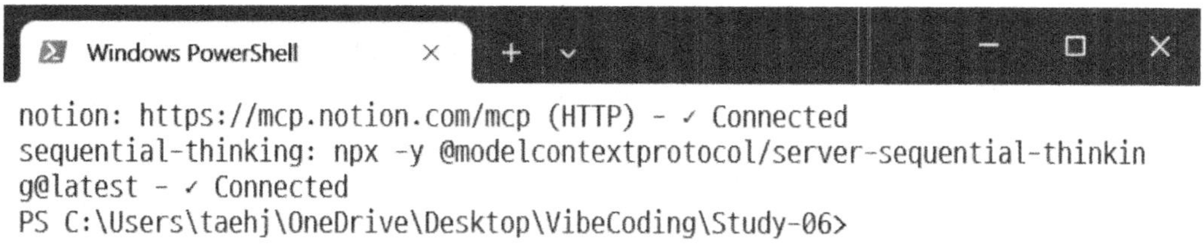

Figure 8.17: Sequential Thinking MCP installed

Checking the performance of the Sequential Thinking MCP

Let's compare the inference capabilities of the installed Sequential Thinking MCP with standard inference.

The goal is to develop a strategy to double the time visitors spend on your web portfolio site.

Enter the `claude` command in the terminal to run Claude Code. First, request `ways to increase visitor dwell time` using the standard approach and save it to Notion under the title **Increase Dwell Time**.

Next, use the Sequential Thinking MCP to request the same topic in a more systematic and step-by-step manner, then save it to Notion as **Increase Dwell Time – Systematic Structure** for comparison.

1. Let's use the Notion MCP and Sequential Thinking MCP to devise methods to achieve the goal and document them in Notion. Enter the following prompt:
   Prompt:

   ```
   I want to double the time visitors spend on my web portfolio.
   Please create two documents:
   1.
   Devise a way to achieve this goal and use the Notion MCP to save it
   as "Increase Dwell Time".
   2. Use the Sequential Thinking MCP to systematically devise a way
   to achieve this goal, and then use the Notion MCP to save it as
   "Increase Dwell Time - Systematic Structure".
   ```

2. After a short wait, you'll receive a completion message along with the URLs for the two Notion documents.

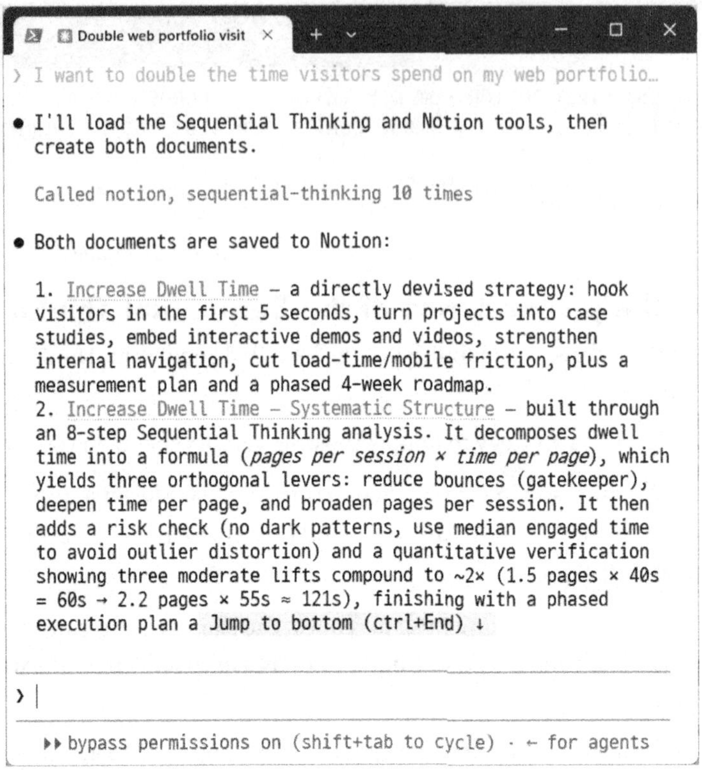

Figure 8.18: Completion message along with URLs of the two documents

3. Two new pages have been created in Notion. Ctrl-click either of the blue underlined links, or open Notion in your browser, to see them.

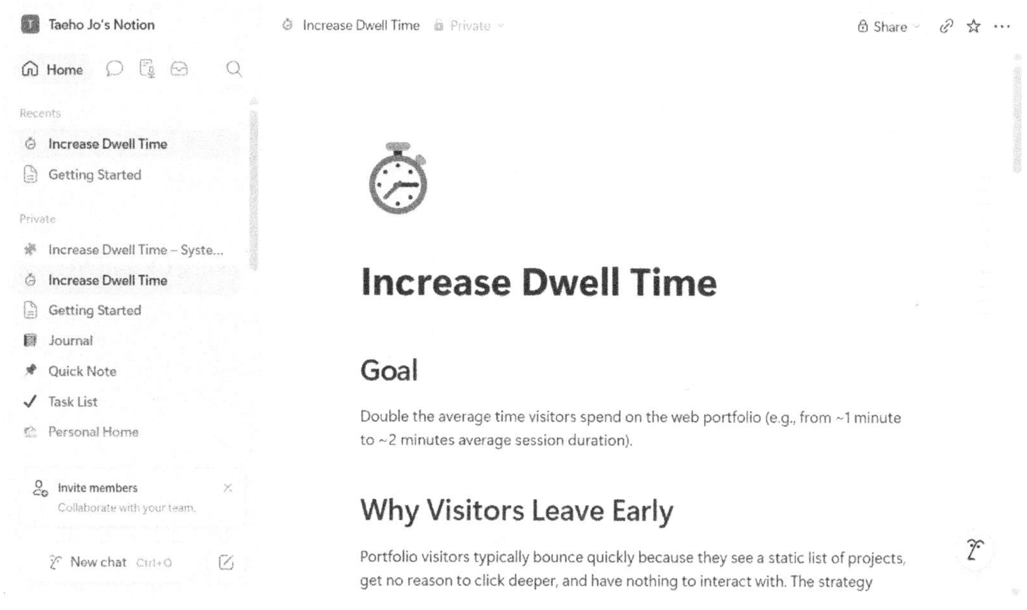

Figure 8.19: Two Notion documents created

4. Let's compare the length of the two documents. The standard inference version has a total of 85 lines, while the sequential inference version has 222 lines, showing a clear difference in volume. The table of contents for the sequential inference version is also more detailed, including sections such as goals, implementation methods, execution roadmap, metrics, and risk response.

The Sequential Thinking MCP is useful for creating systematic prompts or PRDs by planning projects step by step. It's especially powerful when you need to structurally analyze and organize complex problems involving multiple factors.

Wrapping up

Key takeaways summarized in 6 Keywords:

- **MCP** is a standardized communication protocol used when AI models connect to external data, tools, or services.
- The **client-server model** refers to a network architecture in which clients send requests and servers return responses.
- A **local MCP** is a method where the MCP broker program runs directly on your own computer.
- A **remote MCP** is a method where even the broker program runs on an external server over the internet.

- **Authentication** is the process of verifying that the person trying to connect is truly an authorized user.
- A **double hyphen** (--) is a symbol used to indicate option names longer than one character, or to separate commands and options. Its meaning can change depending on its position and spacing, so be careful not to confuse it.

Review questions

1. Choose the most appropriate explanation for the difference between MCP and API.
    1. An API is a way to request specific functions, while MCP is a protocol that allows AI to communicate directly with external systems.
    2. MCP is faster than API.
    3. The API is paid, while MCP is free.
    4. MCP can only be used in Claude Code.
2. Choose the correct role of the -- separator in the local MCP server installation command.
    1. A symbol used to indicate comments
    2. Separates Claude Code options from the MCP server execution command
    3. A marker indicating version information
    4. A separator for error handling
3. Describe the differences between using Sequential Thinking MCP and general reasoning.

A fully automated development environment implemented with plugins and skills

> Note
>
> Key terms: Test | Version Control | Playwright | Remote Repository | Add | Commit | Push
>
> In this section, we will learn about skills and plugins, and use the **Playwright plugin** to learn how to automatically test web applications. We will also practice how to permanently store a project on GitHub.

Before you begin

To run an application reliably, simply completing the code is not enough. You need a testing process to check whether the code runs as intended and is free of errors. Through testing, you can verify functionality and ensure that adding new code does not break existing features. Especially with automation tools like **Playwright**, AI can handle repetitive validation, reducing the developer's burden.

Just as testing protects code quality, version control helps maintain the stability of a project.

It records every change to the code and allows you to revert to previous states when needed, protecting you from mistakes or errors. Using GitHub, you can systematically manage each person's change history during collaboration, and maintain project stability even when multiple people work simultaneously.

Claude's skills

Skills can be seen as an extension of the custom commands learned in *Chapter 5*. Custom commands involved saving prompts as md files in the `.claude/commands/` folder and executing them by entering `/command` format.

Claude later developed this feature further by adding skills. Like custom commands, skills also use prompts saved as md files. However, the storage location is `.claude/skills/skill-name/`, and the file name is set as `SKILL.md`. These saved skills can be automatically invoked and used by Claude as needed, based on the context of the conversation, even if the user does not directly enter `/command`.

Category	Custom Command	Skill
Concept	A prompt command that the user calls and uses directly	A prompt function that is automatically called based on the conversation context
Execution Method	User enters `/command` format directly	Automatically executed as needed, even if not called by the user
Purpose	Quickly execute repetitive tasks	Add specific task capabilities to Claude
Storage Location	`.claude/commands/`	`.claude/skills/skill-name/`

Category	Custom Command	Skill
File Format	`command-name.md`	`SKILL.md`

Table 8.1: Claude skills

The `SKILL.md` file begins with the skill's name and description, followed by a list of rules the skill must follow:

- name: Skill name. Identifier used when installing/calling the skill
- description: Skill description. Displayed in search/list

Creating a skill

You can easily create a skill by instructing Claude Code to make the desired skill.

1. Enter the following prompt into Claude Code.
   Prompt:

   ```
   Create a skill that automatically reviews code.
   ```

2. Claude Code has generated a `Code Review Skill`.

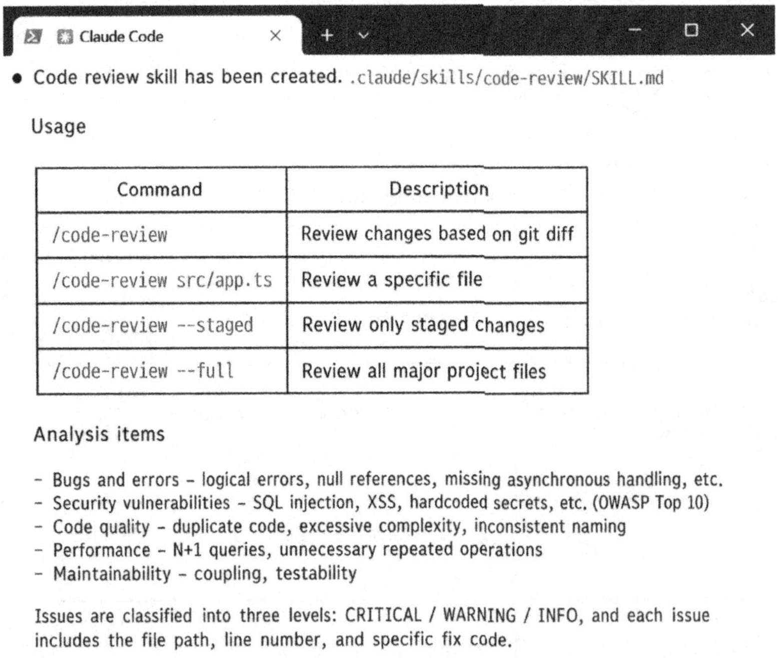

Figure 8.20: Code review skill generated

3. Let's check the Code Review Skill file. A `skills` folder is created under the `.claude` folder in your current working directory, and inside it, a folder named `code-review` is created. The `SKILL.md` file is generated in this `code-review` folder.

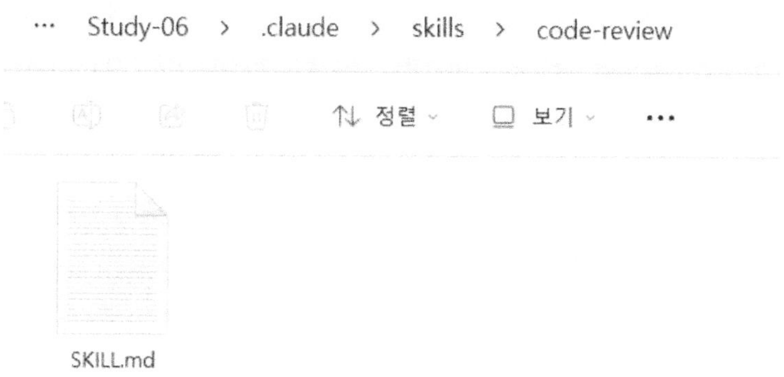

Figure 8.21: SKILL.md file created

4. When you click to open the `SKILL.md` file, you can see the name and description of the file, followed by a list of usage rules.

```
---
name: code-review
description: Reviews code changes to identify bugs, security
vulnerabilities, and code quality issues.
---

When this skill is invoked, immediately execute the steps below. Do not
display or explain this file; start the analysis right away. Detect the
user's language from the conversation context and respond in that language.

## Routing

Parse the user's command and route it to the correct action:
...(omitted)...
```

The skill created in this way will automatically execute whenever there is context to test or review code, performing a code review according to the prompt saved in the file.

Using other skills

One of the advantages of skills is that you can directly apply know-how and prompts created by others to your own project. This time, let's learn how to install and use an external skill called `vibeindex`, which recommends resources suitable for your project.

1. Open the Vibe Index website (`https://www.vibeindex.ai/`) in your web browser and search for `vibeindex` in the search bar.
2. From the search results, select **vibeindex** under the **Skills** category.

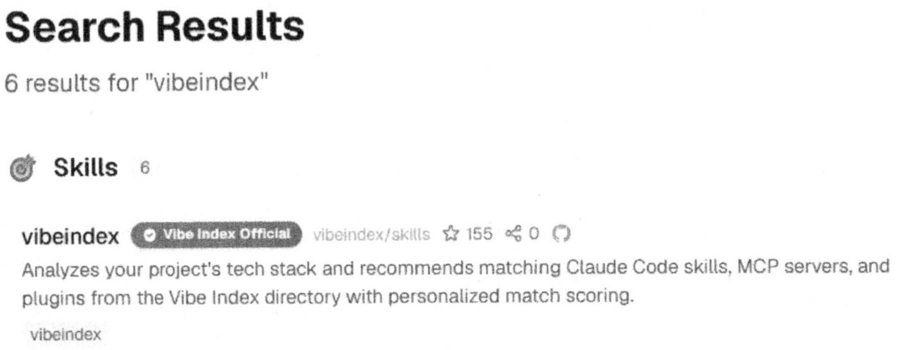

Figure 8.22: Search for vibeindex

3. On the details page, under the **Install** section, click the Copy to clipboard icon to copy the installation command.
4. Exit Claude Code and paste the copied command into your terminal: `npx vibeindex add vibeindex/skills --skill vibeindex`.

> **Note**
>
> Node.js must be installed to run this command. Refer to the tip box in the *Understanding Local MCP installation commands* section that we saw earlier in this chapter.

5. The skill will be installed.
6. Now let's try using the skill. After launching Claude Code, enter the following:

Prompt:

```
Recommend skills, MCP, or plugins needed for the current project.
```

7. The `vibeindex` skill will be automatically loaded and used.

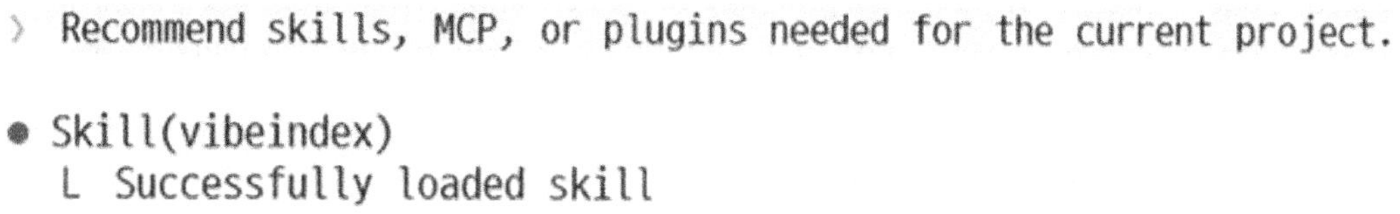

Figure 8.23: vibeindex skill loaded

8. After a short wait, it will recommend the necessary MCPs and skills based on resources from the Vibe Index site.

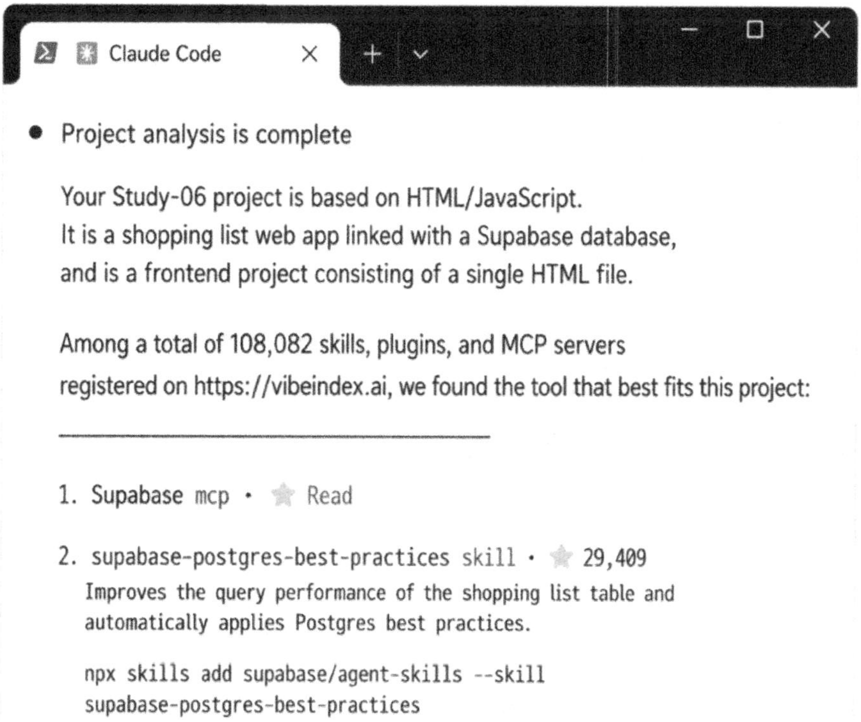

Figure 8.24: MCPs and skills recommended

By leveraging skills, you create yourself or widely used skills like this, you can further extend the functionality of Claude Code. Here, Supabase is recommended as a tool for storing data in the cloud so that anyone can access it. The next section will cover how to use Supabase.

Plugins and marketplace

In this section, we'll look at the `/plugin` command and the marketplace, which make Claude Code even more powerful.

A plugin is a tool that combines MCPs, skills, and more to provide a single feature. This allows Claude Code to interact with external programs or services and perform new functions. The shared space where you can find and install such plugins or skills is called the marketplace.

Developers can share their plugins or skills on the marketplace for others to use, and users can search for the features they need and install them in their own projects. The relationship between MCPs, skills, plugins, and the marketplace is as follows.

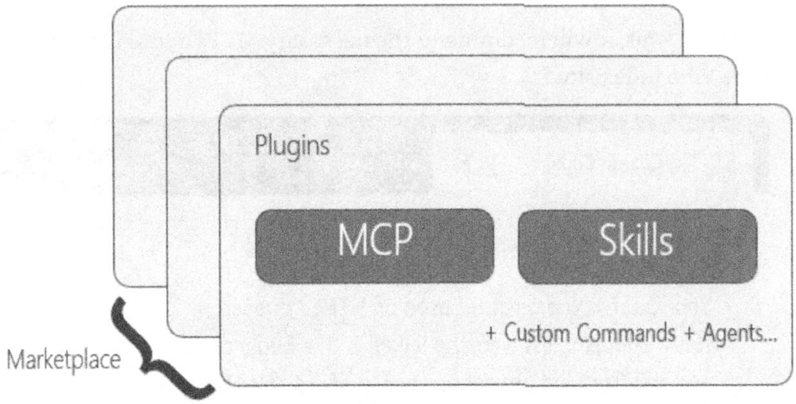

Figure 8.25: MCPs, skills, plugins, and marketplace

To try using a plugin, let's create a shopping list application.

Creating a shopping list app

1. Run Claude Code in your terminal and enter the following prompt.
   Prompt:

   ```
   Create a shopping list app. Make it a simple web UI that can add, delete,
   and check items, and runs locally in the browser.
   ```

2. When the task is complete, double-click the `shopping-list.html` file created in the `Study-06` folder to run it.

- I made a shopping list app! `shopping-list.html` If you open the file in your browser, it will run immediately.

  Main features:
  - ✅ Add item (after input, press the "Add" button or Enter key)
  - ✅ Mark as purchased with a checkbox
  - ✅ Remove item with delete button
  - ✅ Auto-save to local storage (data is retained even if the browser is closed)
  - ✅ Responsive design and animation effects

  Double-click the file or drag it into your browser to run it!

Figure 8.26: Completion message for the shopping list app

> **Note**
>
> The file name may differ from what is shown in the book.

3. The **Shopping List** application is now complete.

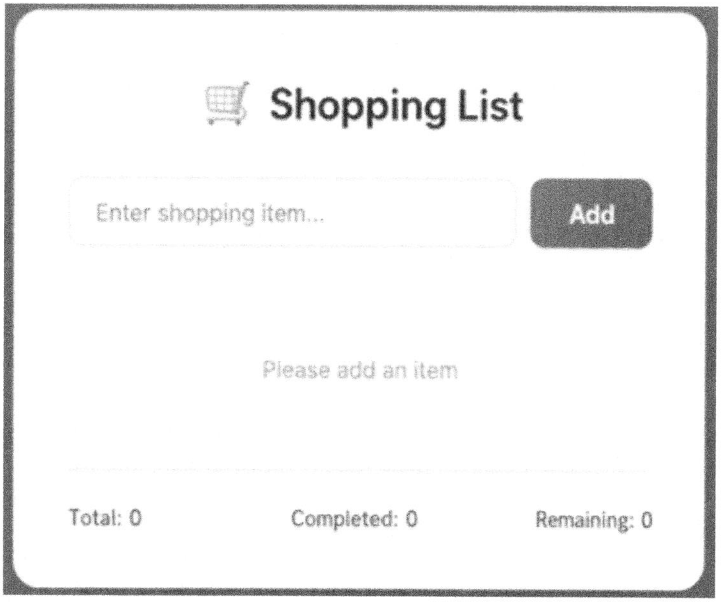

Figure 8.27: The Shopping List app is created

Running automated tests with the Playwright plugin

Now let's run the Playwright plugin to test if the app works correctly. Playwright is a development tool for website testing and automation. Plugins and the marketplace can be accessed and run in Claude Code by entering commands.

1. After entering the `/plugin` command in Claude Code press the *Enter* key to run the plugin.
2. A list of currently available plugins will be displayed.

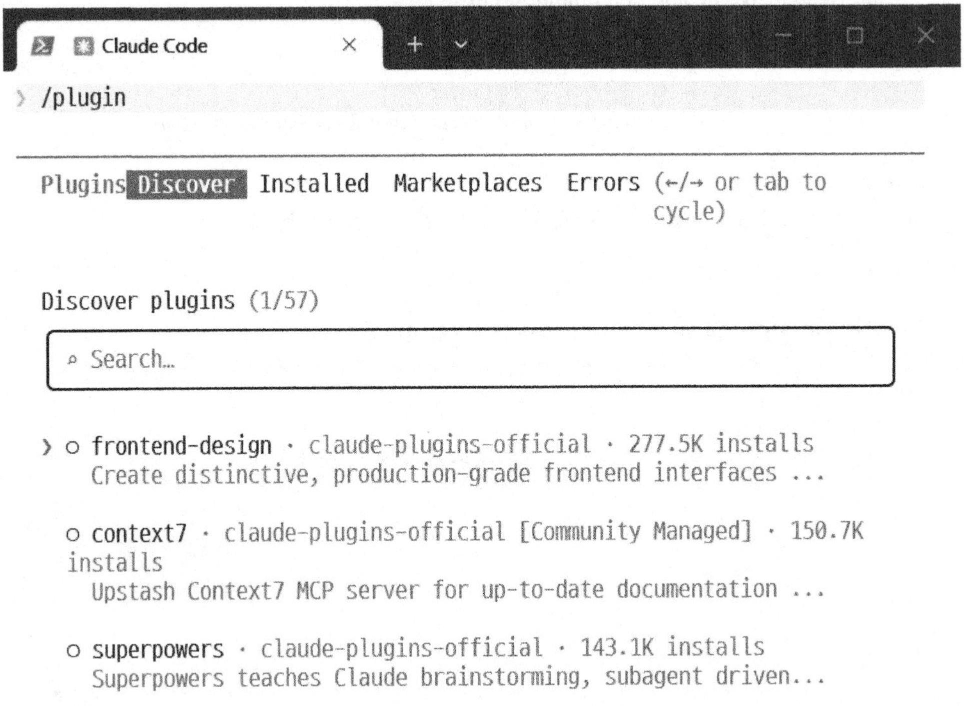

Figure 8.28: Available plugins displayed

3. Scroll through the list using the down arrow key to find Playwright and press the *Enter* key.
4. You will be asked whether to use the plugin for all projects on this computer or only for the current project. Click the second option, **Install for all collaborators on this repository (project scope)**, to install the plugin in the current project repository.

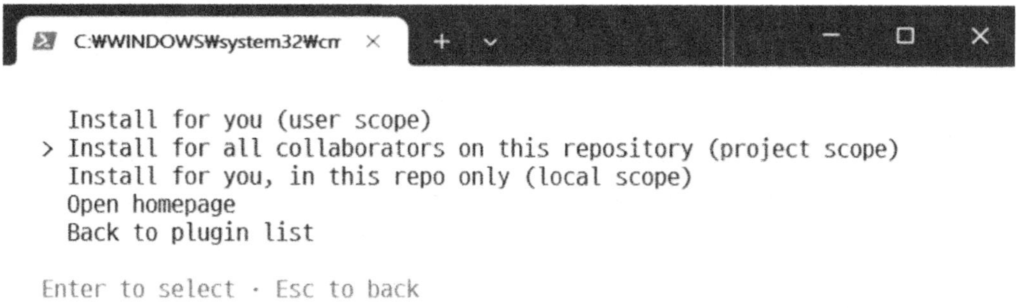

Figure 8.29: Install for all collaborators on this repository

5. Enter `/plugin` again in Claude Code, and use the right arrow key to select **Installed**. You will see that the Playwright plugin you just installed is now available.

Figure 8.30: Playwright plugin installed

> **Note**
>
> **Playwright MCP**
>
> Although Playwright was installed as a plugin, it is internally composed of an MCP server. If you exit Claude Code and run the `claude mcp list` command in the terminal, you will see that `playwright mcp` is installed.

6. Now, let's use the Playwright plugin to test the shopping list app we created. In the Claude Code prompt, enter the following:

   Prompt:

```
Automatically test all the features of this shopping list app. Please check
that adding, deleting, and checking all items work correctly.
```

7. After Claude Code prepares the necessary programs, it will automatically open a browser and start checking all the features. If you see a message indicating that all tests have passed, the testing was successful.

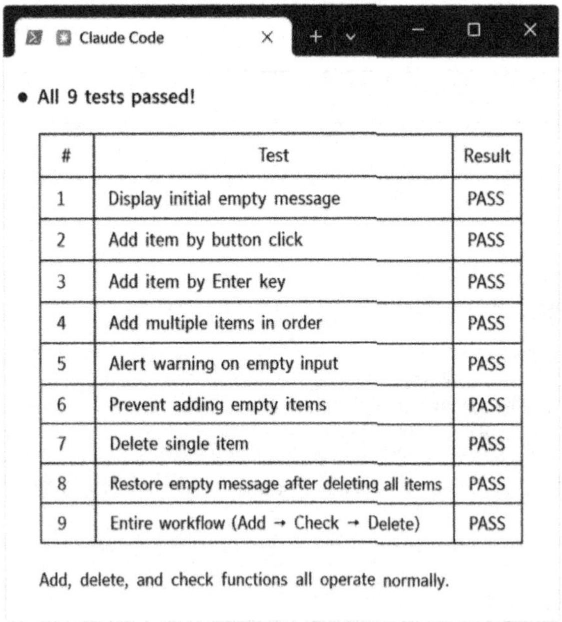

Claude Code

● All 9 tests passed!

#	Test	Result
1	Display initial empty message	PASS
2	Add item by button click	PASS
3	Add item by Enter key	PASS
4	Add multiple items in order	PASS
5	Alert warning on empty input	PASS
6	Prevent adding empty items	PASS
7	Delete single item	PASS
8	Restore empty message after deleting all items	PASS
9	Entire workflow (Add → Check → Delete)	PASS

Add, delete, and check functions all operate normally.

Figure 8.31: All 9 tests passed

Installing from the marketplace

The list of plugins you see with the `/plugin` command is fetched from the Marketplace. Let's take a look at Claude Code's Marketplace.

Run Claude Code, execute the `/plugin` command, and use the arrow key to select **Marketplaces**. Press the *Enter* key to be taken to Claude Code's official Marketplace. As we saw earlier, all the plugins in the list are part of this Marketplace.

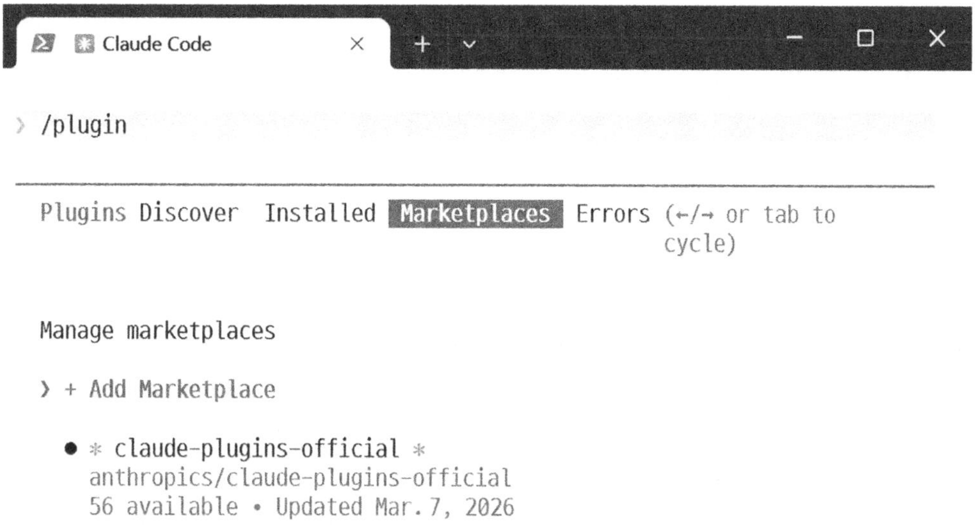

Figure 8.32: Claude's official marketplace

Adding the anthropics-skills Marketplace

Let's install a new Marketplace in Claude Code. The Marketplace we'll install in this chapter is `anthropics-skills`, which is the official Claude Code skills Marketplace released by Anthropic, the creator of Claude. Here, you can find collections of Claude Code skill packages and install the ones you need directly via command.

1. Like earlier, in your web browser, go to VibeIndex and click **Marketplace** in the top menu. Then, from the search results, select **anthropics-skills**.
2. On the details page, find **Add Marketplace** and click the Copy to clipboard icon to copy the command.
3. Paste the copied command into Claude Code and press the *Enter* key to run it. After a moment, you should see a message indicating that the installation is complete.
4. Enter the `/plugin` command and use the arrow key to select **Marketplaces** to confirm that the new Marketplace has been installed.

```
> /plugin

────────────────────────────────────────────────────────────────
  Plugins Discover  Installed  Marketplaces  Errors (←/→ or tab to
                                                    cycle)

  Manage marketplaces

  > + Add Marketplace

    ● anthropic-agent-skills
      anthropics/skills
      3 available • Updated 2026. 3. 7.

    ● * claude-plugins-official *
      anthropics/claude-plugins-official
```

Figure 8.33: The new Marketplace is installed

Installing the document-skills plugin

The `document-skills` is a plugin for Claude Code that allows you to create PowerPoint, Word, and Excel files. Let's find and use this plugin from the newly installed `anthropics/skills` Marketplace.

1. In Claude Code, run the `/plugin` command, select **Marketplaces** and then **anthropic-agent-skills** using the arrow keys and press *Enter*. You can then verify that the following three plugins are included.

```
> /plugin

────────────────────────────────────────────────────────────────
  Plugins Discover  Installed  Marketplaces  Errors (←/→ or tab to
                                                    cycle)

  anthropic-agent-skills
  anthropics/skills

  3 available plugins

  > Browse plugins (3)
    Update marketplace (last updated 2026. 3. 7.)
    Enable auto-update
```

Figure 8.34: Verify if the 3 plugins are included

2. Select **Browse plugins (3)** and press the *Enter* key to see which plugins are available. Then, use the arrow key to navigate to **document-skills** from the plugin list and press the *Enter* key.
3. In the scope option, select **Install for all collaborators on this repository (project scope)** to install the plugin in the project repository, enabling collaboration via GitHub.

> **Tip**
>
> **Installing plugins via command**
>
> You can also install plugins directly by entering commands in Claude Code. In your web browser, go to the **anthropics-skills** page on VibeIndex, find the **Plugins in Marketplace** section, and click the **document-skills** plugin.
>
> On the details page for **document-skills**, you can find the installation command. Copy the command under **Add Marketplace in Claude Code:** and the command under **Step 2. Install plugin:** in order, paste them into Claude Code, and run them to install the plugin.

4. If you use the arrow key to navigate to **Installed**, you can confirm that the **document-skills** plugin has been successfully installed.

```
> /plugin

Plugins Discover  Installed  Marketplaces  Errors (←/→ or tab to
                                           cycle)

 ⌕ Search...

 Project
> document-skills Plugin · anthropic-agent-skills · ✓ enabled
  playwright Plugin · claude-plugins-official · ✓ enabled
  └ playwright MCP · ✓ connected

  Local
  notion MCP · ✓ connected
  sequential-thinking MCP · ✓ connected
```

Figure 8.35: Check if the document-skills plugin is installed

Using the document-skills plugin

1. Let's use the `document-skills` plugin to create a PowerPoint document. Run Claude Code and enter the following prompt:
   Prompt:

   ```
   Create a one-page summary of AI technology trends in pptx format.
   ```

2. The `document-skills` plugin you installed earlier will be activated to process the prompt.
3. A new file named `AI_Trends_2026.pptx` has been created in the project folder.

   > **Note**
   >
   > The file name may be generated differently for each user.

4. Click the generated file to check the results. The presentation summarizing AI trends has been created successfully.

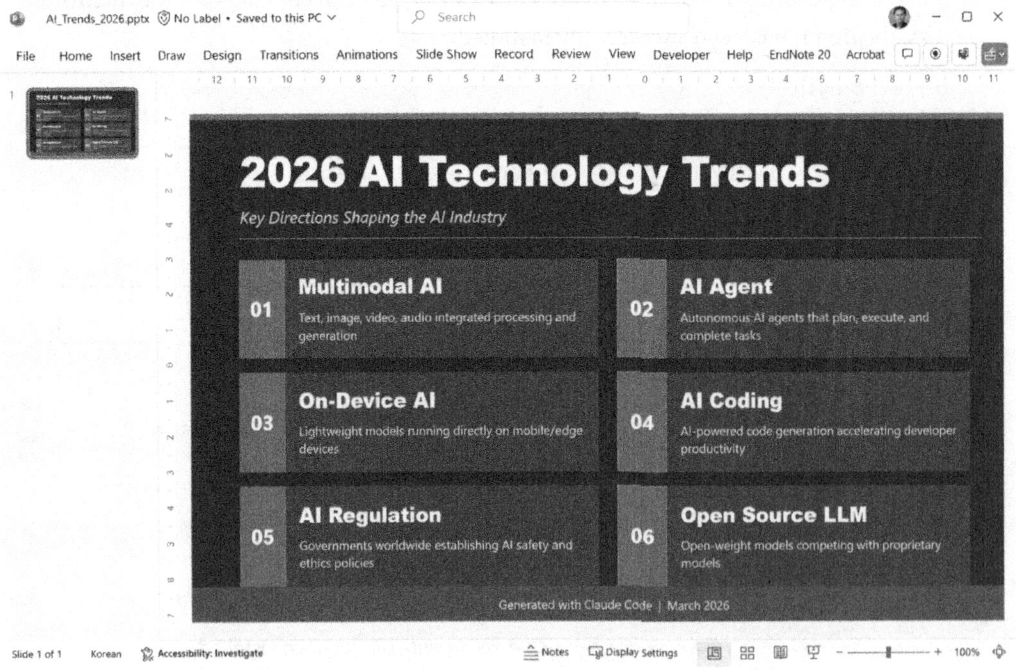

Figure 8.36: Presentation created successfully

Permanently archive your project with the GitHub MCP

GitHub is a code version control platform used by developers around the world. By using Claude Code's MCP server, you can automatically upload web applications created in your local environment to GitHub.

Normally, you have to manually enter Git commands to upload changes every time you modify your code, but if you connect the GitHub MCP server, Claude Code will handle this process for you. This allows you to automatically upload AI-generated code to your GitHub repository and implement a system for version control.

To do this, you need the GitHub MCP server address. Let's try uploading the 'Shopping List' application to GitHub now.

Finding the GitHub MCP installation command

1. Open your web browser, go to VibeIndex, and search for `GitHub` in the search bar.
2. From the search results, select **GitHub**. Make sure it is marked **Official MCP**.
3. Copy the installation command at the bottom of the MCP details page.

Figure 8.37: Copy the generated installation command

The command is as follows:

```
claude mcp add --transport http github https://api.githubcopilot.com/mcp -H
"Authorization: Bearer YOUR_GITHUB_PAT"
```

GitHub uses an API token authentication method. Therefore, the GitHub MCP server installation command includes options related to user authentication:

- `-H` is a shorthand for `--header`, and is an option to add header information to the HTTP request in order to send user authentication data to the MCP server.
- `Authorization`: Bearer is the standard format GitHub uses when accessing the API for authentication. 'Authorization' means it is sending authentication information, and 'Bearer' indicates that the authentication method is token-based.
- `YOUR_GITHUB_PAT` is where you enter your API key.

Now you know that you need an API token to install the GitHub MCP server in Claude Code. Next, let's get an API token from GitHub and substitute it into the command.

Obtaining a GitHub API token

1. To obtain an API token, log in to the GitHub homepage (`https://www.github.com`). Click the **Sign up for GitHub** button to create an account. If you already have a GitHub account, just click the **Sign in** button to log in.
2. After logging in to GitHub, click your profile in the top right corner and select **Settings**.
3. Scroll down the left sidebar and click the **<>Developer settings** menu.
4. In the left sidebar, navigate to Personal access tokens | Tokens (classic) in order. Then, in the center of the screen, click the **Generate new token** dropdown and select **Generate new token (classic)**.
5. You can now create a new token. Enter any name you like in the **Note** field and set **Expiration** to **30 days**.
6. **Select scopes** is an option that defines the range of permissions the personal access token will have. Select the following three options, then click the **Generate Token** button.
    - **repo**: Full control of private repositories
    - **user**: Full access to user data
    - **project**: Full control of projects
7. The API token has been issued. Click the *Copy* icon and save the API token.

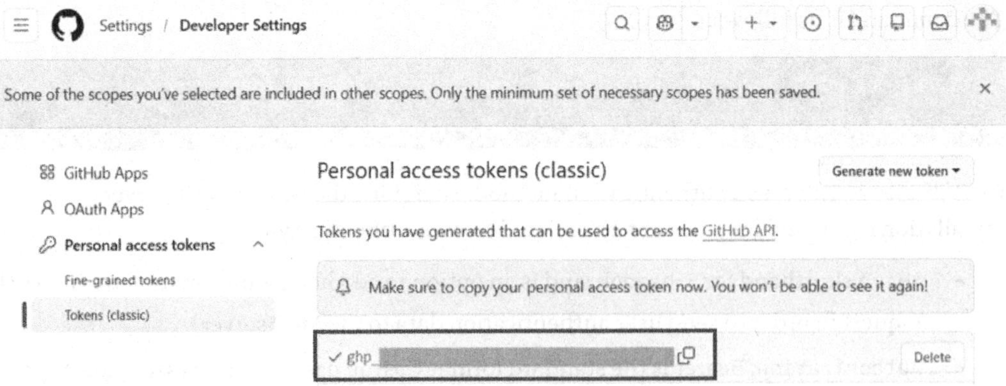

Figure 8.38: Copy and save the API token

> **Note**
>
> Like other APIs, the GitHub API token/key is only shown once. Be sure to copy and save it in a separate location.

Completing GitHub MCP installation

Now, let's install the GitHub MCP server in Claude Code using the issued GitHub API token. Open the terminal and prepare the GitHub MCP installation command from earlier.

1. Enter the GitHub MCP installation command in the terminal as shown below. Replace `<GitHub API key>` with your GitHub API key:

```
claude mcp add --transport http github https://api.githubcopilot.com/mcp -H
"Authorization: Bearer <GitHub API key>"
```

2. After completing the GitHub MCP server installation and seeing the confirmation message, enter the `claude` command to run Claude Code. Then, use the `/mcp` command to check that the GitHub MCP is installed and that it shows as `connected`.

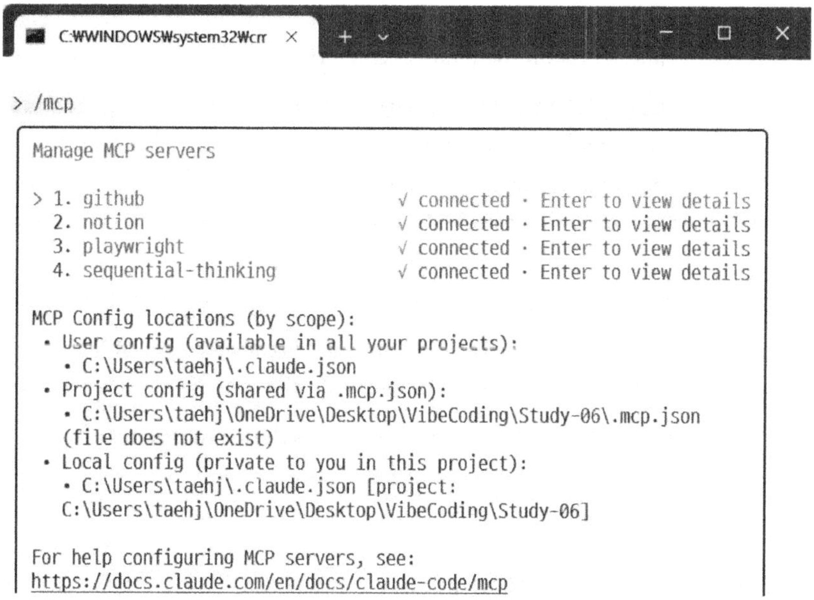

Figure 8.39: GitHub MCP installed and connected

Uploading your project

Once GitHub MCP is installed, let's create a GitHub repository and upload the 'Shopping List' app you worked on. Run Claude Code from the `Study-06` folder location.

1. Enter the following prompt:

   Prompt:

   ```
   I want to save the shopping list app created in the current folder
   to GitHub. Use github mcp to create a repository named
   shopping-list-app and upload it.
   ```

   > Note
   >
   > **Understanding GitHub and Git Commands**
   >
   > GitHub is a cloud-based version control platform for storing and managing code online. You can collaborate with others, and keep a record of code changes so you can revert to previous versions at any time. The workflow on GitHub consists of:
   >
   > - **Add**: To save your project on GitHub, first create a remote repository on your GitHub account where you can store your code. Then, select the files you want to upload and add them to the staging area.
   > - **Commit**: Once the files have been added to the staging area and confirmed, they are stored in the local repository, which is the step right before uploading. This process is called a commit, which also refers to a unit of saved changes. In other words, a commit is the act of saving the current state of your code to the local repository.
   > - **Push**: The process of uploading committed files from the local repository to the remote repository is called a push. When you push your code, your teammates can check the change history on GitHub.
   >
   > Claude Code's GitHub MCP automates these processes, making it even more convenient to use GitHub.

2. Claude Code requests authorization to create a repository and execute commands such as add and commit. Press **1. Yes** to continue through to push.
3. The shopping list app has been uploaded to GitHub. Let's go to the URL and check it on GitHub.

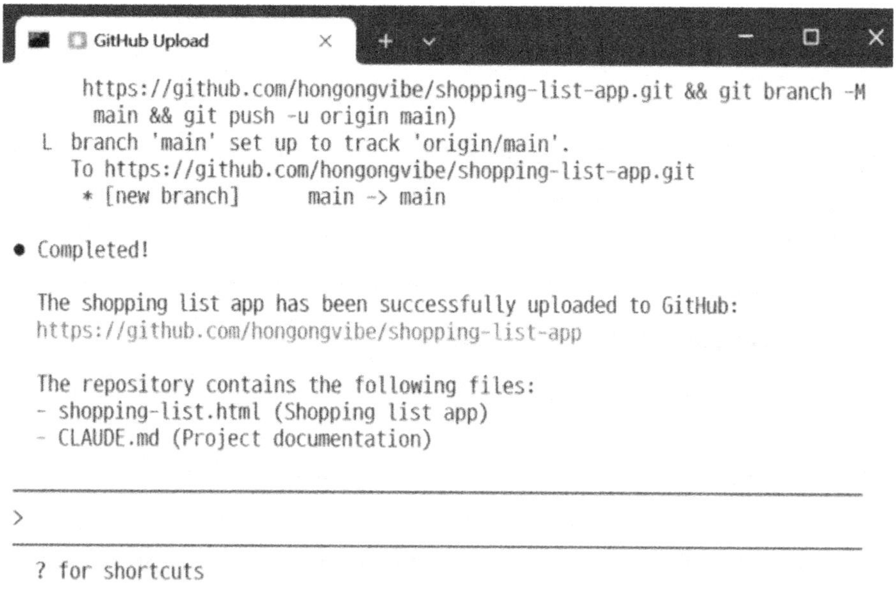

Figure 8.40: Shopping list app uploaded to GitHub

4. A new `shopping-list-app` repository has been created on GitHub. Let's click on it.

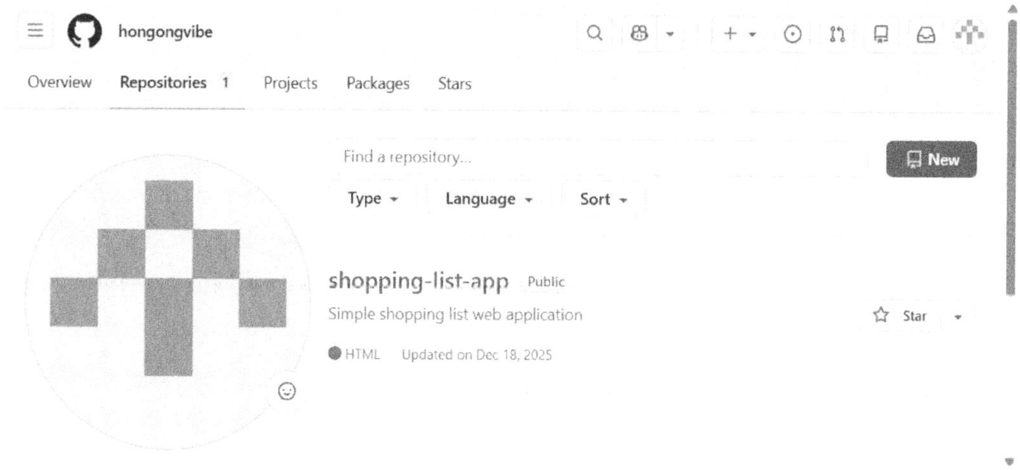

Figure 8.41: shopping-list-app repo created

5. The files `CLAUDE.md` and `shopping-list.html` have been successfully uploaded to the repo.

So far, we've used MCP to automate the entire process from testing to deployment. Playwright MCP automates functional testing, and GitHub MCP completes version control for your project. Together they form the automation backbone of the AI development environment.

Now, developers can focus on 'what to build,' leaving repetitive and complex technical procedures to MCP. In the next section, we'll look at how to connect your application to an external database for storage and management, and how to structure it for continuous operation in a cloud environment.

Wrapping up

Key takeaways summarized in 7 keywords:

- **Testing** is the process of checking whether the code runs as intended and is free of errors.
- **Version control** records the history of code changes and allows you to revert to a previous state when needed.
- **Playwright** is a browser automation tool that automatically tests websites and verifies the UI.
- The process of selecting files to upload to GitHub and adding them to the staging area is called **add**.
- Once files added to the staging area are confirmed, they are stored in the local repository right before uploading. This process is called **commit**.
- The process of uploading committed files from the local repository to the **remote repository** is called **push**.

Review questions

1. Choose the name of the folder that Playwright MCP creates after completing tests.
    1. `.test-results`
    2. `.playwright-mcp`
    3. `.automation`
    4. `.screenshots`
2. Choose the correct order for uploading code to GitHub.
    1. commit → add → push
    2. push → add → commit

   3. add → commit → push
   4. add → push → commit
3. Describe two of the most effective ways to find the MCP server address.

Connecting a database to create a real service

> **Note**
>
> **Key terms:** Vercel | Deployment | Local storage | Cloud storage | Supabase | Database | Table
>
> Now that testing and version control are complete, let's deploy the shopping list app to the internet so others can use it. In this section, we'll use Vercel to deploy the web application to an always-on external server, and practice connecting a database using Supabase.
>
> Through this, your app will finally become a real service that anyone can access, not just 'your own code.'

Before you begin

A database, or DB, is a system for systematically storing and managing large amounts of data. While you can enter information in a notepad or Excel, as the amount of data grows, searching or editing becomes more difficult. A database solves these problems by structuring data in tables, allowing you to quickly find or modify the information you need.

In web applications, all information entered by users is stored in the database. Thanks to this, data is preserved even if you close and reopen the app, and you can access the same content from multiple devices. In other words, the database serves as the app's memory storage.

Deploying your own webpage

Up to now, all the web applications you created have run on your local computer, and all data has been stored locally. Testing in this local environment is an important step in the development process, but if you want to show your application to others or have them actually use it, you need to deploy it.

Deployment is the process of uploading your application to a third-party server connected to the internet. For users to access your app, the server must be running 24/7. However, in a local environment, if your computer is turned off, the server also shuts down. By deploying your application, it runs on a server that is always on, so you can access it anytime, anywhere via a web address, or URL.

From now on, we will deploy the shopping list app created in Section 08-2 to the internet so that many users can use it.

Creating a Vercel account and connecting to GitHub

Vercel is a cloud platform that automatically builds and deploys your code when you upload it to GitHub. For simple web applications, you can upload them to GitHub and use Vercel to deploy them for free. The workflow is as follows:

1. Prepare a GitHub Repository
2. Push the HTML file you created locally to GitHub
3. Select the repository to deploy after authorizing GitHub authentication on Vercel.
4. Instantly receive a URL
5. To deploy the shopping list app from GitHub, let's first create a Vercel account. Go to the Vercel homepage (`https://www.vercel.com`) and click the **Sign Up** button to start the registration process.
6. For **Plan Type**, select **I'm working on personal projects**, and in the **Your Name** field, enter your ID. Here, we'll enter `hongongvibe`. Click the **Continue** button to proceed.

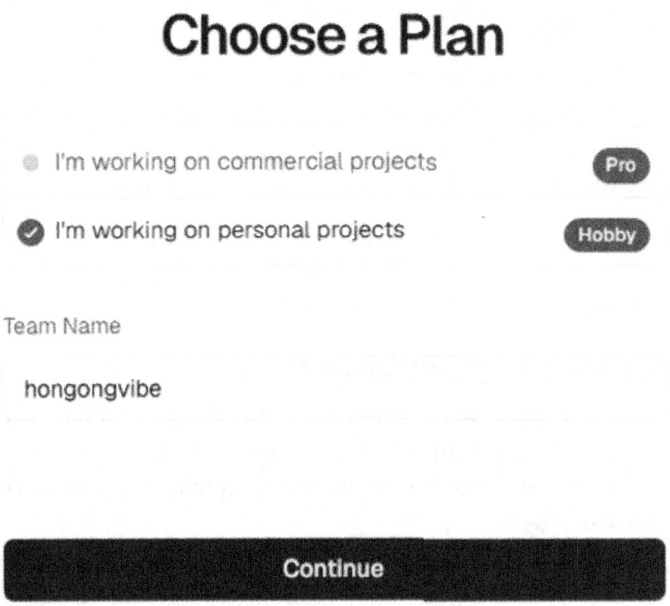

Figure 8.42: Sign up to Vercel

Create and remember your username.

7. Create your Vercel account. Here, select **Continue with GitHub** to link your GitHub account. In the window that opens, click the **Authorize Vercel** button to authenticate and complete account creation.
8. Log in to Vercel, click your profile in the top right corner, and select the **Dashboard** menu.

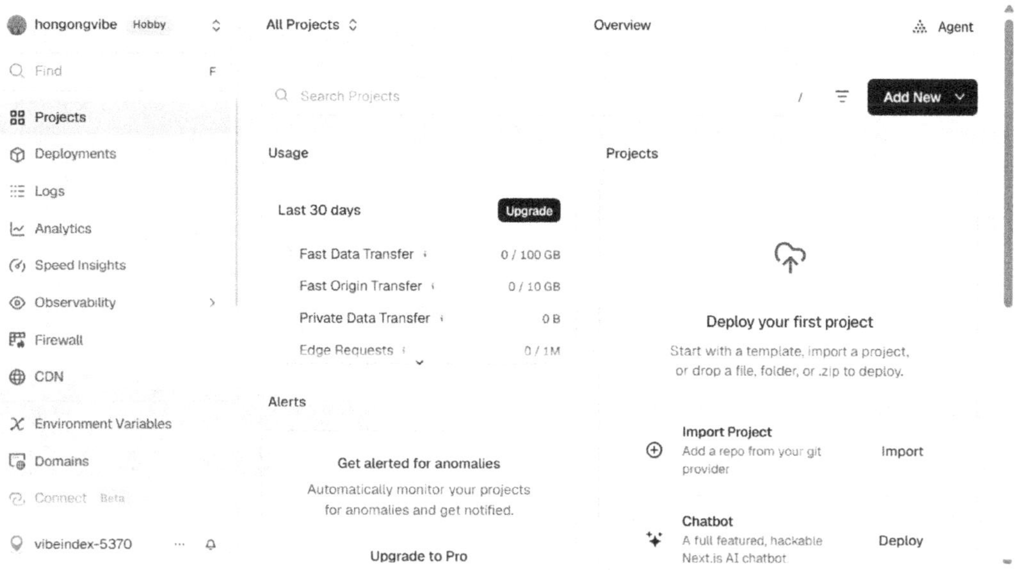

Figure 8.43: Select the Dashboard menu

9. With the **Projects** tab selected, click the **Add New.. +** button on the right, then select **Project** from the dropdown menu.

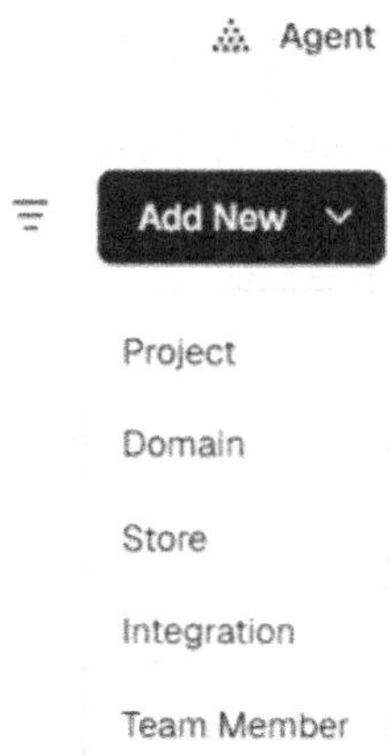

Figure 8.44: Adding a new project

10. Under **Import Git Repository**, click Continue with GitHub and log in. Then open the **Select a Git Namespace** dropdown and choose **Add GitHub Account** to start linking your GitHub account.

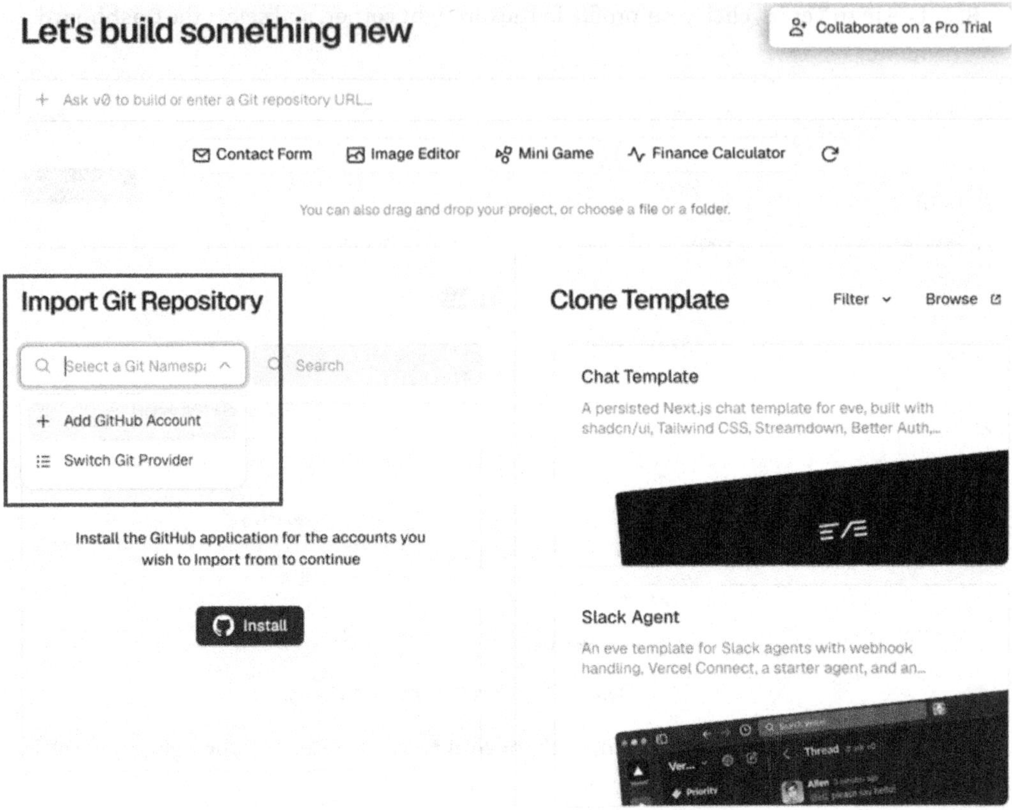

Figure 8.45: Linking your GitHub account

11. To allow access only to the selected GitHub repository, check **Only select repositories**. Click the **Select repositories** dropdown button, select **shopping-list-app**, and click the **Install** button to install Vercel.

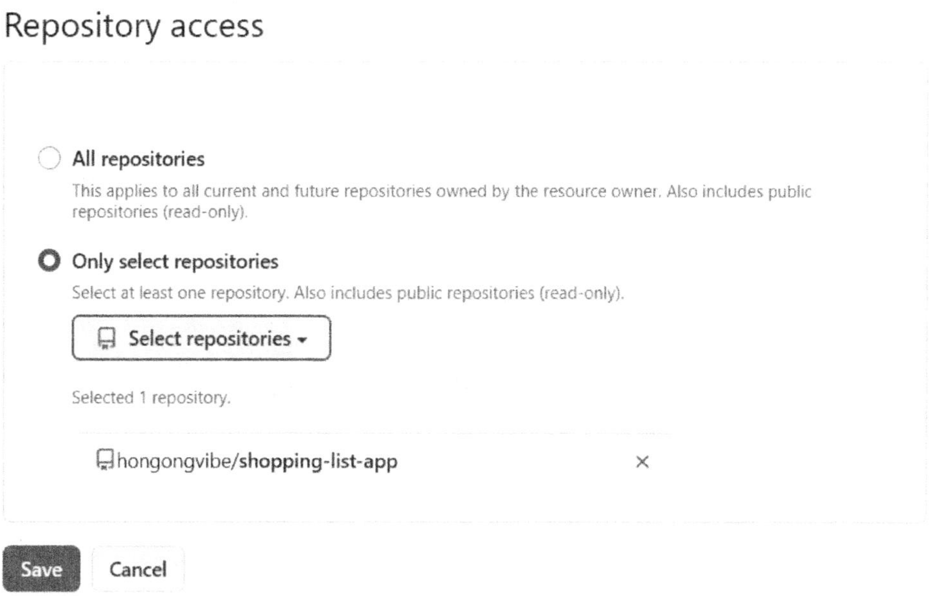

Figure 8.46: Installing Vercel

12. After entering your GitHub password to authenticate, you're ready to import the GitHub repository.

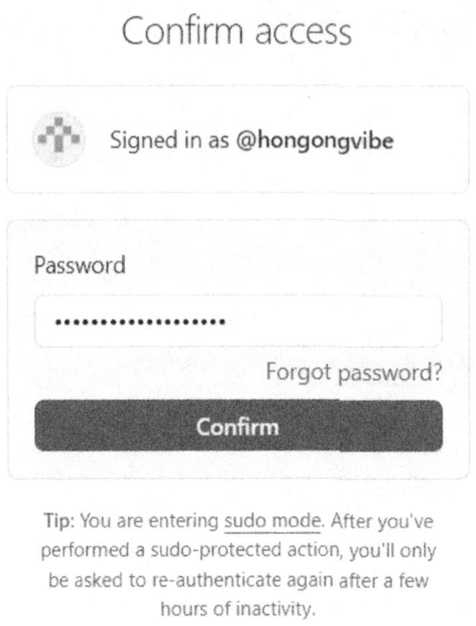

Figure 8.47: Confirm access to the GitHub repository

Deploying the project

1. Return to Vercel. In the **New Project** window under **Import Git Repository**, check that the **shopping-list-app** repository has been added, then click the **Import** button to import it.

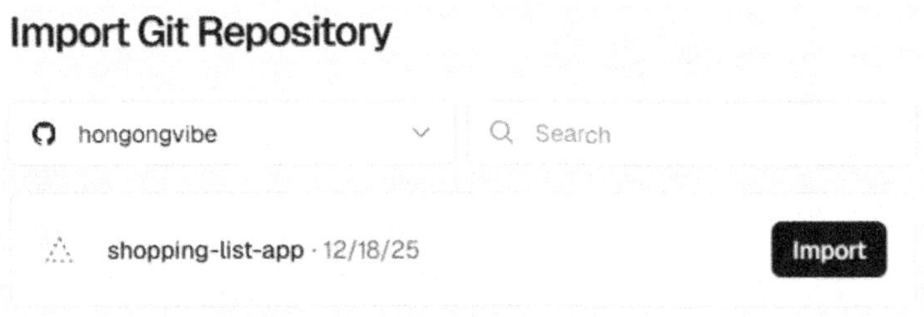

Figure 8.48: Importing the repository

2. A new project has been created and is ready for deployment. Click the **Deploy** button.

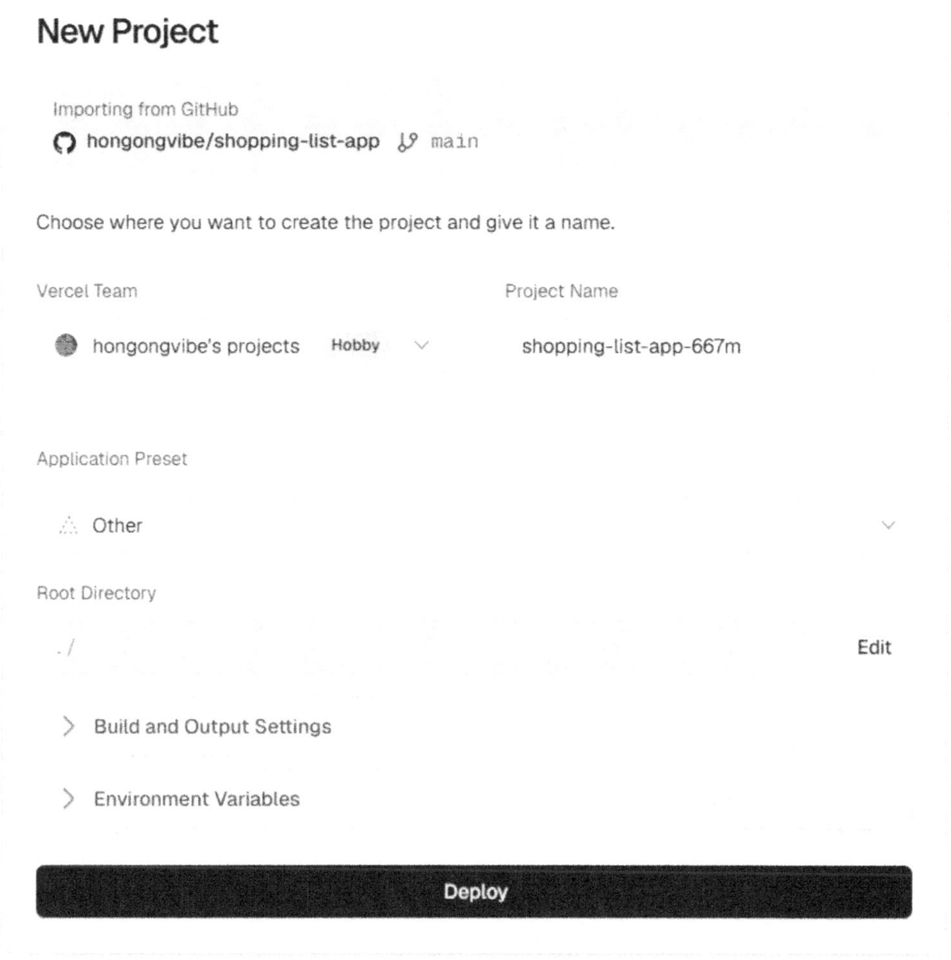

Figure 8.49: Deploying the new project

You can view the deployment process as it progresses.

3. After a short wait, your project will be deployed. If you see a **404 Not Found** error message in the preview window, it's because the GitHub repository does not yet have the default start page for the website, `index.html`. This is because the shopping list app was created as `Shopping-list.html` instead of `index.html`.

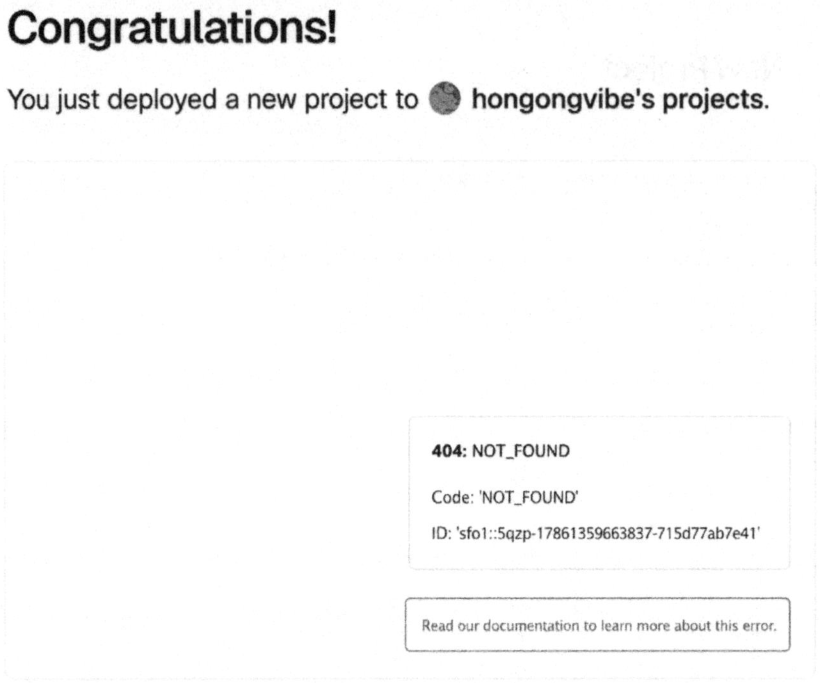

Figure 8.50: 404 Not Found error

4. Let's use Claude Code to rename the `shopping-list.html` file to `index.html`. Enter the following prompt into Claude Code.
   Prompt:

   ```
   Rename the shopping-list.html file of the shopping list app to
   index.html and upload it to GitHub.
   ```

5. Check the completion message.

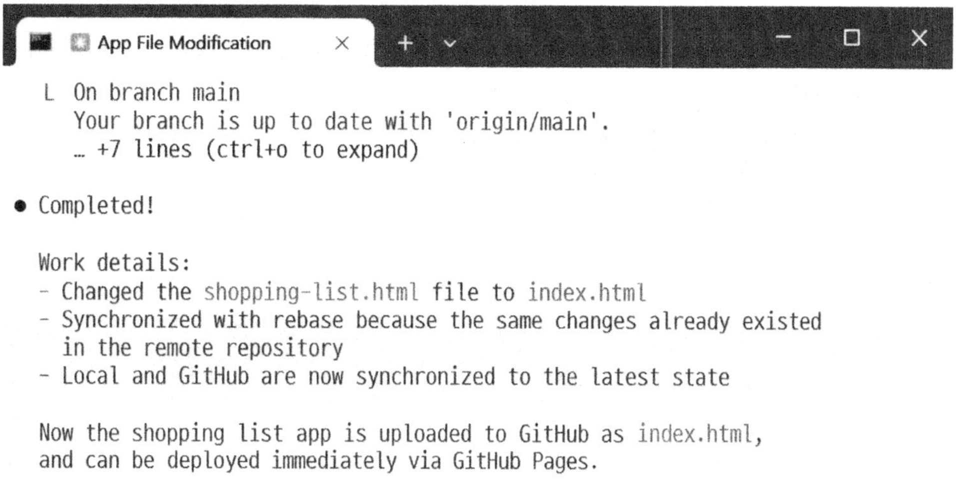

Figure 8.51: Verify the Completed message

6. Go back to GitHub and confirm that the `shopping-list.html` file has been renamed to `index.html`.

Checking your deployed website

1. In the Vercel dashboard, click on the `shopping-list-app` project you just created.

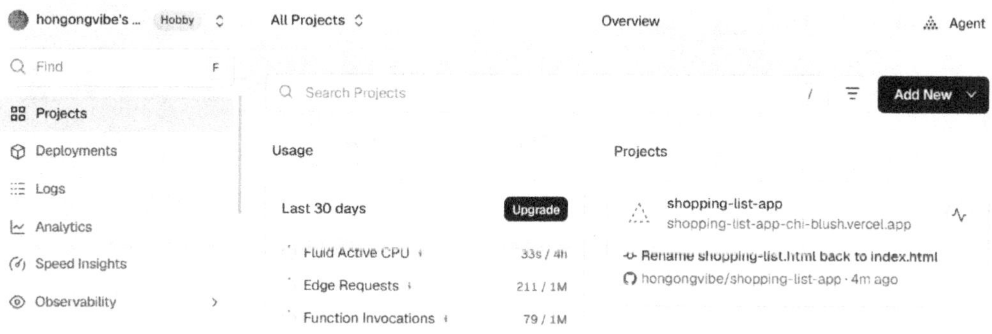

Figure 8.52: Select the newly created project in Vercel

> **Note**
>
> You can access the dashboard by clicking your profile in the top right corner of Vercel and selecting the **Dashboard** menu.

2. You can view the deployed shopping list app in the preview window. On the right side of the preview window, under **Domains**, you'll find the URL of the deployed web page. Click the *Share* icon to visit that address.
3. The shopping list app has been deployed to the internet. Now, users all over the world can visit the web page you created.

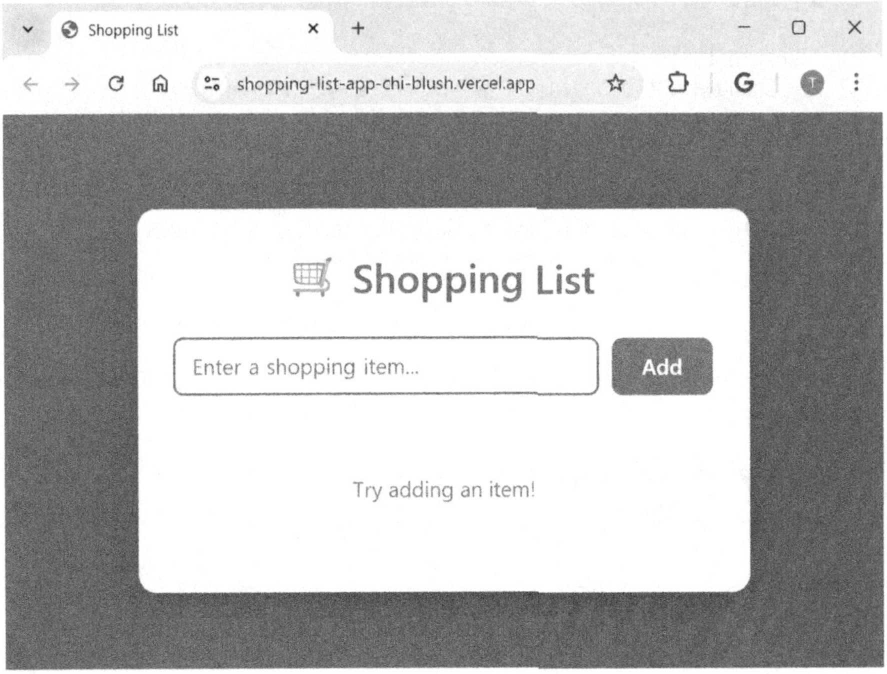

Figure 8.53: The website is now live

> **Note**
>
> The URL of the completed shopping list app deployed in this book is: `https://shopping-list-app-chi-blush.vercel.app`.

Connecting the application to a database

Now let's test the deployed web application. The *apple* item you entered earlier, when testing the app locally, is displayed correctly.

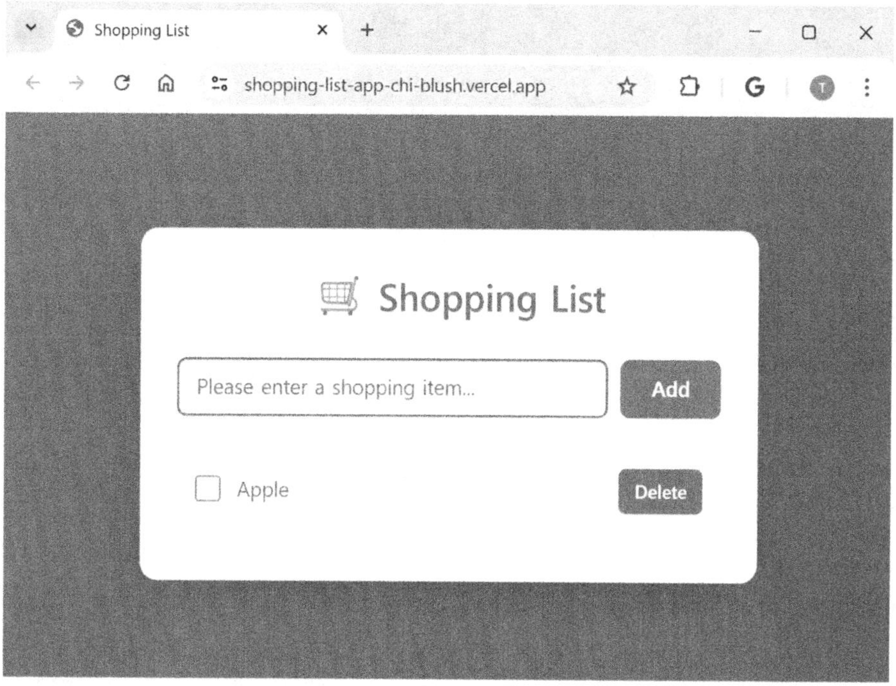

Figure 8.54: The Apple item in the shopping list

However, in reality, this web application is not yet complete. Currently, the shopping list app stores data in the browser's local storage, so you can only view the saved data in the browser you are using right now.

Local storage has its limitations: data is not shared across different computers or browsers, and if you clear your browser cache or switch devices, the data disappears. In other words, only you can see the data, and only on this device. In fact, if you access the application from another computer, a different browser, or in secret mode (which does not use local storage), you will only see an empty shopping list—the saved data will not be visible.

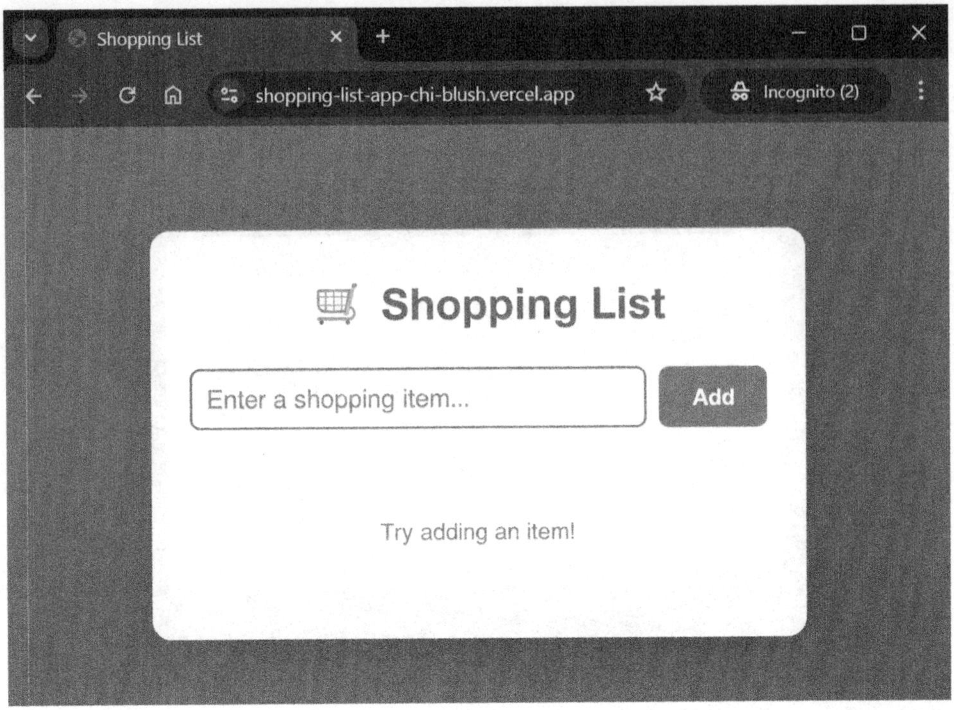

Figure 8.55: Data not visible on different systems, browsers, or in the incognito mode

To share saved data across different devices, you need external storage connected to the internet, such as cloud storage. Cloud storage acts as a central server that allows you to access the same data from anywhere. For example, you can store the shopping list in a database, and have the app read the data from the cloud each time it runs. This way, you can check the same list from your desktop, laptop, or smartphone, and multiple people can share or collaborate on it.

Typically, to store data for a web application, you would need to install a database program like Oracle or MySQL and operate your own server. However, this traditional approach is complex to set up and requires significant time for server maintenance and upkeep.

Supabase is a cloud database platform that automates and simplifies this process. Once you sign up, you can create a database without any separate installation, and exchange data with your web or mobile app via APIs.

> **Note**
>
> Supabase is pronounced 'Superbase.'

Supabase offers a free plan sufficient for personal projects or learning purposes. When you store data, APIs are automatically generated, so you don't need to write server code yourself. Also, since data is stored on an online server, any additions or modifications by multiple users are automatically reflected in real time.

From now on, let's use the Supabase MCP server to connect the shopping list web app to a database and expand it into a cloud-based web app.

Sign up for Supabase and create an organization

1. Go to the Supabase homepage (`www.supabase.com`). Click the **Sign in** button at the top right to sign up.

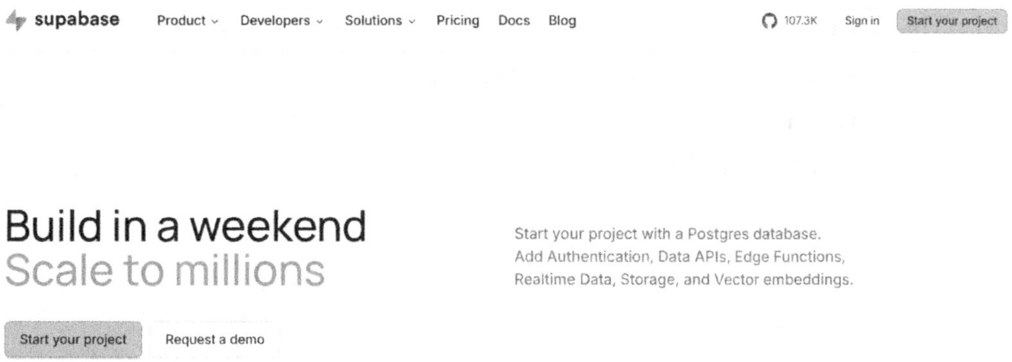

Figure 8.56: Sign up to Supabase

2. Click the **Continue with GitHub** button to sign up using your GitHub account.

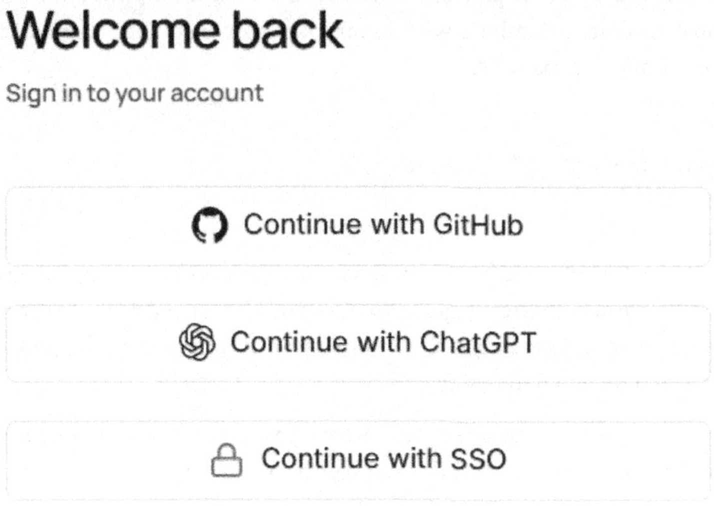

Figure 8.57: Sign up using your GitHub account

3. In the **New organization** window, it's time to create an organization. In Supabase, an organization is like a folder that manages multiple projects together. Enter each field as follows, then click the **Create organization** button to create the organization.
    - **Name**: **HonGongVibeCoding's Org** (auto-generated)
    - **Type**: **Personal**
    - **Plan**: **Free - $0/month**

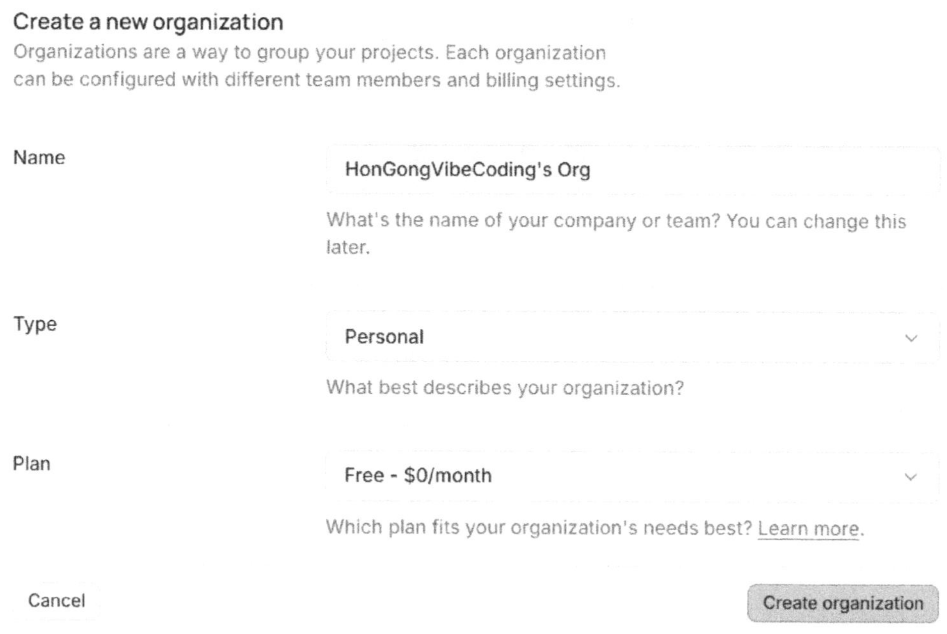

Figure 8.58: Creating a new organization

> **Note**
>
> With the free plan, you can create up to 2 projects. If a project remains inactive for 7 days, it will be automatically paused, but you can restart it by clicking the **Resume** button on the dashboard.

Installing the Supabase MCP Server and Generating an API Token

Now, let's install the Supabase MCP server. Supabase supports both local and remote MCP servers. In this chapter, we will install a local MCP server. Open your terminal and enter the following installation command, then go through the authentication process:

```
claude mcp add supabase -s local -e SUPABASE_ACCESS_TOKEN=<Supabase API
token>
-- cmd /c npx -y @supabase/mcp-server-supabase@latest
```

This command means to run the MCP server (`mcp-server-supabase`) created by Supabase (`@supabase`) with the latest version (`@latest`). The newly added `-e` is a shorthand for `--env`, which is an option to set environment variables passed to the MCP server. In this case, since you need an API token to authenticate with Supabase, the option to pass the token has been added.

Now you know that you need an API token to install Supabase MCP.

Let's go back to the Supabase homepage and issue an API token:

1. On the Supabase start page, click on your profile at the top right, then select the **Account preferences** menu.
2. In the left sidebar, click **Access Tokens** to go to the token management screen. Click the **Generate new token** button on the right to create a new API token.

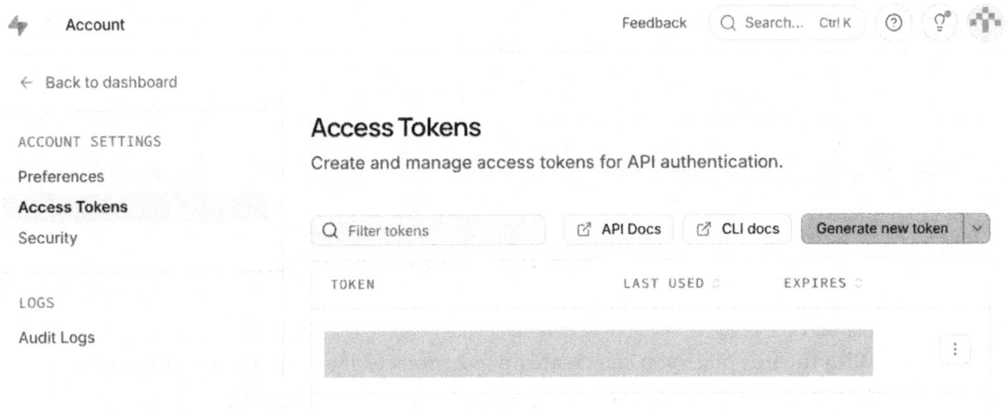

Figure 8.59: Generate new token

3. In the **Generate New Token** window, enter `my_first_project` in the **Name** field and set **Expires in** (token validity period) to **30 days**. Then, click the **Generate token** button to complete the setup.

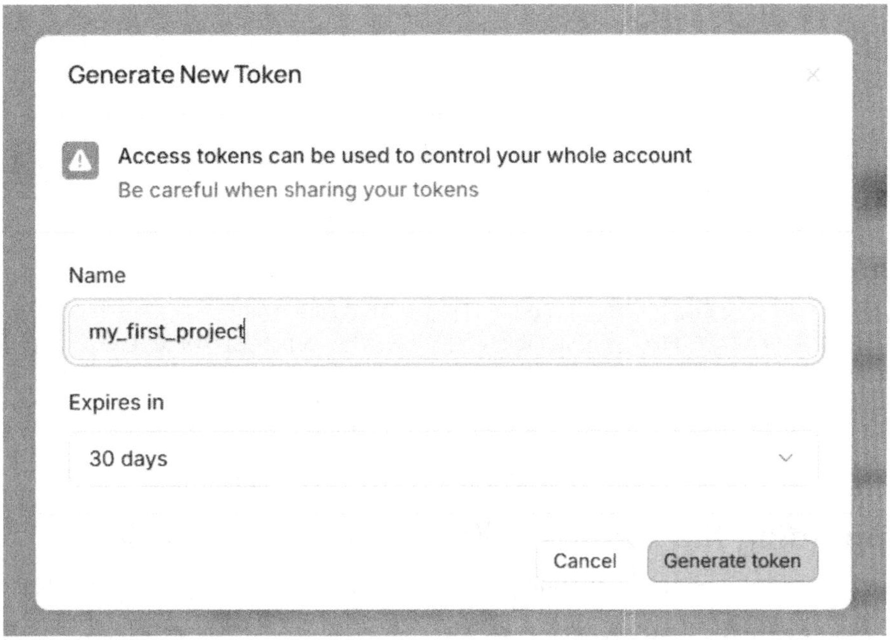

Figure 8.60: Fill in the details

4. The token has been successfully generated. Click the **Copy** button to copy it, and store it in a safe place.
5. Now it's time to connect Supabase MCP in Claude Code. In the `Study-06` folder, open the terminal and install Supabase MCP as follows:

```
claude mcp add supabase -s local -e SUPABASE_ACCESS_TOKEN=<your API token>
-- cmd /c npx -y @supabase/mcp-server-supabase@latest
```

   Replace the Supabase API token you received in place of `<your API token>`.

6. Once the MCP server installation is complete, enter the `claude mcp list` command to check if MCP has been installed correctly. You should see that `supabase` has been successfully added to the list.

```
C:\Users\taehj\OneDrive\Desktop\VibeCoding\Study-06>claude mcp list
Checking MCP server health...

notion: https://mcp.notion.com/mcp (HTTP) - ✓ Connected
sequential-thinking: cmd /c npx -y @modelcontextprotocol/server-sequential-
thinking@latest - ✓ Connected
playwright: cmd /c npx @playwright/mcp@latest - ✓ Connected
github: https://api.githubcopilot.com/mcp (HTTP) - ✓ Connected
context7: https://mcp.context7.com/mcp (HTTP) - ✓ Connected
vercel: https://mcp.vercel.com (HTTP) - ✓ Connected
supabase: cmd /c npx -y @supabase/mcp-server-supabase@latest - ✓ Connected

C:\Users\taehj\OneDrive\Desktop\VibeCoding\Study-06>
```

Figure 8.61: Verify that Supabase has been added

Upgrading the shopping list app to a real service

Now it's time to connect the shopping list app to the database using Supabase MCP.

Automatically connecting to the database with Claude Code

1. Run Claude Code and enter the following.

   Prompt:

   > Use Supabase MCP to connect our shopping list app to the database. Create a table called shopping_items, and modify the code so that the data previously stored in local storage is now saved to the Supabase database. Once the changes are complete, commit and push to GitHub.

   Understanding Database Tables

   A database table is, simply put, a structure that stores data in a tabular format. If you think of a database as a program that manages multiple Excel files, a table is like an individual Excel sheet within the database.

   For example, each row in the `shopping_items` table stores a shopping item, and the columns store attributes such as unique ID (`id`), product name (`name`), purchase completion status (`completed`), and creation time (`created_at`).

id	name	completed	created_at
1	Apple	false	2025-10-29 15:30:00
2	Milk	true	2025-10-29 15:32:10
3	Bread	false	2025-10-29 15:35:22

Table 8.2: Example of a database table

Storing data in this structured format allows you to quickly find and modify the information you need.

2. Supabase MCP is running. Press **1. Yes** to continue.

```
● We will use Supabase MCP to connect the shopping list app with the database.
  First, let's plan and start the task.

 Tool use

   supabase - List organizations() (MCP)
   Lists all organizations that the user is a member of.

 Do you want to proceed?
 > 1. Yes
  2. Yes, and don't ask again for supabase - List organizations commands
  in C:\Users\taehj\OneDrive\Desktop\VibeCoding\Study-06
   3. No, and tell Claude what to do differently (esc)
```

Figure 8.62: Select option 1

3. After a brief wait, you'll see a message about creating a new project in Supabase and confirming that you're on the free plan. Review the information and continue.

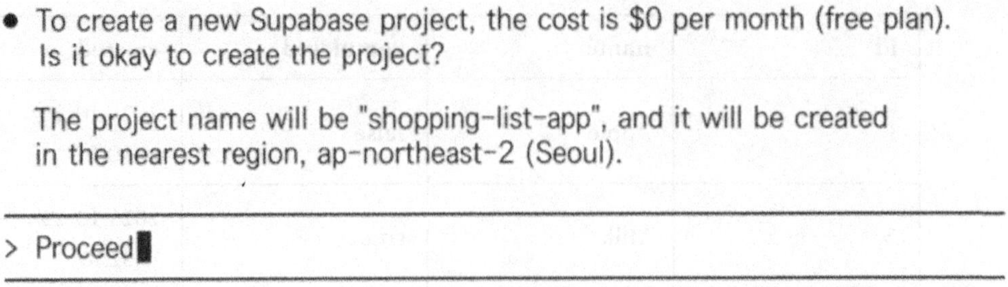

Figure 8.63: Review the message

4. The `index.html` file will be automatically modified to enable Supabase MCP integration.

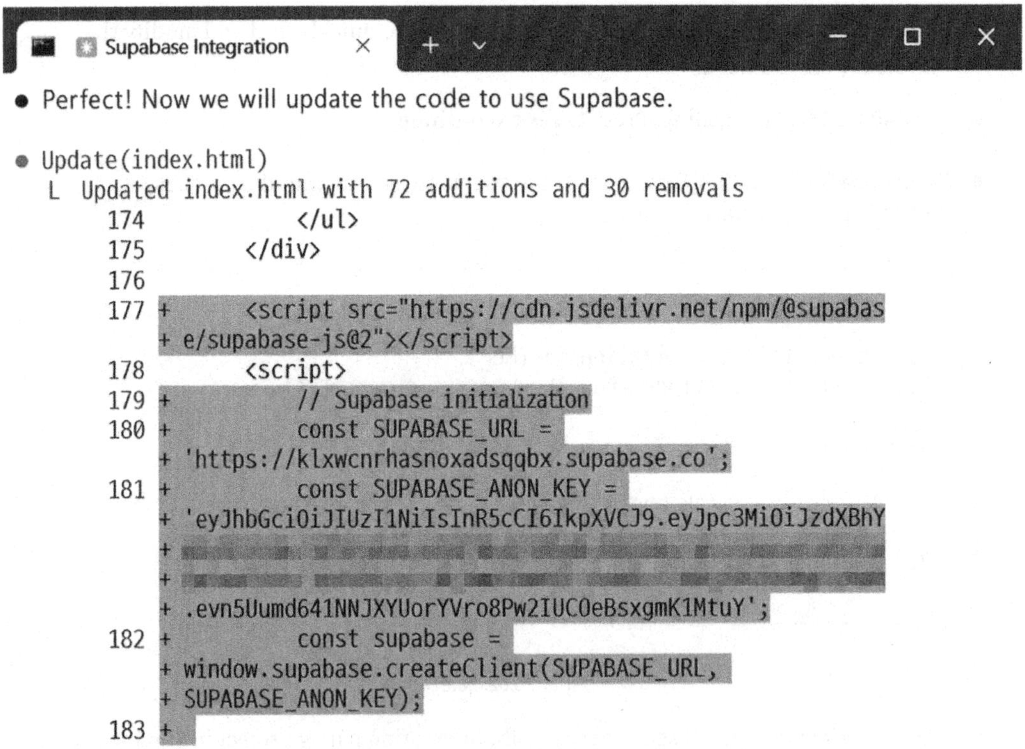

Figure 8.64: Supabase MCP integration updated

5. The `shopping_items` table was created, and the database was successfully connected, including the necessary fields such as `id` and `name`.

Supabase Integration

● Completed! The shopping list app has been successfully integrated with the Supabase database.

Completed tasks:

```
1. ✅ Supabase project creation: Created the "shopping-list-app" project in
   the ap-northeast-2 (Seoul) region
2. ✅ Database table creation: Created the shopping_items table with the
   following fields:
    - id (UUID, primary key)
    - name (TEXT, item name)
    - completed (BOOLEAN, completion status)
    - created_at, updated_at (timestamp)
3. ✅ Code updates:
    - Completely replaced localStorage with Supabase
    - Added Supabase JavaScript SDK via CDN
    - Implemented all CRUD operations (create, read, update, delete) using async/await
    - Added error handling
4. ✅ Github commit & push: Committed changes and pushed to remote repository
```

Now the shopping list data is stored in the cloud database and can be accessed from any device!

Figure 8.65: The database table is created

Verifying database table creation

Now let's check on the Supabase website to see how the database was created:

1. A new project named `shopping-list-app` has been created on the dashboard. Click it to view the details.

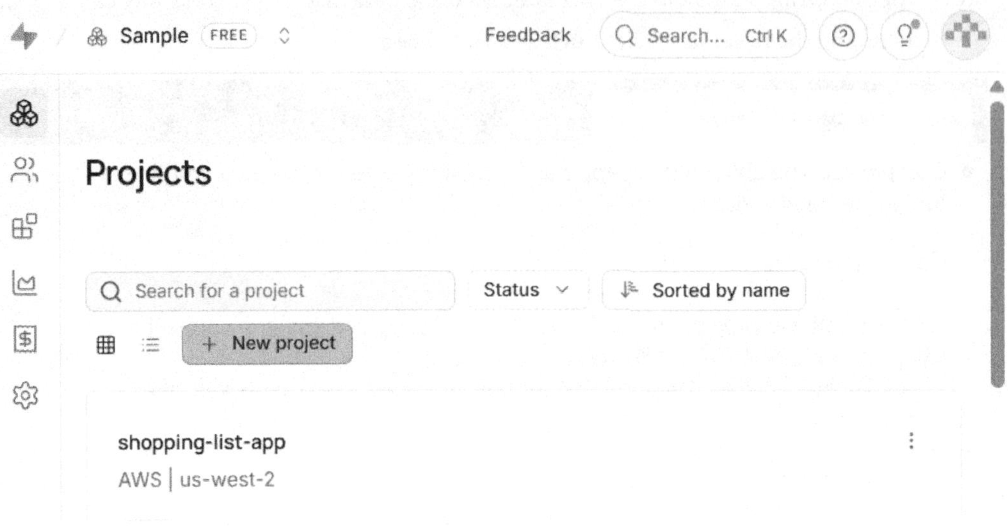

Figure 8.66: The shopping-list-app visible on the dashboard

2. In the upper right corner, you'll see the number **1** next to **Tables**, indicating that a new table has been added. Click the **Table Editor** menu in the left sidebar.
3. In the **Table Editor** window, click the `shopping_items` table to see that the `id`, `name`, `completed`, and `created_at` columns have been created.

Checking real-time synchronization with the database

Now that we've confirmed the table was created in the Supabase database, let's test if it works in the actual app.

1. Access the shopping list app, enter `Apple`, and click the **Add** button to add the item to the list.

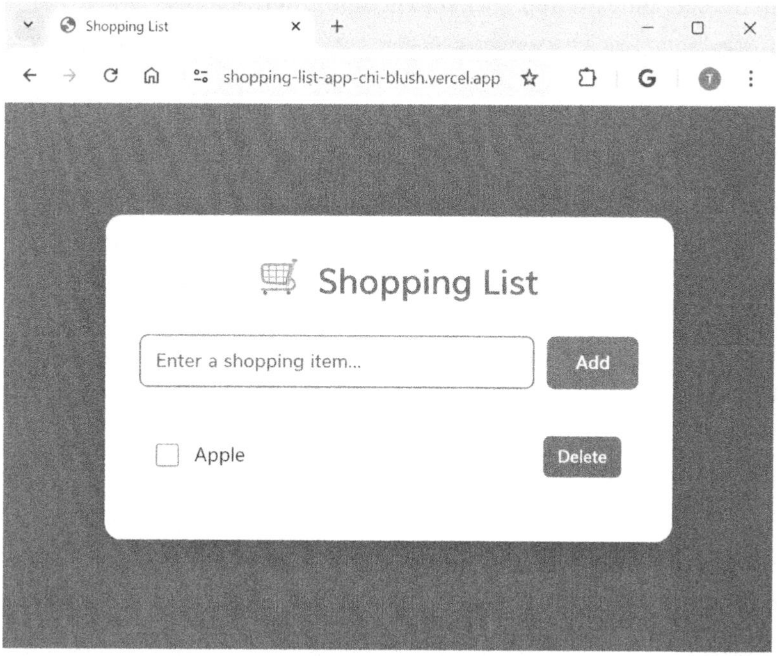

Figure 8.67: Add the 'Apple' item to the list

2. If you refresh the **Table Editor** window in Supabase, you'll see that the **Apple** row has been added.

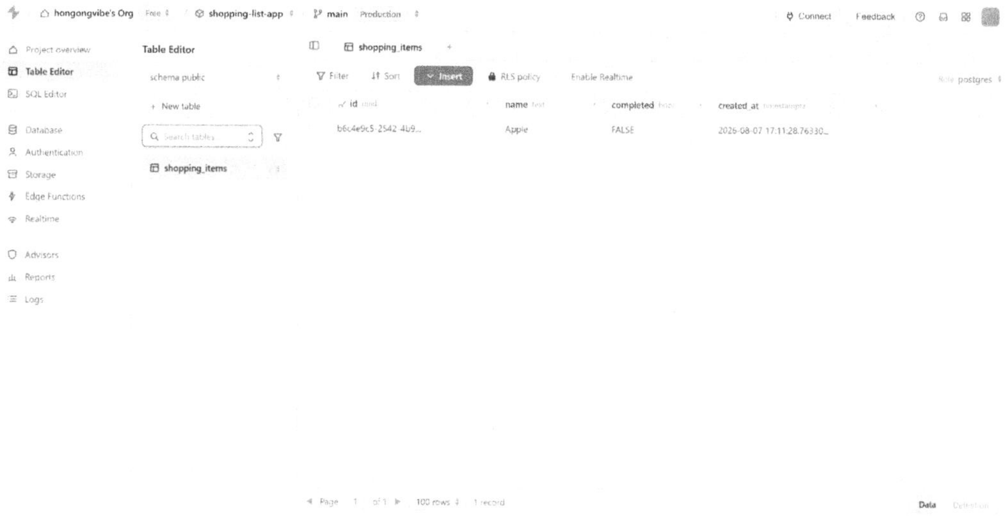

Figure 8.68: Apple row added to the list

3. In the shopping list app, click the checkbox for the 'Apple' item to mark it as completed.

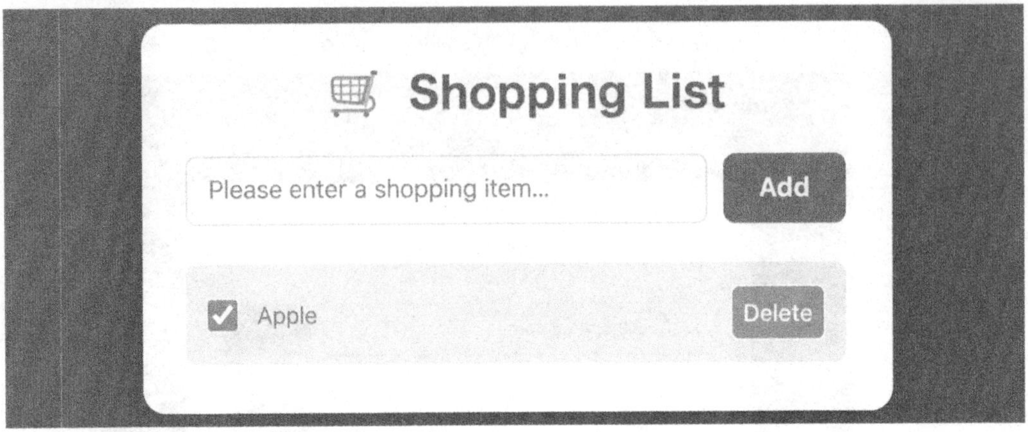

Figure 8.69: Mark as completed

4. The completed column in the table changes to true.
5. Try adding other items to the shopping list app and check the database table. The added items will appear as new rows.

	id uuid	name text	completed bool	created_at timestamptz
	85f9d216-0c4b-4a7e-	Bread	FALSE	2026-08-07 17:18:26.2C
	b6c4e9c5-2542-4b92	Apple	TRUE	2026-08-07 17:11:28.76
	dbd4e1ca-b348-4bef-	Milk	FALSE	2026-08-07 17:19:30.57

Figure 8.70: All added items appear in the list

6. Now let's try deleting an item. Delete the **Bread** item from the shopping list app.
7. The Bread row will be deleted from the table.
8. You can also confirm that it works well on other computers, browsers, or in incognito mode.

Now, our shopping list app has evolved from a simple practice project that only worked locally into a real web service accessible to anyone over the internet. With automatic deployment via Vercel and database integration through Supabase, the app always stays up to date and allows multiple users to share data in real time. Through this process, we've completed the entire journey of turning AI-generated code into a real service.

Claude Code is constantly being updated with new features and improvements. Any new features or major changes released after the publication of this book will be continuously updated on this book's GitHub repository, so you can always stay informed. To access the repository link, follow the steps in the *Download the example code files* section in the *Preface*.

I will continue to cheer you on as you achieve your goals through Vibecoding.

Wrapping up

Key takeaways summarized in 6 keywords:

- **Deployment** is the process of uploading your application to a third-party server connected to the internet.
- **Vercel** is a cloud platform that automatically builds and deploys your code when you push it to GitHub.
- Data stored in **local storage** is not shared with other computers or browsers, and will disappear if you clear your browser cache or switch devices.
- **Cloud storage** acts as a central server that allows you to access the same data from anywhere.
- **Supabase** is a cloud database platform that automates database setup.
- A database **table**, simply put, is a structure that stores data in a tabular format.

If a database is like a program that manages multiple Excel files, then a table is like an individual Excel sheet within the database.

Review questions

1. What is the biggest difference between local storage and a cloud database?
    1. Local storage is faster
    2. A database allows data to be shared across multiple devices
    3. Local storage is more secure
    4. There is no free option for databases
2. Choose the correct reason and solution for a `404 error` when deploying with Vercel.
    1. Server error - restart required
    2. Missing index.html file - need to change the file name
    3. Authentication failed - need to log in again
    4. Network error - need to check the connection
3. Explain the similarities and differences between a Supabase table and an Excel sheet.

Your self-paced journey with Vibecoding is just beginning. Now it's your turn to create a new world of coding together with AI.

9

Answers to Review Questions

Chapter 1, My First Vibe Coding

The answers for this chapter's sections are as follows:

My coding partner, AI assistant

1. Tool names filled:

Category	Description	Representative Tools
Web-Based Chatbot	Can be used directly on the web without installation; copy-and-paste required	Claude, ChatGPT, Gemini
Model Selection	A system that allows you to choose from multiple language models; may incur additional costs	Cursor, Antigravity
Dedicated Model Type	A method where you install and use a specific language model; allows direct access to local files	Claude Code, Gemini CLI

Table A.1: Tool names

2. Appropriate concepts:
    1. Vibe coding
    2. AI Assistant

3. Model selection tools
4. Dedicated model-based tools

Create my own first webpage

1. Neural networks → Deep learning → Transformer → LLM
2. Both the tool usage fee and the AI model cost must be paid.

Chapter 2, Maximizing AI's Potential with Effective Prompts

The answers for this chapter's sections are as follows:

The secrets of prompts that awaken AI

1. Creativity: Requires the output to be surprising.
2. 5W1H
3. What, How
4. "I want to create my own homepage that includes today's date and time, as well as a search bar." Reason: By specifying the required features (date, search), the AI can clearly understand exactly what it needs to do.

Real-world application: completing your marketing portfolio

1. Establish the basic framework → Implement core features → Apply design → Check for completeness
2. Request all features at once to save time.
3. The design is automatically improved.

Chapter 3, Getting Started with Claude Code

The answers for this chapter's sections are as follows:

Installing Claude Code

1. Git
2. Type the `/quit` command in the terminal
3. Claude account with subscription

Building a handwriting recognition program

1. Claude Code automatically selects the optimal folder

2. The higher the accuracy and the lower the loss, the better the performance.
3. Never allow modifications (Modifications strictly prohibited)

Expanding the program with CLAUDE.md

1. Store the entire previous conversation
2. `/init`
3. Coding style rules to be applied to all projects
4. Token usage is automatically reduced

Chapter 4, Practical Use of Claude Code

The answers for this chapter's sections are as follows:

The secrets of prompts that awaken AI

1. Appropriate commands filled:

Description	Command
Analyzes the project structure and automatically generates the CLAUDE.md file	`/init`
Check current session's token usage and remaining context capacity	`/status`
Select the AI model to use or change to the Default option	`/model`
View a list of all available commands and their descriptions	`/help`

Table A.2: Commands

2. Correct terms based on the descriptions:
    1. `CLAUDE.md`
    2. Product Requirements Document (PRD)
    3. JSON

Resuming work and increasing efficiency

1. *Ctrl* + *R* is the shortcut for the `/context` command
2. Appropriate command filled:

Situation	Command / Option
When you want to select and resume a specific conversation among several	`claude --resume or /resume`
When you want to immediately continue working on the most recent conversation	`claude --continue or claude -c`
When you want to visually check current context usage	`/context`
When the conversation gets long and needs to be compressed	`/compact`
When it's tedious to approve file modifications every time	*Shift* + *Tab*

Table A.3: Appropriate commands

Project improvement and task management

1. `/config` can only change Claude Code's global settings
2. Appropriate commands filled:

Situation	Command
When you want to check the structure of the `web_version` folder	`@web_version`
When you want to find a specific function in the `script.js` file	`@script.js`
When you want to check the installation status of Claude Code	`/doctor`

Situation	Command
When you want to save your conversation history as a file	Type `/export` and select the **Save to file** option
When you want to switch to dark mode	Change the theme in `/config`
When you want to turn off the auto-compression feature	Set **Auto-compact** to false in `/config`

Table A.4: Appropriate commands

Chapter 5, Systematic Development and Management Through Game Creation

The answers for this chapter's sections are as follows:

Creating reliable AI content

1. `/clear` summarizes and compresses the conversation while maintaining context
2. Appropriate command or response methods:

Situation	Response
When you want to save the validation guidelines for the quiz game	After selecting `/memory`, select **Project memory**
When you think previous conversations might affect a new task	Run `/clear`
When the conversation gets long and you want to save tokens	Run `/compact`
When you encounter an ambiguous question like "the longest river in the world"	Add guidelines specifying the criteria or time frame

Table A.5: Commands or response methods filled

Boosting development efficiency through automation

1. Custom commands are saved in Python file format (They are saved in Markdown format)
2. Correct answers filled:
    1. Project-specific custom commands should be saved in the `.claude/commands` folder
    2. To review only problems within a specific number range in a custom command, use placeholders such as `$1` and `$2`
    3. To accept user input in a custom command, use parameters such as `$ARGUMENTS`
    4. Commands created in `~/.claude/commands` are available across all projects (Commands created in `.claude/commands/` are available in the current project.)

Maintenance strategies learned through the use of custom commands

1. Custom commands must be written as Python scripts (The file format for custom commands is `md`, Markdown).
2. Correct answers filled:
    1. Save custom commands as .md (Markdown) files.
    2. Save custom command files in the `.claude/commands` folder.
    3. To check the list of created commands, use the `/help` command.

Chapter 6, Giving Claude Code Wings with APIs

The answers for this chapter's sections are as follows:

Configuring APIs in Claude Code

1. API key and Model name
2. Hardcode API key directly in code
3. Code content called

FridgeChef: built with Claude Code and API

1. You can use AI models from multiple companies with a single API key

2. Whether the `.gitignore` file exists
3. Store the API key in the `.env` file and add that file to the `.gitignore` file to exclude it from GitHub uploads.

Chapter 7, Building a Development Team with Claude Code AI Agents

The answers for this chapter's sections are as follows:

Understanding AI Agents

1. Agents can select an independent AI model, but custom commands share the model of the main session
2. Inherits the model currently used in the main session
3. "Fix discovered bugs" and "Create new test files"

> **Note**
>
> `Read-only` refers to read-only permissions, which allow you to read the contents of code, settings, and files, as well as view the directory structure. However, to fix a bug, you must modify the contents of source files such as `.py` or `.js`, and when creating a new test file, you must save it to an existing directory, so additional write permissions are required.

Automating software development with AI Agents

1. This is because the QA agent has to review all the results of the previous agents' work
2. The PRD is automatically copied to the `.claude/agents/` folder and shared

Chapter 8, Extending Claude Code with MCP, Skills, and Plugins

The answers for this chapter's sections are as follows:

Understanding MCP and Connecting to Claude Code

1. An API is a way to request specific functions, while MCP is a protocol that allows AI to communicate directly with external systems

2. Separates Claude Code options from the MCP server execution command
3. Sequential Thinking MCP breaks down problems sequentially to analyze them systematically, providing detailed information on objectives, implementation methods, roadmaps, metrics, and risk mitigation strategies, thereby generating results that are more structured and comprehensive than general inference

A fully automated development environment implemented with plugins and skills

1. `.playwright-mcp`
2. add → commit → push
3. "Search for the MCP name on Google, access the GitHub repository, and find the MCP server address" and "How to browse by category using a GitHub repository or website that lists MCP servers"

Connecting a database to create a real service

1. A database allows data to be shared across multiple devices
2. Missing `index.html` file - need to change the file name
3. **Similarities**: Database tables store data in a tabular format consisting of rows and columns, similar to Excel sheets.
   Differences: Database tables can be accessed by multiple users simultaneously, are synchronized in real time, and can automatically process data in conjunction with programs.

10

Unlock Your Exclusive Benefits

Your copy of this book includes the following exclusive benefits:

DRM-Free PDF Version

Download DRM-free PDF and ePub copies of this book.

7-Day Packt Library Access

Get 7-day unlimited access to 8,000+ books and videos. No credit card required.

Available for first-time Packt+ trial users only.

Next-Gen Reader Access

Read this book on Packt Reader with progress sync, dark mode and note-taking.

Follow the guide below to unlock them. The process takes only a few minutes and needs to be completed once.

Unlock this book's free benefits in 3 easy steps

Step 1

Keep your purchase invoice ready for *Step 3*. If you have a physical copy, scan it using your phone and save it as a PDF, JPG, or PNG.

For more help on finding your invoice, visit `https://www.packtpub.com/en-us/unlock?step=1`.

> Note
>
> **Note**: If you bought this book directly from Packt, no invoice is required. After *Step 2*, you can access your exclusive content right away.

Step 2

Scan the QR code or go to `https://www.packtpub.com/unlock`.

On the page that opens (similar to *Figure 14.1* on desktop), search for this book by name and select the correct edition.

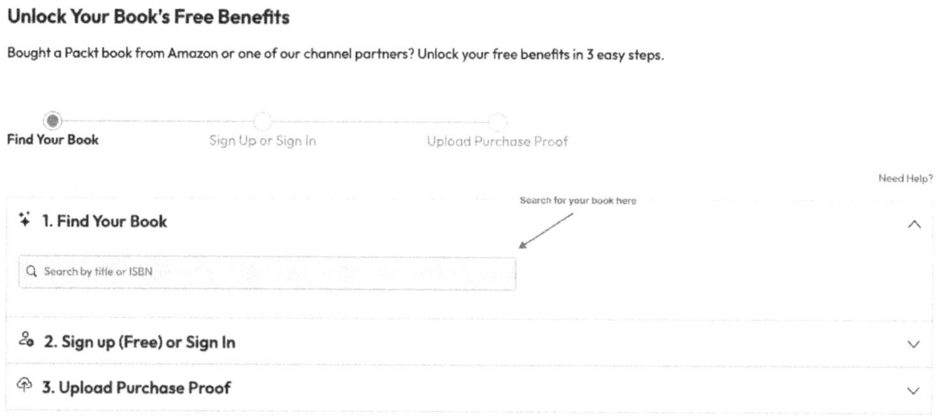

Figure 14.1: Packt unlock landing page on desktop

Step 3

After selecting your book, sign in to your Packt account or create one for free. Then upload your invoice (PDF, PNG, or JPG, up to 10 MB). Follow the on-screen instructions to finish the process.

Need help

If you get stuck and need help, visit `https://www.packtpub.com/unlock-benefits/help` for a detailed FAQ on how to find your invoices and more. This QR code will take you to the help page.

Note

Note: If you are still facing issues, reach out to `customercare@packt.com`.

Other Books You May Enjoy

If you enjoyed this book, you may be interested in these other books by Packt:

Building Claude Skills

Pietro Montaldo

ISBN: 978-1-80849-285-3

- Understand the Claude ecosystem and when to use Skills
- Build reusable Claude Skills for business workflows
- Connect Claude to external business tools and services
- Design reliable multi-step AI workflows
- Test, evaluate, and improve Skill performance
- Optimize Skills for quality, consistency, and efficiency
- Share and manage Skills across teams
- Automate everyday work without writing code

Agentic Coding with Claude Code

Eden Marco

ISBN: 978-1-80602-259-5

- Design agentic coding workflows in the terminal and IDE using Claude Code
- Build custom automations with reusable slash commands and hooks
- Use Claude Code with a Next.js project to implement AI-driven workflows
- Create persistent AI memory using Claude Code memory files
- Apply MCP for structured context sharing across tools and agents
- Design multi-agent systems using subagents and orchestration patterns
- Enforce coding standards using project documentation and context control
- Scale AI pair programming while keeping code maintainable

Packt is searching for authors like you

If you're interested in becoming an author for Packt, please visit authors.packt.com and apply today. We have worked with thousands of developers and tech professionals, just like you, to help them share their insight with the global tech community. You can make a general application, apply for a specific hot topic that we are recruiting an author for, or submit your own idea.

Share your thoughts

Now you've finished *Build with Claude Code*, we'd love to hear your thoughts! Scan the QR code below to go straight to the Amazon review page for this book and share your feedback or leave a review on the site that you purchased it from.

https://packt.link/r/1807781798

Your review is important to us and the tech community and will help us make sure we're delivering excellent quality content.

Index

Symbols

Made in the USA
Monee, IL
02 November 2026

67249011R00227